Thinking Pro/ENGINEER®

Mastering Design Methodology

David Bigelow

Thinking Pro/ENGINEER®
Mastering Design Methodology
David Bigelow

Published by:

OnWord Press
2530 Camino Entrada
Santa Fe, NM 87505-4835 USA

All rights reserved. No part of this book may be reproduced or transmitted in any form or by any means, electronic or mechanical, including photocopying, recording, or by any information storage and retrieval system, without written permission from the publisher, except for the inclusion of brief quotations in a review.

Copyright © 1995 David Bigelow

SAN 694-0269

First Edition, 1995

10 9 8 7 6 5 4 3

Printed in the United States of America

Library of Congress Cataloging-in-Publication Data

```
Bigelow, David
   Thinking Pro/ENGINEER: mastering design methodology / David Bigelow
 -- 1st ed.
     p.   cm.
   Includes index.
   ISBN 1-56690-065-4
   1. Computer-aided design 2. Pro/ENGINEER 3. Mechanical drawing
 I. Title
 TA174.B54 1995
 670'.285'53--dc20                                              94-48551
```

Trademarks

OnWord Press is a trademark of High Mountain Press, Inc. Pro/ENGINEER, Pro/MANUFACTURING, Pro/SHEETMETAL, Pro/NC-CHECK, Pro/MOLDDESIGN, Pro/REPORT, Pro/CABLING, Pro/DETAIL, Pro/DESIGN, Pro/CASTING, Pro/SURFACE, Pro/MESH, Pro/FEM-POST, and Pro/HARNESS-MFG are trademarks or registered trademarks of Parametric Technology Corporation. Many other products and services are mentioned in this book that are either trademarks or registered trademarks of their respective companies. OnWord Press and the author make no claim to these marks.

Warning and Disclaimer

This book is designed to provide information about Pro/ENGINEER. Every effort has been made to make this book complete and as accurate as possible; however, no warranty or fitness is implied.

The information is provided on an "as-is" basis. The author and OnWord Press shall have neither liability nor responsibility to any person or entity with respect to any loss or damages in connection with or rising from the information contained in this book.

About the Author

David H. Bigelow received a Bachelors of Science Degree from Purdue University School of Engineering and Technology. Having a strong background in math, fluids, and thermal engineering, in 1993 he presented to the American Society of Mechanical Engineers (ASME) an original work on the analysis and solution of parallel flow in piping networks using frictional iteration.

Having designed parts and assemblies for a number of manufacturing processes, such as sand and die castings, forgings, PM products, plastics, and stampings within the automotive and consumer-based industries, he has been exposed to numerous design and manufacturability problems. In a continuous effort to reduce costs and development time while increasing the "quality" of the final product, he has coordinated the use and execution of Pro/ENGINEER's tools, in conjunction with any analysis, manufacturing, and documentation requirements. Currently he is working as an Engineer for Harman-Motive, Inc. in Martinsville, IN, a manufacturer of audiophile automotive sound systems for several major auto manufacturers.

Acknowledgments

The author is grateful to the many people who have assisted in the technical support, editing and production of this book. Without a pool of experienced, resourceful, and energetic individuals, the completion of this book would not have been possible. A special thanks is due to Parametric Technology Corporation and the following people:

High Mountain Press

Margaret Burns
David Talbott

Technical Reviewers

Peter Barbee
Jim Schulze
Steve Levin
Dennis Steffen
Guy Edkins

The Indianapolis offices of Information Decisions, Inc.

Tim Weatherford
Bill Walters
Todd Hussong

Harman-Motive, Inc.

Ernie Latham-Brown
David Seidl
Edward Trachman

OnWord Press

OnWord Press is dedicated to the fine art of professional documentation.

In addition to the author who developed the material for this book, many members of the OnWord Press team contribute to the book that ends up in your hands. In addition to those listed below, other members who contributed to the production and distribution of this book include Frank Conforti, Jean Nichols, Joe Adams, Robin Ortiz, James Bridge, Roxsan Meyer, and Bob Leyba.

Dan Raker, President
Kate Hayward, Publisher
Gary Lange, Associate Publisher
David Talbott, Acquisitions Editor
Margaret Burns, Project Editor
Carol Leyba, Production Manager
Michelle Mann, Production Editor
Janet Leigh Dick, Marketing Director
Lynne Egensteiner, Cover Designer and Illustrator
Kate Bemis, Indexer

Introduction

This book was written for users to learn about how Pro/ENGINEER can truly capture the design intent while producing a quality database that can be used for more than documentation purposes. It is not intended to act as the "Pro/ENGINEER Bible" or to lay down the law as to how you should conduct your development procedures for designs. However, it was written to emphasize the importance of obtaining "quality" input, not only for Pro/ENGINEER, but for the entire design process, and how that information can affect numerous areas that interface with the design.

Overall, the book is laid out to follow the phases of a development cycle, starting with obtaining new ideas for the conceptual layout of a design and ending with the manufacturing of the final product. Some of the methods that are explained in the chapters may not apply to your needs. With this in mind, I encourage you to experiment with a number of design modules and procedures to find the tools and techniques that satisfy your design and documentation requirements.

Enjoy the book!

For her continued patience and loving support in everything I do, I dedicate this book to my wife Judith.

*Love always,
David*

Table of Contents

Chapter 1: Planning Your Design 1
Introduction 1
Things To Do Before You Touch the Computer 3
    Think! 4
    Weathering a Brainstorm 5
    Planning the Plan 6
Selecting the Tools for the Job 8
Touch the Computer 10
Summary 10

Chapter 2: Managing Designs with Layouts 13
Introduction 13
What Are Layouts? 14
Putting Layouts To Work for You 19
Layouts and the Design Intent 22
Multiple Layouts and Assemblies 24
Summary 29

Chapter 3: Starting a Design with Seed Files 31
Introduction 31
What Are Seed Files? 32
Why Use Seed Files? 33
Developing Your Seed File 33
    Creating a Seed File 33
    Creating a Seed Script 34
Developing Your Seed File Using Trail Files 35
Deciding What Should Be Seed Data 37
    Turning Seed Data into a Seed File 39
Optimizing Seed File Execution 42
    Macro Execution Methods 42
    Menu Execution Methods 43
Adding New Parameters 45
    Adding New Information to Old Models 45
    Updating the Seed Script with New Information or Requirements ... 49
    Improving the Update Execution 52
Summary 53

Table of Contents

Chapter 4: Corporate Standards and Contracted Resources 55
Introduction 55
What Are Corporate Standards? 56
Why Have Corporate Standards for Pro/ENGINEER? 61
The Effects of Having No Standards 62
    Perpetual Remodeling, No Communication, and Using the Wrong Tools for the Job . . . 62
Standards and Contracted Resources 65
    How To Avoid Getting Stung 66
    Contracted Resources and Corporate Standards 69
Developing Your Corporate Standards 70
    Educate Others in Your Capabilities 71
    Involve Other Departments in Developing Modeling Standards 71
    Define Approved Methods of Model, Assembly, and Drawing Development 72
    Use the Hot Shots 72
    Obtain Supplier Input 73
    Use the Right Tool for the Job 73
    Alternative Module Selection 75
    Keep Standards Flexible 75
What Are the Ramifications of Having Corporate Standards? 76
    Uniformity: Everyone Working on the Same Page 76
    People Must Be Educated on Standards 76
Summary 78

Chapter 5: Capturing Design Intent 79
Introduction 79
"It's beginning to look a lot like Christmas..." 81
Parent/Child Relationships and Design Intent 86
How About a Game of Chess? 89
Use the Right Tools for the Design Task 92
Which Components Should Be Modeled First? 98
Which Mode Is Right for You? 99
Summary 105

Chapter 6: Design Verification and Manufacturability 107
Introduction 107
Verify the Parts and Assemblies 108
Verifying Manufacturability 112
    To Section or Not To Section, That Is the Question 112
    Does the Design Satisfy the Process Requirements? 118
Apply the Tolerances 121
Summary 130

Chapter 7: Modifying Designs 133
Introduction 133
Assembly Modifications Using a Layout 134
Assembly Modifications in Assembly Mode 138
Simplifying Your View of the Design. 148
    Configuration States or Simplified Representation 148
    Using Layers 150
    Component Simplification 151
Modifying Designs from the Drawing 153
Part Modifications. 154
    Finding the Design Options 154
    Learning by Trail Files 157
    Just Query the Features 158
    Parent/Child Relationships 158
    Making the Changes 158
Summary 170

Chapter 8: Detailing 171
Introduction 171
Before You Detail. 174
    Apply Tolerances to the Right Features. 175
    Develop Parametric Notes 179
    Using Seed Data 184
    Parametric Formats and Seed Data 188
Developing Parametric Formats. 192
    Manually Placed Text. 192
    Symbols 194
    Tables, Tables, and More Tables. 196
Proper View Development 198
Showing Off. 203
Summary 210

Chapter 9: Improving Design Execution 213
Introduction 213
Options For Initiating Repetitive Execution 215
    Macros 215
    Menu Items. 227
Running Multiple Configurations 232
    Making the Transitions Slick. 236
Summary 239

Table of Contents

Chapter 10: Analysis ... 241
Introduction ... 241
Improving Communication ... 242
Meshing ... 246
Design Optimization ... 248
    Using the Design for Optimization ... 252
    Topology Optimization ... 260
Who Should Conduct the Analysis? ... 262
Summary ... 266

Chapter 11: Rapid Prototyping ... 269
Introduction ... 269
Which Technique Is Right for You? ... 270
    Price, Quantity, and Process ... 273
    Using CNC ... 274
    Other Options ... 276
The Common Link: The Database ... 277
    Geometry Errors ... 277
    Geometry Errors and CNC ... 280
Summary ... 283

Chapter 12: Pro/MANUFACTURING ... 285
Introduction ... 285
Adapting To Change ... 289
    Patterns ... 293
Ease of Use + Powerful Tools = Productivity ... 295
    Sketching Mill Volumes ... 296
    Surfaces for Mill Volumes ... 300
Design Quality and Manufacturing ... 305
    Inaccurate Data ... 305
Configuration State and Simplified Representation Machining ... 312
Pro/NC-CHECK ... 319
    Clipping Planes ... 322
Postprocessing ... 325
Summary ... 326

Appendix: Hardware Configurations ... 329
Memory, Graphics, and Processing ... 329
    Bottlenecks ... 330
The Price of an Optimal Configuration ... 332

Index ... 335

Planning Your Design

Introduction

Remember feeling like an expert just after you completed your first classes in Pro/ENGINEER? If you are like most people, you felt as if you could model almost anything. But as time went on, the feeling of modeling superiority seemed to diminish, and you noticed that you were not using the tool as efficiently or expertly as you once were. If this is the case, then the following may seem familiar.

After having completed the novice level courses in Pro/ENGINEER and spending lots of time working on solving modeling problems, you have reached a point where you must learn more about Pro/ENGINEER's capabilities and functionality. With your time at a premium and your projects ramping up to a near critical stage, you make the difficult decision to leave work to attend some advanced classes in Pro/ENGINEER that will save you some time in the long run.

After setting aside a week's worth of work to attend the advanced classes, your projects have fallen slightly behind, which will require you to work harder and faster to bring the projects back on schedule. With all the new information from the classes under your belt, you sit down at the computer and try to apply some newly learned lessons in advanced modeling. Everything seems to be moving along just fine until you hit a virtual wall where the results of your commands are not what you were expecting. The clock has still been ticking and your projects continue to fall behind. With the sweat running down your brow, you revert to some tried and true but poor modeling techniques and continue your model's development by performing illogical operations that will eventually result in the "picture" that you are looking for, but not the "functionality." You have made the conscious decision, under stress, to act as a "sculptor," rather than an engineer, to cover up and solve your problems.

During your modeling of the design, you received the attention of several others in the department. All those wire frame and shaded images of your sculpted design were impressive and may have even caught the eye of a few department heads. But the excessive number of features, the poor parametric relationships, and all the "workarounds" hold the untold story of your frustrations.

With a design review around the corner, you quickly generate a drawing in Pro/ENGINEER. Because your method of modeling did not use a logical and functional approach, you lay in some driven dimensions to quickly describe the key dimensional relationships. To finish the drawing for review, you add some tolerances and overall package descriptions of the design, and then submit the drawing for review. After the review, the design is returned with a number of important dimensional and tolerance modifications, along with a request to find the maximum and minimum clearances with a separate component in the assembly.

Under normal conditions, when models in Pro/ENGINEER are logically developed, capture the design intent, and are capable of adapting to change, the requests (as outlined by the design review) would not take long to investigate or integrate, but because you have cut corners throughout your design and development process, you will have to work very hard to finish the design. As you investigate each of the design changes, you find that because (1) your dimensioning scheme on the drawing was not the same as the staggered dimensioning scheme that was used for the model's generation and (2) parent/child relationships that resulted from the poor modeling were mismanaged, you end up spending twice the time fixing what you originally developed. In the end, it would probably have been easier to just start over.

This scenario may not seem far from your current situation. You either have experienced this problem or worked with other engineer's models where the same problems have occurred. Believe it or not, this type of situation happens more than most people are willing to admit, and if you are not prepared to perform your design and documentation tasks properly, then the above situation may choke your capabilities to design quality components and assemblies.

In the end, it all comes down to your ability to generate *quality* input before you even sit down at the computer to model a design. As with any other CAD/CAM/CAE system, the quality of the design is directly related to the amount of information available about what the design environment and expectations will be. Basically, outline the design intent, then satisfy it while considering all of the process, manufacturing, quality, and inspection requirements. Sound like a lot, doesn't it? It is!

Things To Do Before You Touch the Computer

Just as babies must learn to crawl before they can walk, and walk before they run, in Pro/ENGINEER, you must first decide what you are going to do, understand the design problem and how to overcome it, and then do it. Pro/ENGINEER does not follow the same rules and guidelines that you used during your explicit modeling days. Each and every feature that you develop must have purpose, be functional, and be logically placed in the model to ensure maximum flexibility with minimum effort.

You may have noticed that the most experienced users and application engineers can make Pro/ENGINEER virtually sing, but remember, they have the ability, experience, and expertise to analyze the overall design, sit down at the computer, and work it all out on the fly. There is no reason that you can't do the same, but first you have to have an understanding of what you and your department need to accomplish with the design: the *quality input*. Generating quality input is *not easy*, but once it has been generated, you are over 60% through the battle and ready to win the war on remodeling (a rather common experience for Pro/ENGINEER designs that are not capable of adapting to change).

Basically, there are three steps to generating *quality* inputs for Pro/ENGINEER: (1) think through the design, (2) brainstorm problem areas of development, and (3) plan the necessary steps to satisfy the design's requirements. The following discussions may seem unimportant, but they represent some of the fundamental techniques of engineering problem solving that are commonly overlooked. There are literally thousands of ways to generate input; this list represents a direct and relatively efficient method. If you and your engineering department are satisfied with your current methods of generating input, then by all means continue to use them.

Think!

One of the most common mistakes revolves around the urge to sit down at the computer and sink hours, if not days, into free-form modeling in Pro/ENGINEER; basically, plugging and chugging features until the user is left with a very impressive picture of a potential design option. There is, of course, a lot of thought and energy that goes into modeling components right out of the air; unfortunately, you may be losing valuable time that could be spent doing more important things. Therefore, it is important, before you even grab the mouse and begin modeling, that you think about what the overall objectives are and how you can satisfy those objectives. You need to understand the processes available for manufacturing and the proposed working environment of the component. Outline what is given to you—the work envelope—and what you need to find—the design's requirements. Looking at these two things can help you to develop preliminary sketches of what the design might look like or a list of how the design may perform.

Be sure to sketch and list your ideas on paper, so you won't forget them later. Even the most experienced engineers cannot remember everything. Also, by putting your ideas on paper, you will be able to communicate simple and complex designs to other people more efficiently and effectively. To minimize confusion, keep your concepts clear and separate from other design options. This will ensure that all of those 30-second ideas will not be lost or garbled when it comes time to discuss the design.

Things To Do Before You Touch the Computer

Use any *like* physical models for improving your concept development. Having a physical model to work with, especially when your design is a retrofit to an existing design, is an excellent way to visualize your design options. The computer is a great tool for visualization of a concept or design option. However, the computer alone cannot give the engineer a tangible understanding of the volumes, weights, or material attributes that actual production designs will have. Once you have a sizable list of design options, some sketches, and a list of objectives that need to be satisfied, prepare to generate more input through a brainstorming session.

Weathering a Brainstorm

One of the best ways to boost your level of input is to bring together the parties who will be affected by the design (internal/external manufacturing, production, design, inspection, and so forth) and give them the opportunity to help solve the design problems. If you perform your own little reality check, you will see that you alone will not be able to solve all of the design problems. Use the invaluable experience of the people who have to live, and have lived, with the decisions that you make. Giving others the opportunity to vent historical frustrations is one of the best ways to generate *quality* input and make the overall design more realistic and functional.

Gathering all the resources at the right time is essential for efficient design. If the people are called together too early, that is, before the design requirements have been established and understood, they will not be used with full efficiency. If they are pulled in too late, the overall design may suffer from a lack of useful input. Unfortunately, there is no real formula for *when* to pull the people together. To ensure that all parties have opportunities to assist in the development, you should plan a series of brainstorming sessions to discuss the design and give the participants time to think of additional design options.

> ✪ *TIP:* **Some hints for successful brainstorming:** *If you have never been involved in a brainstorming session, you are in for a treat; they don't always go as planned. Basically, you bring together a select group of individuals and outline the problems that the design should overcome and the boundaries of your design's existence. Prompt them for several designs and document the suggestions and sketches for everyone to build*

on. Make sure that all of the ideas are documented and available for review, no matter how far out they may seem.

There is always the risk when you bring together a diverse group of people, especially when those people have frustrations with other departments, that your brainstorming session can veer off to other topics (take off on the proverbial tangent). In most cases, it is better to manage or mediate the meeting and let everyone else do the work for you. The advantage in this is that you will be able to set the tone of the meeting without getting swept up in the discussions. Your information should be a catalyst for discussion, not a topic for debate. If you are not comfortable with the mediator role, ask someone else to guide the discussions.

Overall, this method of obtaining input can be very effective and produce mountains of information. One risk is that you can obtain a consensus too early in the design process. This effect is commonly called group think, where everyone is in total agreement and continuously takes the position that, "We can do no more, and no one else could do better." This is not common, but a skillful devil's advocate should actively challenge design options once they have been presented.

Once these meetings have exhausted all potential design options, review, critique, and openly discuss each option that has been suggested. This will eliminate a lot of design options and really bring a design into focus. The results will translate into better communication of the design's requirements and intent and ultimately give you an explicit list of goals and objectives. Once this valuable information has been generated, it is time to move on to the planning stage.

Planning the Plan

Once a consensus has been achieved during the brainstorming sessions as to what the design should be and how to accomplish it, make sure that everyone understands the direction of the design by publishing the minutes of the meeting, along with a copy of the final markups. This is an essential step, especially when there are a number of different inputs that have affected the design's direction and intent. Once this is done, outline a rough sequence of events for the design's development. These items may include which components should be developed first (usually the longest lead items), who is responsible for what, and what time frames, processes, and modules will be involved. Basically, develop a project outline of development, highlighting time frames and milestones.

Another key to successful design development, especially in Pro/ENGINEER, is to outline (prior to modeling) some of the key inspection and dimensional relationships for each component. This can be accomplished by simply asking, "What aspects and relationships of the design must remain flexible and how?" The answer to this question is often found in the component's fit and function with other components. You alone will not be able to satisfy or outline all of these requirements, so use the people who will affect your development.

Finalizing the design requires you, your design checker, and inspection resources to evaluate each component or aspect of your design and constrain the design dimensionally to truly capture the design intent and ensure it can be manufactured. Historically, this phase occurred several weeks into the modeling, after an initial drawing was submitted for dimensional layout. Remember, with Pro/ENGINEER, in order to develop flexible and useful designs, you must spend time up front deciding what your final requirements will be. That is where the input from your design checker and inspection personnel will be most valuable. After all, they are the ones who will be the first to criticize your efforts.

The outcome of your discussion with the design checkers should be a marked up layout of the component or components that you are designing. This markup should not be excessively detailed, but should give you a target for what your final drawing will look like, and therefore your final model. Layout work can cover the inspection techniques and what information should be included, basically outlining which aspects of the design are critical and which are not.

A few hours spent discussing which dimensions and tolerances will affect the overall design and how the final product will be inspected can give you a plan of attack for modeling simple and complex components. If you are too impatient to research what your interdepartmental requirements are, then you deserve to rework your models and assemblies. Remember, the tough part is deciding what to do, the easy part is telling Pro/ENGINEER how to do it.

Chapter 1: Planning Your Design

Selecting the Tools for the Job

Once you have amassed this great input, decide which modules will solve your modeling problems with the greatest flexibility in the least amount of time. This is not always an easy task, and there is always the chance that your assumptions for a module will *not* satisfy your design's requirements. For example, Pro/SHEETMETAL has functionality that can make complex designs simple and easy to manipulate. The following illustration of a metal bracket was completed using conventional modeling techniques in Pro/ENGINEER.

Bracket developed using surfaces with thin protrusion.

Even though, dimensionally, the previous illustration satisfies the design intent, there is a lot of baggage to manage due to the modeling technique. To further complicate the design, all of the bends in the bracket are to be controlled from one side of the bracket, where the surface geometry is. Generally, stamping facilities like to see and inspect to the inside radius of a bend or form. The following illustration shows the same component, after it was developed using Pro/SHEETMETAL.

Selecting the Tools for the Job

Bracket developed using Pro/SHEETMETAL.

This bracket captures the design intent without a lot of parametric management problems. As an added bonus, this model was completed in about a quarter of the time, with at least 10 times the flexibility. This is because the user can independently manipulate the location, size, and form direction of sheet metal features, such as the form feature, with relative ease. Performing these types of modifications with conventional surface features would require a significant amount of remodeling of the same form with very little flexibility, and you may have to oversize the surface geometry to compensate for material thickness direction.

As you can see, module selection is important to the development and flexibility of your designs. You may be thinking, "Yes, but we don't have a full package of Pro/ENGINEER." The answer to this can be as simple as, before you buy a module, test it. I will be the first to admit that it is painful to drop $5000 to $10,000 on a module of Pro/ENGINEER and then find out that it was not what you expected. Be sure to understand each module and look for cross-functionality, that is, a module developed for one industry may have a new application in your area of expertise.

Touch the Computer

Now that you know what your dimensional and tolerance constraints will be, have selected the modules that will be used, and have an understanding of process-related requirements and expectations, you are ready to touch the computer. But where do you start and how sophisticated do you want to get? The answers are generally dependent on existing corporate and departmental requirements or standards and the level of sophistication of your design, that is, is it a part, an assembly, or will it be integrated into another assembly?

If the design is a part, you may want to look at the options for each module as well as any components with which it may interface. Developing parts in Pro/ENGINEER can be a simple operation, but making sure that you are taking full advantage of Pro/ENGINEER is difficult. There are several titles from OnWord Press that discuss, in detail, modeling techniques and Pro/ENGINEER (see the listing at the back of the book for additional information).

If the design is an assembly, you may want to consider some assembly functionality, such as component development in an assembled position or incorporating some type of interchangeability. Another option for planning assemblies is Layout mode. Again, you should understand the basics of each option and base your decisions on your current and future design requirements.

Summary

There are a number of critical steps to ensure that your designs are functional, flexible, capture the design intent, and can be manufactured. The rest of this book shows how to effectively plan, execute, modify, and analyze your design. You will learn how to use the strategies outlined in this chapter to produce efficient and flexible solid models. You must be proactive in your efforts to develop designs in Pro/ENGINEER that satisfy all the corporate, interdepartmental, and external requirements. Some steps to success are (1) thinking through the design, (2) brainstorming about problem areas of development, and (3) planning the necessary steps to satisfy the design's requirements.

Pulling together internal and external resources to discuss and develop concepts and design options is one of the fastest ways to bring a design into focus. Once you have a consensus on the design, all you have to do is lay out and identify the dimensional requirements and relationships and you basically have a road map for modeling the design in Pro/ENGINEER. Sitting down at the computer and modeling a part without understanding the design intent can be a waste of time and can put you on the road to remodeling land.

Once you have gathered the preliminary information, and understand the boundaries within which your design must exist, all you have to do is put it in the computer. If you and your engineering department are going to share information and develop functional and flexible designs in Pro/ENGINEER, you must capture the design intent by using the proper tools for the job. If you used a pipe wrench to remove an oil filter, you could have a real mess on you hands. The same goes for Pro/ENGINEER; if you don't use the right tools for the job, you could have a large and inflexible design that no one wants to use.

Managing Designs with Layouts

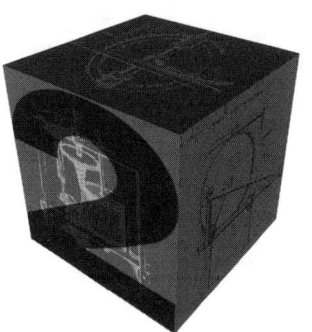

Introduction

Have you ever gone from department to department with stacks of prints, searching for input on a new design, only to be turned back to look for additional information? Most engineers, especially in larger companies, seem to spend most of their time on a quest for that one missing document. You may have the best software and the fastest computer, and above all, you can model parts and assemblies faster than anyone in your department. But how effective are you at managing all of this power and flexibility? This is a big question, one that engineers generally do not look at or even think about.

Have you ever developed or worked on an assembly where every time you modified a part, you lost an assembly constraint? This often causes a time-consuming reassembly of all of the components that were children of the modified component. This can not only be very frustrating, but a real time vacuum, especially on larger assemblies.

Another favorite management scenario is that perfect assembly that has been fully constrained with parametric relationships in the assembly. The only problem is, you have no idea where "d5" and "d255" are and how or why they were constrained. The worst cases of poor design management are those where the entire design is constrained with indirect relationships. An indirect relationship may be in the form of a boss controlling the size of a screw hole on another component. I know there is probably that one rare case where this may be desired, but in general it may not be practical and can be a management nightmare. Can you imagine querying all the logical selections for the driving parameter, only to find it on a feature that has nothing to do with that portion of the design? Believe me, it happens.

If you are like most experienced engineers who use Pro/ENGINEER, you most likely appreciate the flexibility and intelligence that you can program into your designs. However, when it comes to managing assemblies, even the small ones, it can be very difficult to document and track all of the relationships that you have developed during your construction. Pro/ENGINEER has powerful tools for controlling geometry. However, if misapplied, they can create problems in your design. The layout module is an effective tool for the documentation and management of complex assembly and parametric relationships.

What Are Layouts?

Layout mode is coupled with the optional module Pro/DESIGN and can be accessed as a standard mode within the Pro/ENGINEER menu structure. Layouts are basically a two-dimensional environment that is used to establish the design intent and capture key dimensional and geometric relationships. This is a powerful tool and is like a virtual scratch pad that can be used to quickly define, calculate, and manage simple and complex relationships; ultimately making your life easier when it comes to managing a design.

But before you even sit down at the computer, you must have an understanding of where you are and where you are going with the design—basically what should the design be able to accomplish or satisfy. Unless you are modeling an existing component or assembly for the first time in Pro/ENGINEER, you probably do not have enough information to be able to just sit down and go right to work. You need a good understanding of the design's requirements and the expectations of other departments and the manufacturing processes.

What Are Layouts? 15

If you have gathered a list of expectations and goals for your design, then all you need to do is lay out the foundation for the design and develop the geometric and parametric relationships. A good way to do this is to analyze the documented requirements of the design and transfer that information into Pro/ENGINEER before you even model the first component. First, you need to understand the key parametric, geometric, and assembly relationships that must be maintained.

For example, your design goal is to ensure that a piston assembly is generated such that the piston is always aligned with the end of the connecting rod and held in place with a pin. The following illustration represents the free-form layout of the components that you will want to manage in the assembly.

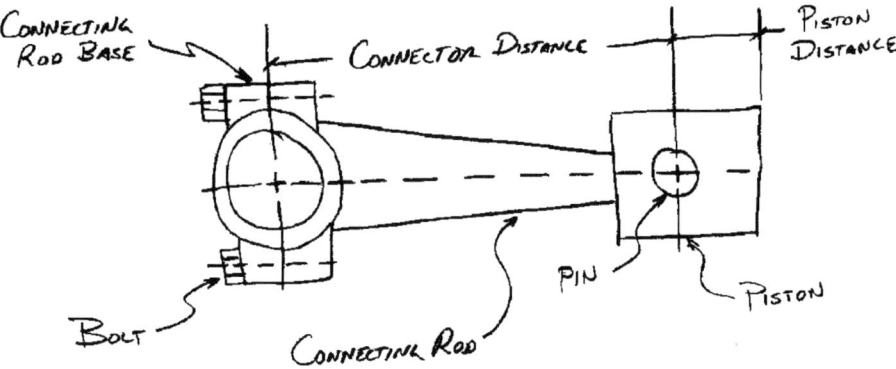

Free-form sketch layout of assembly interface.

The following illustration is the Pro/ENGINEER layout equivalent of the free-form layout shown previously.

16   Chapter 2: Managing Designs with Layouts

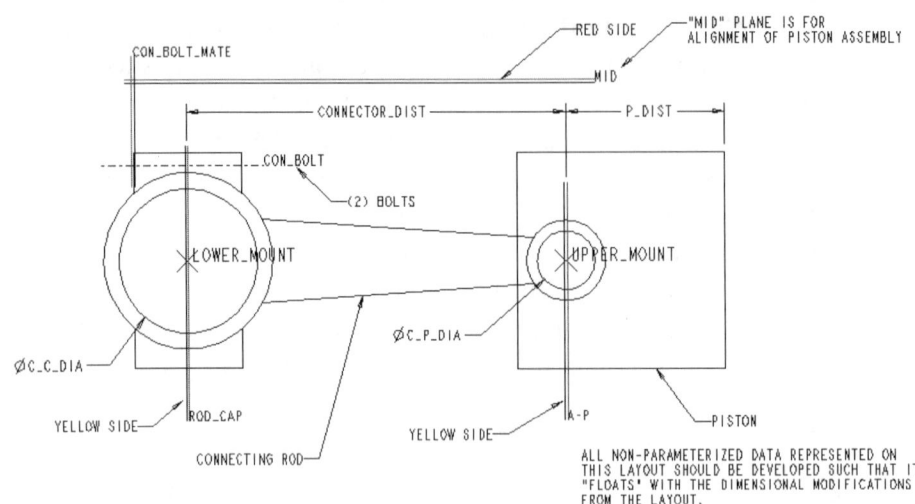

Simple assembly layout.

The previously shown Pro/ENGINEER layout highlights some of the simple relationships for the parts to mate together properly. For this application, Pro/ENGINEER only requires a datum point and some datum planes to locate and control the alignment of the piston to the connecting rod body assembly. This simple geometric relationship constrains piston to connecting rod assembly completely. There are other methods for defining this relationship, but these features work well for this application. Therefore, you will be able to put the computer to work for you and automatically assemble and parametrically manage the relationships. As an added bonus, if you have generated the rest of the layout and associated components properly, you will not have to place each component independently; the software will understand your design intent and constraints and automatically place and manage the assembly based on your layout.

What Are Layouts? 17

Looking at the same simple layout, you can see that the piston and connecting rod can also be defined and managed by simple dimensional relationships. These constraints outline the fundamental design constraints that must be achieved. All you have to do is (1) generate the components, (2) make sure that the components are "declared" to the layout, and (3) ensure that all of the geometric and dimensional relationships have been established and follow the same scheme as the layout. Once these simple requirements have been established, your design can be managed from one simple document. The following illustrations show the final individual components that will be controlled by the layout.

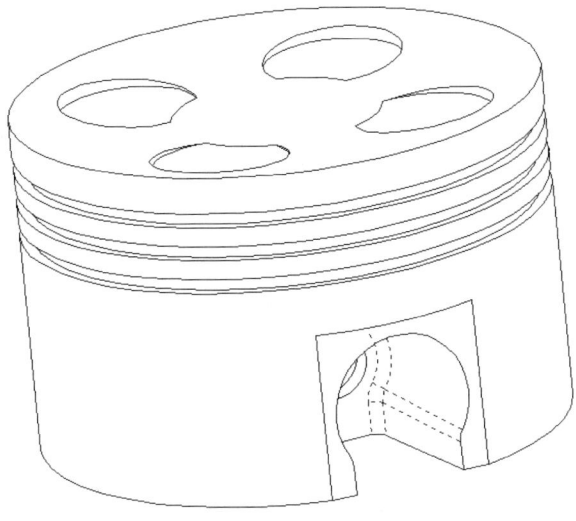

Piston.

18 Chapter 2: Managing Designs with Layouts

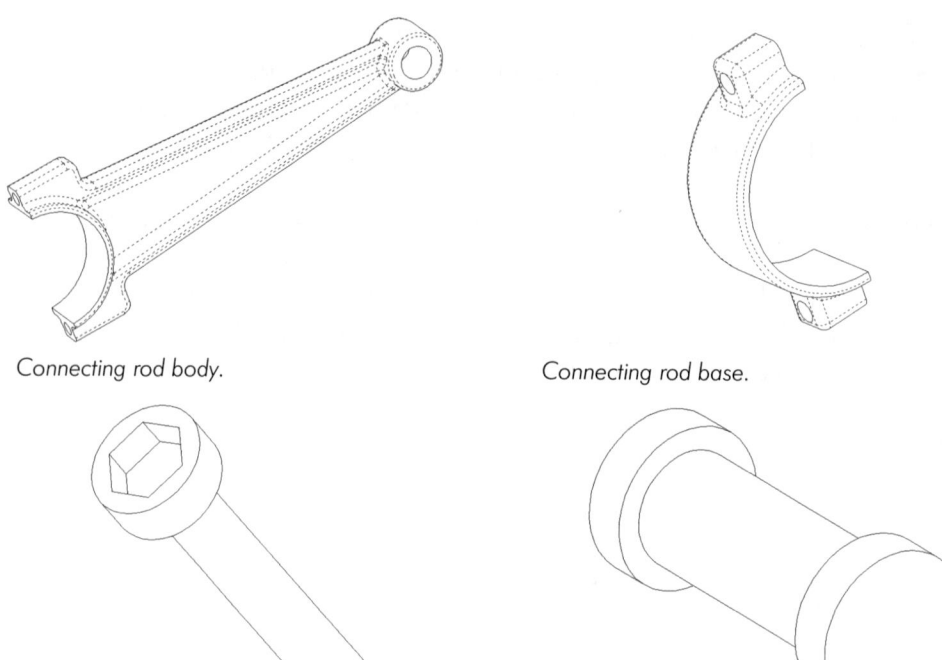

Connecting rod body.

Connecting rod base.

Bolt.

Pin.

Once these components have been completed and declared and any key dimensional relationships related to the layout file, the fun begins when you enter Assembly mode to generate the final assembly of the components.

After you have started an assembly, place your first (or base) component, and you are ready to experience the joys of automatic assembly. The next component that you place in the assembly, the piston, will be automatically assembled to the manifold. Why? Because you have already defined all of the placement and alignment constraints in the layout. The result will be Pro/ENGINEER prompting you for an "Automatic" or "Manual" method of assembly. Automatic will put the software to work for you, eliminating all of that menu picking and querying of each model's datum planes and axes required for placement in the assembly. The following illustration outlines the results of the automatic assembly of all of the components.

Putting Layouts To Work for You 19

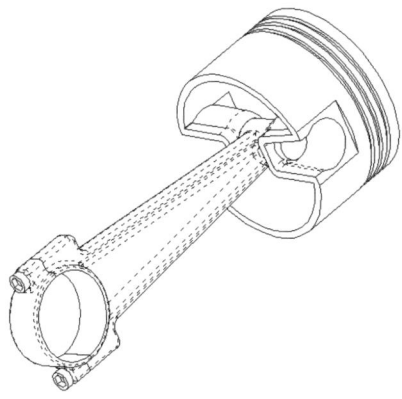

Piston, connecting rod, and pin assembly.

This automated approach to the assembly of subcomponents will continue for each and every component that you have included and related to the layout. Overall, this can save time in both the first assembly and managing modifications to the assembly after a change has occurred. But there is more to it than just automatically placing your components in the assembly.

Putting Layouts To Work for You

The key to developing effective designs lies in the quality, not the quantity, of information that you put into Pro/ENGINEER. When preparing to manage a large or small assembly, you must be careful not to turn your layouts into detail prints. Keep things simple and easy to manage. Pro/ENGINEER can handle complex calculations and even be programmed to warn you if your design inputs exceed the packaging or fundamental limits of the design. Your job, when using layouts, is to input only what is significant to the overall design. Think of this as putting up the Christmas tree and then hanging the ornaments. The Christmas tree in this case would be the fundamental parametric equations for the design and geometric relationships that must be maintained. The ornaments would be things that assist in the manufacture of

20 **Chapter 2: Managing Designs with Layouts**

or improve the load-bearing capabilities of the components such as ribs, gussets, cores, etc.

Here is a simple example of an engine block and piston assembly layout.

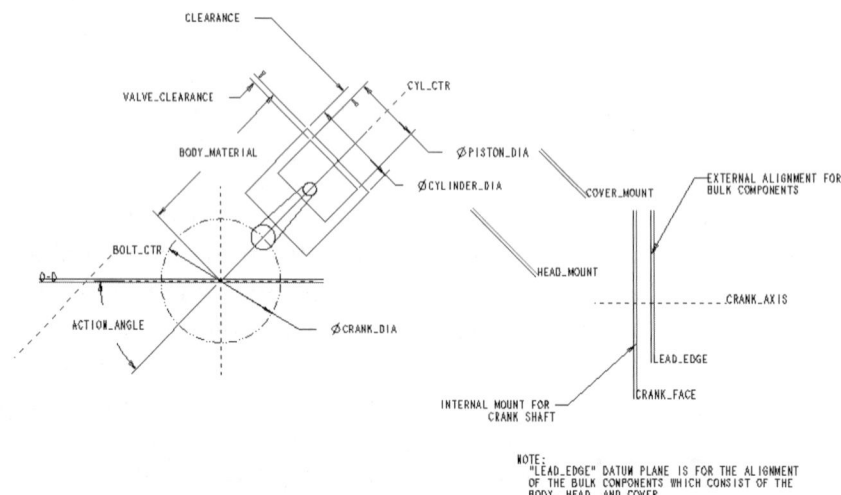

Engine block and piston assembly layout.

As you can see from the previous layout of this hypothetical engine application, only the critical assembly requirements and dimensional relationships have been laid out. They are the crank diameter (which establishes the stroke), piston diameter, cylinder diameter, and all of the axial and planar relationships for the assembly. Notice how the layout does *not* describe every single aspect of the interfacing components; only those aspects that are significant or relevant to this level of design are included. You do not need to have a lot or very accurate geometry for this phase of your design. The geometry that you see in the layout is purely for visual communication purposes. They will not change as you massage the dimensions, unless of course you are performing a Case Study.

The Case Study is a way of graphically validating your dimensional calculations. You can evaluate your design options by either (1) selecting the sketched layout geometry or (2) developing the geometry in the Sketcher session, which is used for the Case Study. Once the geometry has been established in the Sketcher, all you have to do is add dimensions, relate them to the layout using basic parametric relationships, and then regenerate the sketch. What you will see is the layout's dimensional outputs for the component. This is a quick and efficient way to look at your dimensional relationships and make sure that your relationships and equations make sense.

Taking a closer look at the table information that was generated in this layout, you can see several things being managed at once. Tables are very efficient for visualizing key relationships for the assembly. Tables permit you to localize all of the dimensions and be able to quickly locate and view the results of your modifications. The table shown in the following illustration was developed within the layout and uses the same techniques used to create tables in drawings. Please refer to the *Pro/ENGINEER Drawing User's Guide* for additional information on developing tables. Overall, the table in the following illustration explicitly outlines the relationships and what state the dimensions are in (either driving or driven). All of these data were developed to simply enhance the communication of the dimensional relationships.

Engine Assembly & Constraint Designation					
Stroke & Orientation		Actuator Calculations			
Stroke Dist.	Action Angle	Desired Clearance	Cylinder $\varnothing$	Piston $\varnothing$	
50.000	45.000	1.250	50.000	47.500	
			DRIVEN		
Body Material		Valve Clearance			
137.500		2.500			
DRIVEN					
Sub-Layout Parameters *(Values shown are driven)*					
Connector Dist.	Rod/Crank $\varnothing$	Rod/Piston $\varnothing$	Piston Distance		
80.000	22.000	12.500	30.000		

Dimensional and tolerance table for engine assembly.

If you have never managed an assembly with a layout before, you probably have either (1) generated an assembly relationship in Assembly mode or (2) just tried to remember how much to add or subtract from the interfacing component. Managing an assembly with a long list of complicated relationships can be a nightmare for two simple reasons:

1. Any small assembly relationship modification that you make can have a compounding effect on other components and subassemblies (leaving you with your mouth wide open as you watch the computer adjust the whole assembly).
2. You need an "Assembly" to generate the relationships! Isn't that putting the chicken before the egg?

Both of these management methods are valid; however, you must keep some kind of record of how and why these relationships were developed and what their impact is on the assembly. By using the layout, you can eliminate second guessing by visually displaying the dimensional relationships and outlining which component controls or drives the relationship. This is one of the biggest reasons why you should take a close look at this module; it will help you manage and document your overall designs much easier with less effort; permitting you to focus on capturing the design intent.

Layouts and the Design Intent

As you can see from the last section, layouts can be an effective tool for managing your work. But remember, in order to really put the tool to use, this module should be used as a front end to the design before you even model the first component. The use of layouts can go much further than just acting as the foundation for your design. If you have done the best that you can do in generating as much quality input as possible, you will have the perfect foundation upon which to develop your models and assemblies.

Once all of the key design parameters have been outlined in a layout, use the layout as a conversation piece to bring closure to your quest for input. Obtain a final blessing from all of the departments and personnel involved in your design. It is possible that the design's direction will change during this process. This is not unusual in the engineering field. But late changes do not hurt as much as if you had spent 2 to 3 weeks in front of your workstation modeling components and assemblies, basically generating pretty pictures. The layout gives you an opportunity to turn a stack of notes, scribbles, and general input into a rough, but functional, layout of the constraints, fits, or whatever else you wish to manipulate.

When you have all of your information pulled together, a layout that has been discussed, and all of the dimensional and tolerance relationships defined and approved, you are ready to sit down and model your components. This is where layouts can truly help you and your department launch and concurrently develop a design. I use the word *concurrently* because once you have all of the key parameters, relationships, and geometric constraints outlined in the layout, every engineer in the department has a schematic of what each component must have as a minimum foundation to satisfy the design. Hence, all the engineers have to do is select the right tools for the job, build the Christmas tree, and hang the ornaments. And that is the easy part.

Once the models have been completed they should (1) have a dimensioning and reference scheme that follows the dimensional relationships for the design or assembly, (2) be flexible, and (3) be linked ("declared") to your layout file. With these three fundamental requirements satisfied, the models and assemblies can be completely driven by the layout. This is the one area of using the Layout module where a minimal amount of work will pay off in a big way.

If all parties involved in the modeling of the components use modeling techniques that ensure model flexibility, satisfy the manufacturing requirements, and declare all of the assembly references properly, assembling components will be a pleasant (if not blissful) experience. I have worked on some large assemblies where every item had to be oriented and placed back into the assembly after a parent component was modified. Losing a parent placement constraint can create some major problems, the results of which can cause any engineer to loose another 1000 hair follicles on the spot. The automatic assembly of the components saves time, but the bigger payoff is the ability to *truly* manage the assembly from a single or multiple documents.

As an added bonus, the next engineer, a month or two from now, will be able to understand and manipulate your work with relative ease, eliminating the urge to remodel components that he or she may not understand. Nothing is more frustrating than going back to a model you generated, only to find that another engineer remodeled it.

Multiple Layouts and Assemblies

If your company or division is like most, you produce one type of component or group of like components. For example, referencing the first sets of layouts, your company may produce 10 different types of engines. The only major differences between the units are the physical size, load-carrying capacity, some electronics, and the number of connections that must be made. Each final unit is basically comprised of the same components. The only differences between the components may be their size and location in the assembly.

Assume for a moment that your department is in charge of bringing all of the components together and laying out the final product. Should you be responsible for the definition of each and every subassembly and how all of those components are assembled and managed? In a way, yes. However, you should not be the sole person to tell everyone else how their components should be developed. Fortunately, because you are working with similar assemblies, you can use these assembly characteristics to help you. Like components and assemblies generally have like interfaces and assembly procedures. You and your company can use this to your advantage.

If you have done your homework, you know what the general layout of each assembly will be. Once you have all of this data pulled together, you can standardize the assembly process for each and every assembly that your company or division produces. In essence, your assemblies are basically the same. The only difference is the size and general location. Therefore, you can send out a minimum sublayout requirement to all of the departments who are working on assemblies for the final product. Your minimum requirement may look like the illustration on page 16.

Basically you and your departments define how each of the component's layout parameters should be developed and managed. For example, you do not want the department in charge of piston assembly development to develop their assembly requirements by using datum axes when you have planned to use datum points. This is counterproductive to your design requirements. You also may require that some dimensional relationships be used consistently to minimize the amount of rework to an existing assembly that will be adapted to a variation of an existing design. By simply using the same terminology for the description of geometry and key dimensions (such as "connector_dist"), you will be able to quickly and efficiently incorporate design changes on the

Multiple Layouts and Assemblies 25

fly, rather than reworking the entire assembly every time you have a design change.

The term *sub-Layout* may be a little confusing, and here is what I am getting at: With the Layout module comes the ability to develop multiple layouts that may add information to the overall assembly. This is useful when two or more departments develop subassemblies to interface with the main assembly. You can access their layouts, which manage their designs, to incorporate critical information into your assembly. For example, you may not want to totally redevelop the distance of material required to satisfy the stroke of the piston. Because you can access the other department's layout, you can generate a link to their data and have their design drive yours, capturing the design intent of mating components (see the following illustration).

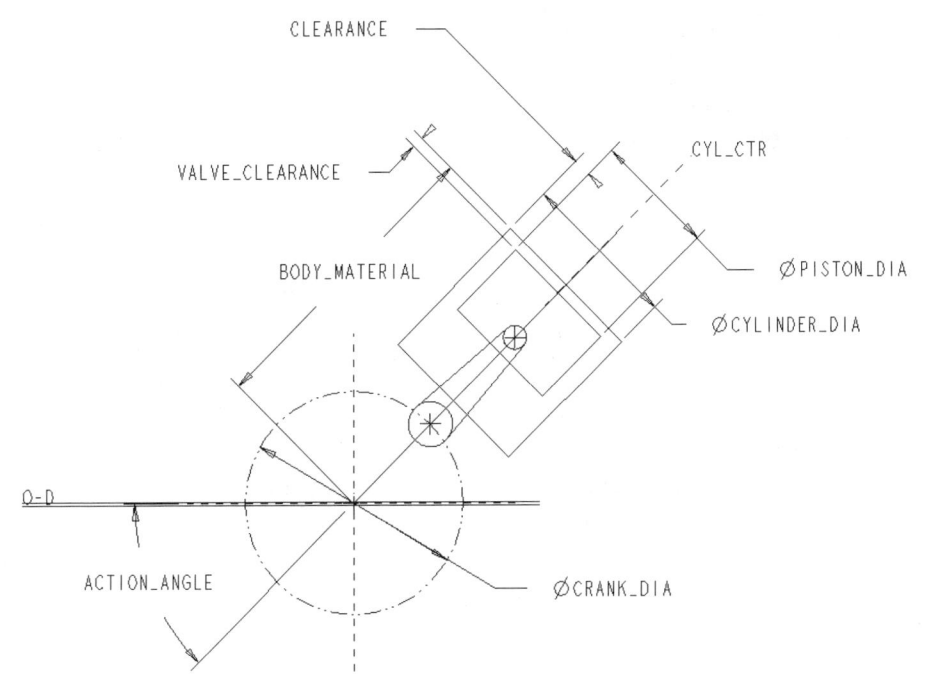

Driving your design with someone else's layout.

The relationships that govern the relationship for body_material shown above are as follows:

Chapter 2: Managing Designs with Layouts

```
cylinder_dia=piston_dia+clearance*2
body_material=p_dist+crank_dia/2+connector_dist+valve_clearance
```

The tabled results of sharing information between the layouts is shown in the figure on page 21. The resultant assembly is shown in the following figures (with the crank shaft added).

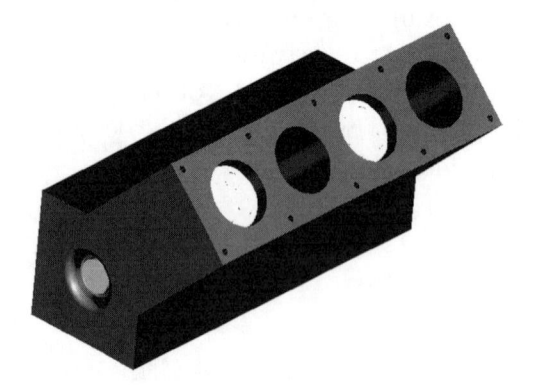

Front isometric view of final assembly.

Rear isometric view of final assembly.

Having this ability to access other departments' design parameters and integrate and manipulate that information on the fly is one area where Pro/ENGINEER really excels. This is a simple step and basically involves you "declaring" their layout to yours; just as you would declare your parts to your own layouts. This gives you even more power to quickly manage and alter the design and will generally improve your use of Pro/ENGINEER. Here is

Multiple Layouts and Assemblies 27

another example of how this module can improve your communication of the design intent.

For example, another department indicates that one particular assembly will not be able to handle the operating and assembly requirements of the overall design. They have proposed an alternative design and given you the name of the layout that governs the new design. Your job is to package the new design and make sure that it satisfies the overall requirements. This can be done fairly easily with minimum effort. By "un-declaring" the old layout and declaring the new layout, all you have to do is reestablish the dimensional relationships that govern any assembly constraints. If it is a like component, and the datum references are the same for the assembly, you will not have to adjust or add any alignment or assembly constraints; they all should be there. The Engine Assembly and Constraint Designation (page 21) and the illustration of the front isometric view of the final assembly highlight the effect of a change to the connecting rod length and action angle.

Engine Assembly & Constraint Designation				
Stroke & Orientation		Actuator Calculations		
Stroke Dist.	Action Angle	Desired Clearance	Cylinder ⌀	Piston ⌀
50.000	75.000	1.250	50.000	47.500
			DRIVEN	
Body Material		Valve Clearance		
107.500		2.500		
DRIVEN				
Sub-Layout Parameters (Values shown are driven)				
Connector Dist.	Rod/Crank ⌀	Rod/Piston ⌀	Piston Distance	
50.000	22.000	12.500	30.000	

Original layout tolerance table with the new design's layout declared (shorter connecting rod than original design).

Chapter 2: Managing Designs with Layouts

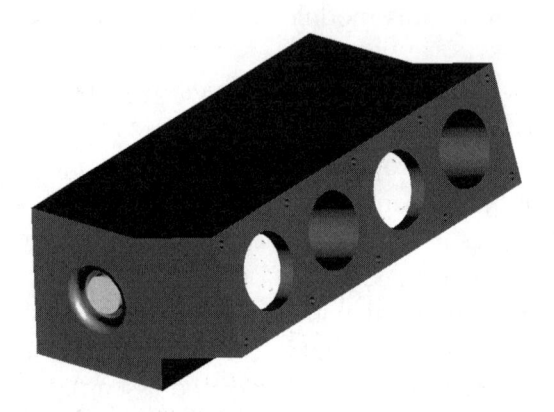

New assembly after new design's layout has been declared and the design assembled. (The engine block's action angle was also modified from 45 to 75 degrees.)

The only required change from the original design to the new design was for the engineer to assign any parametric relationships that needed to be included. However, if the original design's layout and the new design's layout used the same format and definition for control variables, no reprogramming would be required. In this particular example, the only changes that were made to the assembly were as follows:

1. The un-declaring of the original piston assembly layout from the master layout.
2. The removal of the original design from the assembly (all four piston assemblies were deleted).
3. Declaring the new design's layout to the existing design.
4. Declaring the new design's components and assemblies to the existing layout.
5. Changing the "Action_angle" value.
6. Regenerating the current layout and assembly to reflect any new changes in geometry that will occur (the Body_Material Distance changed due to the shorter connecting rod).
7. Assembling the new piston design into the assembly (Pro/ENGINEER can "automatically" place all of the piston assemblies because the new design uses the same assembly parameters and dimensioning scheme).
8. Sitting back and grinning.

✍ **NOTE:** *Since the new piston design that was assembled in the previous example uses the same references as the previous design, you may have also used the "REPLACE" command to replace the current design for the new one.*

As you can see, this particular method of managing a design is a lot more powerful than you probably imagined.

The previous example took only a few minutes to modify and update. Using conventional methods to perform the same changes could take up to a week due to the number of components that must be managed. The example outlines some of the positive effects of having like assembly references for like components. You may want to earmark this to improve your company's use of Pro/ENGINEER. If your components have like references, then you will have the ability to quickly interchange components without much work. The results are faster analysis of your design and packaging options.

Summary

You can have the best tools and fastest computers at your fingertips, but all of that power will be useless if you cannot manage your designs efficiently and effectively. Layout mode is one of the best tools for outlining and managing your designs in Pro/ENGINEER. However, as with any design in Pro/ENGINEER, you need to have quality input and a solid (no pun intended) understanding of where you are and where you are going with the design. If you are not prepared to design your components in Pro/ENGINEER, then all of your efforts may be wasted.

The Layout module can be used to formally transfer conceptual and key dimensional requirements into Pro/ENGINEER. Once in Pro/ENGINEER, the layout can be used as a conversation piece to generate more input or to obtain the final blessing on the design. This is important, because you can avoid days, if not weeks, of modeling only to scrap large portions of the design.

Once a layout of the design is completed, you will have a schematic of the minimum requirements for each component to be developed. This can act as the foundation for the design and prompt concurrent development of each component in the design. Because everyone responsible for the design has his or her requirements outlined in the layout (the Christmas tree), all he or she needs to do is pick the right tools for the job and model the components (hang the ornaments).

Above all, the layout can be used to assign and manage complex dimensional relationships over numerous components and subassemblies. This gives you the opportunity to truly manage the design through one living document, instead of tracking complex indirect parametric relationships in an assembly or part.

Starting a Design with Seed Files

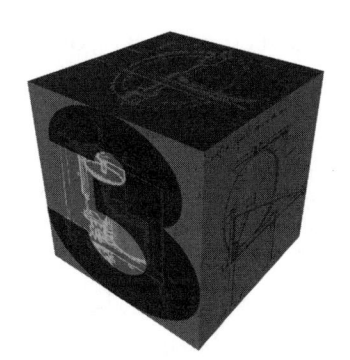

Introduction

You are in an engineering department where you are responsible for the design and verification of several components and assemblies. These designs require extensive amounts of time to research and develop, but you have a limited amount of time to accomplish these tasks. This scenario probably resembles your everyday work load.

In addition to your day-to-day responsibilities, you must follow corporate guidelines for the modeling and documentation of your designs. These guidelines require, in some cases, a significant amount of time to develop and maintain. This chapter examines the use of seed files to kickstart your design and development requirements by automating time-consuming and redundant premodeling tasks.

Chapter 3: Starting a Design with Seed Files

What Are Seed Files?

A *seed file* is a specific file or script that contains the fundamental information that you need for modeling in Pro/ENGINEER. This seed data usually consists of a set of default or offset datum planes, some basic parametric relationships that are used to link the model to the drawing, and any other user-specific requirements such as saved view orientations. The following illustration is an example of a parametric link between the model and the drawing, based on parametric relationships established by the seed file and modified by the user.

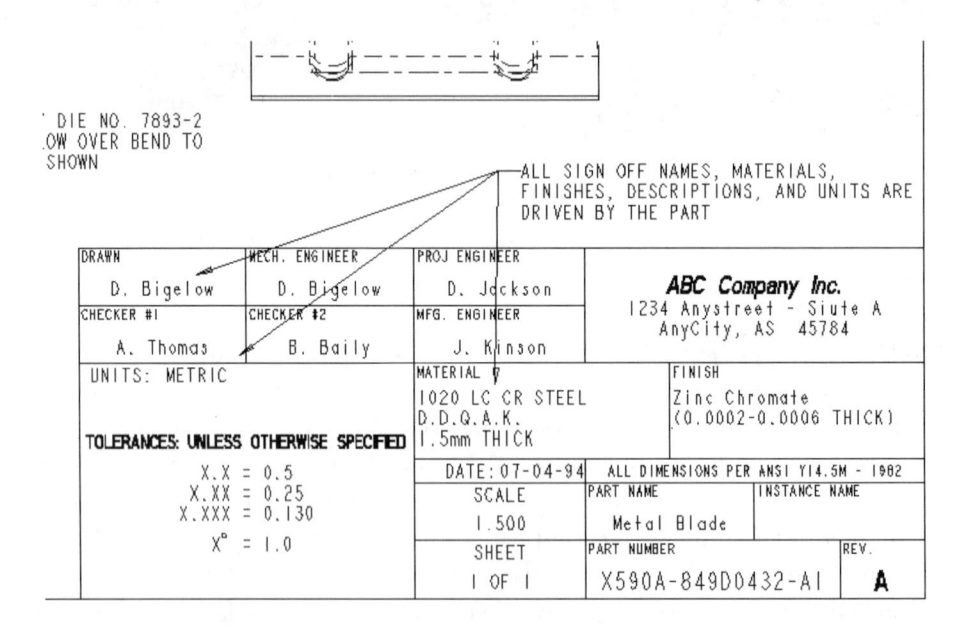

A parametric link.

The amount of information included in this file is directly related to the company's modeling and documentation requirements and how many redundant, initial tasks you want the computer to do for you.

Why Use Seed Files?

When you enter a part or assembly for the first time, you are presented with nothing. You are at ground zero with no datum planes, user-defined parametric information, or view orientations that you may query during your modeling sessions. Generally, the first thing you do is develop the information to satisfy the company's and your personal requirements for modeling and documentation.

Entering this preliminary information can take anywhere from 2 to over 10 minutes before you start to model a part. If you model six parts in a particular day, you can waste an hour of your time entering redundant data. Spread this over a week or two and you have lost valuable engineering time doing nonproductive tasks.

The development of a seed file can eliminate these repetitive tasks altogether. In addition to making your job easier, the implementation of a seed file will give you more time to engineer.

Developing Your Seed File

There are a lot of very slick and impressive methods for implementing seed files. Primarily there are two methods of implementation: (1) developing a specific seed file that you copy to new designs and (2) developing a script that executes all of the Pro/ENGINEER menu calls and numeric and alphanumeric user inputs for the seed data. Both methods are flexible, can evolve with new versions of Pro/ENGINEER, and do have advantages over each other, depending on your implementation requirements. You can experiment with each option to find the tools that satisfy your requirements.

Creating a Seed File

One easy way to implement a seed file is to develop a centrally located file that contains all of the seed data required for the development of your model or assembly. You start a new design by copying and renaming this file. Once this is done, you can load this new file into Pro/ENGINEER and begin modeling.

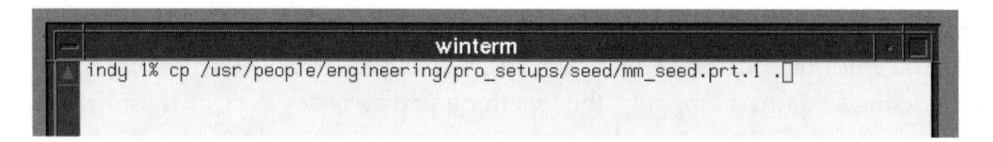

```
indy 1% cp /usr/people/engineering/pro_setups/seed/mm_seed.prt.1 .
```

Centrally located seed file being copied to a local design directory.

Even though this method saves time and ensures that the engineer is working with the latest seed file updates, it can be a hassle. If the seed file is located somewhere on a large network, typing in all of those path names could slow you down.

Developing a centrally located file works well for new designs, but as seen in the previous illustration, you can spend a lot of time locating and duplicating files. An alternative to this file management is the use of seed scripts.

Creating a Seed Script

Another way to enter seed data in your new design is to use trail files to create a seed script. The *trail file* is a recorded history of your model's development. Comprised mainly of the movements and actions of your mouse and any numeric or alphanumeric inputs, this file can be edited, manipulated, and played back, just like rewinding an audio tape and playing it back again.

The trail file is essentially a "script" of user-defined and executed events for Pro/ENGINEER to follow. Using a trail file as a method of execution is quick and can be almost seamless to the engineer. The advantage of this method is its flexibility. These scripts, as with your seed file, must be updated as Pro/ENGINEER continues to grow from version to version. The advantage of using a script is that your scripts can be used for more than simply developing your seed data when you begin a design. The same techniques can be applied to maintain existing databases, which must be updated as your requirements evolve for Pro/ENGINEER. Let's look at how trail files are developed and executed in Pro/ENGINEER and how to develop seed scripts and explore some applications of this powerful tool.

Developing Your Seed File Using Trail Files

Whenever you start up Pro/ENGINEER, a trail file is generated in your default directory (unless your *config.pro* file specifies a different location). This file records all of your operations and serves as a backup in case of a system crash. If you ever have a core dump or system crash you will learn to appreciate these files.

Let's experiment with trail files by developing a junk part. Start up a session of Pro/ENGINEER and create a part called *junk*. Once in this part, develop a set of default datum planes, add a few protrusions, cuts, and whatever else you want. Shade and rotate the model a few times and then exit Pro/ENGINEER. Once you exit Pro/ENGINEER, change to your default directory and locate the trail file that was just generated. It should look like the following:

```
trail.txt.#
```

where # is the version number of the trail file.

Rename the trail file to another file name with a *.txt* file extension. The *.txt* file extension is not required for the execution in Pro/ENGINEER. However, you may find it easier to locate and manipulate these files in a large directory by querying only *.txt* file extensions. For example, you may change the file name from *trail.txt.#* to *myfile.txt*. Be sure *not* to call the file *trail.txt*.

Now that you have saved the trail file under a new name, all you have to do is test the file by playing back the recording. To play back the trail file, enter Pro/ENGINEER and select the Trail menu selection on the MISC menu.

After selecting the Trail command, type in the name of your renamed trail file at the prompt and press return.

```
Enter File Name:myfile.txt
```

Every feature that you sketched, created, or modified will be replayed, including any shading or rotations that you performed during the part development. Eventually, at the end of your modeling session, Pro/ENGINEER will exit.

✪ **TIP:** *If Pro/ENGINEER does not replay all of the features one right after another, without pausing or stopping, check your config.pro file and make sure that the "set_trail_single_step" option is set to "No."*

Chapter 3: Starting a Design with Seed Files

Remember, the last step that you performed in your junk part was to Exit Pro/ENGINEER. Because the trail file records your menu selections, mouse locations, and actions, exiting Pro/ENGINEER was also recorded in the trail file. To keep the system from exiting Pro/ENGINEER you must remove this last set of commands from the renamed trail file.

To remove the Exit command and confirmation from your trail file, edit the file using whichever text editor you are comfortable using. When you have loaded the trail file, go to the bottom of the file and you should see some text like that in the following illustration.

```
!Regeneration completed successfully.
#VIEW
#ORIENTATION
#SPIN
!Left button to select, right button to reset, middle button to abort.
0.657961 0.403040 M
#Change_Window 0
0.720033 0.261310 M
@@Dynamic Drag
@@ 0.9304880306 0.1412622681 -0.3379896396 0.0000000000
@@ 0.2205521678 0.5206541913 0.8247884301 0.0000000000
@@ 0.2924872068 -0.8420001097 0.4533067936 0.0000000000
@@ 0.0000000000 0.0000000000 0.0000000000 1.0000000000
0.003988 0.020322 L
@@Rezult Box
#EXIT
!Do you really want to exit? [N]:
YES
@ confirm 1
```

At the bottom of a trail file.

Once at the bottom of this file, look for the first line that contains the Exit command. Delete that line and all of the lines below it. Your trail file should look like the following illustration.

Deciding What Should Be Seed Data

```
!Regeneration completed successfully.
#VIEW
#ORIENTATION
#SPIN
!Left button to select, right button to reset, middle button to abort.
0.657961 0.403040 M
#Change_Window 0
0.720033 0.261310 M
@@Dynamic Drag
@@ 0.9304880306 0.1412622681 -0.3379896396 0.0000000000
@@ 0.2205521678 0.5206541913 0.8247884301 0.0000000000
@@ 0.2924872068 -0.8420001097 0.4533067936 0.0000000000
@@ 0.0000000000 0.0000000000 0.0000000000 1.0000000000
0.003988 0.020322 L
@@Rezult Box
~
~
~
~
~
:
```

Trail file edited to remove Exit command.

This single change to the file tells Pro/ENGINEER that when you get to the end of this file, sit there and wait for the next command. Save your trail file with this change and reenter Pro/ENGINEER.

Once in Pro/ENGINEER, access the MISC menu and select the Trail menu selection.

`Enter File Name:myfile.txt`

The system will prompt you for the file name to run. As in the previous example, enter the file name of your trail file and press return. Pro/ENGINEER will take off replaying the trail file. You should see all of the menu selections, sketches, rotations, and shading that you performed in your junk part flash before your eyes. This will continue until Pro/ENGINEER reaches the end of the trail file, and then it will wait for your next command.

Now that you have a basic understanding of how trail files are created and developed, let's apply them to the development of your seed file.

Deciding What Should Be Seed Data

Before creating a working seed file, you need to determine what types of information need to be included in the file. What you select as seed data will be dictated by the methods of modeling, your company's requirements, and anything extra that you personally require.

Compose a list of the variables that must be included in the seed file. Talk to other users in your company about parameters or requirements that are already established or currently being developed.

Once this information has been gathered, lay out the order of input into the file. You may want to enter information in the following order:

1. Set the datum planes

2. Read in a parameters file

3. Set some commonly used views.

The order of placement in the file is not critical, provided that you do not attempt to perform operations that are dependent on other features for their performance. However, the entire process will be less frustrating if you develop blocks of information for entry or execution.

Let's say you are required to enter ten parametric relationships and a set of default datum planes. If you set up the datum planes and then enter the relationships one at a time, you will not be using your time efficiently. A better way is to write a generic text file that contains all of the generic parametric relationships. All you'll have to do is read in that single file instead of typing in every relationship.

Now, what happens when your assembly models and drawings require a completely different set of parametric relationships? Don't worry, even though these models and drawings often require their own types of information, the same seed file or script implementation techniques may be applied for entering the data.

> ✪ *TIP: Generating a text file of the parametric relationships simplifies the input of the information. This text should be stored in a special place, independent from Pro/ENGINEER and your models and assemblies, so that it can be updated and reread into later versions of the seed file.*

A detailed discussion of parametric relationships occurs in Chapter 8. For now, you should know that parametric relationships in a text file are defined using the following simple equation:

```
variable="value"
```

A complete relationships text file could look like the following:

Deciding What Should Be Seed Data

```
design_engineer=""
design_checker=""
quality_engineer=""
department_manager=""
```

✍ **NOTE:** *Each relationship in the previously listed text does not contain any value between the quotations. This value may be entered in Pro/ENGINEER once the seed script has been executed and the relationships read into Pro/ENGINEER.*

Suppose that your manufacturing engineers require that a fixture be included in a table on the assembly drawing for your design. Your parametric relationship in the assembly may look like the following:

```
Fixture_Number="KX-5560"
```

As you can see, the variable portion of this relationship is the *Fixture_Number* and the value is *KX-5560*. Please note that the value portion of the relationship is in quotes. This is important, because it explicitly defines the relationship, guaranteeing that the value portion of the equation will be passed from the assembly to the drawing table.

Turning Seed Data into a Seed File

Remember that whenever you start to work in Pro/ENGINEER a trail file is generated in the default directory (or wherever your *config.pro* file instructs Pro/ENGINEER to write these files). Once you have decided what you need for seed data and you have written the parametric relationships into a text file, start up Pro/ENGINEER and create a part. Call it whatever you wish. Once in the part, follow these steps:

1. Create a set of default datum planes.
2. Access the RELATIONS menu, edit the relationships, and read in the text file that contains all of your parametric relationships.
3. Save a couple of view orientations from the default datum planes, if you would like them saved.
4. Once you have developed all of the seed data that you require for every file that you will be creating, exit Pro/ENGINEER with or without saving the file.

Chapter 3: Starting a Design with Seed Files

5. Change to the default directory and locate the trail file. Rename and edit the trail file to remove the Exit command sequence.

Now you can test your seed script. Enter Pro/ENGINEER and select the Trail menu selection under the MISC menu.

At the command prompt, type in the trail file name that you just created and press return.

```
Enter File Name:myfile.txt
```

You should see Pro/ENGINEER replay that trail file and stop at a point just prior to exiting. At this point you will have all of your datums set, parametric notes established, and any other user-specific requirements in place and ready for you to begin your modeling and development.

However, your job is not complete. When you entered Pro/ENGINEER and began to model a part, your menu selections and file name were recorded in the trail file. Therefore, whenever you enter Pro/ENGINEER and run your trail file, you are creating and naming a part. So every time you run this file you are creating a part with everything you want, only with the wrong name. Unless of course you want every part to start out with the same name. One solution would be to simply rename the part to a new name in Pro/ENGINEER. However, even this task requires time and would be considered a redundant task. To get around this nuisance, you must reedit your modified trail file and remove the mode selection and naming portion of the file.

Because these operations were performed at the beginning of the modeling session, they will be at the beginning of the trail file, just below the header. See the following example.

> **NOTE:** *Pro/ENGINEER automatically generates a header for each trail file. You must leave the header alone. Pro/ENGINEER will not run a trail file without it.*

Deciding What Should Be Seed Data 41

```
HEADER ──┐
         ├─ !trail file version No. 731
         ├─ !Pro/ENGINEER  TM  Release  13.0  (c) 1988-94 by
         └─ !Select a menu item.
            #PART
            #CREATE
PART DEFINITION ── !Enter Part name [PRT0001]:
            seed-file-01
            @ ok
            #FEATURE
            #CREATE
            #DATUM
            #PLANE
```

Original trail file with part definition.

Once these lines are deleted from the trail file, your file should look like the following:

```
!trail file version No. 731
!Pro/ENGINEER  TM  Release 13.0  (c) 1988-94 by Param
!Select a menu item.
#FEATURE
#CREATE
#DATUM
#PLANE
#DEFAULT
!DATUM PLANE has been created successfully.
#DONE
#RELATIONS
!Select a feature to display parameters, or select fr
```

Modified trail file, with part definition removed.

Once these changes have been made, save the file. Now you have a file that will execute within a user-created and named part, instead of executing the trail file immediately after entering Pro/ENGINEER. Test this file by entering Pro/ENGINEER and starting a part; call it anything you wish. Once in the part, select the MISC menu and then the Trail menu selections from the menu and enter your modified trail file name. After you press enter, you should see all the seed data replayed into your new part.

Congratulations! You have just developed your first seed script. Now that you have a tool to quickly load all of the seed data, let's analyze some methods of improving the execution of this information.

Optimizing Seed File Execution

There are primarily two methods for executing commands in Pro/ENGINEER: macros and menu selection. Overall, these two methods do the same thing; the difference lies in the way the information is presented to the user. One method relies on the user to remember the command sequence, and the other method incorporates the functionality directly into the Pro/ENGINEER menu structure.

Each of these methods has advantages and disadvantages, and you will have to decide which method of execution best satisfies your requirements. Please note that it is important to review any changes in the Pro/ENGINEER menu structure and the methods of trail file development from one version of Pro/ENGINEER to the next. This ensures that you are always incorporating the latest functionality into your files. Chapter 9 contains an in-depth discussion of macros and menu selection modifications. For this discussion we will be looking at how they can be linked to the seed file.

Macro Execution Methods

Pro/ENGINEER has a sophisticated set of tools for the development of user-definable functions, commonly called macros. Macros are a small, one-lined script of commands that are to be executed by Pro/ENGINEER. Our overall goal is to streamline the input and execution of the seed file in Pro/ENGINEER.

Let's say that you have chosen to use a macro to execute the seed script that you have developed. To incorporate this functionality, you must edit your *config.pro* file and add the following line of information:

    mapkey mcro #Misc;#Trail;"*yourfilename.txt*"

This one line of information tells Pro/ENGINEER that you will be assigning a key sequence called *mcro* to the list of commands from the MISC and Trail menu selections, with a final entry of your trail file's name. Once you reread your *config.pro* file into Pro/ENGINEER, whenever you type `mcro` in the keyboard Pro/ENGINEER will load your seed script.

The key advantage to using macros for the execution of the seed file is that the seed file can be called by a few simple keystrokes. The big disadvantage to this method is that the keystrokes must be memorized. If you have a lot of macros for executing functions in Pro/ENGINEER, there is always the risk that you will actually call the seed script late in the development of a file.

Accidentally executing the seed script late in the design's development can cause some headaches and in some cases cause a core dump. The reason for this is simple; once the seed data has been read into the system you do not need to read the information in again (unless you are executing an update script; this is covered later in the chapter). When you tell Pro/ENGINEER to reread and execute the information that has been developed for the beginning of a file, some of the functionality may not be available later in the modeling session. During the execution, Pro/ENGINEER may not have access to some default functionality that your seed script indicates should be there; the result often is a core dump or a system hang.

✪ ***TIP:*** *If macro execution of a seed file is desired, make the macro's keystrokes totally independent of any other macros that you may have written. Avoid any opportunity for late execution of the seed script.*

Menu Execution Methods

Menu execution of a seed file is an efficient and visually obvious method. This involves the incorporation of a new menu selection within an existing Pro/ENGINEER menu structure. Chapter 9 contains a detailed discussion of menu selection development. A menu selection will act as a small script that is executed from the menus instead of blindly by a macro. This is the key advantage of using a menu selection for this application.

To avoid accidental execution, I generally place this menu selection in the MISC menu; Pro/ENGINEER automatically locates the user-defined menu selection within the menu. Here is an example of the menu before and after the addition of the user-defined menu selection.

44   Chapter 3: Starting a Design with Seed Files

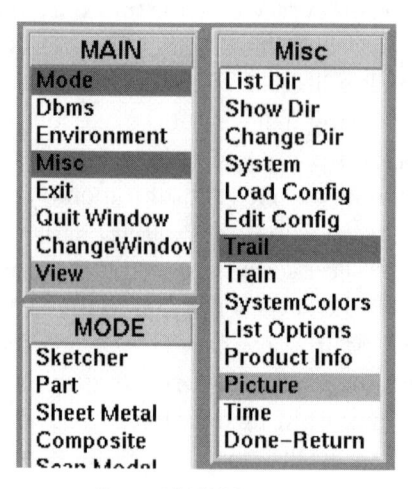

Original MISC menu.

Modified MISC menu with added SEED menu item.

From the previous example, you could simply execute the entire seed script from the click of a button on the added SEED menu selection.

Because you do not want to accidentally select this added menu selection when you are modeling a component, try to place this added selection on the MISC menu or any other submenu under the MAIN menu. Even though you do access these menus quite a bit during your modeling sessions, it is important to limit your chances of accidental selection by keeping it as separate as possible.

Adding New Parameters

As your company continues to use Pro/ENGINEER and more departments become literate with Pro/ENGINEER, your overall standards will most likely change. Adapting to this change can be a challenge, especially if your company has several hundred parts already developed using existing modeling standards, seed files, and requirements.

Generally, most changes or improvements to existing files and seed data will be department- or process-specific modifications.

For example, your manufacturing department may require that a layer called "MECH" be added to all new and existing casting files so that machining operations can be selectively suppressed by a layer. Their request is based on a need to improve the model filtering time for the machining of casting blanks. In addition to the development of a layer, they have requested that a clamp offset relationship be added to the model so that it appears in a table on the drawing. The following explains a useful method for developing an updated script using the trail files generated by changing or adding to an existing model.

Adding New Information to Old Models

Adding information into a new design is easy, and can be made almost seamless. But what happens when you must add new variables to an existing design or a whole set of designs? If you or your company has standardized the information that is input and maintained with your parts and assemblies, you are in luck. Modifying or adding information to an existing model will be much easier. Problems occur when one person is modeling their parts and developing parametric relationships independent of the company's standards and requirements. These differences can manifest in the form of additional and unnecessary datum planes in the part or a completely different set of relationship callouts relative to the seed data.

Chapter 3: Starting a Design with Seed Files

If everyone in the department, or company, has used the same seed data in their designs, adding to or modifying existing models can be almost effortless. Once again we will access the functionality of the trail file to help us accomplish these tasks.

Referring to the previous example, manufacturing requires that an additional layer be developed called "MECH" within every sand cast part. Manufacturing also has requested that an additional set of clamp offset distance relationships be included in the file to ensure that the information will appear in a table on the drawing.

With the required modifications outlined by another department, all you have to do is develop, test, and implement the modifications. To do this, start up a Pro/ENGINEER session, access an existing part, and add the other department's requirements. Set up the layer called "MECH," add the new relationships for the part, and then Exit Pro/ENGINEER.

Caution: When you edit your relations in Pro/ENGINEER, your trail file will record your complete list of existing relations within the file you are editing. The following illustration shows how editing an existing component's relations writes all of the relationships into the trail file.

```
                              winterm
#RELATIONS
!Select a feature to display parameters, or select from Relation menu.
#EDIT REL
!results of editing rel.ptd
@ edit
^/*********************************************
^/******* General Relationships ***********
^/*********************************************
^
^/***** General Information *****
^drawn="D. Bigelow"
^m_engineer="D. Bigelow"
^checker_1="A. Thomas"
^checker_2="B. Baily"
^mfg_engineer="J. Kinson"
^p_engineer="D. Jackson"
^date="07-04-94"
^/***** Material Definition *****
^material1="1020 LC CR STEEL"
^material2="D.D.Q.A.K."
^material3="1.5mm THICK"
^/***** Finish Definition *****
^finish1="Zinc Chromate"
^finish2="(0.0002-0.0006 THICK)"
^finish3=""
^/***** Component's Name *****
^name="Metal Blade"
^/**** Model Revision Letter *****
^revision="A"
^/***** Units *****
^units="METRIC"
^/***** Added Parameters *****
^clamp1_dist=""
^clamp2_dist=""
^clamp3_dist=""
^
@ endedit
```

Adding relationships in an existing file.

Adding New Parameters

Editing an existing model to add new parameters can create some problems due to that file's current relationships being written to your trail file, just by editing the relations. Since all you will be doing is adding some new variables and defining a new layer for an existing model, take the direct approach and develop your layer followed by using the "Add" option in the RELATIONS menu.

```
MODEL REL
Assem Rel
Part Rel
Feat Rel
Pattern Rel
Done

RELATIONS
Add
Edit Rel
Show Rel
Evaluate
Sort Rel
Show Dim
Switch Dim
Add Param
Del Param
Component Id
User Prog
Where Used
```

The Add option in the RELATIONS menu.

This will allow you to append an existing set of relationships, without letting any existing relationships be written to the trail file. Once you have input your new relationships, exit Pro/ENGINEER and change to your default directory or wherever your trail files are written to. Locate the trail file that was just created. If you edit the file, it should look similar to the following illustration.

48   Chapter 3: Starting a Design with Seed Files

```
winterm
!trail file version No. 731
!Pro/ENGINEER  TM  Release 13.0  (c) 1988-94 by Parametric Technology Corporatio
n  All Rights Reserved.
!Select a menu item.
#LAYER
#CREATE
!Enter layer name [QUIT]:
mech
!Layer MECH was added to BLADE. Enter again [QUIT]:

0.604166 0.465112 R
#DONE/RETURN
#RELATIONS
!Select a feature to display parameters, or select from Relation menu.
#ADD
!Enter RELATION [QUIT]:
added_param1=""
!Enter RELATION [QUIT]:
added_param2=""
!Enter RELATION [QUIT]:

#DONE
#EXIT
!Do you really want to exit? [N]:
YES
@ confirm 1
```

Edited file.

As in our previous examples, rename the trail file to a different name with a *.txt* file extension, remove the Exit, mode, and naming command sequences from the trail file and re-enter Pro/ENGINEER. Once in Pro/ENGINEER, load up the part that you just used for your trail file's development.

✍ **NOTE:** *Because you did not save the modified part, all of your changes will not be in the model.*

Run the trail file just as before. During this file's execution, you will see the layer created and the relationships added to your general set of relations. Once this trail file has been executed, you have successfully updated your Part File to the new requirements and Pro/ENGINEER will await your next command.

✪ **TIP:** *The incorporation of new information into existing files can be difficult and risky if you are not careful. Generally, you should test any modifications that you will be making to existing seed files or scripts before they are released for public use.*

This technique can save you and your colleagues a lot of time updating older databases to current standards.

Updating the Seed Script with New Information or Requirements

If you are using a seed script to execute or input all of your seed into a new design, and new requirements are to be added to your seed data, should you recreate the seed script? For most updates that don't require geometry additions or modifications, the answer is no. Most of your updates can be accomplished by simply manually appending your existing seed script to add the latest requirements. The seed script file, as we have discussed, is simply a file that Pro/ENGINEER plays back like an audio tape in a tape recorder. This file, like an audio tape, can be edited to remove portions of unwanted command sequences. The opposite is also true; these trail files can be edited to add information to update the script without recreating the entire trail file. The types of information that can be updated manually is limited to alphanumeric inputs from the user, meaning you will not be able to manipulate existing solid surface geometries from the trail file.

Using our previous example with the manufacturing departments' additional requests, we will modify the existing seed script to add the new layer and parametric relationships.

To add the new parametric relationships to the existing script, edit the current file and go to where the relationships are defined in the script. Once you have located the relationships, you have one of two choices for adding the new relationships. You may either (1) copy an existing relationship and replace it with your new relationship or (2) develop an Add sequence that will mimic the Pro/ENGINEER menu selections and alphanumeric inputs.

Copying and replacing an existing relationship is a quick and effective method for adding new relationships. A typical copy, add, and replace sequence would start out as shown in the following illustration.

Chapter 3: Starting a Design with Seed Files

```
winterm
#DONE
#RELATIONS
!Select a feature to display parameters, or select from Relation menu.
#EDIT REL
!results of editing rel.ptd
@ edit

^/********************************************
^/******* General Relationships ************
^/********************************************

^/***** General Information *****
^drawn=""
^m_engineer=""
^checker_1=""
^checker_2=""
^mfg_engineer=""
^p_engineer=""
^date=""

^/***** Material Definition *****
^material1=""
^material2=""
^material3=""

^/***** Finish Definition *****
^finish1=""
^finish2=""
^finish3=""

^/***** Component's Name *****
^name=""

^/**** Model Revision Letter *****
^revision=""

^/***** Units *****
^units=""
```

Original trail file.

Once a line is selected, copied, and added to the script, your file should look like that shown in the following figure.

```
winterm
#DONE
#RELATIONS
!Select a feature to display parameters, or select from Relation menu.
#EDIT REL
!results of editing rel.ptd
@ edit

^/********************************************
^/******* General Relationships ************
^/********************************************

^/****** THIS IS THE ADDED INFORMATION IN THE SEED FILE ******
^new_param1=""
^new_param2=""

^/***** General Information *****
^drawn=""
^m_engineer=""
^checker_1=""
^checker_2=""
^mfg_engineer=""
^p_engineer=""
^date=""

^/**** Material Definition *****
^material1=""
^material2=""
^material3=""

^/***** Finish Definition *****
^finish1=""
^finish2=""
^finish3=""

^/***** Component's Name *****
^name=""

^/**** Model Revision Letter *****
```

Finished sequence (with new parameters).

Adding New Parameters 51

As you can see, the only difference is that the new relationships were added to the existing script by copying an existing line and entering the new relationships within the script. Once these relationships have been added, save the script. The next time you enter Pro/ENGINEER and execute your seed script, you will see these new relationships in your list of parametric relations.

Another method for adding information to an existing seed script would be to mimic Pro/ENGINEER's menu selections while adding your new relationships. Before you do this, create a part and manually add some parametric relationships using the Add menu selection in the RELATIONS menu. Exit the part and take a look at the trail file that was created. Your file should look like the following example.

```
^finish3="Yellow Chromate"
^
^/***** Component's Name *****
^name="BRACKET ASSEMBLY"
^
^/**** Model Revision Letter *****
^revision="C"
^
^/***** Units *****
^units="METRIC"
^
^
^
^
^
^
@ endedit
#ADD
!Enter RELATION [QUIT]:
additional_param1=""
!Enter RELATION [QUIT]:
additional_param2=""
!Enter RELATION [QUIT]:
#DONE
```

New trail file with newly added parameters.

The previous example shows the relation's Add sequence for a parametric relationship. The goal is to add the same menu and key sequences to your existing seed script, adding new relationships without complete redevelopment of the seed script.

Edit your seed script and go to a point below your original relation's development in the file. This is done to ensure that these modifications will occur after the relationships are added to the part. Type in the exact text sequence for adding a relationship to the file, as shown in the previous example. Once this has been added to your seed script, it should look like the following illustration.

```
                              winterm
^finish3=""

^/***** Component's Name *****
^name=""

^/**** Model Revision Letter *****
^revision=""

^/***** Units *****
^units=""




@ endedit
#ADD
!Enter RELATION [QUIT]:
additional_param1=""
!Enter RELATION [QUIT]:
additional_param2=""
!Enter RELATION [QUIT]:

#DONE
```

Manually adding parameters to an existing seed file.

Once you have completed this addition to the script, save it and test the script in Pro/ENGINEER. You should see the seed data and then the additions load into the part relations. Once this has occurred, you can edit the relations and they will be added at the bottom of the file.

Although not recommended for simple additions and modifications, there is one other option for updating the seed script—regenerating the entire file from scratch. Use this as a *last resort* for these types of updates. Once the script has been proven to be successful and accurate, it is always better to build on that foundation than to tear down the building and start over. Please note that you may be required to recreate a seed script to incorporate new functionality from one revision to the next of Pro/ENGINEER, just as you may have to do with seed files.

Improving the Update Execution

Updating and adding information to an existing model can be a simple process for you and your fellow engineers. Please keep in mind that the only differences between your seed script and update script are the operations that you are performing. One script, the seed script, is designed for jump-starting your designs by eliminating redundant tasks. Whereas the other script is designed to improve and update your models as new requirements are developed.

Just as you have improved the execution of your seed script, you can improve the execution of your update script. Generally, engineers are not willing to change or incorporate small details of information for another department, unless absolutely necessary. By using an update script, you can automate this entire update process, just as you automated the execution of the seed script.

For example, you have developed and renamed a trail file that incorporates another department's design and documentation requirements. By adding a menu selection for the update file, just as in the seed script, you will be able to update your files at the click of a button. This added menu selection could look like the following figure.

```
Misc
List Dir
Show Dir
Change Dir
System
Load Config
Edit Config
Trail
Train
SystemColors
List Options
Product Info
Picture
Time
Done-Return
SEED
UPDATE
```

Update menu selection.

Summary

Seed files contain all the basic modeling and relationship requirements for a design's development, which are based on your company's modeling and documentation standards and can act as the foundation for your design's development.

You have better things to do besides inputting redundant information into every model you develop. A seed file can eliminate redundant tasks and requirements by automating the development of datum planes, generic sets of relationships, view orientations, and any other user-specific requirements, while giving you more time to engineer.

Efficient implementation of the seed data into the models can be accomplished by either (1) actually developing a file or (2) developing a script that executes the necessary Pro/ENGINEER menu calls. There are a number of methods for implementing this information; one of the more impressive methods uses trail files. The trail file basically replays all of the information that you have input into the model.

Once the seed file or script has been developed, the execution of the information must be developed. Macros and menu selections are two efficient methods for implementing the seed data into a model. These same general techniques can be used to update existing models in Pro/ENGINEER.

It is important that you update your seed files and seed scripts as new functionality is added to Pro/ENGINEER. This ensures that you're working with the latest file formats and variables that have been incorporated into Pro/ENGINEER.

Corporate Standards and Contracted Resources

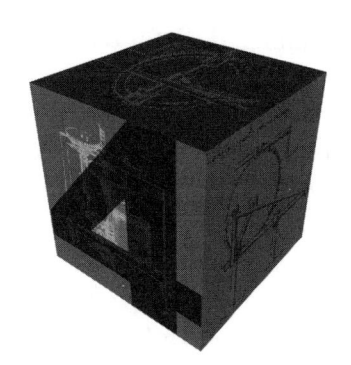

Introduction

Suppose that your company primarily develops one type of product, a gauge panel for the automotive industry. This product is constantly being redesigned and updated to satisfy the industry's demand for new products. Overall, the primary variations in the product are the placement of the instrumentation, packaging, and styling of the face plate and its associated assembly components.

Because your company has invested heavily in Pro/ENGINEER, it will be expecting results from you and your engineering department that are just as quick and efficient as a PTC demo. In addition, you are expected to improve the current and future design process further by sharing information in the form of parts, assemblies, and drawings by developing libraries of your current and past designs.

After working on an assembly for a few days, you are ready to include a subassembly component from another engineer in the department. As the component is loaded, you notice that your system has slowed down tremendously; it takes several minutes to regenerate the image of the design, and you can't even see the part that you assembled. After closer inspection, you find that your fellow engineer has over 150 datum planes obstructing your view of the component and over 600 features to describe the relatively simple plastic component. Most of the features are short, simple, wedge-like cuts that emulate draft for the component's surfaces.

With a deadline approaching fast, you opt to retrieve the original print and recreate the needed component. Upon completion of your remodeling, the component is down to approximately 7 datum planes and 70 features. In the end, your time for product development was improved by totally redeveloping a component that would otherwise have acted like an anchor to your assembly, dragging down your system's regeneration time and performance, and potentially placing your overall design in jeopardy.

There are a lot of reasons why this situation could exist in companies that have invested in Pro/ENGINEER. This chapter discusses some of the reasons why problems exist, how to recognize the problems, and how to develop future solutions for this important corporate issue.

What Are Corporate Standards?

Corporate standards can be as simple as having a set of requirements for each and every model that your company develops. Examples of these requirements are listed below:

1. Parts and assemblies that are not using data from other CAD/CAM systems will have a set of default datum planes as the base feature for the design.
2. Parts and assemblies that use data from other CAD/CAM systems will use a set of offset datum planes as the base feature for the design.
3. All parts and assemblies will have a default (Cartesian) coordinate system.

What Are Corporate Standards?

4. All parts will have the following layers included in the file:
   - ROUNDS: all nonessential rounds for FEA modeling and machining
   - W_IGES: Wireframe IGES inputs
   - S_IGES: Surface IGES inputs
   - P_DRAFTS: Primary drafts for the design (bulk geometry)
   - S_DRAFTS: Detail drafts for manufacturability
   - HOLES: Patterned holes for design
   - CONSTRUCTION: Construction datums and features
   - D_CURVES: Datum curves
   - D_POINTS: Datum points
5. All appropriate geometry shall be layered on the appropriate layers shown above.
6. All new designs are to be started with the company's seed file to load the latest variables and default file requirements.
7. All existing designs that you may be modifying will be updated to current standards by using the "update" script.
8. All drawings are to be completed using the fully parametric formats.
9. All Pro/ENGINEER reports are to be generated using Pro/REPORT.
10. All parts, assemblies, and drawings are to be completed in metric units.

This list could continue for another few pages as to what the bare minimum requirements would be for an engineer to develop a new design or update an existing design to the latest set of corporate standards.

Corporate standards can also be as broad as which modules to use for certain types of parts, or when layouts are to be used and how they are to be set up and maintained. Looking at an even larger picture, corporate standards could also be used to define how parts are to be assembled, what types of tools and equipment to use for one type of manufacturing process over another, or even what types of inspection (linear dimension exclusively or the use of GD&T) are to be used for one type of part versus another.

From the approach to modeling the design, to the dimensional or feature relationships that must be maintained, there is no doubt that the design process described previously could have benefited from the use of corporate standards. A corporate standard, for the above example, could have been used to define the key geometric and dimensional relationships for mounting features or the alignment of the dial portion of the gauge relative to the mountings for the vehicle. These represent some primitive characteristics of the design, but could be very important and functional to your assembly needs and your customers.

But looking back at the previous example, the key issues were how the subassembly component was developed and how that method of development directly affected the efficiency of others. Here lies another opportunity to implement corporate standards. The definition of key feature relationships and flexibility for the design is a good place to start. But when dealing with parts and assemblies, especially when you are working with designs that will be used many times within a family of designs, it can be very helpful to optimize the method of development, document the key dimensional relationships, the tools used for development, and how the model should be expected to react to changes in the design intent (the list, of course, can be expanded to the manufacturing, analysis, and inspection requirements). This is not an easy task and takes time to develop, but can, if done properly and with enough quality information, improve the speed and efficiency of completing designs for a specific application.

Above and beyond the minimum part, drawing, and assembly requirements for all users of Pro/ENGINEER at your company, optimally capturing the design intent for standard components may be your next big hurdle. Essentially, the corporate standard for model development would serve as a list of instructions, or a "recipe," of the tools, modeling approach, key relationships, and a list of other designs or manufacturing functions with which the design must be able to interface. A lot of this information, especially the processing of the design, can be captured on the detail drawing for the design. But there are a number of areas of the design's development that just can't be put on a detail drawing: that information (i.e., modeling tools, techniques, approaches, etc.) generally do not add any value to the manufacture of the design. The following is a brief example of a corporate standard.

What Are Corporate Standards? 59

XYZ Company, Inc.
Pro/ENGINEER Corporate Standards Worksheet

Annotated Picture of Optimized Design

Part Information
Reference Part Number:
Drawing Number:
Part Name:
Units for Design:
Is Database a Design or User-Defined Feature (UDF):

Database's Location:
Under PDM Server Control: Yes/No
Network Node Location:
Off-line Location:

First Used:
Material:
Approximate No. of Features:
Dimensional Relationships:
Global Relationships:

Application(s)
Developed Using Pro/ENGINEER Rev. No.   CD No.
Pro/ENGINEER Modules Used for Development:

Note on model development (where to start, modeling tools used, basic layout of feature-by-feature development, any user-defined features, etc.):

Manufacturing
Will the database be used for manufacturing purposes? Yes/No
Will Pro/MANUFACTURING be used? Yes/No
Pro/MANUFACTURING databases?
     Under PDM Control: Yes/No
     Network Node Location:
     Off-line Location:

Analysis
Will the database be used for analysis purposes? Yes/No
Is Pro/MESH used for mesh generation and constraint definition? Yes/No
What types of meshes will be used?
Does FEA model use symmetry? Yes/No
Where are the output files and results databases located:
     Under PDM control? Yes/No

--Continued--

Corporate standard worksheet.

Think of the corporate standard worksheet as a living document of how to optimally develop specific components in Pro/ENGINEER. This process of optimization and documentation takes time to develop and may require that some sections of the design be dumped from your screen and included in the package. But the purpose of this is to document what tools and techniques capture the design intent of the design as well as any dimensional or process limitations. This document, or whatever mechanism your company uses for maintaining its corporate standards, can be very helpful in the reduction of the "trial and error" approach to solving a design or modeling problem.

One direct effect of using a corporate standards worksheet to document an optimal method of development is a transcript of model development that could be reviewed by others to change the design easily. These worksheets can be very helpful when a design has been completed, released, and is in production. Suppose that you are required to make a change to an existing design that was developed by another engineer using a mutually agreed upon corporate standard. If you simply pulled the corporate standard for this type of part that was developed, you could learn quite a bit about the development techniques, modules, manufacturing or analysis files that may be dependent on this model. This is invaluable information when it comes to making changes to existing databases. If this information is not available and everyone is doing his or her own thing for modeling designs, do you think you would be able to quickly make a change? Or would you eventually break down and remodel the design to your personal preferences? Mark down another plus for having corporate standards.

This may seem like a lot of work, but once you have a design developed, optimized, tested, and documented, the next person who needs to develop a similar design will have a library of standards to draw from, instead of trying to tackle all the design challenges on his or her own.

This is just one approach to the solution of establishing and maintaining corporate standards for Pro/ENGINEER. There are many different approaches to the solution of this problem, and some methods work better than others; the bottom line is that you must find what works best for you and your company. The long-term benefits outweigh the short-term frustrations of implementing corporate standards.

Why Have Corporate Standards for Pro/ENGINEER?

When used properly, Pro/ENGINEER is a fantastic modeling and documentation system. However, one of its great strengths, its flexibility, makes the maintainence of company standards a challenge. In many cases, Pro/ENGINEER provides different ways to accomplish the same tasks. This flexibility is good for solving tough modeling problems, but can hamper the sharing of information.

Many companies that purchase Pro/ENGINEER previously had a CAD/CAM system of one type or another. These companies, especially larger ones, generally have an established methodology or standards for the generation of drawings and manufacturable databases. These standards ensure that (1) all of the documentation for the company is as uniform as possible, that is, every drawing has the same title block, revision block, text heights, etc., and (2) the next engineer or department to access the information will be able to locate areas of interest quickly and easily.

Because a lot of companies who use Pro/ENGINEER have had other CAD/CAM systems as their primary design and documentation platform, making the transition from an explicit to a parametric modeling environment may seem easier than it is. You can customize Pro/ENGINEER to satisfy the bulk of your documentation requirements; that is the easy part. Getting the models to follow the same rules that your explicit modeling systems were capable of conforming to is a different task; prepare yourself for developing new standards.

The example in the introduction may not seem far from your current situation. Implementing corporate standards for Pro/ENGINEER will help you to streamline the development of specific, or like, components and assemblies in Pro/ENGINEER.

Corporate standards can act as the foundation (or cookie cutter) for everyone's part and assembly development, ultimately ensuring uniformity, flexibility, and a global understanding of what your design is and how it can be modified. Therefore, corporate standards are essential for efficient communication, recycling of existing databases, and your piece of mind. It is much easier to complete your work, and use other people's, if you are all on the same page for modeling and documentation.

The Effects of Having No Standards

The effects of having no standards are simple: (1) your company will loose significant amounts of time due to the seemingly perpetual remodeling of completed components, (2) there may not be sufficient communication between engineers and other departments, and (3) the wrong tools may be used for the job. This short list could continue....

Perpetual Remodeling, No Communication, and Using the Wrong Tools for the Job

Knowing that there are many different ways to accomplish the same design tasks in Pro/ENGINEER, the following illustration is a layout of the design intent for an electronics housing that will be used in the gauge panel from the introductory example.

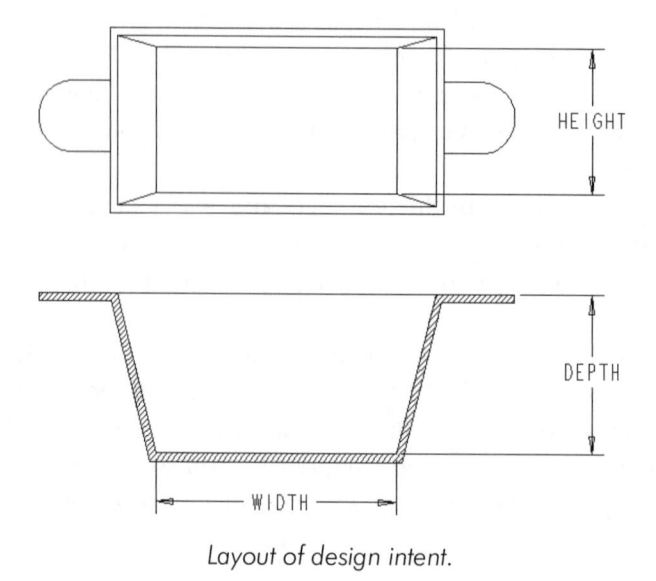

Layout of design intent.

The Effects of Having No Standards

This component has been laid out to be modeled such that the functional aspects of the design are controlled from the inside of the part. This is an important piece of information for the proper development of this component in Pro/ENGINEER. If, because of time constraints, you were not able to sit down and model this part, and you simply passed off the layout and some dimensional information for the parts that this component will interface with, your final model may not be what you expect.

Suppose that your only requirements were that: (1) the part mated with a group of other components, and (2) the dimensioning scheme and size of the inside of this part were maintained. Can you think of all the possible methods that could be used to generate this part? I'm sure that you could probably name at least five different methods of model development, and if you really thought about it, you might be able to come up with over 15 methods to obtain this same basic model. Some of the fundamental differences in the approach to modeling can be seen in the following illustrations.

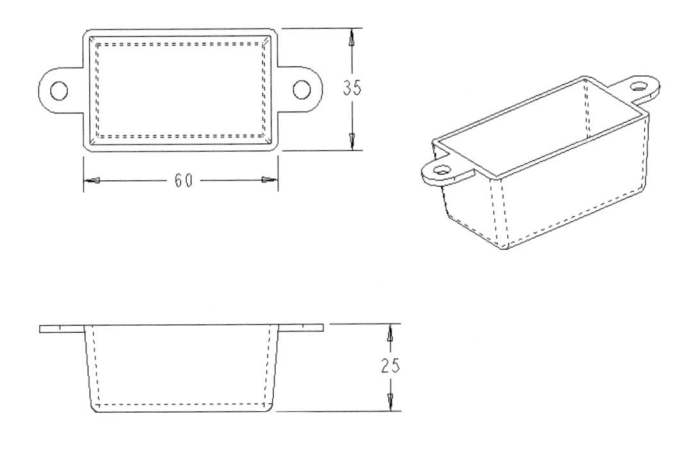

BLOCK & SHELL METHOD

Block and (internal) shell method, which is functional to the outside of the part.

Chapter 4: Corporate Standards

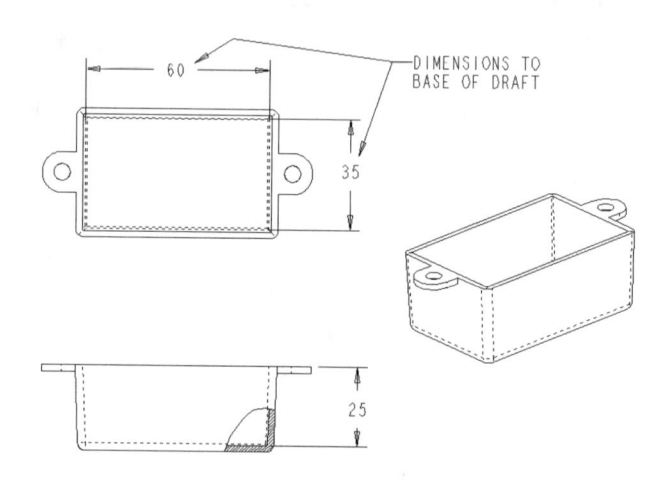

Surfaces and thin protrusions, which are functional to the inside of the part.

If you were to receive either of the above two designs, or any of the other options available to develop this same part, how long do you think that you would spend trying to modify the design to the proper size, develop functional geometric dimensioning and tolerancing in the model, or track down unexpected design variables that the previous user added to ensure the model would adapt to a change? For this simple part, you may have tolerated some minor rework or alterations to better capture the design intent, but if the design was not easy to modify, had problems adapting to changes, or used an illogical method of development, what do you think the chances would be of you giving up on that design and remodeling the entire part to save time? Probably pretty good.

This simple modeling problem is a good example of how corporate standards can be used to reduce the chances of you remodeling the part, through improved communication skills and using the proper tools for modeling this type of component. If a corporate standard was set up for this type of component, where the optimal model had been developed and documented using the Corporate Standards Worksheet, any user of Pro/ENGINEER would be able to reference an optimal model for this part. Therefore, each and every user knows what methods were used for the development of the part and how to change or modify the model in the future. These types of standards can also be used by others outside of your company, who you may hire during peak work loads.

Standards and Contracted Resources

Using contracted resources or service bureaus can help you get up to speed in the following ways:
   1. Modeling established components in Pro/ENGINEER.
   2. Acting as a coach to aid in the implementation of Pro/ENGINEER.
   3. Providing additional design help during peak work loads.

Using these people or companies can either help or hinder your company as a whole. Pro/ENGINEER is still a relatively new and aggressive player in the CAD/CAM/CAE market. Therefore, there are not many companies or individuals out there who really know it all or are a "one stop shop."

There are plenty of contract firms who claim to have experts capable of assisting your company in getting up to speed or supporting design tasks. Buyer beware! Sometimes your prospective resource may have a shop full of what I call "Boolean Heads"—people who have never used anything except explicit modelers and have little or no understanding of parametric modeling or constraint management. If you have ever worked with a model that has be done by a learning Boolean Head, you will probably never forget it; they usually have hundreds upon hundreds of shortcuts and protrusions, skillfully placed to resemble the final component. There are some quality firms across America who are the genuine article and are worth every penny you pay them, but unfortunately there are some companies who have the people, but not the experience using Pro/ENGINEER.

You must keep in mind that the people who will be doing work for you have their own ideas, and bad habits, for modeling your components. The major risk is that the long, and expensive, hours that they spend modeling will result in components that may not be useful to your design process. This is an unpleasant thought and has been a nightmare for some companies who were misled by inexperienced companies and individuals who promised the unobtainable.

How To Avoid Getting Stung

When it comes to the selection of a resource to work on your designs, don't be afraid to run a benchmark with your potential help. You benchmarked Pro/ENGINEER and the workstations that it runs on to ensure that your purchase would give you the most bang for the buck; so you should also benchmark the people and companies who will be working for you. You can have the fastest and best-handling car in the world, but how that car is used is directly dependent on the driving skills and experience of the operator. Here are some guidelines for benchmarking potential resources.

Run a Benchmark Test

1. **Ask for a short list of companies that the contract company has done work for in the past and some contact names at each of those companies.** Do a background check on the work that individuals from your potential contract firm have done. This is important because some people at a company have a higher level of experience with Pro/ENGINEER. You do not want your components to be sent to a person who just completed his or her introductory class in Pro/ENGINEER. That person will most likely take two to ten times longer to complete the same design tasks. You should not have to pay them to learn on your components. After all, you gave the company or individual the work because you needed the help.

2. **Send out some test parts.** If you are planning to use the services of a company or individual, and your project requires several weeks of work, spend a couple of hundred dollars and send out a component that your company has already modeled and optimized in Pro/ENGINEER. You may want to even include some design requirements to help them understand the design intent. Give them a date that the component must be completed and returned to you.

3. **Don't tell them it is a test.** This is the last thing that you want to do. If they know that your parts are a test of their abilities, you may get the fastest and cheapest modeling of components you have ever seen. Do not expect this awesome turnaround to stay so productive if you award them a contract. It is best to take the wounded bird approach, saying that you have a component or two that you need modeled within a

certain amount of time. They do not need to know that you may have copious amounts of Pro/ENGINEER work just over the horizon.

4. **Let each potential company figure out the component on their own.** Give no modeling hints or assistance to the solution of the problem. This portion of the benchmark will give you raw data regarding the amount of time to complete the modeling task, the costs involved, and overall flexibility of the end product. Remember, the goal here is not to trick the potential resource; it is to give you an understanding of their thought processes and techniques for modeling your components.

The results of the benchmark will show you how fast, accurate, and cost-effective each company or individual is. This information is most important because your goal in hiring additional temporary personnel is to inject additional expertise to complete your design and documentation tasks. As an added bonus, you will have a database of contract services to draw from for future work.

Analyzing Benchmark Results

The things that you should look for when evaluating the results of the benchmark are as follows:

1. **Accuracy of the model.** Are there geometry errors, such as overlaps, thin edges, unattached geometry, etc.? These can be frustrating to work with and can, in some cases, cause problems for some rapid prototyping and manufacturing processes.

2. **Do the models capture the design intent?** All of the dimensions should be functional to your overall design. The dimensions and geometric dimensioning and tolerancing (GD&T) should be properly and logically developed in relation to your prints. Any parent/child relationships should be manageable, that is, you do not want to see one round, at the beginning of a model, be the parent of 75% of the rest of the model, unless that is the intent.

3. **Models and assemblies are flexible and easy to manipulate.** Dimensioning schemes should be properly laid out such that the geometry will react to changes as you would expect after a modification. Patterned features and groups are flexible and can be modified with successful regenerations.

4. **Components can be fully detailed with a minimal amount of or without manually adding dimensions (there are cases where driven dimensions are required).** The final components should follow the prints that you have supplied them, to the letter. If the model was completed properly, and your prints are manufacturable, the person modeling the components should not have any trouble successfully remodeling the components, without adding any new dimensional constraints.

5. **The final models should be of a manageable file size.** Even though there is more than one method or approach for modeling components, the final database should not be much larger than what you were able to optimally model. You should not see hundreds of datum planes in the final part, unless there is a need for it. Feature selection and placement in the order of modeling should be well thought out. For example, on a vertical wall, you do not want to see draft applied to the model after a round.

6. **How much time did it take?** Even though this test of potential resources is not a race to see who completes the modeling tasks first, time is important. The amount of time allocated for the modeling of components is dependent on how you have arranged the payments. Some companies and individuals will give you a quote that is the maximum that you will pay for the work. Others will bill an hourly charge, with an approximate amount of time to complete the task. Either way, it is up to you and your company's payment preferences. Keep in mind that if company A quotes 5 hours and company B approximates 10 hours at an hourly rate, company B may complete the work in 4 hours. Overall, the results of this test will give you an indication of who is faster and more cost-effective.

All of the above items can have a major impact on your future designs, manufacturing processes, and any number of other areas where you may be using the database as the master. Therefore, it is important that your investment in contracted resources produces a product with which you are more than satisfied. Don't fall for slick salesmen who promise you the world when their company can't even deliver the quality databases that satisfy your company's needs. Do your homework and make sure that you outline what you expect for your investment.

Once you have narrowed your search, and have a list of companies that will produce what you are looking for quickly and accuracy, you will have the following results:

1. Reduced time to market by implementing experienced modeling services.
2. Liquid employment by harnessing the design and modeling skills without the long-term overhead.
3. Off loading peak design and documentation requirements, etc.

There are many more positive elements to implementation of this useful and flexible work force. For every negative experience, there are twice as many positive ones. Overall, it comes down to their ability to follow directions.

Contracted Resources and Corporate Standards

Your Role in the Relationship

With this additional help comes the additional time that you must spend overseeing the efforts of the contracted resources. They are not intimately involved with all of the design process, manufacturing requirements, and time frames. They need to be educated and updated as changes occur in the design, just as you would a member of your design team. They will be sensitive to design changes, and you must be as open as possible with them as to what you expect from the models on completion, that is, flexibility, accuracy, and manageable size. You do not want to be a negative statistic, so set aside the time to help, answer questions, and understand any deviations from the paths that you have laid out.

Don't be afraid to sit down with the designer and go over a strategy for modeling your components. This is your opportunity to set the ground rules for what you and your company expect, especially if you do not have a formally documented set of standards in place. If your company does not have guidelines, it is important that you establish and enforce the design and modeling boundaries.

Document your expectations and any changes that you may have to make for each part as they occur. This gives you a living document that your contracted resource will be able to follow as the models are developed. This ensures that you will get what you expect. If you do not get what you expect, you have a document that backs all of your agreed upon design and modeling requirements, so the cards are stacked in your favor if you need to get the models fixed without any additional cost.

Their Role in the Relationship

A good contract resource will fulfill the following promises:

1. Follow and fulfill your corporate standards for modeling and documentation.
2. Pay attention to every detail, that is, make sure component A mates properly with component B.
3. Make sure that all of the components for which the contract personnel are responsible are up to date and accurate.
4. Keep their word and meet the deadlines at or under projected cost.

I am sure that you can add to this short list. These are some general positive results that you should expect from day one of your working relationship.

The company or individual who you hire should be reliable, maintain contact with your company at all times, and be aggressive when it comes to obtaining information about design modifications or changes. The best of these resources employ both degreed and shop engineers who have experience in manufacturing, some forms of analysis, and inspection.

Experienced resources have been exposed to a number of design problems over a broad spectrum of engineering and manufacturing problems and can act as an "encyclopedia" to assist and improve your designs. Please note that not all companies can offer this highly sophisticated and educated help. A lot of these companies employ people with basic technical draftsman degrees, not engineering degrees. Buyer beware once again!

Developing Your Corporate Standards

Corporate standards for Pro/ENGINEER should be a company's number one long-term goal for internal and external resources. The benefits of having everyone on the same page will outweigh the free-form and independent development of models, assemblies, and drawings. Most companies who use Pro/ENGINEER are not highly diversified, and the primary product, or group of products, encompasses an entire family of similar products. For example, the components for an engine are basically the same, with variations in the physical size, number of cylinders, horse power, mountings, and so forth.

With this in mind, it is possible to optimize and standardize each component and its methods of development and assembly for a product family. With the standardization of like components from a modeling, assembly, and drawing standpoint, a general set of guidelines can be developed: a corporate standard.

Corporate standards are not easy to establish and maintain, especially with a software package that is on a rapid development cycle. Some of the keys to the development of a corporate standard for Pro/ENGINEER are described in the next section.

Educate Others in Your Capabilities

Pro/ENGINEER is an awesome design and documentation tool, and you should let people know about your capabilities and what types of information are important for a design. If others in the company understand what your requirements are for a ground zero design or modifying an existing design, you will be able to make changes faster due to the more accurate and higher quality inputs from others in the company.

Involve Other Departments in Developing Modeling Standards

If other departments use Pro/ENGINEER for analysis or manufacturing, it is important to understand their requirements for Pro/ENGINEER. For example, the analysis group may require a specific layer within a part that is used for the placement of rounds so they can be suppressed to simplify the model for mesh generation and analysis.

Other departments' requirements will not be difficult to integrate into your existing models or into new designs. Taking the time to simplify all departments' use of the tool means that you will, eventually, obtain a faster turnaround.

As an added bonus, those departments will know what to expect from your, and everyone else's, department because you all are required to follow the same rules.

Define Approved Methods of Model, Assembly, and Drawing Development

There are literally hundreds of paths you can take to obtain the same results. This flexibility generates some difficulties for the definition of how components, assemblies, and drawings are to be developed. Analyze several methods for modeling and documenting your components. This is just too large a task for one individual to solve. Answering all of the process, manufacturing, and modeling questions that come up requires input from all areas and experience levels. Experienced individuals and groups can investigate the positive and negative aspects of several methods and concurrently develop an optimal method of development in Pro/ENGINEER, in a reasonable time frame.

Use the Hot Shots

It is often the case that people just learning the software do not have enough global experience or understanding of Pro/ENGINEER to act as a guiding light for the development of corporate standards. Obtaining their input in the form of suggestions and involvement is important, and every participant is an asset to the development of corporate standards. Unfortunately, this lack of experience and understanding can hamper the development process.

You may be wondering what a *hot shot* is, and you may even think of yourself as the answer to your own question, and that's good! Hot shots are the people who have taken to Pro/ENGINEER like a duck to water. They experiment continuously with optimizing designs to test flexibility and general modeling fluidity. You can find these people staying after work and coming in on the weekends just to experiment (or play around) with the software on top of their normal work load.

Generally, these people know a lot of obscure facts and methods for the modeling, assembly, and documentation of designs. A lot of this experience comes from reading the manuals and then trying to find out each feature's and module's limitations. The number of iterations that these people perform when testing each feature, and how they interact with other features, is what makes them so valuable. They understand when and how to use features, modules, and techniques to achieve fast, accurate, and flexible designs. Every company has at least one individual like this; do all you can to keep him or her. These people are an asset to the development of a corporate standard, and others who may not have a high level of modeling experience with Pro/ENGINEER can only benefit from learning about unfamiliar functionality.

Obtain Supplier Input

A supplier's input can help to bring the details of a developing corporate standard into focus. The companies and people who manufacture or make prototypes of your components and assemblies have an in-depth understanding of what is required to turn the computer models into physical components. Obtain input relative to their historical frustrations, that is, tolerances, inspection techniques, dimensioning scheme, material and process requirements, and so forth. This valuable information could reduce the amount of time you spend preparing your data for rapid prototyping, manufacturing, or inspection; and, it is hoped, improve the definition of the component and assembly relationships.

Use the Right Tool for the Job

Nothing can be more frustrating than to have a two-minute job turn into a two-day hair loss session. The reasons for this are simple and usually are the result of a limited amount of experience or understanding of system-wide capabilities. I am not saying that Pro/ENGINEER can model everything, but using the right tools for the job can certainly make a big difference.

For example, you may have a steel bracket that you need to develop in an assembly. The problem is that this component requires a number of bends that will not be easy to describe using conventional modeling techniques. For this application you decide to use the sheet metal module to generate the component in Assembly mode. The advantage of using this module is that when you are through modeling the component, you can (in this particular application) generate a flat pattern, reducing the amount of time required to calculate the flat pattern manually. The result is a faster prototype and

74   Chapter 4: Corporate Standards

production turnaround time; all of this from just implementing a module at the right time for the right application. For comparison, the following illustrations demonstrate the two methods of generation. The first illustration is a component generated using the surfacing and feature modules, and the second is the component that was developed using the sheet metal module.

Bracket developed with surfaces and thin protrusion: total number of features, 40; time to generate, approximately 3 hours; flexibility, average to poor.

Bracket developed with sheet metal module: total number of features, 20; amount of time to develop, 30 minutes; flexibility, average to excellent.

This is a classic example of how the tools within Pro/ENGINEER can directly affect the design time and flexibility of the database. This type of modeling or module standard has a number of positive and negative causes and effects. A positive effect of this type of standard may be modeling uniformity for specific component types. A negative effect may be the relative experience levels of the users who will be developing a new or modifying an existing design in an unfamiliar module.

Alternative Module Selection

You should keep a close eye on both current and emerging modules within the Pro/ENGINEER product line. Each module has some kind of special functionality that differentiates it from the other modules. These modules have been developed to satisfy customer and engineering requirements and do not have to be industry specific. Your design may have a need that the basic design packages do not satisfy easily. Investigate your options, obtain evaluation copies of the modules that you are interested in, and find out for yourself if they will help simplify or improve your design. This is not necessarily a corporate standard issue, but the results of your investigations could result in a modification of your existing standards due to new capabilities and functionality.

Keep Standards Flexible

Because new functionality is continuously being incorporated into the software, it is important that modeling, assembly, and documentation standards remain flexible. The reason for this is that new techniques for managing feature development and parametric relationships can dramatically simplify or automate an established standard. Therefore, it may be worth revising the standard to incorporate the new functionality, once it is fully understood.

This flexibility goes beyond your department's doors. You must also be willing to revise and update your standards for interfacing with other departments. Believe it or not, Pro/ENGINEER is not the only software that upgrades its methods of processing and user interface.

What Are the Ramifications of Having Corporate Standards?

Uniformity: Everyone Working on the Same Page

Everyone being on the same page is probably the biggest advantage to having corporate standards for Pro/ENGINEER. However, it is only an advantage if the engineers, designers, and contracted resources understand what is expected of them and apply the standards properly.

Enforcing compliance with corporate standards is not an easy or pleasant job, but enforcement is necessary to ensure that further designs or modifications to existing designs will be easy and pleasant for the next engineer who comes into contact with your department's work.

Standardization can save a company literally tens of thousands of dollars annually in lost time spent remodeling other people's or company's work, just to ensure that the models, drawings, and assemblies can adapt to change with a minimum amount of effort, not to mention all of those people who remodel a design to satisfy their own approach to a modeling problem.

People Must Be Educated on Standards

Standards Effect on Novice Users

Just learning Pro/ENGINEER seems tough enough without trying to conform to corporate standards at the same time. If you have successfully developed some corporate standards for parts, assemblies, and drawings, the novice will be overwhelmed with the requirements.

How the standards are implemented and maintained can frustrate engineers and designers to the point where they will fight against the standards tooth and nail. A solution to this is to get novices up to speed on components that will contribute to the design effort, but do not require an expert level of experience. This may require the novice user to learn an additional module or two and advanced functionality on the fly. I strongly recommend that an advanced user with a lot of patience be used as the crutch to bring a new user up to speed. If your company is like most, these advanced users are kept busy, but a few minutes here and there can make the transition from novice to experienced user much easier in less time than having the new user sit at the computer for hours at a time with little productivity.

Standards Effect on Contracted Resources

Contracted resources are employed for their expertise in modeling, engineering, and expedient use of Pro/ENGINEER. However, like the novice, your corporate standards will be overwhelming until they grasp the techniques, procedures, and general requirements. Contracted resources require less attention from you, after all they already know how to use Pro/ENGINEER; they just don't know how you want it used.

Which Aspects of a Standard Should Be Enforced?

It would be easy to say, "All of them," but this is not realistic. Some, but not "all of them," apply to the function of the design. You should not have to, or expect others to, memorize every single detail of a corporate standard. The standards that you have established must be simple and easy to follow and understand. Above all, they should not require too much time to implement. It is possible to develop standards that are so detailed and rigid that your own documentation and modeling requirements stifle the productivity of your design group. Ultimately the enforcement of standards and which standards are not significant enough to enforce is up to the company. Either way, the acceptance and rejection criteria must be outlined for all parties involved.

Future Use of Company Information

With standards established and maintained, you are effectively preserving the information for future use. Components that are modeled today will be the reference components for future designs and assemblies. Establishing standards for each component's development and adhering to those standards is the key to reducing future questions and preserving the information that you and your department have worked so hard to develop. You will be able to access another engineer's materials and understand the methods of creation and, even more importantly, how to modify the design so that in the end, you may not have to remodel.

Summary

To improve and support the continuing development of concurrent relationships within a design, engineering, and manufacturing environment, engineer A must be able to easily understand and use engineer B's materials. Being able to understand and use other people's work goes beyond the walls of the engineering department into all areas of the engineering and manufacturing community, including contracted resources. Initiating and maintaining corporate standards for modeling, assemblies, and documentation and constraint management can eliminate the guess work on how to modify and rework developing or developed designs. Remember, what you see is not what you get. Pretty pictures are not an indication of design flexibility or conformity to any established standards.

Contracted resources can be a tremendous help in supporting design and documentation tasks. However, these resources can hinder a design project by not following your corporate standards for using Pro/ENGINEER correctly. The use of unacceptable procedures and processes can cost a company thousands upon thousands of dollars annually and virtually halt some design and manufacturing operations. Therefore, it is important to optimize component and assembly development and standardize them to establish guidelines for all parties to follow.

Establishing corporate standards can simplify design development, reduce costs, lower frustrations, and save money. Corporate standards must remain flexible and continuously be updated to incorporate new functionality as it becomes available.

The development of design standards requires an in-depth understanding of your design and manufacturing process requirements and how those requirements affect component and assembly development. Design standards also require an understanding of how Pro/ENGINEER maintains information links and how that information is manipulated.

Capturing Design Intent

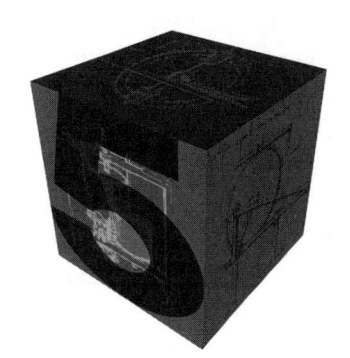

Introduction

Your manager has outlined the project time frames for a new design. You find that you only have 10 months to bring a totally new design from a concept, through prototype, manufacturing, building, testing, and shipping to your customer. Your schedule for design is even more compressed than you thought due to the lead times of some of the components in your design. Actually you have 1.5 months to develop and finalize the design to meet your tooling kick-off requirements.

Taking the initiative, your first step in the development of your design is to sit down at the computer and go to work, quickly designing your components based on the rough design goals that have been outlined. After a week of modeling and development in the computer, you have some very impressive pictures and assemblies that "wow" the entire department, as well as your supply base who will produce your designs. You then spend another week generating the drawings and associated documentation for discussion and dimensional analysis.

With two weeks gone out of your development schedule, you discover that your designs will require some modifications to improve the manufacturability and inspection characteristics of the entire design. On top of that, the manufacturing process requires some fixturing lands and holes to be incorporated that will affect your current design. As you sit at your desk reviewing the mountain of changes and redesigns that you must accomplish within the remaining 4 weeks, you learn that it would be easier to just restart the entire design from scratch. Your remodeling decision was made in an attempt to avoid all of the predictable Regen Fail messages you will knowingly encounter due to the sculpted, nonparametric models that you have created.

NOTE: *Sculpted models are the results of the master Pro/ENGINEER users who start with a glorious solid block and skillfully carve out chunks of material, one feature at a time, until they are left with the final part. These people have missed their calling in life.*

During a documentation and design review with the department head, you hear that one comment that will bring you to your knees, "All you should have to do is change the dimension values." If there was ever a comment that summed up people's perception of Pro/ENGINEER's capabilities, I would definitely cast my vote for this one. After your meetings and design reviews, reality hits you full force and you call your significant other and let him or her know that you will not be home this weekend.

If you have really read the book up to this point, you should know that it is not the pretty pictures that make your designs functional and useful. It is the quality of the information that you put into Pro/ENGINEER and how well you manage that information. Anything else is just processing mistakes and errors. The previous example may not seem too far from the truth for a lot of engineers reading this book. Especially if you have been through this situation more than once. The problems can be compounded when a team of engineers and designers are working on the same design. Picture engineers working on an assembly, each engineer with his or her own techniques and preferences for developing and managing each and every component designed. When this situation exists, there is always the risk that another engineer may remodel or bastardize a model developed by a team member to satisfy a design change requirement. Unfortunately, this *does* happen and can be a real pressure point for some departments as to which method or technique is correct.

The focus of this chapter is not to reiterate all of the previous chapters. Instead, it focuses on modeling techniques and approaches to solving some common problems. This will not be a case by case analysis of what button to push or when to push it. However, I hope to convey some fundamental concepts so that you will have a better understanding of how to manage your designs from ground zero.

"It's beginning to look a lot like Christmas..."

Picture some frost on your window, a fireplace roaring in the background, and your family gathering together to set up the Christmas tree. Ever since you can remember, each and every year you have set up the tree a little different, some years with red tinsel and homemade ornaments, other years with multicolored lights and purchased ornaments. But every year your family gathers together to set up the tree. Modeling in Pro/ENGINEER is just like putting up a Christmas tree; you must first establish the foundation for your design (the tree) and then integrate the manufacturability and inspection characteristics (hang the ornaments). This is what I affectionately call the "Christmas tree" approach to modeling.

There are literally thousands of command combinations that can be executed to develop a component or assembly. Each method of development has merit, and often the final results will be dimensionally accurate, that is, the same pretty picture on the computer screen. The big question is: how flexible are the designs that have been generated?

As we have seen in previous chapters, there are many methods available for keeping designs flexible and manageable. A lot of these methods are somewhat elaborate and generally functional for the overall design. But the scope of this chapter is a micro discussion on how to ensure that globally controlled and modified designs are capable of adapting to design changes. The Christmas tree approach to modeling involves the development of the base, or package, model, basically the bulk of the model without any extreme detail. Once this bulk geometry has been developed (the Christmas tree), hang the ornaments, the features such as draft, rounds, and ribs, which must

Chapter 5: Capturing Design Intent

be incorporated to ensure the manufacturability of your designs. This approach is especially true for plastic injection and die cast components, even though some of the "ornaments" must be structured early in the database. A classic example of this is the fillet at the base of a drafted wall.

The following illustration shows the outlined design intent of the wall and flange intersection for the component you will be designing.

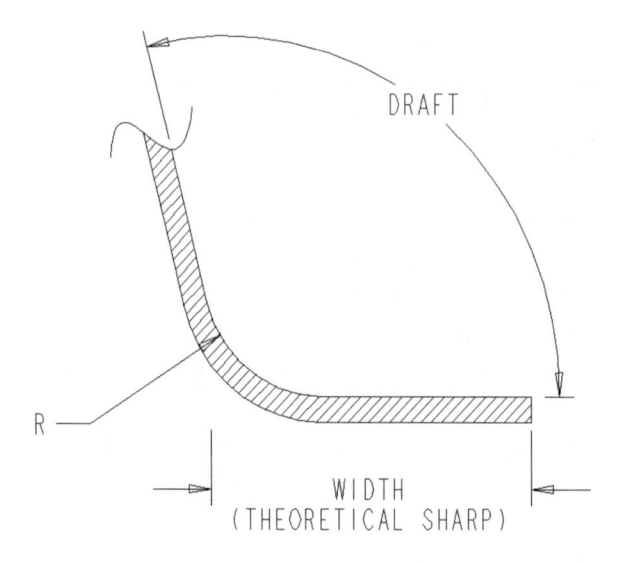

The design intent.

Given the information shown in the figure for a typical plastic component, you develop a flange based on the design's requirements and define the overall package (the Christmas tree) using protrusions. Your design at this stage may look like the following:

"It's beginning to look a lot like Christmas..." 83

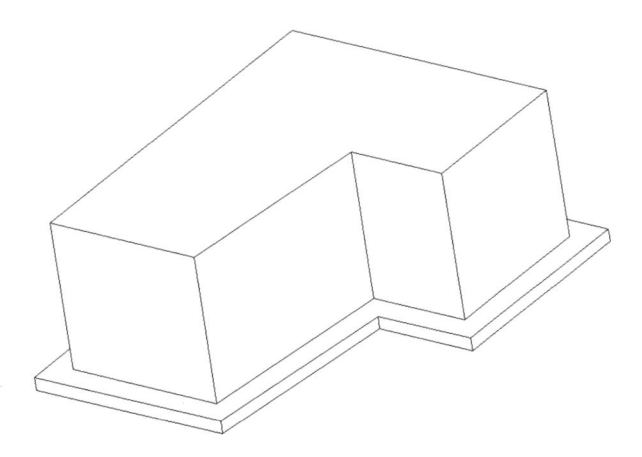

Stage 1 of capturing the design intent: a developed Christmas tree.

Once you have all of the basic geometric information for the design developed, finish the design by making it manufacturable (hang the ornaments). The following illustrations outline the steps that were taken to capture the design intent of the vertical walls intersecting with the flange.

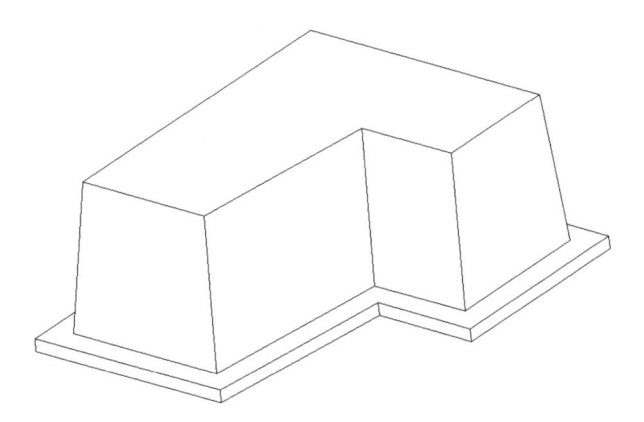

Draft the model as required for the design.

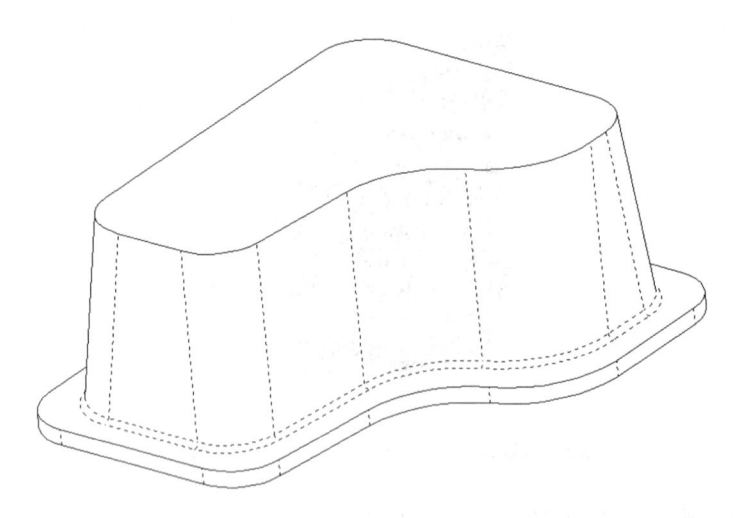

Add the rounds at the base of the drafted walls and the flange.

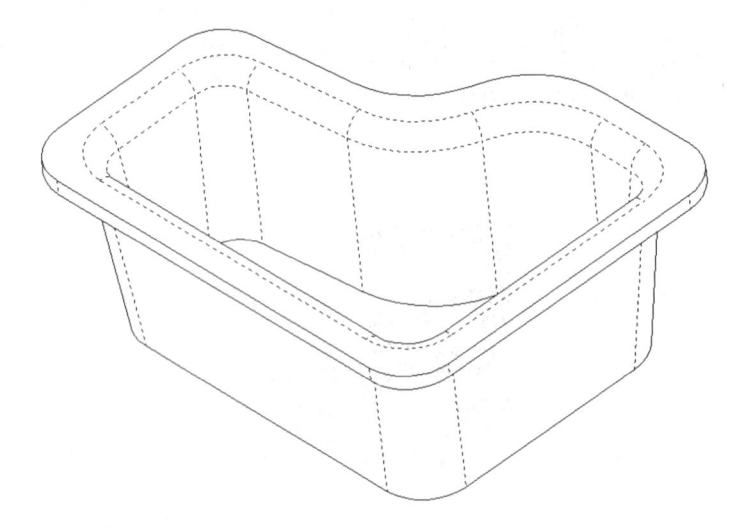

Shell the model.

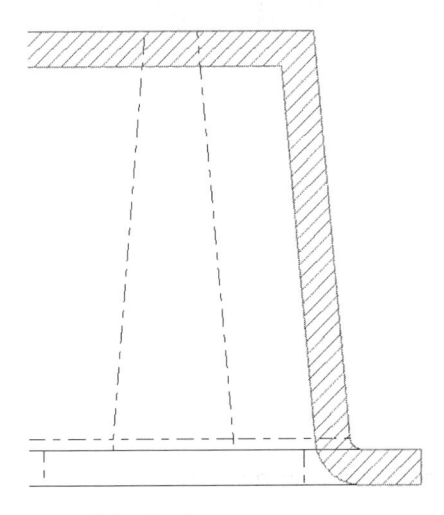

Cross-sectional view of the final component, capturing the design intent.

Once the steps shown in the figures have been completed, you will have a model that is responsive to design intent modifications. Why? Because the features that were applied, in the order that they were applied, will result in a model that will produce expected results after a modification is made.

The previous example is nowhere complete, it only outlines what was needed to ensure that this single aspect of the design intent has been captured. You may still need to continue your development by adding internal ribs, runners, bosses, cuts, holes, or whatever else you need to hang on your Christmas tree. As an added bonus, if you have thought out the design's requirements and what dimensional and feature relationships must be maintained, you can have Pro/ENGINEER manage feature relationships automatically, by selectively developing functional parent/child relationships. All of which will have a significant impact on the design intent of the component.

Parent/Child Relationships and Design Intent

As stated in previous chapters, design flexibility is a must for design modifications and future revisions. Designs are kept flexible simply by capturing the design intent of the component or assembly that is being developed. This means that your development work in Pro/ENGINEER must have just as much, if not more, thought and planning than the actual design. At this particular phase in your development, you should have all of your design and constraints outlined and laid out. This phase centers around taking those inputs and requirements and choosing the right tools, approaches, and methods for the job.

When you are modeling your components in Pro/ENGINEER, it is very easy to slip into the role of a "sculptor." Quite honestly there is a fine line between actually *using* and *sculpting* with Pro/ENGINEER. The difference lies in how well you manage your design's development, how flexible the results are, and whether or not you cut any corners just to get the job done. You must always remember that every feature that you generate must (1) have a functional purpose in your design, (2) be properly placed in the database's development, and (3) any parent/child relationships must yield desirable results if the rest of the part changes. A classic example of a parent/child relationship may be in the form of a boss with a concentric hole through it. The following illustration outlines this particular type of geometry combination.

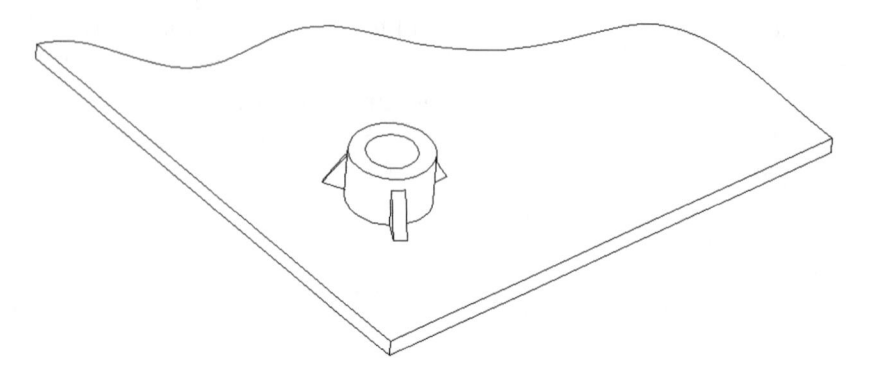

Boss with a concentric hole.

Parent/Child Relationships and Design Intent 87

As you can see from the previous illustration, the boss has a concentric hole. The big question is: how is that hole being kept concentric with the boss? And does that method truly capture the design intent?

There are many ways to establish a hole such that it maintains a concentric relationship with a boss. Looking at the previously shown illustration, you may assume that the user simply selected a straight hole that was coaxial to the boss. That of course would be the most direct approach; the hole would move with the boss, and therefore maintain its concentric relationship. But the picture does not always tell the complete story. Upon investigation, you may discover that the person who modeled the component choose to create a sketched cut with a *thru all* option, and then dimensioned the hole back to the datum planes to control each hole's location, independent of the boss.

If you were to look at each feature by modifying the boss and the hole, you might see something similar to the following illustration.

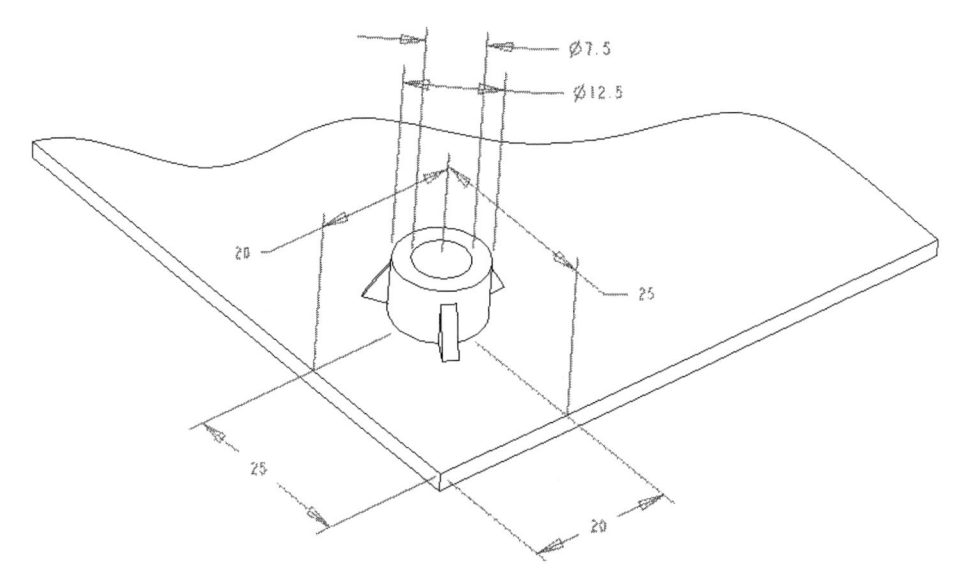

Boss and hole dimensions.

You may also find that the boss and hole relationship was maintained by using parametric relationships. Is this really what the engineer was looking for, or is it an example of immature Pro/ENGINEER modeling techniques? In a way, both. I really like this example because it can support both approaches to modeling components while trying to capture the design intent, and the design intent is what we are concerned with. On one side of the coin, the engineer's intentions may be that there always be a hole at that location, even if there is not a boss. In this case, the method shown may be satisfactory but not optimum. On the other side of the coin, having that hole developed by using a coaxial hole would make the hole a child to the boss geometry. The results of which would be that (1) the hole would follow the boss wherever it moved, and (2) if the boss was deleted, the hole would also be removed. The following illustration shows how the parent/child relationships are generated relative to the method of model development.

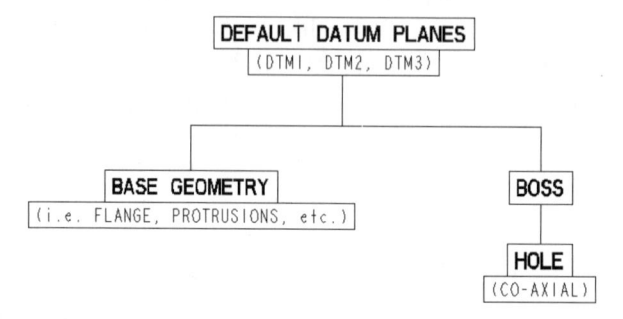

```
              DEFAULT DATUM PLANES
                (DTM1, DTM2, DTM3)
              ┌──────────┴──────────┐
        BASE GEOMETRY              BOSS
    (i.e. FLANGE, PROTRUSIONS, etc.) │
                                    HOLE
                                  (CO-AXIAL)
```

Parent/child relationships: coaxial hole with boss as reference.

The tree of events shown previously highlights the fact that the hole is in series, or a child of the boss, and the boss is a child of the datum planes. The following illustration outlines the same example, only using different references and methods of development.

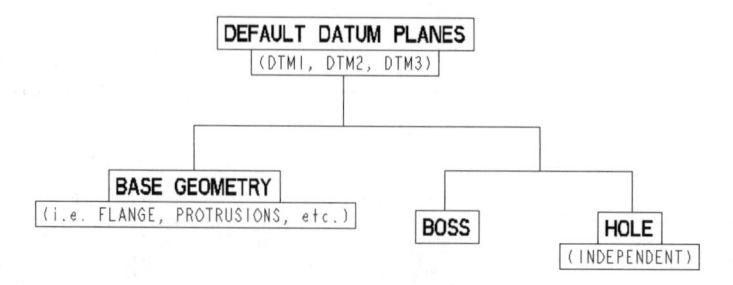

```
              DEFAULT DATUM PLANES
                (DTM1, DTM2, DTM3)
              ┌──────────┬──────────┐
        BASE GEOMETRY    │          │
    (i.e. FLANGE, PROTRUSIONS, etc.)
                        BOSS      HOLE
                              (INDEPENDENT)
```

Parent/child relationships: hole references datum planes with relationships.

In this case, the hole was developed as an extruded cut and only references the datum planes. Hence, the holes are parallel to the boss in the development tree. When this case exists, if you delete the boss, the hole will stay in the same place. Whereas in the previous development tree, if you deleted the boss, Pro/ENGINEER would prompt you that the hole was a child of the boss and list some options for how you would like to handle this child. If the design intent was to have the hole removed if the boss was removed, then this would be the optimal relationship to have for these features.

As you can see from this example, there is a lot of luggage that you must carry when you are developing your geometry. This reinforces the need to understand the design intent of the components that you and your engineering department are developing. If you are using Pro/ENGINEER as your first method of solving design problems, essentially bypassing the generation of quality input, you may find yourself constantly fighting unwanted (dysfunctional) parent/child relationships during model regeneration. In short, you must spend the time to properly model your components in Pro/ENGINEER. A little effort put into understanding each feature's relationships can mean the difference between a 2-minute modification and 2 days of remodeling at a later date.

How About a Game of Chess?

As you know, the models developed in Pro/ENGINEER are mathematically defined, and parent/child relationships will always have an impact on capturing the design intent. Because of this, you must pay close attention not only to how each feature is developed, and what their relationships will be, but also how features developed early in the model will affect features later in the database structure. Because you cannot put the wheels on a car before you have all of the suspension system designed and developed, you must plan ahead by looking at what your design intent and goals are. To do this you must ask yourself, how will this next feature impact my design 5 to 10 features later and will it be flexible? Essentially you are playing a game of chess with Pro/ENGINEER.

I know what you are thinking, "Chess?! Surely there could be a better analogy than that! I hardly ever play the game." Believe it or not, if you have

Chapter 5: Capturing Design Intent

used Pro/ENGINEER for any length of time, you have been using the same types of logic, reasoning, and general thought processes that are required to play chess. In chess you are playing against your opponent; with each move you are trying to gain the board advantage to secure *checkmate*. When you are using Pro/ENGINEER, you are not competing with the computer or the software, you are competing against yourself and your modeling skills. However, in this case you win by developing a model that is flexible, easy to understand, captures the design intent, and satisfies all of the documentation and database requirements of your company.

To do all of this you must be able to understand and anticipate the consequences of each and every feature that you generate in Pro/ENGINEER. By understanding the features' applications, the consequences of your instructions, and how the order of execution can affect the component's development, your skills and abilities will increase. The following illustration outlines how feature placement within your database can make all of the difference in efficient design execution.

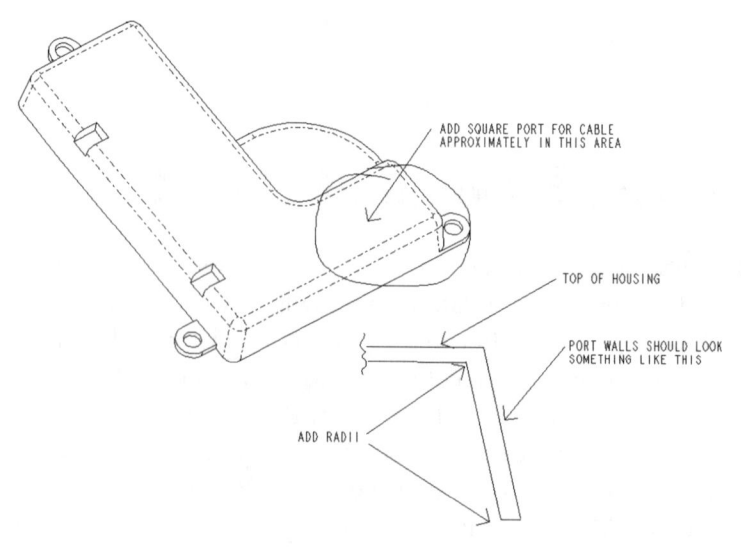

Design intent: have a cable port in the top of a plastic housing.

From the design intent, this opening is basically an inverted chimney that helps to guide some cables out of the enclosure that this covers. There are a lot of ways to accomplish this design task, and each method is valid given its own specific set of circumstances. In this case, you are presented with a number of options to solve this modeling problem. You could continue to develop the base geometry by making a cut, adding a thin protrusion, and applying some additional drafts to obtain the final geometry. This works; however, there is a lot of baggage associated with this particular method of modeling. In the end you are just adding more features to your database, which increases the file size and lengthens the amount of time to regenerate your parts. The results of this modeling would look like the following illustration.

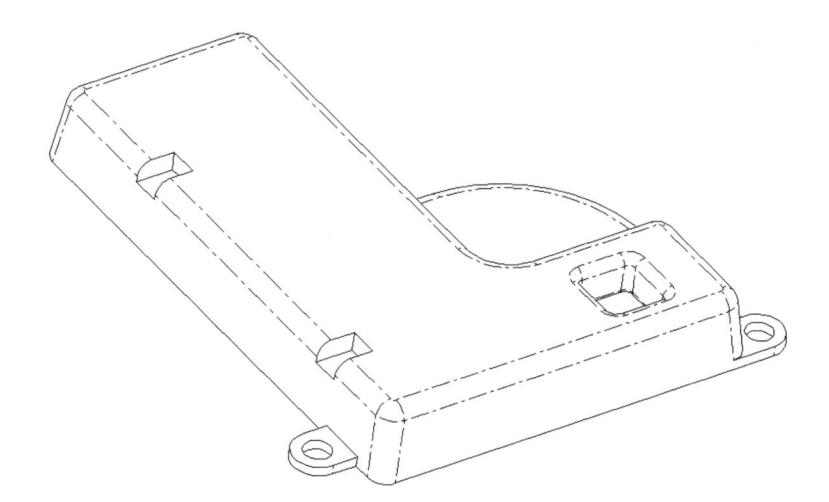

Finished component: using modeling method 1.

A more fundamental approach is to think about where you want the design to end up. To do this you need to select what types of tools (features) you are going to use to accomplish the modeling tasks and how and when those features should be placed in the model. Another possible answer to this problem is to use the power of a shell to do a lot of the dirty work for you. The same problem can be solved by using each feature more efficiently and effectively. By using Insert mode to add features prior to the shell for the part, perform a blind cut for the location and depth of the opening, adding draft from the base of the cut, and ultimately modifying the shell to break out the bottom of the chimney, the results will look like the following illustration.

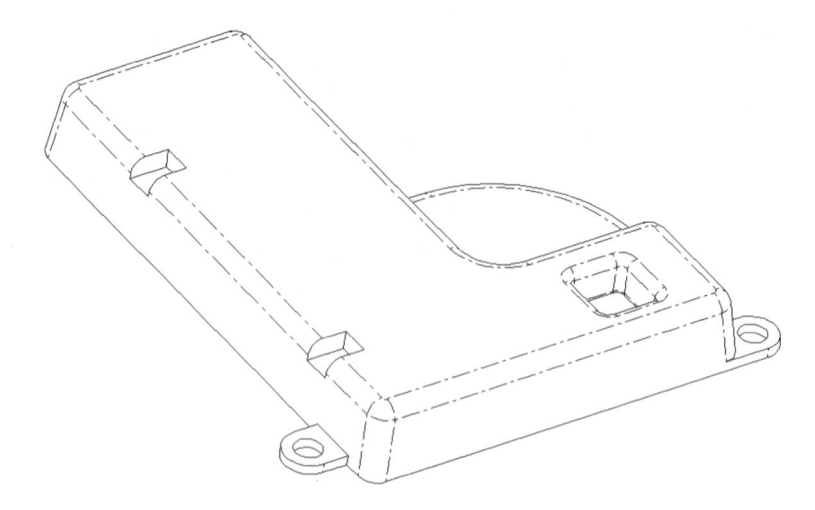

Finished component: using modeling method 2.

As you can see from the two modeling methods, your feature selection and usage can reduce the amount of modeling while making your designs more flexible. Just as in the game of chess, by planning your moves in advance you can improve your use of Pro/ENGINEER. When you apply the proper tools for the job, you will have components that are more responsive, better capture the design intent, take up less space on the hard drive, and are easier to manipulate by other users.

Use the Right Tools for the Design Task

As you can see from the previous section, feature selection and placement are more important than just hacking out and adding features to solve a design problem. This example carries over into the global spectrum of using Pro/ENGINEER. Just as modeling in Pro/ENGINEER is like playing a game of chess, proper module selection is just as, or more, important than what steps you are taking to solve a modeling problem.

Use the Right Tools for the Design Task

The basic modeling package is great, but it is not the optimal tool for every design problem or application. Management, and other decision makers within a company can often be mislead by inexperienced individuals as to which packages and modules are useful and which are not. This myopic understanding of Pro/ENGINEER's capabilities can create a lot of friction between the department and management; not to mention the friction among engineers within a department. Therefore, it is important that users have a basic understanding of each of Pro/ENGINEER's modules. The reasons for this are simple: (1) the basic modeling and assembly modules for Pro/ENGINEER do not do everything, (2) some functionality within an unrelated industry-specific module may solve some of your difficult design problems, and (3) each module of Pro/ENGINEER does certain things very well, which can improve design flexibility and documentation.

A classic example of using the right tool for the job is the routing of cables in Pro/ENGINEER. I have seen a number of very slick methods, and some painfully complex attempts, to route cables in Pro/ENGINEER. All of the methods (excluding Pro/CABLING and Pro/HARNESS-MFG) that I have seen to date have been *time vacuums*. The following illustration outlines the routing of a wire harness to an array of solenoids in a vacuum assembly.

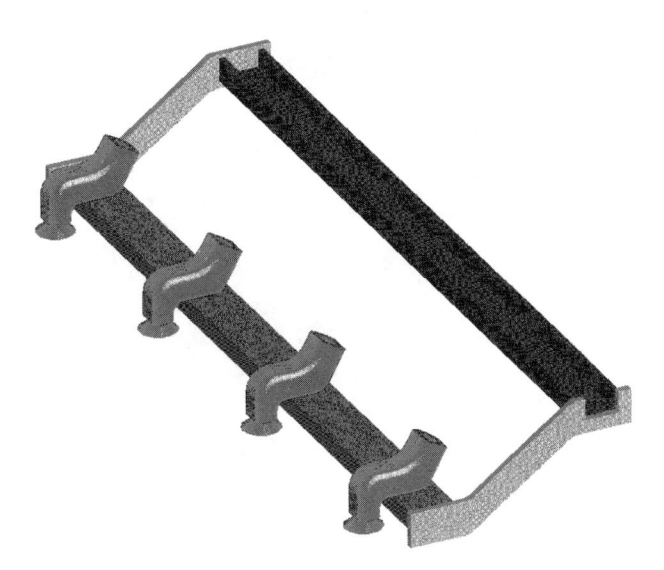

Vacuum array, before wire routing.

Some of the more involved attempts to route the cables have been the use of two surfaces to develop a datum curve through the surface intersections. Once the curve has been generated, a solid cross-section was swept along the datum curve, and that was the wire. Another attempt is the use of datum points to "pipe" the solid geometry through the assembly or part. Either method required a significant amount of time. Generally, the amount of time was in increments of a few days to over a week for a simple two-wire harness. It is those significant amounts of lost time that really hit home and add pressure to an entire development program. Using the right tools for the job, whether they are modules or features, can make all of the difference in the world when it comes to quickly defining and managing your work.

The Pro/CABLING module was selected to solve this modeling problem. After establishing all of the fundamental requirements for routing wire, you simply define the harness on the fly by picking which cables you want to use and how they are to be routed in the assembly. The results of this exercise are shown in the following illustration.

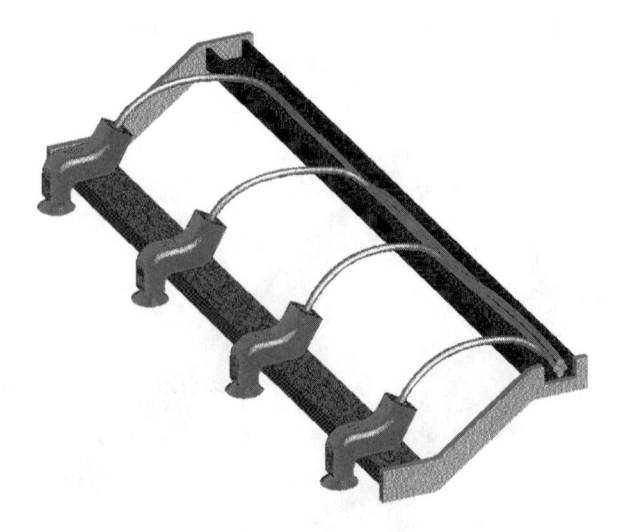

Vacuum array, after wire routing.

Because the proper tool was selected for the job, you are able to quickly define and modify any aspect of this harness. In addition, you can use Pro/HARNESS-MFG to lay out and detail the entire harness assembly. Ultimately, the total amount of time required for development and detailing of this component was reduced from weeks to just hours by the proper tool selection. You may be thinking, "OK, I can see where this particular module may be advantageous for this particular example, but these modules are many thousands of dollars." Yes, these modules are not cheap. But you must look at what you are getting for your investment. You may be thinking that you can produce similar designs within a reasonable amount of time. But what will you do when you are required to make a change? Will you tell your customer that the change will be complete in a couple of days? Or would you prefer to let them know that you will send a package with the redesigned components by overnight mail.

Making changes is another good reason to use the right tools for the job. Using the proper tools will increase your accuracy, better capture the design intent of the components that you are working on, and reduce the amount of time that you would have spent using alternative methods.

Having an in-depth understanding of each modeling feature and module within Pro/ENGINEER can give you a distinct advantage when you are developing flexible component and assemblies. Understanding when to use a certain feature, how it should be used, and what its limitations are can either make your designs very flexible or stifle the entire modeling process and ultimately your efforts to capture the design intent.

One of the most common mistakes that people make when developing designs in Pro/ENGINEER is the improper selection of a feature or sequence of features to complete a design task. But how do you know when to use a certain feature over another? This is a big question, and it is dependent on the types of flexibility that you are looking for in your designs. Taking the time to experiment and find the limitations and flexibility of each feature in Pro/ENGINEER is a great way to develop a personal understanding of feature and module flexibility. For example, when I am designing plastic components, I know when to apply one type of round over another. The following illustration shows a boss with a round at the base of draft.

Chapter 5: Capturing Design Intent

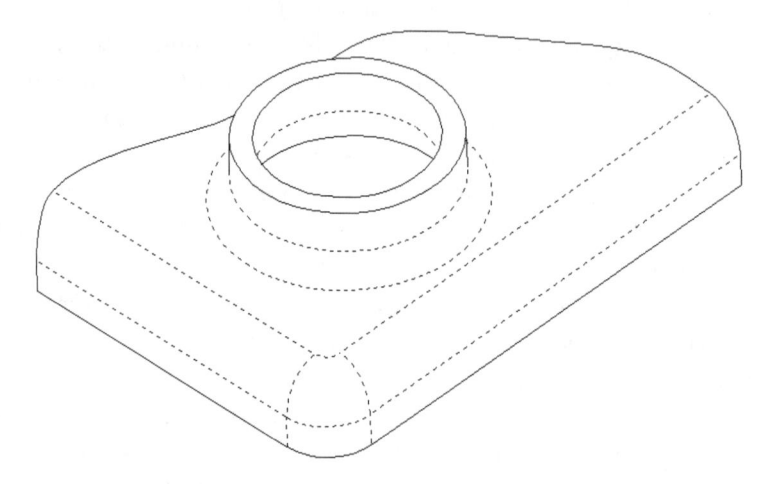

Boss with edge round at the base of draft.

If the boss is moved close to the edge, the feature will fail. Why? Because this type of round is not capable of being calculated with this type of intersection. The results would look like the following figure.

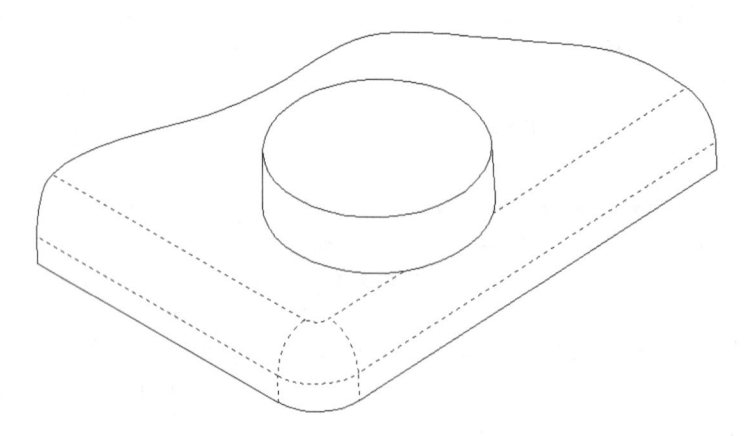

Constant round regeneration failure.

If the round is replaced with another type of round, a surface-to-surface round, the geometry looks the same as the constant round prior to the boss being moved.

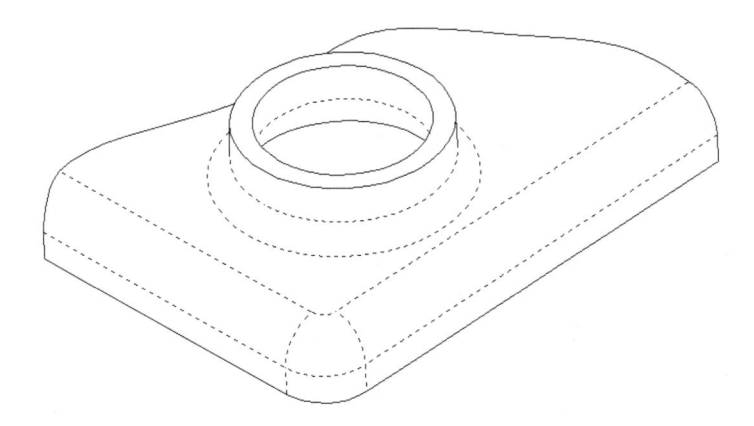

Same boss with a surf-surf round at the base of draft.

In this case, when the boss's position moves, the surface-to-surface round is capable of calculating the intersection, the results of which would look like the following figure.

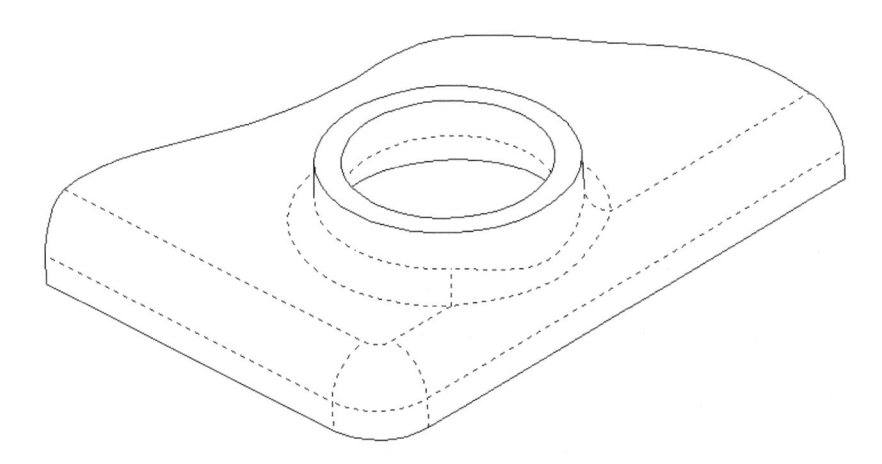

Surf-Surf round after regeneration.

As you can see from the previous example, your work can be more flexible by just using the right tools for the job. The example highlights the need for you, during development, to predict what will change and how, as the design evolves. By selecting the right tools to ensure that your design will adapt to future changes, you will be able to minimize the amount of time spent on debugging regeneration problems when and if the design changes. Just as in the previous example, you must analyze the possibilities of that boss moving and what the effects on surrounding geometry will have on that feature.

Because experience is the best teacher, I strongly urge you take some classes to get your feet wet in the basic and advanced Pro/ENGINEER functionality, but to also spend time pushing Pro/ENGINEER to its limits for each feature of interest. As time goes by, you will find that the time you have taken to experiment will pay off in faster model and assembly development. You will be more productive.

Which Components Should Be Modeled First?

This may well be the $64,000.00 question. After spending a lot of time looking at this problem the answer is balanced between four issues:

1. Lead times for component development
2. Available resources
3. Manufacturing- or process-related requirements
4. Impact on the design intent.

There may be a few other areas that affect this balance or decision. Most managers will tell you that the first component to be modeled should be the longest lead item. It is true that the amount of lead time will definitely affect the design and delivery of your components, and in most cases the longest lead item is the foundation of the design. But should this simple component or group of components be sent to the top of the priority list to be completed? In many cases, no. If you throw all of your resources into releasing a database that has a long lead time, you may be shooting yourself in the foot.

Experience has shown that other interfacing components may have a significant impact on the base component's design, tooling, and inspection, which in turn may push a lead time even further out due to interim tooling modifications required to facilitate a mating component. Ultimately, you and your management must assess the risks involved in any potential design changes for each component that you will be developing. That risk assessment will give you an indication of which components truly need to be developed first; it will also help to set the order for all of the other components to be developed.

One tool that is helpful in determining which components should be modeled first is the layout. As you have seen in Chapter 2, the layout can act as the master controlling document for managing components and assemblies. This document, provided you have done your homework and generated all of the quality input, can act as a schematic for each component that you develop, highlighting key areas of the design that must remain flexible and how. This document can also provide you with additional insight to the interfaces for subassembly components and how those should be developed. This may or may not help you in your selection process and ordering of the components that must be developed. I have found that this document can act as a crutch to ensure that whichever component is developed first, it can be easily integrated into an assembly or as a foundation for other components.

Whether or not your decisions are based on the lead times or the structure of the components and assemblies you are developing, it all comes down to capturing the design intent. Keep this in mind during your development.

Which Mode Is Right for You?

Should you be spending your time in Assembly or Part mode? There are a lot of opinions as to which mode is the *right* mode for component development. In the end, you should do your development in whichever mode enables you to complete your work the fastest while still capturing the overall design intent. For example, the following illustration outlines a small assembly that needs to have a cover designed.

100   Chapter 5: Capturing Design Intent

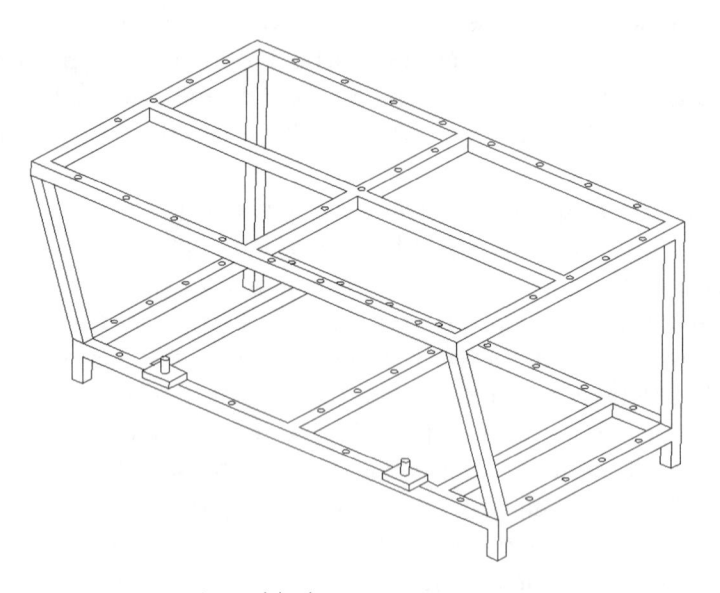

Assembly that requires a cover.

In order to design the cover properly, the mounting locations must be outlined so that whoever designs it will know how and where the cover must be assembled. Those locations are shown in the following illustration.

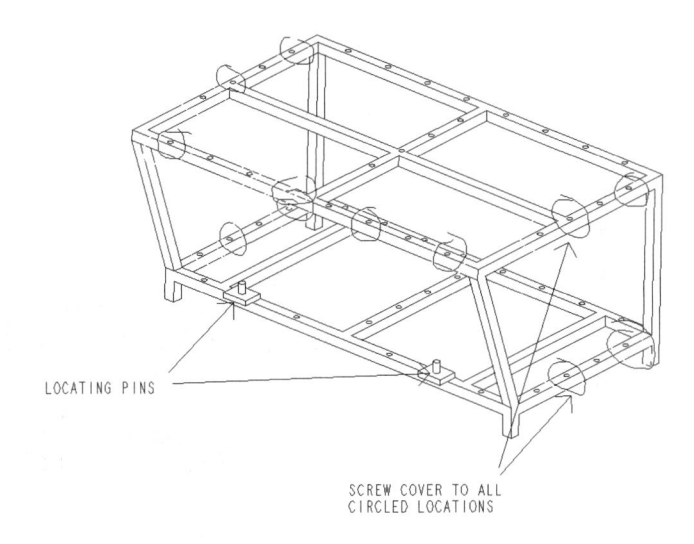

Assembly with the mounting locations for the cover outlined.

Which mode of development should be used for this application? It should be obvious that the component should be developed in Assembly mode. However, it is possible for the same component to be developed in Part mode. The big question is, which method or mode of development will be quickest and most efficient? In this particular case, let's assume that this interface is governed by a layout. Depending on the amount of information included on the layout, you may be able to quickly develop the component without even entering Assembly mode, provided there is enough information included in the layout. A picture of the layout is shown in the following illustration.

Chapter 5: Capturing Design Intent

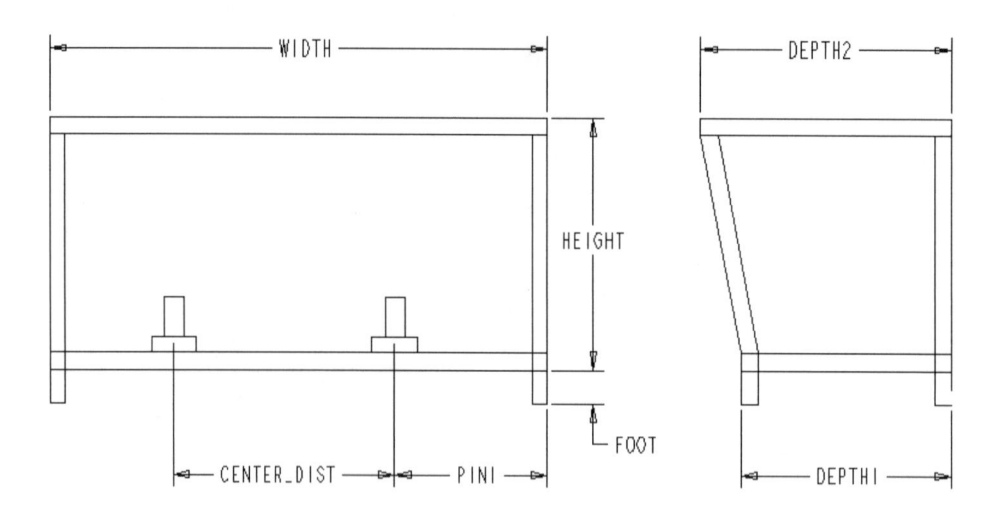

Layout of the assembly.

You will notice that there is sufficient information included in the Layout to manage the part as a single entity. Therefore, you may be able to complete your work in Part mode, without even loading the assembly onto your computer. But what if your design was not using Layout as the method of managing the design? What should you do then? When this situation exists, there are basically two options: document the size of the component that you are to develop, the mounting locations, distances, clearances, etc., then develop it in Part mode. Unfortunately, this method is not always as fast and efficient as you might like. Another method of development, the method that better captures the design intent, is to develop the component in an assembled state. This of course gives you insight as to the overall package and design. Using this technique, you can develop your geometry and align it such that the component will "float" with the design until you disassociate or unalign the feature from the interfacing components. Such a condition is shown in the following figure.

Which Mode Is Right for You?

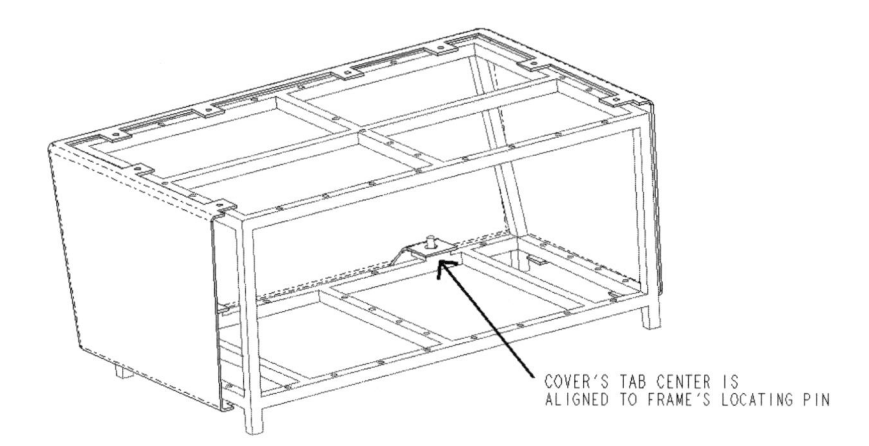

Geometry aligned to interfacing component will "float" with interface.

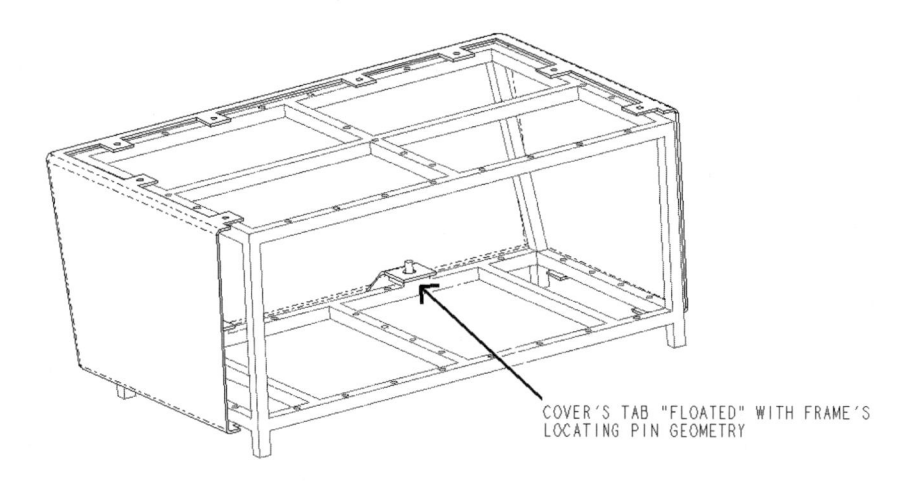

Aligned geometry's movement with interfacing component after modification.

If the geometry was dimensionally constrained such that it moved independent (i.e., would not float with the interfacing geometry), the results of a modification to the interfacing geometry would look like the following illustration.

Chapter 5: Capturing Design Intent

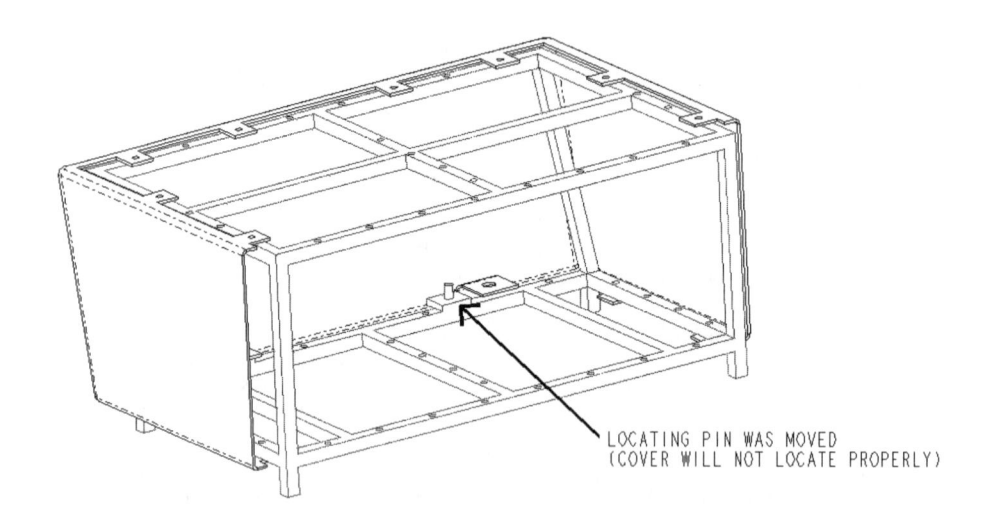

LOCATING PIN WAS MOVED
(COVER WILL NOT LOCATE PROPERLY)

Geometry doesn't move relative to interfacing geometry.

There is always the option to generate a parametric relationship, and this is a valid method of managing this interface. The problems come when it is time to finalize the design. You may have 20 parametric relationships governing the assembly; which ones do you need and which do you not need? Careful documentation of the parameters is important to avoid major problems in assembly management. Overall, it is probably easier to manage the dimensional relationships with a layout or by letting the design float until you are ready to finalize the design and break out the assembly for detailing.

There are many options at your fingertips for the development of components and assemblies in Pro/ENGINEER. You must use the tools that you are comfortable with, can be easily understood by other engineers who may come into contact with the design, and capture the design intent of the component or assembly. It is almost impossible to analyze each method or mode of development. And for every case study or example, there are 5 to 10 different approaches to obtaining the same solution, and some may be faster than others. Ultimately, it is up to your skills and abilities as an engineer to determine which method best describes your components and satisfies your long-term requirements.

Summary

Capturing the design intent is not easy, and it is not because of Pro/ENGINEER. Capturing the design intent involves not only understanding where you are going with your design, but how you are going to get there. This chapter has analyzed some of the fundamental requirements and thought processes required to develop functional designs in Pro/ENGINEER. As we have seen, each model's strengths are not in the pretty pictures that the software can generate, but in the flexibility of the final product. The methods and tools that you select, the time that you select them, and how well you manage the development of parent/child relationships plays a significant role in how well you capture the design intent. If you have taken the time to fully understand each feature's capabilities and limits, you will not only become a better user of Pro/ENGINEER, you will be able to increase the accuracy and flexibility of your designs while preserving that data for future revisions.

Design Verification and Manufacturability

Introduction

You have worked for a number of weeks to complete a plastic component's design and to keep your program's timing on schedule. Now that the design has been completed, you send an IGES database to your plastics supplier for CNC programming. A week and a half later your department head receives a call about your design; your molder has discovered a number of undercuts in the database. Knowing that this fundamental error will cost both time and money for your company, you are embarrassed by the oversights.

With your heart already pounding at the top of your throat, you quickly make the required changes to the design to correct the problems. During your corrections, you uncover another set of undercuts that the molder has not yet discovered. By this time your blood pressure has jumped and you have lost 3 pounds in sweat alone due to the number of manufacturability problems that you are discovering and correcting on the fly. Your timing for the component is now critical and there is a chance that your company will not receive parts on time for a build. Could all of this have been avoided? The answer is, yes.

Verify the Parts and Assemblies

Although it is not stressed as much as it should be, design verification is an important phase of the development process in Pro/ENGINEER. You must remember that just having a shaded picture on your computer does not mean that your design is manufacturable; there is much more to it than that. Use the pretty pictures for visualization and impressing customers. Design verification focuses on whether or not the databases are flexible and satisfy the conceptual, dimensional, inspection, manufacturing, and process-related requirements, and, above all, design intent. In a nutshell, were all of the design's requirements satisfied and will the design adapt to modifications?

As you can see from the introductory example, design verification is very important. If you have had a similar experience, I feel for you; it is not easy to deal with and it does nothing to help your credibility. Undoubtedly you learned from that experience and are now more cautious about your design's development. If you have not gone through this experience, I hope that you learn from the examples in this book and are able to reduce your chances of making these costly mistakes.

One of the first steps in design verification is to determine if your design satisfies the requirements of your company, supplier, and ultimately your customer. This revolves around the inputs you obtained during those early brainstorming and layout sessions. By simply looking at each feature the design has and verifying that the geometric and dimensional relationships satisfy the detailing, inspection, and tolerancing requirements, you can quickly catch any problems on the fly and take the steps to correct them. This simple form of analysis can help to refamiliarize you with the design intent of the component. This is important because you may need to field questions about the design intent and why your designs have been laid out in the fashion that they were.

Once you have verified that the dimensional relationships are correctly established, verify the database's flexibility. To do this, make sure that specific

Verify the Parts and Assemblies 109

relationships that you have developed adapt to the changes that you make. For example, the overall design intent of the connecting rod body shown in the following figure may be to have a constant material thickness of 2.5 mm for a given connecting pin diameter. If the design was developed incorrectly, your database may look like that shown in the following illustration after making a change to the connecting pin diameter.

Piston before modification.

Piston after modification.

As you can see, the wall thickness did not stay a constant 2.5 mm. Therefore, you have discovered an error in the database's ability to capture the design intent. Now that this has been discovered, you can quickly enter a mathematical relationship to ensure that this critical relationship exists. But what if this relationship had not been properly developed; do you think you, or anyone else, would have caught the error quickly if the diameter had only changed by 0.5 mm? Probably not. This is why it is important to verify that the design is responsive to modifications. The same principles apply to patterned and user-defined features for both parts and assemblies. If you have taken the time to carefully develop and manage complex pattern relationships, then those patterns should be flexible and easy to manipulate by the next person to come into contact with your work.

You must be sure that every design intent–related modification is tested and that the results are what you and everyone else expect. When you are testing the database for flexibility, you are not just testing it to see if features maintain their relationships, you are making sure the next person, or company, who will come into contact with the database will be able to adjust the database with ease. By taking the time to verify your design's flexibility, you are saving face in advance.

In the end, if the model is not easy to modify, has regeneration problems, or is just too difficult to figure out, you may find your hard work being remodeled by someone else. This particular aspect of design verification relates back to corporate standards and Pro/ENGINEER. Theoretically, if everyone knows the ground rules for modeling and documentation, everyone will know how to work with everyone else's work.

Another area of design verification is the verification of subcomponents in an assembly. What will your subcomponent do when the design changes? I have worked on enough assemblies where I would change one aspect of the design, and then spend 2 or 3 hours hunting for all of the other component's parameters to ensure that they are updated to reflect the changes in design. For this, you need a copy of any layouts that govern certain aspects of your design, the mating components among other assembly components. For this type of design verification, you are interested in more than how an individual component responds to modifications; you are interested in how flexible the overall design is, and how that flexibility will affect future design modifications. When it comes to modifying component designs, the assembly as a whole should adapt to a change in the design intent. This ensures that all of the components in the design will fit together and truly capture the design intent. It is a lot easier to document the design as a whole and have one or two dimensions govern aspects of the entire design, than to be forced to remember to adjust each and every component in an assembly independently.

That can get old really fast. For example, the following piston assembly is designed such that a layout governs the dimensional relationships for all of the interfacing subassembly components.

Original assembly design.

To ensure that the above design is flexible and can adapt to changes, the lower portion of the connecting rod assembly will be modified. If the design has been properly developed and managed, the lower diameter will adjust to the new value, the wall thickness for both components will stay the same, and the body and bolts will adjust to their proper distances all by changing one dimension. The results of that modification are shown in the following figure.

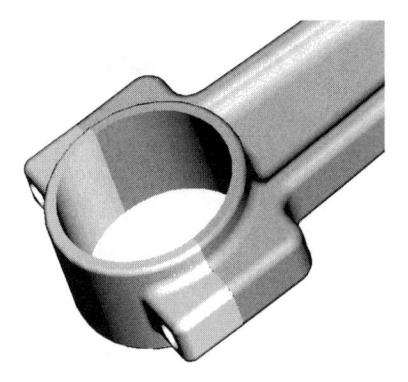

Modified connecting rod assembly.

As you can see from the previous illustration, all of the geometry adapted to the change that was initiated. If the design was not properly developed and managed, you could have gotten any number of incorrect responses from this single change. Nothing is more frustrating than having a design that will not respond to modifications. The above example could be carried even further to ensure that the crank shaft, with which the piston interfaces, adjusts to the design modifications along with the connecting rod assembly.

Both of the previous examples highlight the importance of database and overall design flexibility, but those aspects of verification are for an overall, or macro, verification of your design. There are areas of your design that need to have more in-depth, or micro, analysis—verifying manufacturability.

Verifying Manufacturability

This is one area where you need to have the input of the people who will be actually manufacturing your components. If your supply base has Pro/ENGINEER, you are in luck; they should be able to analyze your designs and make any modifications on the fly with your consent. One the other hand, if your supply base has a totally different CAD/CAM system, you may have to spend more time analyzing your designs up front, with your supplier, to ensure manufacturability.

To Section or Not To Section, That Is the Question

Does design verification for manufacturability mean that you have to cut a million sections through each of your components? Well, sometimes.... There are a lot of tools within Pro/ENGINEER that can be used to analyze your parts, without generating a lot of sections. For example, you are to analyze a plastic component to ensure that there are no undercuts in the design. Cutting a bunch of sections would give you the results you are looking for, but it takes time and often requires you to generate a drawing highlighting each section. Performing a slope surface analysis of the entire component will show you very quickly where any problem areas are in the design. Basically, this

Verifying Manufacturability 113

particular analysis colors each surface on the part. Each color, or color transition, highlights changes in slope relative to a user-definable plane. For example, the following illustration highlights the changes in slope relative to the base of the part.

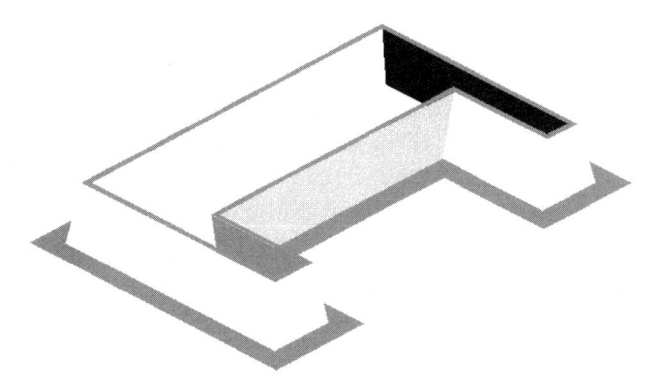

Component with each wall at different draft angles.

The above illustration is a simple example of how different changes in slope are represented with different colors.

The same example with one wall undercut is shown in the following illustration.

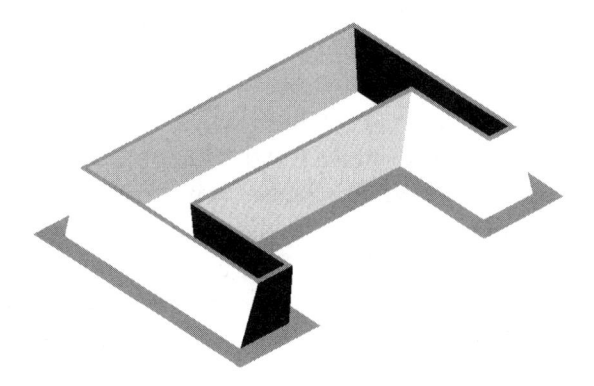

Component with an undercut wall.

A standard shaded image may not have revealed the undercut wall. But with this surface analysis, the undercut was quickly discovered, giving the engineer the opportunity to ensure manufacturability. The above example's draft problem could have been just as easily discovered using *Draft Check* in Part mode or as the mold was being designed using Pro/MOLDDESIGN or Pro/CASTING, unless of course the design intent required that undercut to exist.

These basic tools of analysis are functional and do not require you to be an expert to use them. But what about our original question, "To section or not to section?" Sectioning can be an effective tool to improve the communication of geometry that is difficult to visualize. It is easy to get carried away with the sectioning of a part or assembly. Try to use sections for detailing the design, not analyzing every aspect of how geometry was developed or how much clearance there is between two components in an assembly. I can obtain faster results by quickly measuring the distances from feature to feature or component to component on the fly, rather than detailing every possible problem area of a design.

Most basic components for ejection type manufacturing processes can be analyzed by using either sections, measuring aspects of the part using thickness checking, or some of the basic surface analysis tools that are integrated with Pro/ENGINEER. For those individuals who spend a lot of time working on complex components or data from other CAD/CAM systems, Pro/ENGINEER comes with other nifty tools for analyzing the data and its manufacturability. For components that have complex, contoured surfaces and features, you may find that some of the other surface analysis tools may be helpful. I have found that, especially when I am working with data from other CAD/CAM systems (both single and double precision systems), analysis of complex surface geometry can be a life saver when it comes to prequalifying components for manufacturability. Whether you are working with another CAD/CAM system's data or your own, there are some areas of your development that can create some real problems when it comes time to manufacture the design. Most of these problems occur when you are dealing with free-form geometry, hanging complex surface geometries on scanned datum curves, or trying to maintain tangency (smooth transitions) from one piece of geometry to another.

Verifying Manufacturability 115

Most people will claim that a shaded image will highlight surface discontinuities and give you the opportunity to correct the problem. Most of the time this is true. But there are those cases, usually on larger geometries with more gradual changes in curvature, where a normal shaded image will not reveal a major problem in the design. However, the CNC machine will not miss the errors, and steel is expensive! When you are dealing with another system's data or data that you develop yourself, you must be sure to check complex geometries using tools other than a shaded image. For example, the following surface geometry could be anything from a portion of a head lamp to the front end of a power tool.

Complex surface geometry: wireframe.

Just looking at the image does not indicate any problems whatsoever. Even the shaded image shown in the following illustration does not highlight a problem or variation in surface geometries as outlined by the boundaries of the surface.

116   Chapter 6: Design Verification

Complex surface geometry: shaded image.

But let's put some of the analysis tools to work. The first tool out of the bag would be a Gaussian curvature analysis. Basically this tool will graphically represent the product of the minimum and maximum curvature for every point on the surface or solid geometry. This is a great tool because it can highlight graphically, without the normalized image that a shading produces, what the geometry's topology actually is. As you can see from the following illustration, there appears to be a deviation in the surface geometry.

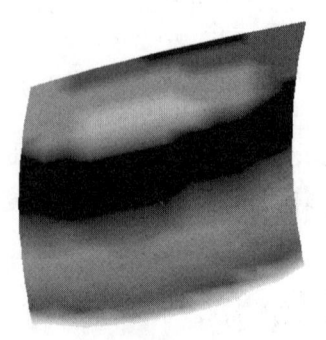

Complex surface geometry: Gaussian curvature analysis.

Another useful tool for analyzing complex geometry is by generating section curvatures using the Porcupine command. This is a surface analysis tool that is included with Pro/ENGINEER. This method of analysis can be used to manually generate either evenly spaced or user-defined section normals of the geometry. The porcupine analysis of the surface shown previously would look like the following.

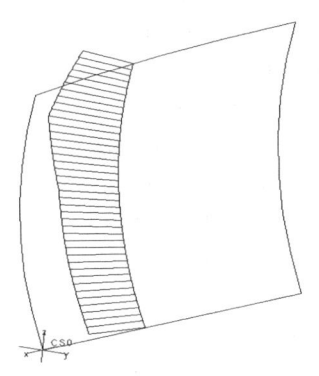

Complex surface geometry: Porcupine.

As you can see, this analysis highlights graphically where some of the surface's problem areas are occurring. These two analysis tools are just some of the tools at your disposal within Pro/ENGINEER. There are a number of reasons why you should use these tools, most of which revolve around verifying that the data that you are working with is accurate. Both of the methods discussed previously brought to light some areas of the geometry that may have caused problems in the manufacturing process.

There are other tools that are useful in your verification of the data and manufacturability of the overall design. I strongly suggest that you investigate each option and analysis feature within Pro/ENGINEER. If nothing else, you will be able to ask the big question: "Is this really what the design's intent is, or is this a genuine error in the database?" Either way, you will be one step closer to producing quality components that capture the design intent.

What will the results of all of this analysis be? And why should you spend the time to verify the data? The answer lies in the following question: Can you afford not to check your work? If you are not bull headed, you know the answer is, No! I have seen a number of expensive and embarrassing submissions to a customer or another department where the database held up entire development programs because of inaccurate data. These are not scare tactics, this is reality.

Does the Design Satisfy the Process Requirements?

Above and beyond the verification of the database that you have developed lies a fundamental process requirement that will affect your bottom line—the cost of the product. You may have spent days or even weeks working on a design that satisfies the overall requirements and is manufacturable. Your design may look like the following illustration.

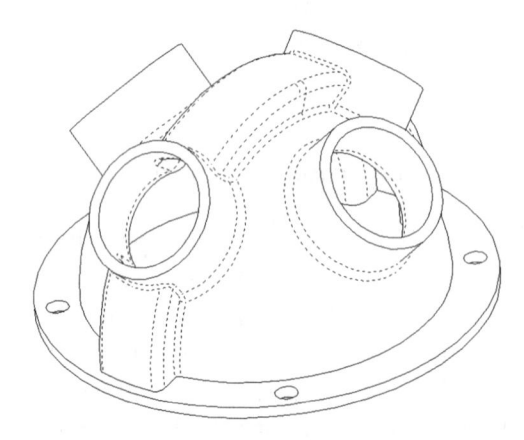

Design that satisfies design objectives.

If the manufacturing process intent was for a lost foam or some type of sand type casting process you may have a good chance of obtaining exactly what you designed. But, what if the component is required to be a magnesium die cast component? This may have an impact on your design. Although this component could probably be developed for a die casting process, it may not be cost effective due to the intensive camming that would be required to capture the design intent. Another area that is not always planned for is the manufacture of the molds or dies that will be used for the production of the component. Will this design require a three- or five-axis CNC machine or will another manufacturing process be an option? This is a big question. Most companies that have a decent supply base do not have to worry about this; it is just a part of doing business. But if you are planning a short in-house run of components on your three-axis CNC machine, you may want to make sure that the operators are capable of quickly and efficiently machining the component.

This subject touches on the fact that there are a lot of people and processes involved in the manufacture of a production-quality component. And each of those people and processes have their own set of design requirements. Verifying that a design is manufacturable may require you to bring them into design reviews. This level of input should go further than just looking at a shaded image on your computer screen. To minimize the amount of corrections on the fly, it is important that your suppliers and manufacturers have a solid (no pun intended) understanding of what they are getting into. I have found that spending a few hours in review before a design is released can mean the difference between an on-time and within budget component, and a late and expensive headache.

These final meetings should not be used to discuss the design in general, unless of course there will be major changes in the design to satisfy the process, but remember, most of the process-related requirements should have been outlined in the preliminary stages of the design. Instead, these meetings should be used to analyze the details and ask such questions as: Are the ribs placed properly? How will the gating affect the filling of the part? Is there enough draft on the part's features? By this time in your development, you should have all of the design's overall requirements satisfied (your "Christmas tree" has been put up and the "ornaments" have been hung). In these discussions you are making sure that the component satisfies the process requirements (making sure that the ornaments are properly placed on the tree and look good). You will get valuable input from your supply base. If their recommendations are satisfactory and will improve the manufacture of the component, incorporate them. Usually when a supplier or tool maker has a request for a component change, it will save your company money.

Be open about tolerancing and dimensioning. Just looking at the database and a set of overall dimensions is not enough. If your supplier is expected to turn in an inspection report on how well the production components match the design's dimensional requirements, the supplier should have the opportunity to give input. This is important because you may be holding down some dimensions too tight that may have an impact on the price of the tooling, inspection, and ultimately the piece price. Most of the supplier recommendations that I have been given in the past have revolved around improving the process and inspection requirements, rarely on the overall design. Their input has resulted in the addition of ribs, rounds, gating, parting lines, tolerancing, etc. This input is invaluable and will help validate the design relative to the process requirements, to insure a smooth transition from the developmental to production stages of the design. In addition to that, their expertise will improve your knowledge of the processes that you will be using, the capabilities of the supplier, and what information is valuable and what is not.

Sometimes, when validating a design for manufacturability, there are suggestions to alter the design to improve processing. When this occurs, it is important for you to verify the validity of the proposed changes to the design. Nothing hurts more than to make a change to a design, without making sure that the design changes will not affect the overall design. Therefore, it is important to understand what each modification will do to the overall design and intelligently address those issues.

> **NOTE:** *If you have done your homework and taken the time to make sure that the design intent of the component has been captured, your designs should regenerate as you would expect after a modification.*

Once the manufacturing considerations have been addressed for the rough design, review the proposed changes with all of the other parties who have contributed to the overall design (i.e., analysis, inspection, design, etc.) Once a consensus has been obtained for any component modifications to improve manufacturability, incorporate the changes. This is important, because when people have taken the time to supply input to a design, they generally don't like to be left in the dark or surprised in the end. To minimize the frustrations, include people in the proposed changes in design.

Once you have completed all of your database, design, and manufacturability analysis, you must prepare the databases for documenting the design. Your design process may require that you use finite element analysis (FEA), design for assembly (DFA), or another type of analysis to verify the strength, ease of assembly, or other design requirements that you may be required to perform. Exploring higher levels of analysis can certainly help you to correlate your predicted performance of the design with the final product, and when applicable, I highly recommend the use of the high-end analysis tools that are available. However, to bring closure to the design verification process, you must produce a final design and document that reflects the requests of all of the parties involved. You must apply the tolerances (both linear and geometric) to the database to truly capture the design and inspection intent of the design.

Apply the Tolerances

Most people who are just learning to use Pro/ENGINEER, especially those who have been spoiled by other CAD system's detailing flexibility, have a hard time detailing components and assemblies in Pro/ENGINEER. I have even heard of companies that heavily invest in Pro/ENGINEER, model complex parts in Pro/ENGINEER, translate the database via IGES to their previous CAD system, and then detail the component. Some of the most common frustrations in detailing the design in Pro/ENGINEER stem from either not creating the model properly or not understanding how to detail in Pro/ENGINEER.

Right about now you are probably thinking, "What does this have to do with verifying the design and manufacturability?" Good question; I'm glad you asked. After taking the time to verify all of the design, manufacturability, inspection, and process-related verifications, you must turn all of the dimensional input into functional and logical linear and geometric tolerances. Basically, outline the limits of the design and constrain them to ensure that the design intent is captured. To do this you must make sure that your database is set up to accept the tolerance constraints. So you must think about what you want to communicate on the final print, and how you want that information to be represented. This entire phase of the development and verification process should be a breeze because you have taken the time to capture the design intent.

This is one area of modeling that is often overlooked. It can be used to verify the design and is generally considered to be a detailing function. After all, if everything has gone according to plan, and all of your design goals have been accomplished, the dimensional references and dimensioning scheme will already be in place. The only thing left to do is apply the tolerances—to the model. The model?!?

A lot of users have not really put Pro/ENGINEER to use, but have certainly gone though mountains of scratch paper calculating fits and clearances for

Chapter 6: Design Verification

interfacing components. Pro/ENGINEER does have the ability to perform a linear stack up analysis of a part or assembly based on your inputs. This is helpful for quickly analyzing how the tolerances affect the overall design.

I have found that when you are working with this analysis, it is often better to perform this analysis in Part or Assembly mode: Part mode for calculating feature stack ups and Assembly mode for component interaction calculations. A drawing can also be used to perform a tolerance analysis, but it is not always optimum for viewing the results, especially in larger assemblies. To perform this analysis, you must first determine whether or not a dimension, or set of dimensions, should use the block tolerance for the part or be controlled independently. I have found that dimensions that vary from the block tolerance values are important dimensions that control interfacing geometry, minimum distance requirements, etc. The block tolerance when in Part mode is located at the base of the graphics window and is shown in the following illustration.

```
X.X     +-0.5
X.XX    +-0.25
X.XXX   +-0.130
ANG.    +-1.0
```

Tolerances in Part mode.

If you look at the following assembly, you can see that all the dimensions on the right have user-defined and controlled tolerances. The dimensions on the left are nominal dimensions that will reference the block tolerance relative to the number of decimal places for which they are defined.

Apply the Tolerances 123

THESE DIMENSIONS USE THE BLOCK TOLERANCE

THESE DIMENSIONS USE USER DEFINED TOLERANCES

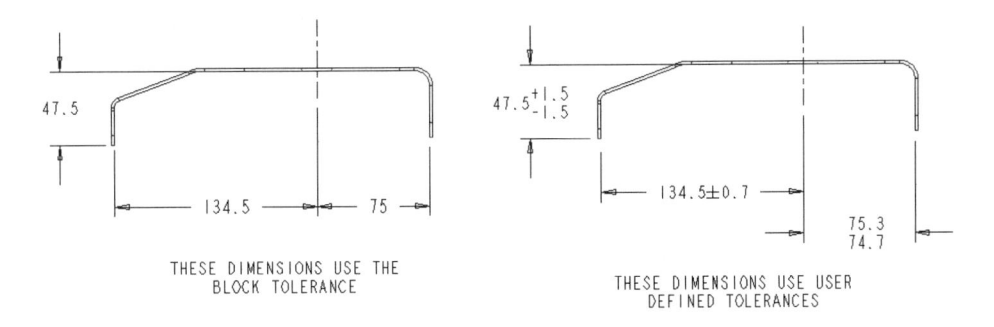

Left: Dimensions reference block tolerance. Right: Dimensions have user-defined tolerances.

If you wish to change the tolerance format, or style, of the dimension from a nominal to a limited, +/-, or +/- symmetric tolerance, all you have to do is select the type of tolerance format that you wish to apply to the dimension. To do this, simply modify the feature, select DIM PARAMS from the MODIFY menu, then Format, and you would see the following menu.

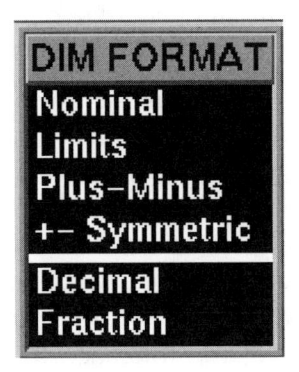

```
DIM FORMAT
Nominal
Limits
Plus-Minus
+- Symmetric
Decimal
Fraction
```

Tolerance format menu.

Simply select the type of tolerance that you wish to apply and then select the dimensions that you wish to change. The results are shown in the following illustration.

124 Chapter 6: Design Verification

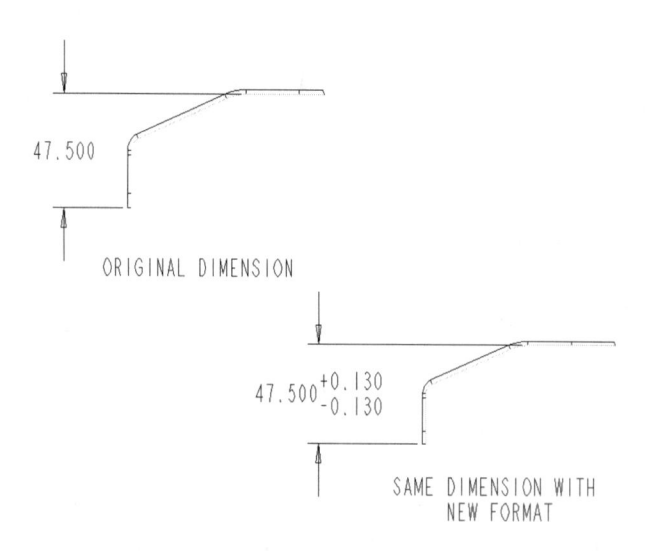

Before and after tolerance format modification.

Notice that Pro/ENGINEER automatically assigned a value to the tolerance. This is the default value for the number of digits that the original dimension was. To change the tolerance, simply modify the tolerance value, just as you modify the dimension itself by selecting the tolerance portion of the dimension. Enter the value that you require, and then regenerate. After you regenerate, notice the nominal dimension value did not change. The reason for this is that Pro/ENGINEER maintains the feature's size at a nominal value until you tell Pro/ENGINEER to set the dimension to a maximum or minimum material condition (apply the tolerance to the dimension).

Why is all of this important, and why should you apply this information in the part or assembly? Because, it is easier to see each feature, and therefore ensure that you are applying the tolerance to the proper dimension. In addition, you will be able to apply either the high or low tolerance to the dimension, regenerate the model, and examine the results. This allows you to verify that the dimensioning and tolerancing scheme will produce functional components and assemblies as the final product. This is accomplished by simply entering the DIM BOUNDS menu within the setup menu.

Apply the Tolerances 125

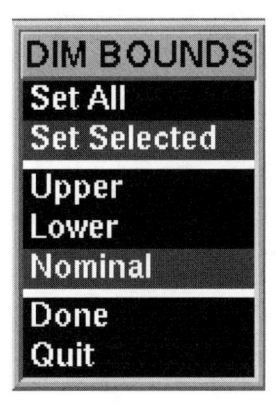

DIM BOUNDS menu.

This menu allows you to alter either all or some of the dimensions to the upper, lower, or nominal dimensional limits. The strengths of this lie in the simplicity of the analysis. For example, you are to analyze the clearance between a small assembly that contains a metal bracket and a plastic pad. The following is an illustration of the assembly before the analysis.

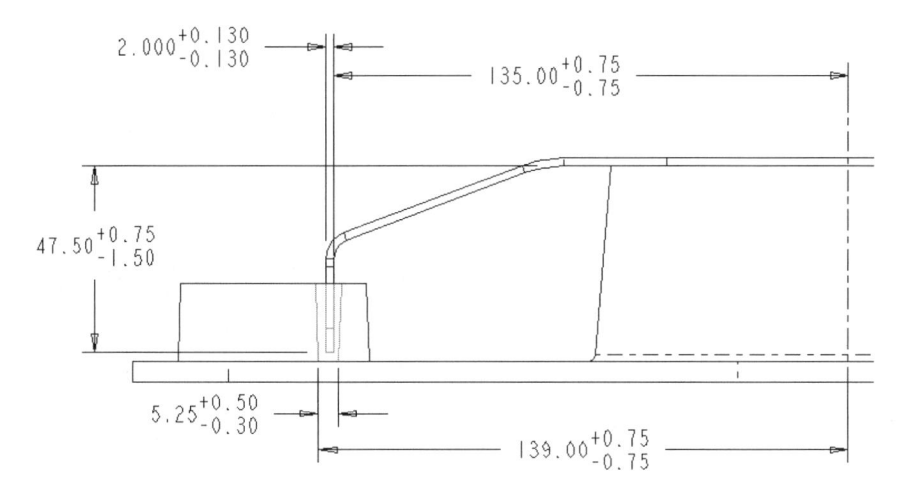

Assembly at nominal dimension values.

Chapter 6: Design Verification

By setting the dimension for the plastic to the lower tolerance value, and the bracket to the upper tolerance value, a regeneration reveals the following clearances in the design.

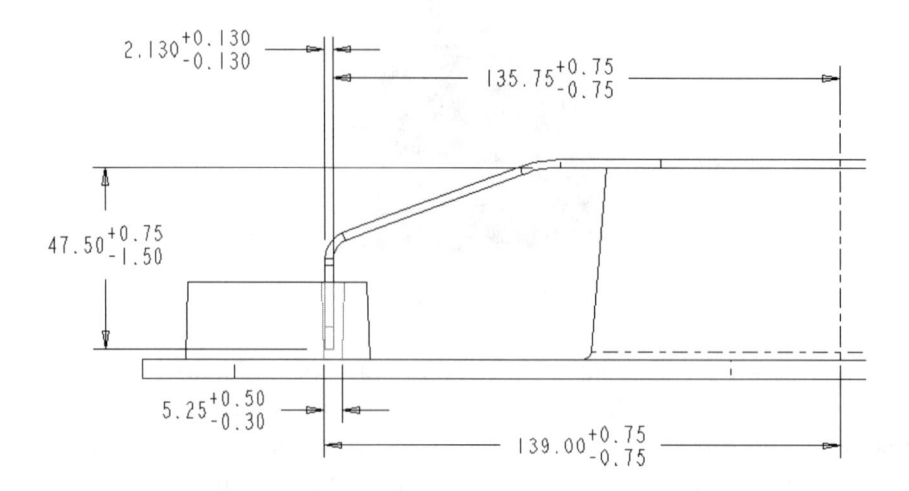

Plastic at lower tolerance and bracket at upper tolerance.

Final measurement between components shows that there is a clearance between the two components at the worst case for the assembly. What does this mean to you? This analysis has highlighted that you have some room to increase a tolerance range, which could reduce the cost of the component. This is a simple problem, and you probably could have figured out that there would have been a clearance in less time than it would have taken you to read this example. But remember, this technique of using Pro/ENGINEER for a linear stack up can reduce errors that can occur by simply transcribing an error from the computer to your scratch pad. Since Pro/ENGINEER completely regenerates the model whose dimensions are altered, the results of the regeneration are a part or assembly that actually measures to the new size, allowing you to truly calculate clearances and ensure fit and function.

One thing that I have found useful is a reference dimension within a part or assembly to minimize the amount of measuring after a regeneration. The previous example can be modified to incorporate a reference dimension, as shown in the following figure.

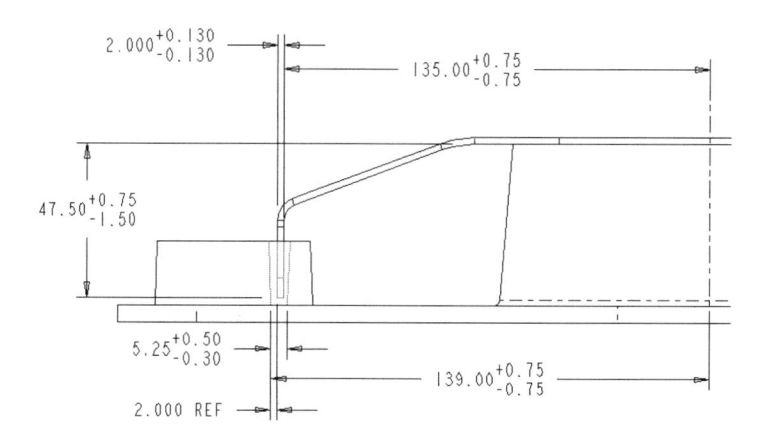

Tolerance analysis using a reference dimension.

You can quickly cycle the dimensional values from upper to lower tolerance values, or even change the tolerance values on the fly, and obtain accurate measurements in half the time of measuring each feature of interest after a regeneration. Because the reference dimensions float, you can quickly obtain useful dimensional results with a minimal amount of effort.

But is this simplistic tolerance analysis solving all of your analysis needs? If you and your company only use linear dimensions to describe your parts and assemblies, then these tools are probably all that you need. However, if your company is currently using, or is planning on implementing, geometric dimensioning and tolerancing (GD&T), then you may need to investigate some alternatives.

Another significant area of verifying the design is the application of the tolerances that define the permissible variability for the features of the part and how features are related to each other. The proper application of GD&T to your databases will result in components that capture the design intent and ensure that component A fits with component B all of the time. If you were to ask someone who has no significant experience in the application of GD&T

128   Chapter 6: Design Verification

to Pro/ENGINEER databases, his or her response would likely discourage you from even attempting to mess with it. Don't be discouraged.

If your design, modeling, and dimensioning scheme have been developed properly, then you should be ready to apply any GD&T you may require. The following illustrations show the untoleranced design, and then the same design with the GD&T applied.

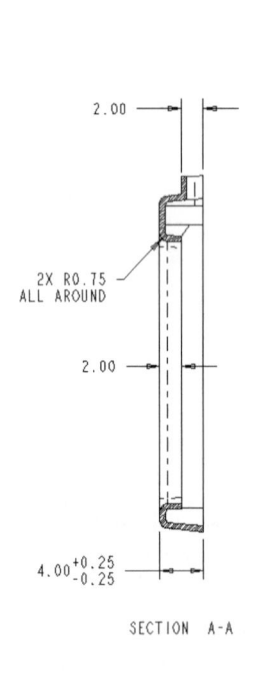

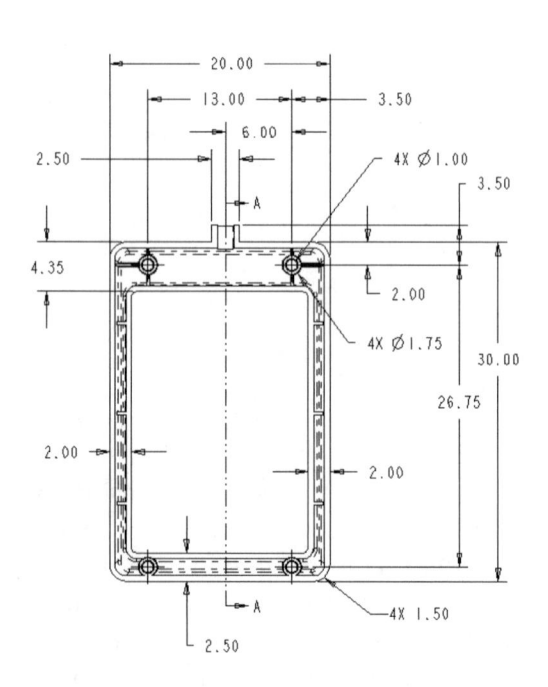

Original design.

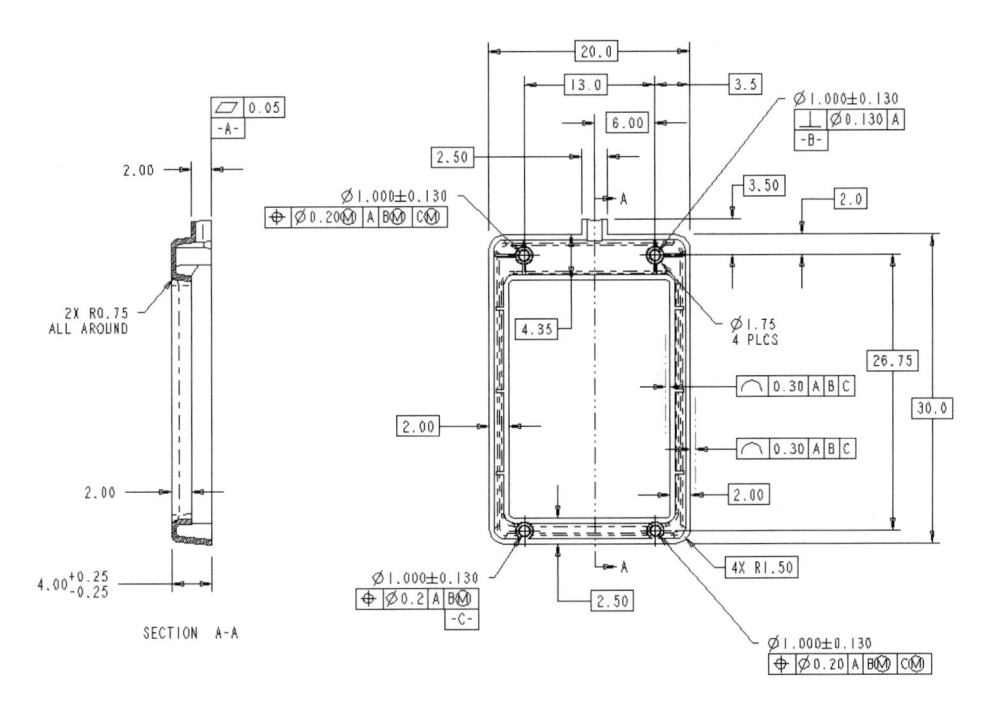

Apply the Tolerances 129

Original design with GD&T.

Unlike the standard toleranced dimensions, which can be set to either a high or low material condition, Pro/ENGINEER does not currently support geometric tolerance analysis of your designs. There are, however, third-party packages available for this type of analysis. If you are interested in using a third-party package, be sure to find one that works directly with the Pro/ENGINEER database. If you are forced to transfer or reestablish all of the dimensional constraints in a different system, you could be losing valuable time for design. Pro/ENGINEER does have some safety features to prevent you from establishing bogus tolerances and feature control frames unless you are set up to add those types of information to your design. I have seen some downright scary methods of applying GD&T to documentation in Pro/ENGINEER. The worst cases have been the application of the GD&T using notes on the drawing or trying to apply the GD&T on the drawing using datum references that are different from the model's. There are a number of problems with this that are discussed in greater detail in Chapter 8, "Detailing."

But what does this mean for the verification of the design? Quite simply, applying both linear and geometric dimensions and tolerances to the database achieves several things at the same time. You will be able to communicate not only (1) what the permissible locations and overall size can be, but (2) what the permissible variations of those features are and how are they related to each other. These two simple reasons will have a significant impact on your design, documentation, and ultimately, the design intent. It is important that this phase of the development and verification process be given the same amount of attention that the entire design is given. The reason is that the tolerances for the design will make or break the design's ability to be manufactured, inspected, fit properly, and above all capture the design intent.

Summary

Everyone who uses or knows about Pro/ENGINEER and its truly awesome modeling and general design capabilities are impressed by the flexibility, simplicity, ease of use, and ability to truly capture the design intent. Putting this tool to use is the easy part, and it will do exactly what you tell it to do. But we are all human and we can make mistakes. This leads to an area of Pro/ENGINEER that is not stressed often enough—design verification and manufacturability. You can be the fastest modeler of components in your department or company, but if you are not producing manufacturable designs, then all your efforts are being wasted.

Pro/ENGINEER comes with a set of analysis tools to assist you in producing manufacturable designs and quality information. Each of these tools can be adapted for analyzing process-related requirements such as draft, curvature, tangency, etc. But beyond the slick tools for analyzing geometry, there lies a requirement to validate your design prior to release. Nothing is more embarrassing or humiliating than having a released design frozen because of a modeling oversight. It is important that your designs not only capture the design intent, but also the process requirements that will be used to produce the components. You may have developed the optimal design to solve your design problem, but if it can't be manufactured cost-effectively, then you may have not spent enough time thinking about the process requirements.

Summary

When verifying a design in Pro/ENGINEER it is important that you pull together the resources involved in the original design's development and layout. The verification process goes beyond whether or not the design captures the design intent. This phase revolves around how the design can be produced. If there are any process-related changes, how will they affect the design and how will the tolerances affect the manufacturability and cost of the component? Verification also means that your data must be accurate.

Modifying Designs

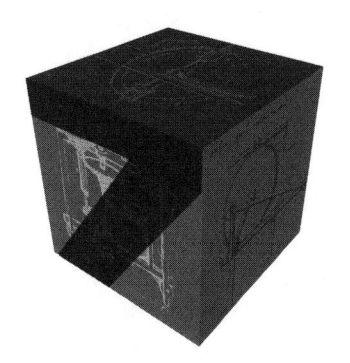

Introduction

Having been given a redesign project, you are forced to adapt an existing design for a new application. Looking at the amount of rework that needs to be accomplished, you are confident that it will not require much time to complete, and you get right to work. As you look into each component and its associated documentation, you discover that the model has been haphazardly developed, with no particular order or logical sequence. There are thousands of complex parent/child relationships, and the dimensioning scheme does not match the drawing that was included in the package. You also notice that, even though the drawing has a substantial amount of GD&T, the model has no *Set Datums*, which would be required to properly develop geometric tolerances. To compound the problems, each feature that was developed has its own set of Datum Planes that were defined as dimensional references, and the previous user has managed to "dig the holes and fill them with dirt," that is, make cuts and then fill them back up with other geometry.

Further investigation yields a long list of problems that will most definitely cause modification problems.

Because the time available for the redesign does not permit a remodeling, which may be the only way out of some major problems, you are forced to sculpt the new geometry into the models. After you have completed your sculpting project, you are left to update the documentation. As you enter the drawing, you are flooded with thousands of notes and manually sketched boxes that represent feature control frames. Because you do not have time to correct the design and associated documentation, you are forced to add to the existing problems by continuing the misuse of Pro/ENGINEER. With your additions to the design, you are exposing yourself to future ridicule and embarrassment, just by placing your initials in the revision block. So what should you do? If you had remodeled the component, you could have missed your deadline. But because of time pressures, you have caved in and helped to perpetuate a problem for which you could be held accountable. Either way, you are at risk.

All of this could have been avoided if the design had been developed to your company's corporate standards. There are a lot of companies who do not have corporate standards, and they are basically playing Russian roulette with a CAD system. This situation could have been avoided if the design's database was properly developed and tested prior to engineering release. But at this point, all of this is obvious. The big question is, how can you work with the designs that have already been developed? This chapter provides some insight into how simple designs can be modified, and what thought processes are involved for using the tools within Pro/ENGINEER.

Assembly Modifications Using a Layout

As we have discussed in previous chapters, layouts are a powerful tool that can make your designs easy to change and manage. Layouts, as you recall, are like an engineering scratch pad within Pro/ENGINEER. They use nonparametric geometry to represent the design, and dimension variables to drive the design. Modifying a design from a layout can be as easy as modifying a dimension value and regenerating the layout and associated databases. For example, the following illustration is a subassembly component that uses

Assembly Modifications Using a Layout 135

shared dimension values with mating components for hole sizes, locations, and so forth.

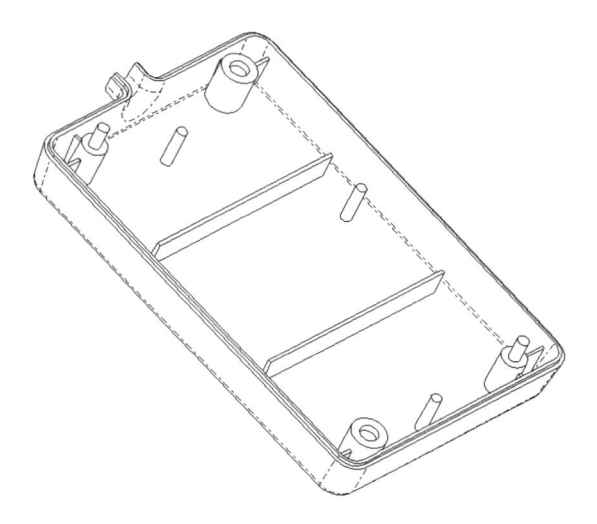

Design that uses shared dimension values.

The following illustration is the layout that governs the design shown previously.

136   Chapter 7: Modifying Designs

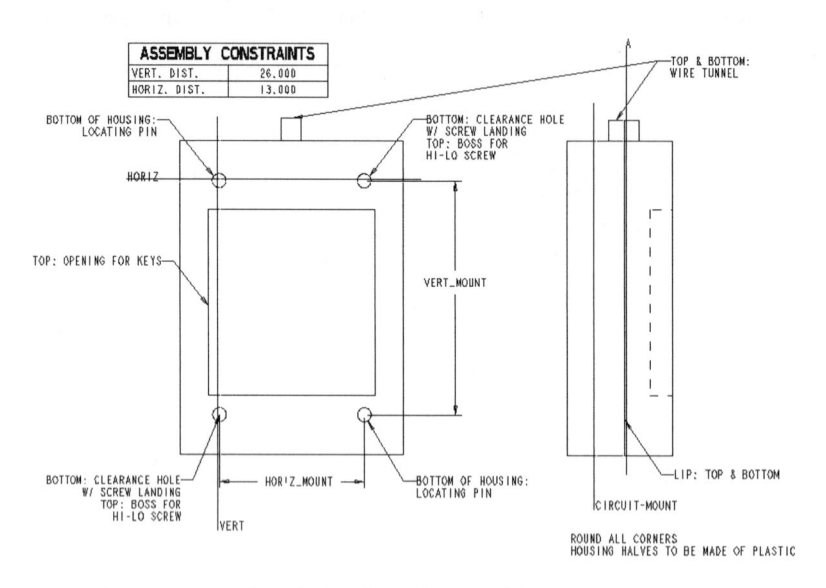

Layout that drives the subassembly component.

As we have seen in previous chapters, simply modifying the dimension values in the layout will drive the subassembly component, and any other component that references the layout's dimension variables. The results of a modification are shown in the following figure.

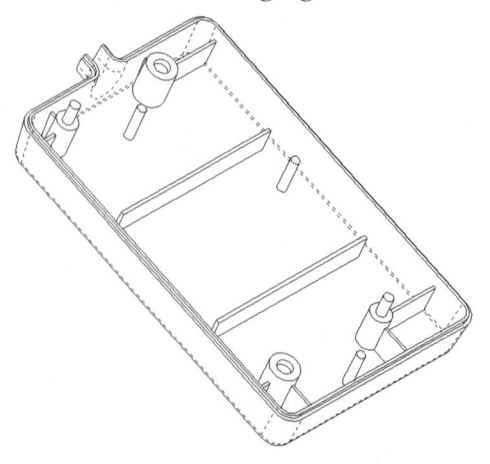

Subassembly component modified.

Assembly Modifications Using a Layout 137

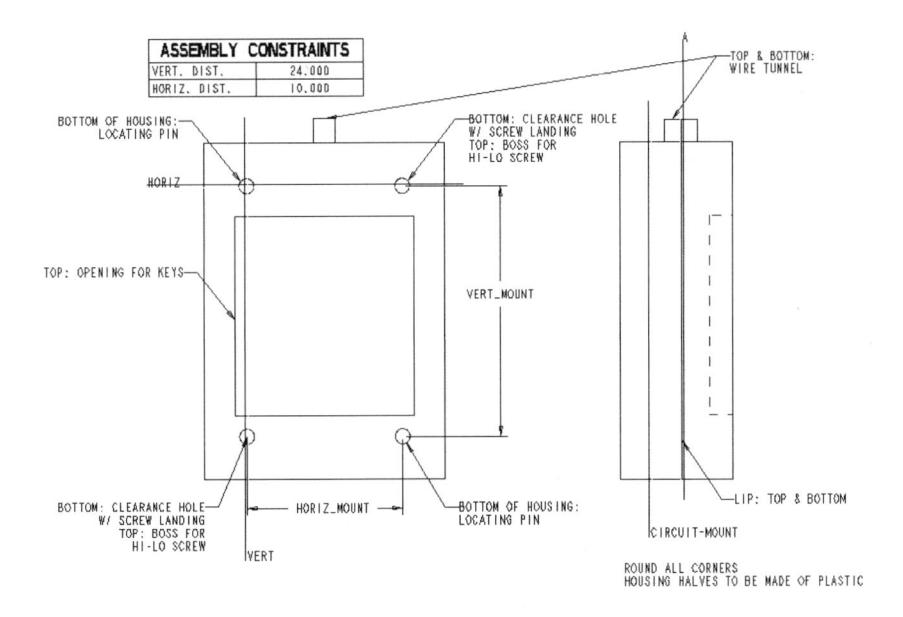

Original layout with new values.

If all of your dimensional relationships are properly established and each component that is declared to the layout has been properly constrained, designs can be modified with ease. This whole area of assembly development, management, and flexibility is one of the most impressive aspects of Pro/EN-GINEER and its ability to truly capture design intent.

Common problems with design modifications occur when a design's dimensioning scheme is changed or features that reference the layout are deleted. Basically, in these situations you are deleting or adding new dimensions to better describe the feature-to-feature relationships. Because the dimensional link to the layout is through a parametric relationship, when you delete a feature's dimensions, you will be deleting the parametric relationship that was established. To ensure that dimensional links are maintained with the layout, you must reestablish the parametric relationship by simply defining a new relationship that links the new dimension to the global variable in the layout.

Another common problem with modifying parts that reference layouts is the loss of geometry references, that is, datum planes, axes, datum points, etc. for the part or assembly. This can happen when a feature is the parent of a datum feature. Another user may have developed some datum axes through some arc centers to maintain a concentric assembly relationship. If the circular feature is deleted, the axis that is referencing the feature will also be deleted. You must be aware of these problems and be able to reroute or recreate the geometric reference. If you lose this reference, you will most likely have a difficult time during automatic assembly of the components.

To ensure that you have all of your dimensional and geometric references intact at the end of a part or assembly modification, access the DECLARE menu and select the *List Decl* menu command. This menu is shown in the following illustration.

```
DECLARE
Declare Lay
UnDeclr Lay
Table
DeclareName
UnDecl Name
List Decl
```

DECLARE menu.

Once you select the *List Decl* menu selection, Pro/ENGINEER shows you all of the dimensional and geometric relations that have been properly established for the part or assembly. This gives you the opportunity to check that the design can be used by other people in the department and easily integrated into existing designs.

Assembly Modifications in Assembly Mode

Modifying an assembly or component in Assembly mode is similar to modifying individual components. The key difference being that the modifications you make can be quickly evaluated relative to the rest of the design. Assume that there is not a master or controlling document or file that governs your design, such as a layout. When you are trying to manage your designs

Assembly Modifications in Assembly Mode

in an assembled state, you must (1) have an understanding of how the assembly was constructed, (2) know what, if any, dimensions or relationships will have an impact on other components, and above all, (3) develop each of the subassembly components to ensure flexibility. Each of these items will have a bearing on how easy the design will be to modify.

To understand how the assembly was developed, you must be able to visualize the sequence in which each component was assembled. Pro/ENGINEER allows you to regenerate the assembly one step at a time to see which component was placed in the assembly and when. This is similar to rewinding an audio tape and then playing it back again. Only in this case, you are playing back the order of assembly. To do this, access the REGEN INFO menu selection within the INFO menu. That menu should be similar to the following illustration.

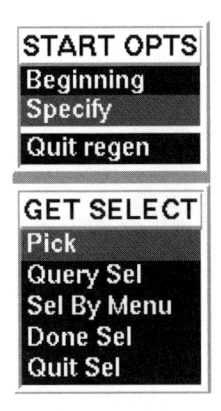

```
START OPTS
Beginning
Specify
Quit regen

GET SELECT
Pick
Query Sel
Sel By Menu
Done Sel
Quit Sel
```

START OPTS menu.

If you select *Beginning* from the menu, Pro/ENGINEER will go to the start of the assembly database (the beginning of the tape) and prepare to go through the assembly's development one step at a time (play back the tape). You do of course have some other options for stepping through the regeneration of the assembly, and I recommend that you look at the Pro/ENGINEER user guides for more detailed information. Basically, what you will see is how the operator developed the assembly. This is important, because you will be able to tell which components will be parents and which will be children. This is significant because if you were to make changes to or remove a component, you would have an idea of which components would

140   Chapter 7: Modifying Designs

be affected by the change and how. For example, the following assembly was developed by assembling the base first (setting up the Christmas tree), then completing the assembly by orienting the components relative to the base component (hanging the ornaments).

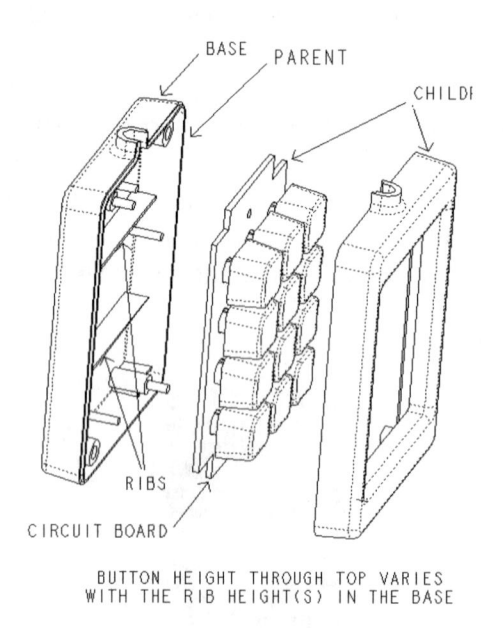

BUTTON HEIGHT THROUGH TOP VARIES
WITH THE RIB HEIGHT(S) IN THE BASE

Base with the components assembled to it.

The assembly shown previously is functional, and the subassembly components will regenerate relative to a change in the base's design. Using the same types of components, but changing the order of assembly, can create a real mess quickly. This is of course dependent on what the person's development intent is for the assembly and therefore the entire design. A restructured development would give you a design like that shown in the following illustration.

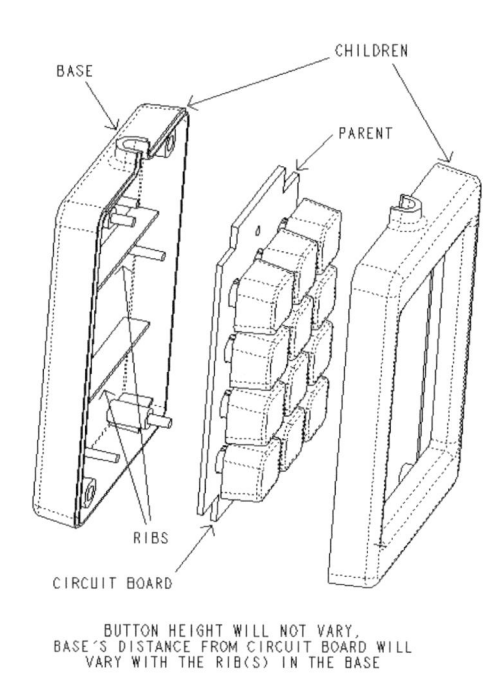

Assembly Modifications in Assembly Mode

Components assembled first, and then the base component.

This method of assembly produces the same visual results as the previous assembly. However, is this technique truly representative of the design intent? There are some people who would argue convincingly that there are cases where this is desirable. But if the design intent of the component is to have the subassembly components move relative to modifications in the base component, this approach may not be desirable. By modifying the base component in this assembly, you can see that the regeneration produces the drawing shown in the following illustration.

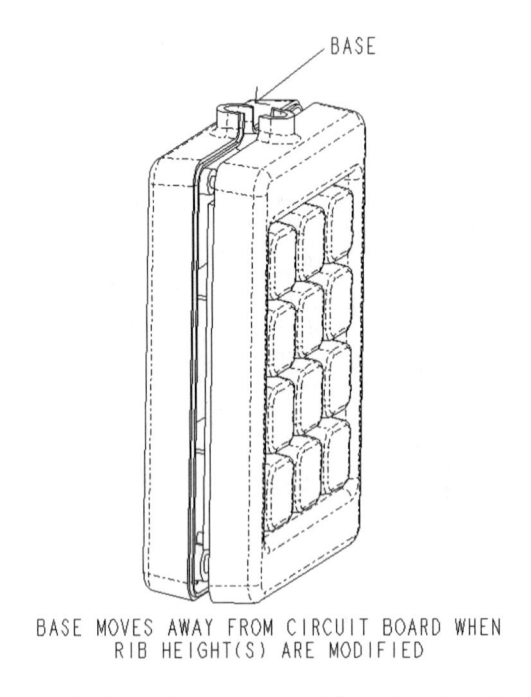

Chapter 7: Modifying Designs

BASE MOVES AWAY FROM CIRCUIT BOARD WHEN RIB HEIGHT(S) ARE MODIFIED

Modification to the base that was assembled after the subcomponents.

This obviously does not provide a functional relationship between the post-assembled base and the subassembly components. To correct this problem, you would have to modify the subassembly component to move it into position relative to the post-assembled base component. If the design was properly assembled by applying the Christmas tree approach, you would assemble the base component, the tree, and then add the subassembly components, the ornaments. Once this has been done, your designs will regenerate to capture the design intent of the component, the results of which are shown in the following illustration.

Assembly Modifications in Assembly Mode 143

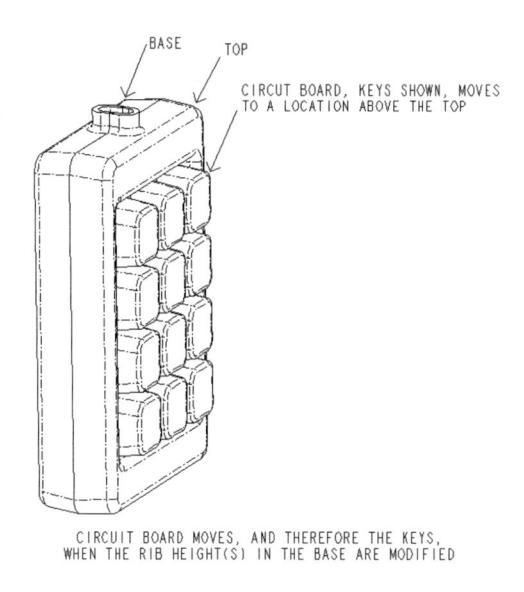

Properly developed assembly after modification.

The key difference is that the subassembly components have been developed such that their location and orientation are children of the base component and its features that are being referenced. The results of which will eliminate second guessing during minor modifications to the assembly. Just as having a properly developed part is important to ensure flexibility and the design intent, a properly developed assembly is just as important. Nothing hurts as much as having expensive prototype, or production intent, components come in for assembly, only to find a millimeter difference in alignment or location that prevents the assembly from going together. Understanding how the assembly was developed can mean the difference between a simple modification and wasting a day verifying your modifications.

There is of course more to assembly modifications than just understanding how the assembly's development is structured. You must have an understanding of how to modify components in both an assembled state and by each component independently, and predict what your modifications will do to the rest of the design.

Modifying components in an assembled state has a number of advantages. You will be able to not only see the results of your modifications to the component, but also what those modifications do to the rest of the assembly. By selecting *Modify* and then *Modify Dim* from the Assembly mode menus, you will be able to select any part's independent features in the assembly. For example, the following assembly will be modified to increase the size of the middle component.

Small assembly before modification.

Small assembly after modification.

Assembly Modifications in Assembly Mode

By simply querying the middle component, and then continuing to query for the feature of interest within that component, you can modify the dimensions necessary to produce the results shown in the previous illustration. Notice that after the assembly has regenerated, the part changed to the reflect the modification. Also notice that the top component maintained its relationship with the middle component. This indicates that the component above the middle component has been assembled such that it maintains this relationship.

If the top component was assembled using an offset to the base component, a modification to the middle component would not have affected the top component, unless of course a parametric relationship was developed in Assembly mode to correct for the interferences that would eventually occur. This is shown in the following illustration.

Small assembly with top component as offset to base component.

As you can see from the previous illustration, an interference would have resulted in a modification to the middle component.

Another way to modify the middle component would be to use the *Modify Part* command under the MODIFY menu selection.

Chapter 7: Modifying Designs

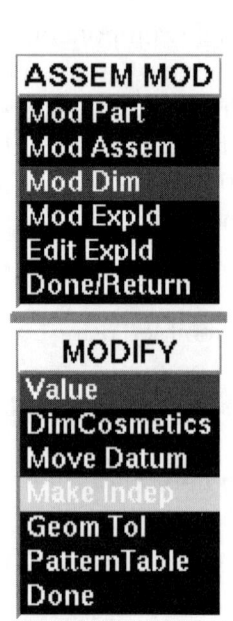

```
ASSEM MOD
Mod Part
Mod Assem
Mod Dim
Mod Expld
Edit Expld
Done/Return

MODIFY
Value
DimCosmetics
Move Datum
Make Indep
Geom Tol
PatternTable
Done
```

MODIFY menu Assembly mode.

Selecting the *Modify Part* menu selection and then selecting the part you wish to work on, presents you with a scaled-down version of the normal part development menu structure. Just as in the previous example, you can modify the part using the *Modify Dim* menu selection within the MODIFY PART menu. By selecting this menu pick, then querying the part for the feature of interest, you will obtain the same results as the previous example. But when should you use one method of modifying part dimensions over another?

To put it simply, you should use the *Modify→Modify Dim* selection combination to quickly change the dimension values of the components. Use the *Modify→Modify Part* combination for modifying the component of interest and for changing the dimensioning scheme, adding or deleting features, rerouting geometry, or any other commonly used part development functionality. This *Modify→Modify Part* combination can also be used to assist in the development of new components that must interface with other assembly components or stay within a packaged volume. For example, the previous assembly needs to have some core outs added to reduce the weight of the components.

Assembly Modifications in Assembly Mode 147

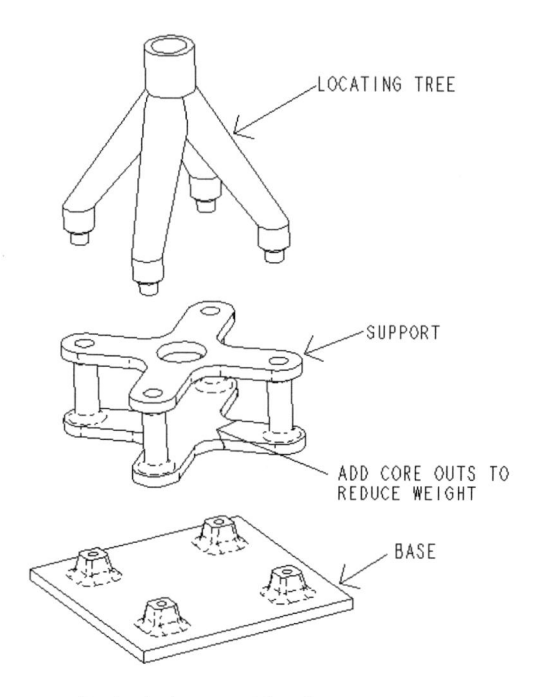

Exploded assembly of components.

For this simple example, how would you incorporate this component change? You could go right into Part mode and incorporate the change, but how would you be sure that you were accurately placing the core out? The alternative would be to incorporate the change on the fly in Assembly mode.

By using the *Modify→Modify Part* combination in Assembly mode you can modify the part while seeing how well you are placing the new part geometry relative to the mating component. The results of your efforts may look like the following illustration.

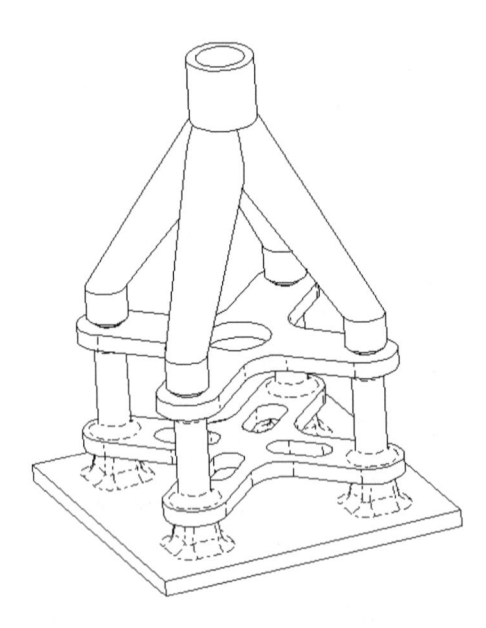

Results of added feature to subassembly component.

This is a simple example of developing part geometry in an assembled state. Many of you already know about this functionality within Pro/ENGINEER, and that's great. I hope that you are using it when applicable. If you have not seen this before, please take the time to attend a class or experiment with the overall functionality; it is worth your time and effort.

Simplifying Your View of the Design

Configuration States or Simplified Representation

One area of frustration for people who modify large components and assemblies is the amount of information that is presented for the modification. If you are only modifying a couple of components in an assembly, you should not have to have the whole assembly up and running on your workstation.

Simplifying Your View of the Design 149

Depending on the level of detail for each subassembly component and the number of components in the assembly, your work can be ground to a halt very quickly. Pro/ENGINEER comes with some functionality that reduces the amount of time required to load and process large amounts of information. The *configuration state* or *simplified representation* enables you to load, visualize, and manipulate only those components of interest.

The implementation of configuration states or simplified representations into Pro/ENGINEER gives users the ability to conserve precious memory, swap drive usage, and regeneration time by accessing only the components or assemblies of interest for a design modification. The beauty of this functionality lies in the user's ability to work with a number of specific components in their assembled state. This means that you will be able to analyze component modifications or new component development, without having to look through other nonfunctional parts and assemblies, which may cloud your view of the important components.

For example, the following assembly may need to have a connecting rod modified to incorporate some locating features to assist the connecting rod's alignment.

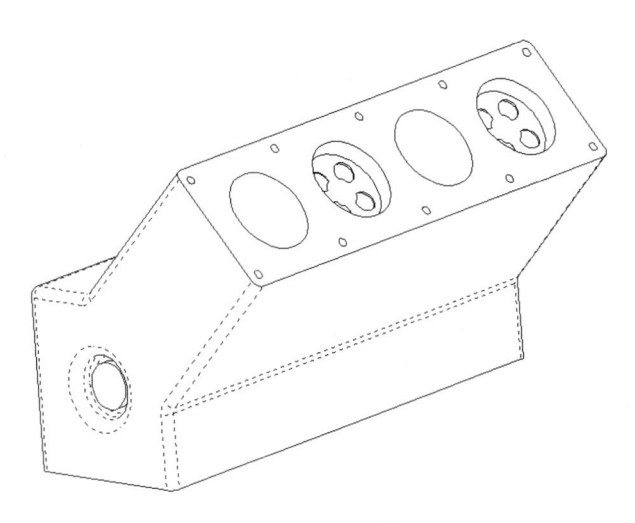

Master assembly.

A configuration state or simplified representation of the assembly shown above that includes only the parts that affect the cover's modification is shown in the following illustration.

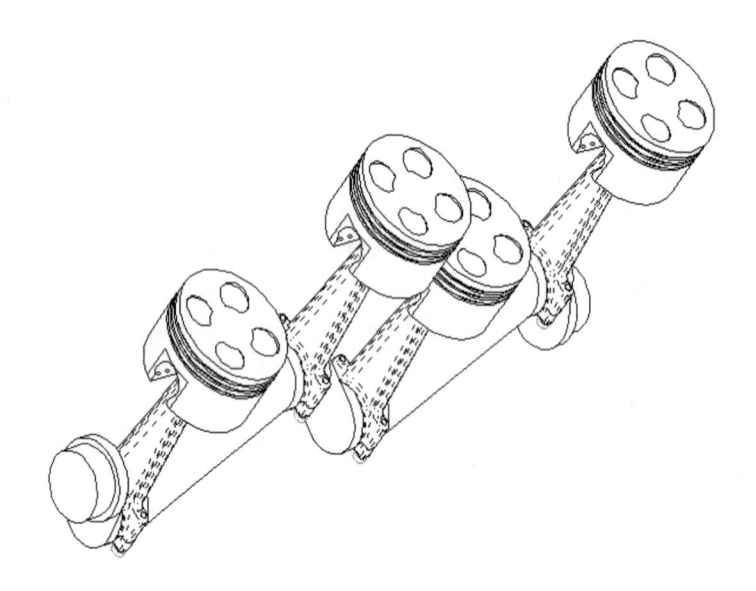

Configuration state (simplified representation) of master assembly.

Now that this configuration state or simplified representation has been established, you can quickly develop the geometry needed to complete the required change by using the *Modify→Modify Part* combination. This functionality is important because it gives you the opportunity to work on only those interfaces that are important. Once the change has been made to the component, you can either keep the configuration state (simplified representation) that you have developed or delete it. Because you may want to work on this interface again, it is a good idea to keep the state with the assembly for future reference.

Using Layers

Using layers is another technique for managing or reducing the amount of clutter that you can be presented with when modifying components in an assembly. This technique was the lifeboat before the implementation of configuration states or simplified representations, because it placed components on layers. Using layers for managing the amount of information presented on the screen was, and still is, effective. The big drawback is that you can't load only those components that are of interest. When you are using layers to manage the viewing of components in an assembly, you are in essence loading the entire assembly into memory, then *blanking* the components that you don't want to see.

Some of you may be thinking, why don't you just suppress the components that you don't want to see? Suppression of components is a viable option for specific cases where there is a minimal number of components that are children of the suppressed component. The use of a layer enables you to control the visibility of one or many components at the same time. This functionality is also available when you are using configuration states or simplifications.

Component Simplification

Another technique for improving design modification in Assembly mode is to simplify components that are being used for reference only. This comes in handy when you are adding a new section to an existing component that must clear a complex component near by. Because you do not want to wait too long for that complex component to regenerate each time you move the geometry, you have the option of simplifying the subassembly component.

Simplifying component geometry enables you to temporarily remove nonessential geometry from a component or subassembly within the assembly you are working on. The result will be decreased regeneration time, while still giving you the opportunity to incorporate changes to unrelated components. Basically, simplifying a component or subassembly gives you a representation of the volume that the component or subassembly occupies.

The following illustrations show how simplification affects components.

152   Chapter 7: Modifying Designs

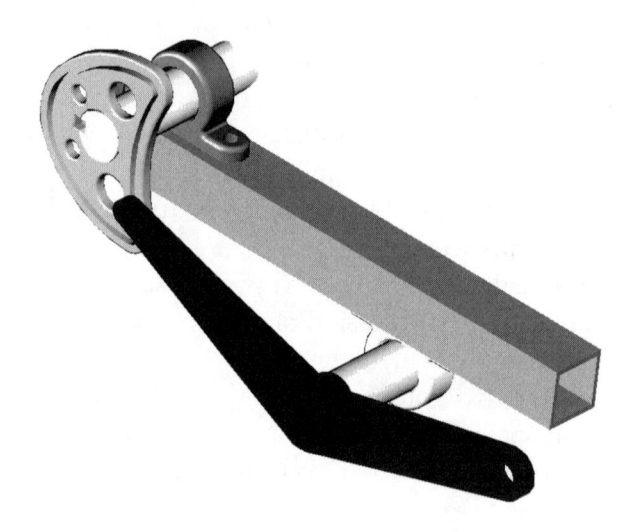

Components before simplification.

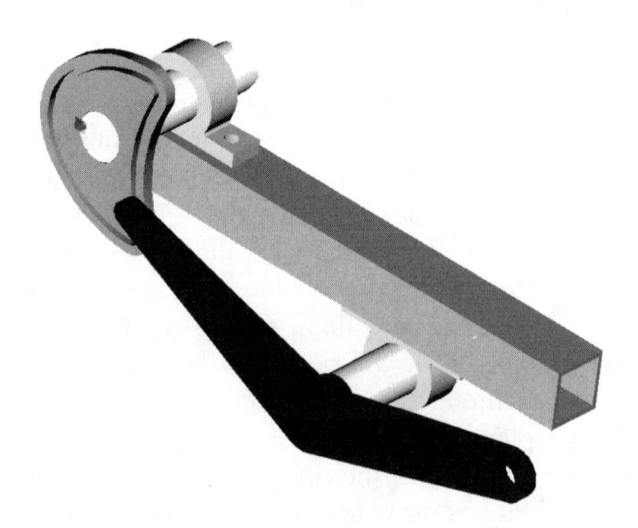

Components after simplification.

You have the ability to store a simplified version of the component of subassembly in the component's or assembly's file for future use and packaging studies. For an in-depth discussion on simplification, please refer to the Pro/ENGINEER users' guides.

Modifying Designs from the Drawing

Reverse associativity between the drawing and the design is a major feather in Pro/ENGINEER's cap. There are not many other CAD/CAM systems that perform this as well as Pro/ENGINEER or with less effort. But just like everything else in Pro/ENGINEER, you must be set up properly to make changes from the drawing and have the design update. Detailing in Pro/ENGINEER is discussed in more depth in Chapter 8, but for this discussion, I will stay with the basic requirements to modify designs.

If your design has been developed such that it satisfies all of the dimensioning scheme and inspection requirements, your drawing should have been developed using parametric dimensions. These are the same dimensions that were defined in Part mode and govern the features of the design. Modifying the design from the drawing can introduce an element of risk to your overall design. One of the limiting factors in modifying the design from the drawing is that you don't have a full understanding of associated geometry that may be affected by your dimensional modifications. Even the most detailed components and assemblies on a drawing will not give you a tangible understanding of the changes that you are making. To truly understand the effects of your modifications, nothing is easier to look at and understand than the three-dimensional model.

Driving part and assembly changes from the drawing is very powerful functionality, but this method of design modification should be used for altering minor dimensional modifications or tweaking the tolerances and locations of features. Changing the design by changing the dimensions on the drawing will undoubtedly save lots of time searching the part or assembly for the dimensions that you need to change. When it comes to major modifications in the design, however, it may be in your best interest to make sure the modifications are done properly, in Part or Assembly mode, so that you can witness the effects of your actions.

Part Modifications

Just as there is more than one way to skin a cat, there is more than one way to change part geometry. This book will not teach you every single aspect of part modification; an overview of that topic alone could take a whole book. But after looking around at how components are developed and modified in Pro/ENGINEER, I learned that a lot of people are just not using the tool properly. Some beginning users remodel the part to incorporate their changes, rather than working with the current design. You may have seen this before, and it can really hit home when someone remodels your work to add a change. Weeks of work can get cut up and destroyed over a two-week remodeling session.

Another problem with part modification is how people sculpt in part geometry to quickly get out of a design problem. To the casual observer, they are working miracles with Pro/ENGINEER, but to the people who must use their geometry at a later date, they are a pain in the butt. Modifying parts in Pro/ENGINEER does not have to be an uphill battle for the users. By simply applying the tools within Pro/ENGINEER, you can learn all you need to know about the part's development and formulate an approach to design modification that incorporates the required changes.

Finding the Design Options

To make changes to existing or developmental databases, especially if they were created by someone else, it is important to learn as much as possible about the database's development and what parent/child relationships exist. For small parts and assemblies, this is not a large task, and you can get up to speed on how the database was developed by looking at how it was generated. To do this, Pro/ENGINEER comes with a handy tool called *Regen Info*. This command is located within the INFO menu, and when executed you are presented with the START OPTS menu, which is shown in the following illustration.

START OPTS
- Beginning
- Specify
- Quit regen

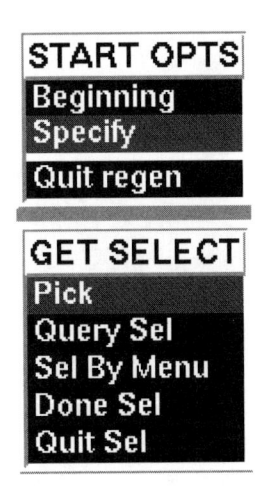

GET SELECT
- Pick
- Query Sel
- Sel By Menu
- Done Sel
- Quit Sel

START OPTS menu options.

As with the assemblies, think of this functionality as a tape player that you can use to rewind and play back your favorite features in Pro/ENGINEER. If you need to jump to a point in the database, like the third feature, which may be DTM3, you can play back all of the features that were developed in the order that they were developed from that feature on. When repetitive tasks occur during the playback of the database's development, such as a large pattern of holes, you have the option to skip ahead, or fast forward, to continue the review of the database's development. This is most helpful for locating features, such as shells, in which you may wish to insert some features and then redefine some later features to accomplish your design goal.

For example, the following design is a plastic component that will require the top of a plastic cover to be recessed to insert a plastic window for an LCD display.

156   Chapter 7: Modifying Designs

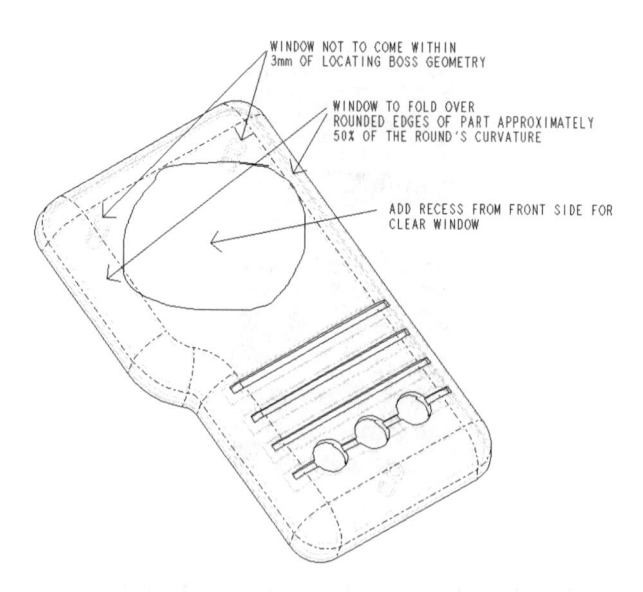

Required design change.

During the investigation, a shell was placed at a point in the database that could be redefined to capture the design change.

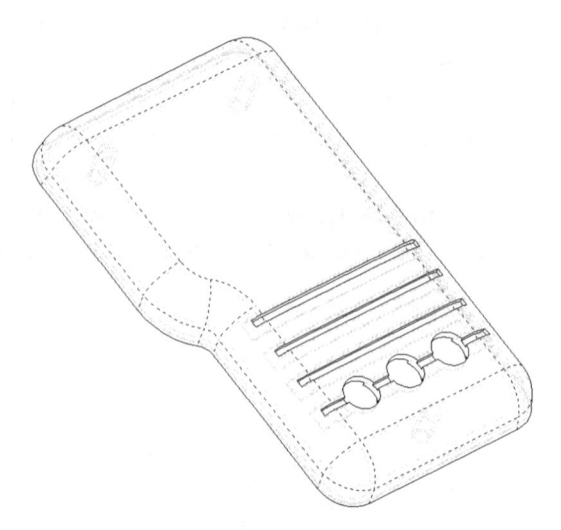

Original design.

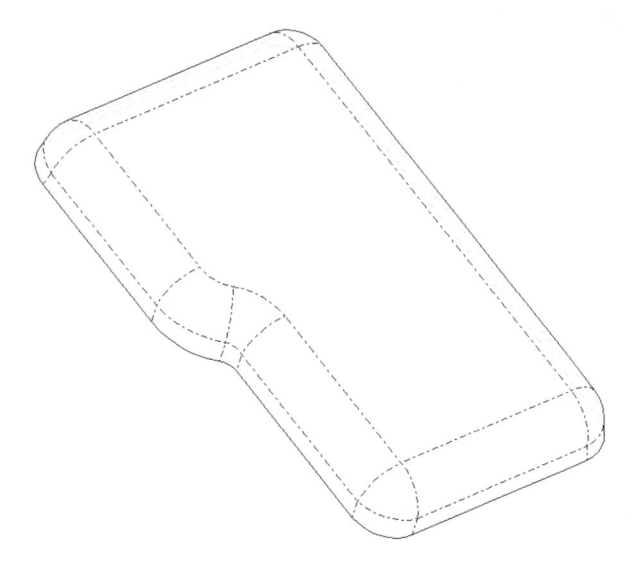

Regen Info. Position in database that could be used to define cut out.

Noting the feature number for the shell, you complete the *Regen Info* by quitting the review. Now that you know the location of the feature in which you will be incorporating your design changes, you can develop your geometry, and then redefine the shell to act on the new geometry. There are alternatives to the *Regen Info* command sequence for learning about the database that you will be modifying. Please review the *Pro/ENGINEER User's Guide* for additional information.

Learning by Trail Files

If you have the trail file that was generated when this component was developed, you could reexecute the trail file and watch, command for command, menu pick for menu pick, how the part or assembly was developed. This is a good way to understand how the geometry was developed, but rerunning the trail file generates the same part over again, and you are not able to just quit the process and go right to the final design. Once you start the trail file, you must wait for the trail file to finish developing all of the geometry before you can incorporate new geometry.

Just Query the Features

An alternative to learning about the database that you are working with is to simple query feature after feature while keeping a mental note of where things are in the database's development sequence. This can be a long process and is fine for small parts where there is not a lot to keep track of. However, when it comes to working with larger assemblies, I recommend that you visualize how each feature was generated and in what order, using *Regen Info*. This gives you a better understanding of the development process and what other geometry was already developed at that stage in the development. Just querying features cannot give you a complete understanding of the relationships.

Parent/Child Relationships

Before you make changes to geometry, you must also have an understanding of any parent/child relationships that have been developed. This is important, because you may want to delete a boss or hole in the part, only to find that half of the database is a child of that feature. These situations can be very frustrating and will contribute to hair loss problems; I have lost a few square inches myself just on parent/child relationships. Pro/ENGINEER comes with another tool to analyze the parent/child relationships within a component. This functionality is located within the INFO menu and enables you to either highlight or write to a file the parents or children of features within the design.

Take the time to review the design, either to refamiliarize yourself with your own work or to develop an understanding of someone else's, so you can formulate a plan of attack for modifying the part.

Making the Changes

The method of incorporating changes to existing designs is just as important as how the design was developed. If the existing design has followed the corporate standards, you should not have any problem understanding the development, and therefore how it should be modified. The real problems occur when changes are made to the design just to get the job done. Just making changes to get a job off of your desk can create major problems for others in the future. Avoid this practice at all costs. I am sure that if you take the time to learn as much as possible about how the design was developed, you will be able to successfully incorporate your required modifications.

Reordering Your Geometry

Pro/ENGINEER gives you a number of options for adding new geometry to a design. One of the most obvious and widely used techniques for adding geometry to an existing design is to develop the geometry and then reorder it to an earlier location in the part. This is effective for changing the part, and on simple parts this is a fast method of making geometry changes and additions. However, when you are working with larger or more complex parts, adding features to the tail end of the database and then reordering them to earlier locations in development, can cause major problems.

When working on larger or complex parts, this technique resembles a blind cannon operator. The operator may not know where the features will land in the structure of the part, but he or she is firing the features from their current location to some arbitrary feature number earlier in the database. This can cause some major headaches during the regeneration and can be a time vacuum for the inexperienced user. By simply reordering your features in the database, you can quickly disrupt the logical development of the design and create unwanted parent/child relationships. This technique for modifying components can be fast and effective. You just have to make sure that you understand where the features are and where they are going.

Insert Mode

The Insert mode within Part mode is one of the most direct and effective means of incorporating new geometry to an existing or developmental design. During the research for this book, I found a number of users, some with several years of tube time using Pro/ENGINEER, who have not yet used this functionality. In a nutshell, this functionality enables you to actively develop new geometry at virtually any point in the design. This is not an easy subject to visualize, but think of it like this. Assume that each feature within the part is a single domino, and because your features are sequentially developed, each domino is stacked on another. Therefore, your part is a stack of dominos.

Chapter 7: Modifying Designs

Using the LCD display modification from an earlier example, your stack of dominos may look like the following illustration.

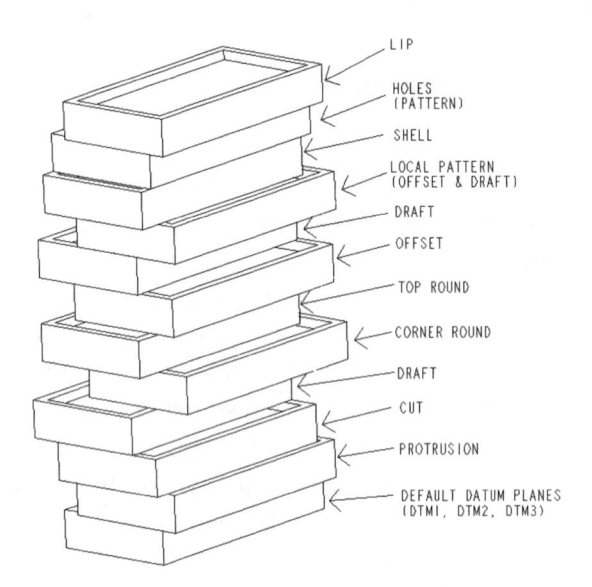

The part represented as a stack of dominos.

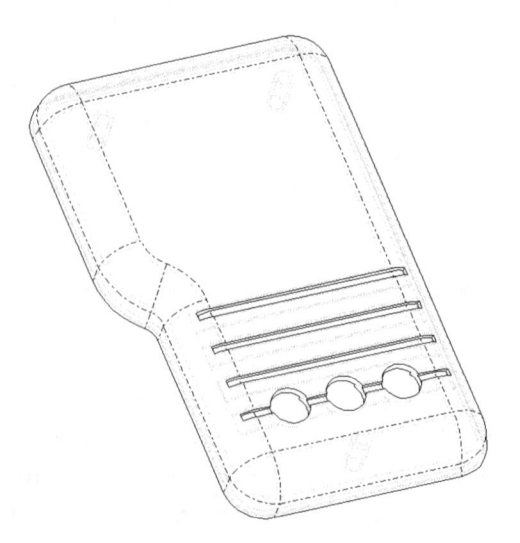

The part before modification.

Part Modifications 161

To incorporate a window into the current design, you will be adding a cut into the top of the housing, and then adding some draft to the walls of the cut for relief. To do this you could just add the cut at the tail end of the database, but you would not be able to easily add the draft. Once that was completed, you would have to reorder the geometry to an earlier stage in the design.

To properly add this new geometry into the design, you can activate the Insert mode, select the feature that you want to insert geometry after, add the geometry, cancel the Insert mode, and complete any other required modifications. Insert mode enables you to go to a point in the database and insert features. This would be like taking the top five dominos off of the stack, adding in three or four, then placing the dominos back on top of the new dominos. This addition of dominos to the stack of dominos for the LCD display modification is shown in the following illustration.

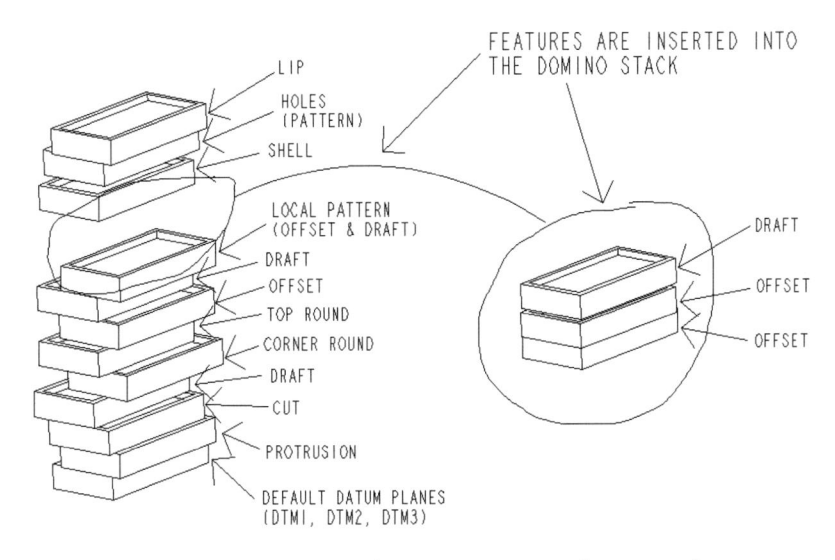

Domino structure with new geometry to be inserted.

The actual part before, during, and after entering Insert mode is shown in the following illustrations.

162   Chapter 7: Modifying Designs

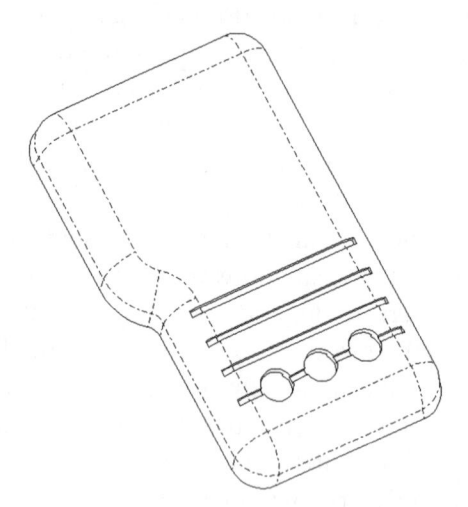

Part before inserting geometry.

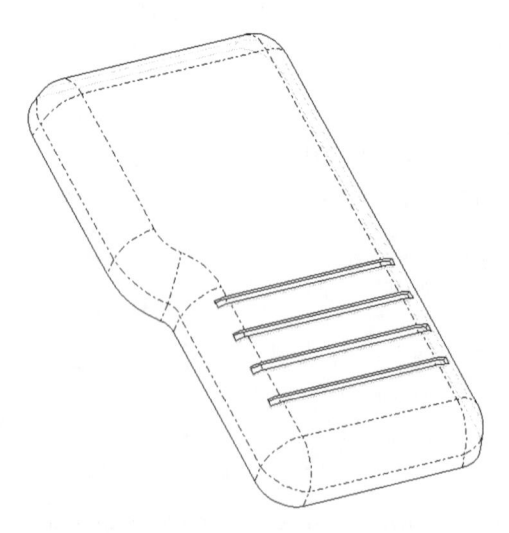

Part during Insert mode.

Part Modifications   **163**

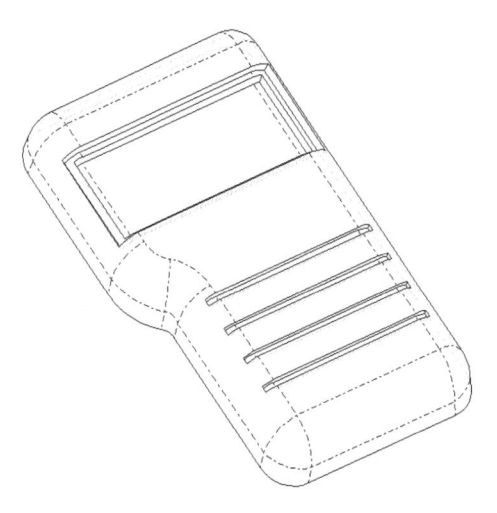

Part during Insert mode with new geometry.

After canceling the Insert mode and letting the rest of the part regenerate, you would have successfully inserted new geometry into the part, the results of which are shown in the following illustration.

Part after canceling Insert mode with new geometry.

Of course, the design may require some additional modifications, such as the addition of a cut for the window geometry or redefining the shell to make the newly developed wall geometry thinner or break out a surface. The final results are that you are able to add new geometry to the part without sculpting the required change for the design. You may be surprised at the number of people who would have added a block of geometry, a few cuts, and some draft to the tail end of the database, just to incorporate the change. Even though this latter approach can visually produce the same results as the part modified using Insert mode, you would probably spend more time and effort in sculpting the changes than in using the Insert mode.

Suppressing and Resuming Features and Simplified Representation in Parts

Suppressing features or using simplified representation of a part can be a quick way to improve the speed of your development and modifications in Pro/ENGINEER. This can be especially useful for working on large parts that have a lot of detail. You may want to use this functionality when you are working in an area of the design that will not need to reference other detail geometry in the design. For example, you may not need to have large hole patterns or all of the rounds for a portion of the design visible for your new geometry development. Because you don't want to wait for the computer to process that geometry that has little effect on your feature of interest, you can suppress those features to gain some regeneration speed for the part.

This can save a lot of time, especially if your system is underpowered, that is, doesn't have enough memory, swap space, processor speed, etc. I have seen some cases in which the computer spends 35 to 50 minutes processing a change in the design of a large and complex part. Of that time, approximately 85% of it is spent recalculating what geometry was hidden and what was not. Talk about a time vacuum. By simply suppressing those features, which will not be affected by your design modifications, you will be able to add to your database without having to wait for long regenerations.

This technique basically takes your stack of dominos, temporarily removes the dominos that you do not want to see, and adds to the total number of dominos. This would look like the following.

Part Modifications 165

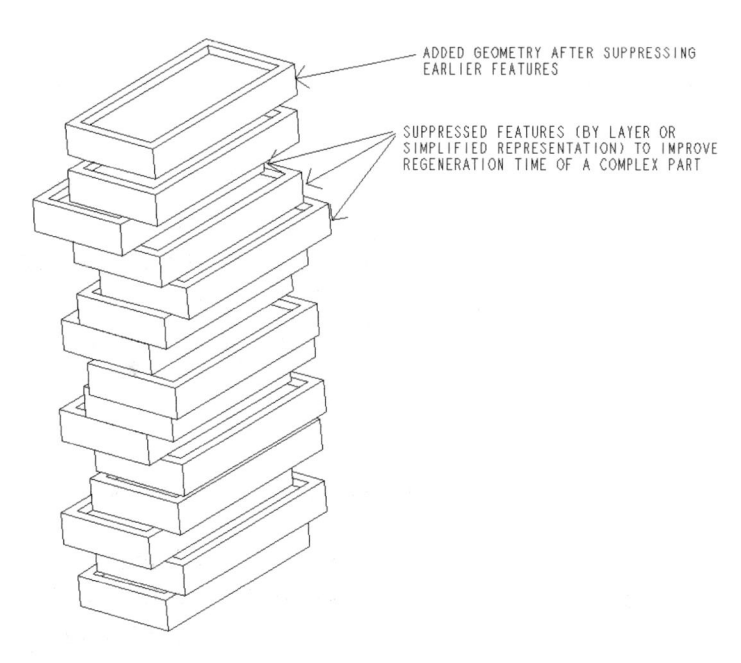

Suppressed dominos with added dominos.

Once you have completed your development, you can simply resume all of the geometry that you have suppressed for the new development or modifications.

✪ **TIP:** *If you will be working on a portion of a large design that will more than likely change a number of times, you may find it to your advantage to place the nonessential or nonimpacting geometry on a layer. By placing this geometry on a layer, you are unofficially grouping all of those features together. Once this has been done, you can then suppress by layer rather than querying through the entire database for all of the features that you do not want to wait for during regeneration, or you could simply maintain several simplified representations of your design.*

✎ **NOTE:** *Whether you opt to layer features and suppress them by that layer or use simplified representations, you must make sure that the method you select fits the needs of those who will be working with your data. For example, analysis may require layer suppression over simplified representations for additional flexibility in mesh generation.*

Rerouting Geometry

Another powerful tool for modifying designs is the reroute feature. This functionality is very powerful and can be your lifeboat when it comes to breaking unwanted parent/child relationships. This is accomplished by simply redefining the references that were used for the feature's original development, that is, the sketch plane, and the placement and dimensional references that govern that feature.

Suppose that you are required to relocate some boss geometry from the lower level to a higher elevation within the part. Your initial and final parts might look like that shown in the following illustrations.

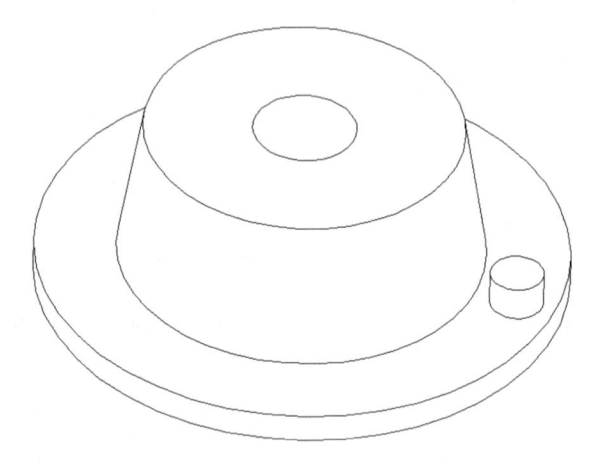

Original part design.

Part Modifications 167

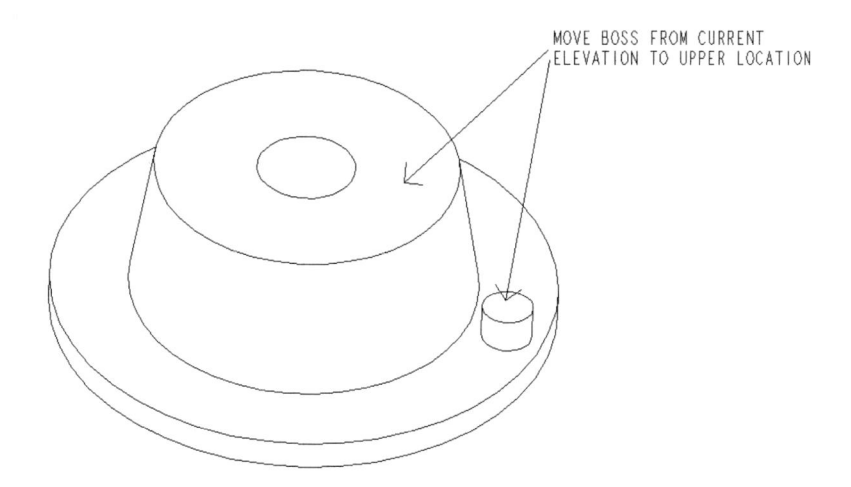

MOVE BOSS FROM CURRENT ELEVATION TO UPPER LOCATION

Final design intent.

Looking at the part shown above, you may just throw in the towel, delete the boss geometry, and add some new features to complete the design change. This is of course a solution to this problem, but is it optimum? Probably not. You would end up introducing the possibility of an error in redeveloping the geometry in the new location. This ultimately could cause some big problems if it is not caught.

The alternative would be to use the reroute functionality within Pro/ENGINEER to quickly translate the geometry from the lower to the upper location. Using the *Reroute* command, the geometry shown previously can be relocated to the new elevation and location using the "elevator" technique. This information can be found in the user's manual, but for the purpose of demonstration, this is what it can do. For this example, you can develop an offset datum plane using the feature's reference plane as the offset reference. By entering an offset distance of 0 you will have a coplanar reference for the feature. The results of this may look like that shown in the following illustration.

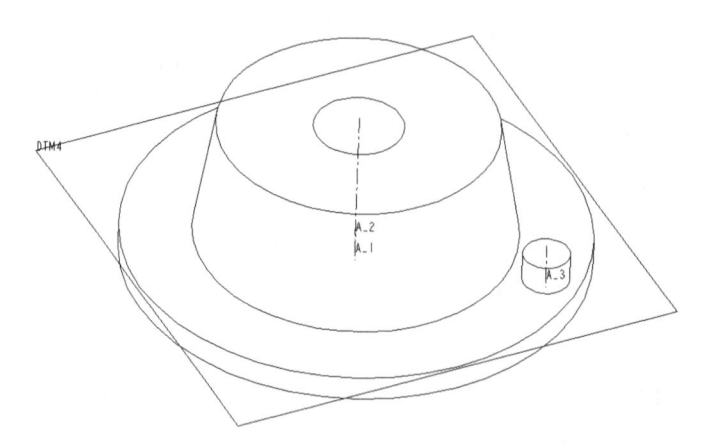

Part with newly created offset datum plane.

Now that the new plane has been created, you can perform a simple reroute from the current base plane to the newly developed zero distance offset plane. Once this has been successfully accomplished, the user can modify the offset distance, and the rerouted feature will follow the new dimensional reference. The results of this are shown in the following illustration.

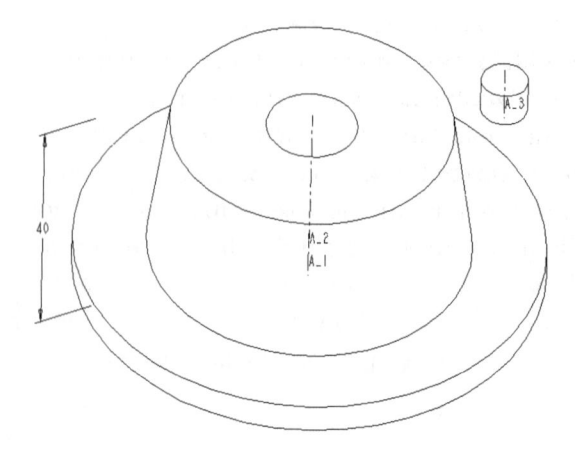

Arbitrary modification of the offset distance.

By simply modifying the offset distance to equal the same distance as the new elevation, you will be able to reroute the geometry once again to the new elevation reference. Once this has been completed, all you have to do is delete the offset datum plane; it no longer has purpose in the design. Your final part may look like the following figure.

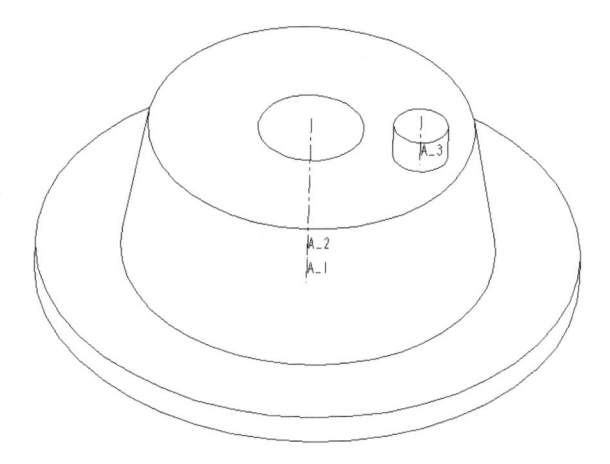

Final design after feature has been rerouted.

Redefining the Dimensioning Scheme

Some of the most common modifications to a design revolve around the dimensioning scheme. But does a change in the dimensional layout mean that you have to spend all of your time rerouting and redeveloping geometry to obtain the required change? Absolutely not.

Pro/ENGINEER can redefine the dimensioning scheme within the feature's sketch, without worrying about accidentally deleting carefully developed geometry. These modifications can be made within the REDEFINE menu, shown in the following illustration.

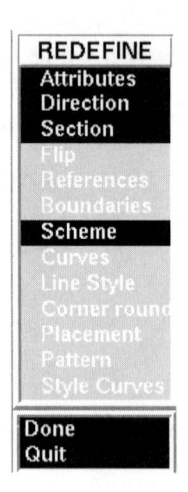

The REDEFINE menu.

By selecting *Scheme* from the menu, you are presented with a limited version of the Sketcher menu structure; some of the menu selections will be grayed out. You can delete and create new dimensions to describe the feature being developed by the Sketcher. This can save a lot of time and does not require you to bend over backward to complete a design modification.

Summary

Please understand that there are a lot of ways to modify geometry, more ways than can be covered in a single chapter. The topics discussed were selected because of the number of instances where people have chosen to fight the software, even when the design modification was just a menu pick away.

Most of the problems that people have with modifying geometry in Pro/ENGINEER come from a poor understanding of the design intent and for whom the design was developed, both of which are important and can mean the difference between an easy part change and major problem for you and the next person who comes into contact with the database. There are a number of ways to learn about how a design was developed, and there are also several ways to modify existing geometry to assist or improve the design change process.

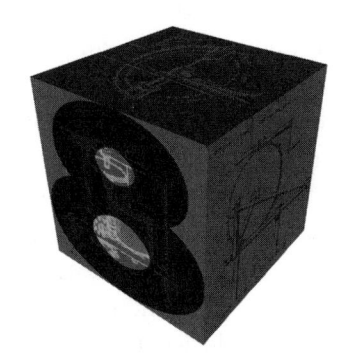

Detailing

Introduction

As usual, you have been given something that needs to be completed by the end of the day, and all of your other projects have been suspended until a few design and drawing changes have been made. Your department head says, "The changes shouldn't take long; all you should have to do is change a couple of dimensions." Because you are always willing to take on new challenges and help your company out of design problems, you sit down at your desk, fasten your seat belt, and get ready to rock and roll on some design changes. But, as you load the drawing into Pro/ENGINEER, you notice that a lot of sketched geometry has appeared on the drawing before the model and dimensions have even regenerated. As you recall, the dimensions are usually the last items to regenerate, so you are suspicious of the integrity of the drawing. Finally, the drawing is fully regenerated and you zoom to the first area that needs to be modified.

Your first change is to adjust the height of some bosses. Because a dimension exists for the feature of interest, you select *modify*, pick the dimension, the dimension highlights (acknowledging that you selected it), and does nothing— no prompt! Knowing that when you perform this command sequence, you should get a prompt for the new dimension value, you find that dimension is a *driven* dimension. Upon further inspection of the drawing, you find that all of the dimensions on the print were independently developed by the previous user. In addition, all of the GD&T that has been applied was manually developed using notes, and the part has no set datums (which are required to properly develop GD&T). After spending over a day working on modifying the database to reflect the design change, you get down to work on completing the title and revision blocks for the design. As you modify the title block information, you discover that each and every item has been independently developed using notes.

It took about five times as long as it should have to complete the design changes, but the drawing and model are now complete. You have come to the conclusion that the model was basically "sculpted" by the previous user, and that the dimensioning scheme for the model's development was not representative of the dimensioning scheme on the released drawing. By your best estimates, you could have completely remodeled the component and finished the design in less time than was required to make the changes.

Curious as to why this drawing was developed in this fashion, you ask the person who generated the drawing why it was developed this way. His responses vary from "The checker made adjustments to the dimensioning scheme" to "Well, that's how I have always done it." Further investigation of the situation reveals a person who has not used Pro/ENGINEER for very long and has been obtaining help from other new users on detailing.

Plagued with the reputation for being difficult to use and inflexible, the detailing module has likely received the most criticism among new users of Pro/ENGINEER. Pro/DETAIL is definitely one module where having *no* detailing experience on other CAD systems can be an *advantage*. Most of the problems that people have can be summed up by how people use Pro/ENGINEER in general. Most new users of Pro/ENGINEER have had some experience with other static CAD/CAM systems in which the approaches to modeling are free form and the final design could have been developed any number of ways. For these static systems, the detailing was also free form; all of the dimensions were independently placed on the drawing and generally had no geometry-driving capabilities. With these systems, the development of datum references, dimension types and locations, as well as the feature control frames are generally developed as a postmodeling function, which left the door wide open for changes in the design intent of the components.

As you are aware, the method of model development is important in Pro/ENGINEER. All of the developmental work, that is, generating quality inputs, was done for a reason—to capture the design intent of the design. If you have developed your database correctly, detailing the design should be almost effortless, at least in the sense that you will not have to manually develop the model's dimensions and tolerances on the drawing. For example, the following illustration is a design that has been developed by a Pro/ENGINEER "sculptor."

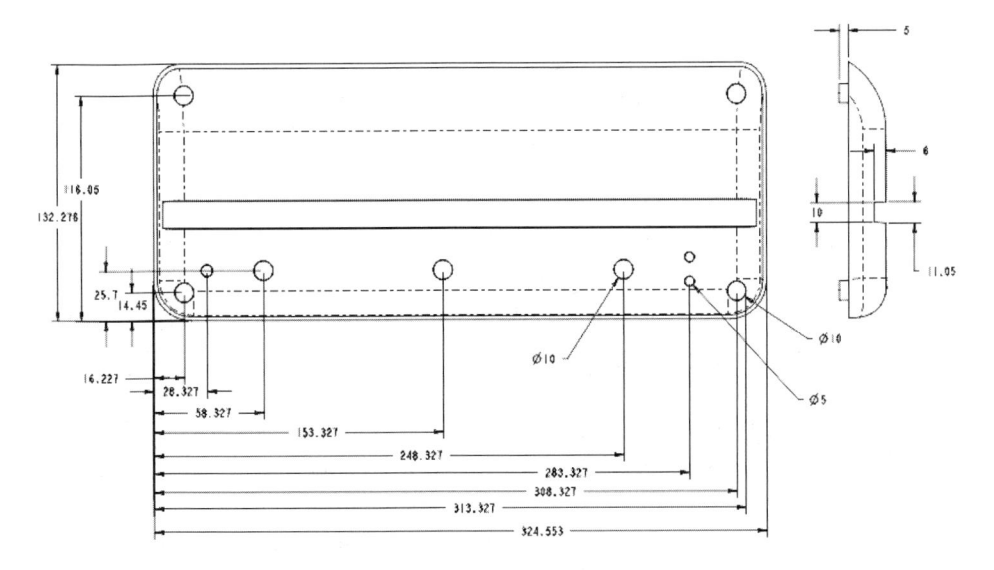

Nonparametric design.

This design cannot be properly detailed because of the improper dimensional call outs. After the detailing of this component was completed, using user-developed (or added) dimensions, the drawing may look like the following illustration.

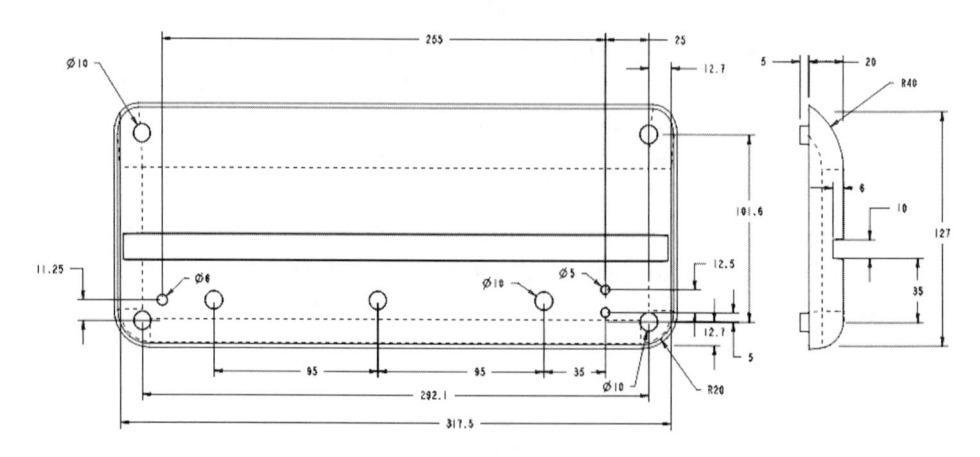

Nonparametric design detail using added dimensions.

The previous illustration does capture the design intent, but the drawing is not parametrically linked to the model. The results of this are obvious; whoever goes to modify this design will have to track down the correct driving dimensions in the model to make adjustments to the design. This situation can become even more complicated when geometry has been developed that has a "stack-up" effect, where unrelated but critical geometry affects your functional geometry when modified.

These are just some of the reasons why a design must be flexible, accurate, and capture the design intent. Most of the problems that people have with detailing in Pro/ENGINEER stem from a deficiency in the development of the design, and the end results can be not only painful but time consuming.

Before You Detail

Make sure that the design has been properly developed and is flexible. It does not hurt to analyze all of the communications and paperwork that you have generated during your review and development sessions. By taking a few moments to make sure that the design is truly ready to be detailed, you may save rework time in the future. It is also a good idea to review the model's development, using Regen Info. This is to ensure that you fully understand where features are located in the database's development and what types of features were used for development. Using Regen Info can be especially helpful if you are going to detail someone else's design. Nothing can be more frustrating than looking for a feature that contains some information you need to include on the drawing and not finding it.

Apply Tolerances to the Right Features

To save time, make sure that any linear and geometric tolerances that will be included on the drawing are properly developed in the model. I know what you're thinking, "The model?! Detailing should be done on the drawing, not the model!" Believe it or not, you can quickly accomplish most of your detailing requirements while you are working in the model. Think of having to place several geometric tolerance feature control frames on your design while you are detailing the part. This can be done fairly easily, and if you have your datum references established and your views set up, you can quickly apply the geometric tolerances to the exact edges, surfaces, and features that require the tolerances. Applying these control frames to the model geometry enables you to interact more efficiently with the database, therefore ensuring the design intent is truly captured dimensionally.

The following illustration highlights a model that requires some geometric tolerances to be applied on the surfaces indicated.

176   Chapter 8: Detailing

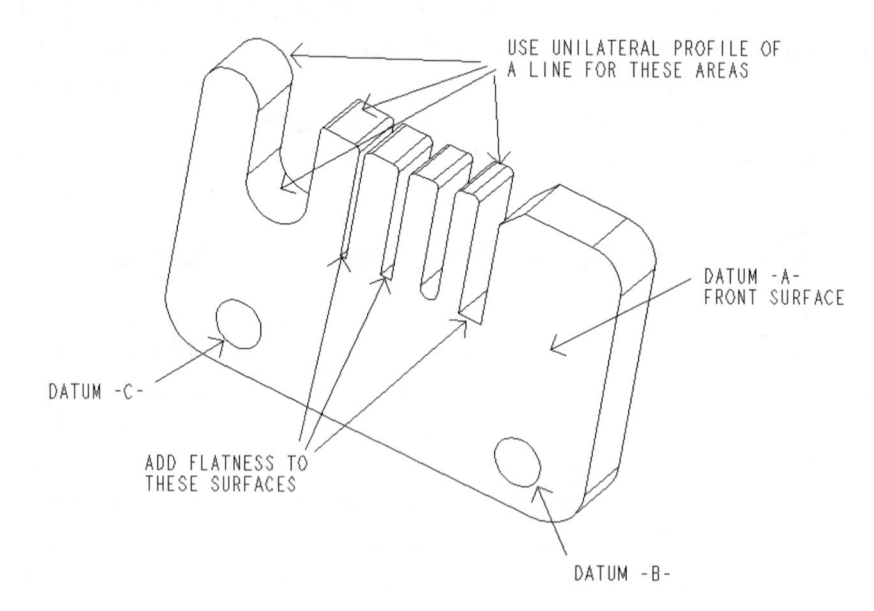

Markup highlighting where flatness and profile tolerances should be applied.

For a moment, assume that you chose to apply the tolerances to the part while in a Drawing mode. An end view of the model is shown in the following illustration.

Before You Detail 177

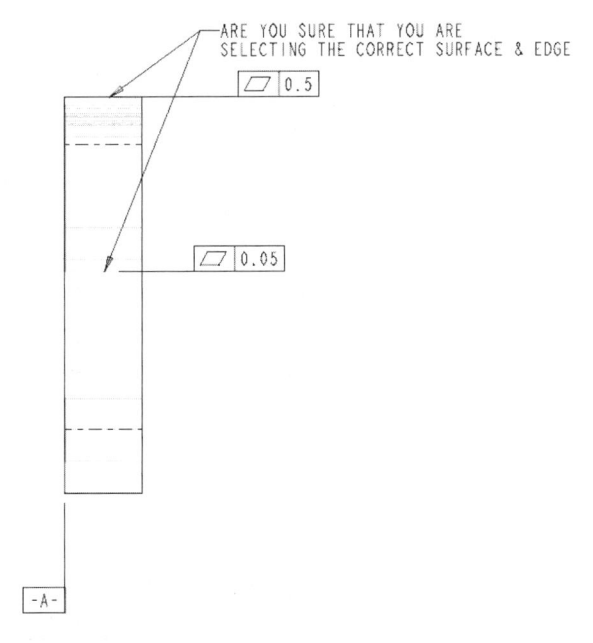

End view of model to apply feature control frames.

Because the datums for the part have been properly set in the Part mode, which permits you to apply and reference geometric tolerances, you have the opportunity to apply a flatness tolerance to the required surfaces. However, if you are going to apply the geometric tolerance to the part and ensure that the tolerance is being applied to the proper surface geometry, you may have difficulty in properly locating and affixing the feature control frame. Based on the previous illustration, you may have difficulty in querying the proper feature to attach the tolerance. In some cases, the feature to which you are trying to apply the tolerance may not be visible on the drawing, which may require you to develop an additional, temporary view in order to apply the tolerance properly. Once the tolerance has been applied to the temporary view, you can simply switch the control frame from the temporary view to the view of interest.

You are probably thinking to yourself, "Who cares whether or not you apply the feature control frame to the correct edge or not? As long as it is on the drawing, the job is done." However, your application of geometric feature control frames, and even surface finish symbols, follows the same rules you

Chapter 8: Detailing

follow when developing geometry. Remember the Christmas tree approach to modeling in Pro/ENGINEER; the same principles apply to the application of feature control frames in both Drawing and Part modes. When you apply a feature control frame to an edge, cut, protrusion, or any feature in general, that control frame is then a child of that feature. Why is this important? If you, or any other user of Pro/ENGINEER, try to make changes to the model, for example, the addition or deletion of features, your feature control frames will be children of the features. The risk is that if you improperly assign a feature control frame to a feature that later gets deleted, that feature control frame will also be deleted. In the end you may accidentally delete an important piece of information from the drawing, all by just making a wrong selection when you applied the control frame.

If you had applied the feature control frame for the previously presented design in Part mode, you would have been able to quickly locate and properly apply the geometric feature control frame to the feature that required it. In the long run, you will be ensuring the integrity of the database and ultimately the drawing. The following illustration highlights the previous tolerance applied to the model in Part mode instead of on the drawing.

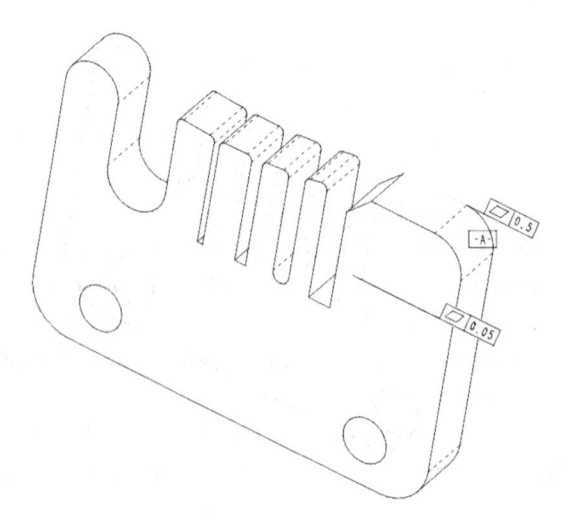

Geometric tolerances applied in Part mode.

Also, for those companies who use Pro/ENGINEER from the design and development through manufacturing and inspection, people who work with your databases later in the development process will be able to look directly at the database for a specific feature's linear and geometric tolerances. This of course does not eliminate the need for a print, but looking at a specific feature or group of features on a large drawing can sometimes be faster than scanning a mountain of documentation. Hence, you will be able to ensure that the design intent is communicated both electronically and physically with a drawing.

Develop Parametric Notes

A common and useful method of reducing the clutter on a drawing while improving the communication of the design is the use of grouping features into notes on the drawing. One of the most common applications is a radial pattern of tapped holes. The amount of information that could be included on the print is shown in the following illustration.

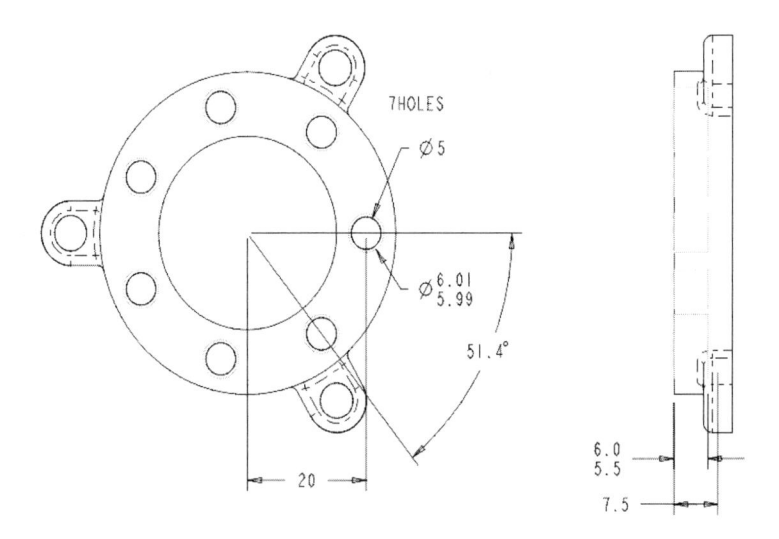

Radial pattern of holes; raw feature data.

Just as applying geometric tolerances can be easier when you are able to interact with the design in Part or Assembly mode, consolidating feature information into parametric notes can be just as effective. The previous illustration is a fairly simple part or group of features, and you may be thinking

Chapter 8: Detailing

that you could consolidate all of this information while working on the drawing. In fact, this may be the case, but to show how you can quickly develop the information within the Part or Assembly mode, we will generate the combined note in Part mode.

The key advantage to this is that you will be able to select only the features in which you are interested. I have seen a number of examples, and I have been in the situation myself, where the user, who has been working on a drawing that has a lot of dimensions, accidentally types in the wrong dimension identification number when consolidating a pattern of features or some other group of features. This can be a little painful, especially when you have to locate which feature's dimension just got pulled from the drawing into a note, and then try to fix the problem by deleting the dimension call from the note and redisplaying the dimension. If there are only a few dimensions on the drawing, you may very well be able to quickly develop a parametric note that groups all of the desired dimensions. But there always exists that opportunity for you to accidentally add an unwanted dimension.

The following is an illustration of a model that has only those features of interest and their dimensions highlighted.

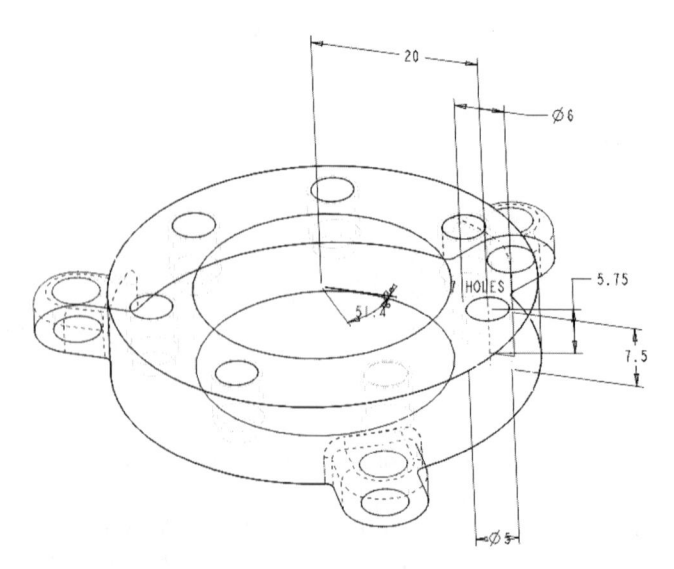

Part with features' dimensions shown.

Before You Detail   181

After you have selected the dimension that you wish to use for consolidating the pattern of dimensions, switch the dimension values to their dimension identification numbers by accessing the RELATIONS menu. If the dimensions don't switch to their dimension identification numbers, you can select the Switch Dim menu selection from the menu (see following figure).

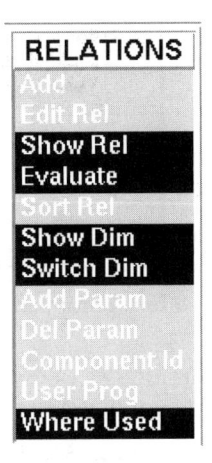

```
RELATIONS
Add
Edit Rel
Show Rel
Evaluate
Sort Rel
Show Dim
Switch Dim
Add Param
Del Param
Component Id
User Prog
Where Used
```

RELATIONS menu, Switch Dim.

Once you have the dimension identification numbers visible, you can edit the dimension that will be used for consolidating all of the features into a single note. Once you have entered into the editor, you can simply add the verbal and dimensional information that you require to describe the geometry. Your new consolidated parametric note may look like that shown in the following illustration.

Chapter 8: Detailing

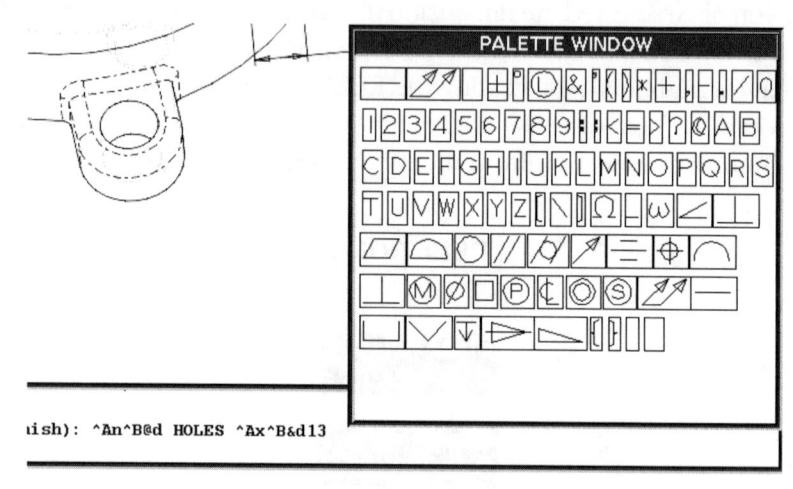

New consolidated fully parametric note in editor.

Notice that the note contains a number of control codes and &d### symbols. Each of these codes and symbols tell Pro/ENGINEER that a dimensional value for another feature is to be located in this note also. Therefore, this note will be a fully parametric note, capable of controlling other features within the part. After you have completed the note and switched the dimensions such that you can see the dimensional values, your note may look like the following illustration.

Before You Detail 183

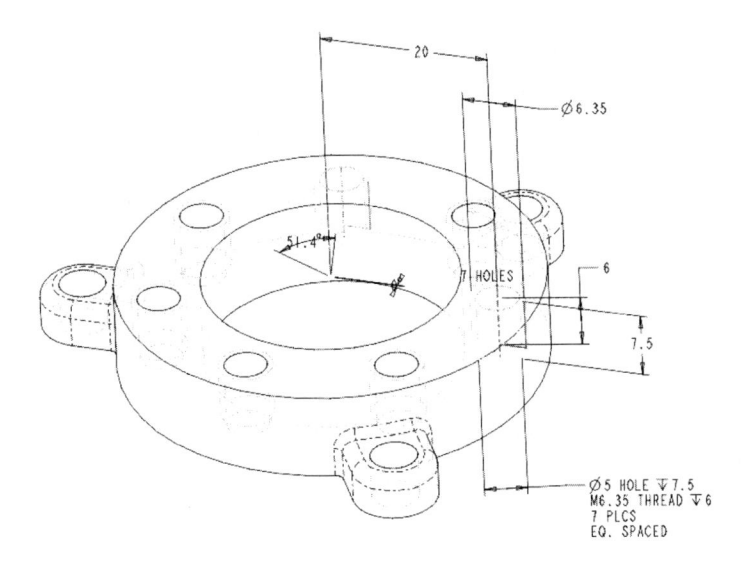

Final parametric note in Part mode.

It is always good to check the notes to make sure that they are working properly. By modifying the number of holes in the pattern and regenerating the model, your part and note will look like the following figure.

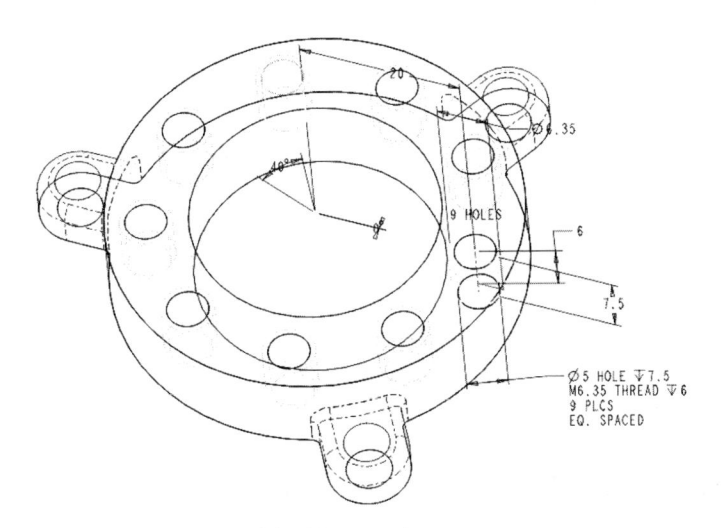

Modified part and new note.

But what about the drawing? If you do all of this work on the model why should you even mess with the drawing? Please keep in mind that there is more than one way to accomplish the same thing in Pro/ENGINEER. This particular technique was demonstrated because it enables you to interact with the model and highlight only those features that are of interest for the development of a simple or complex parametric note. Having the ability to develop fully parametric notes in general is a powerful tool within Pro/ENGINEER. I am sure that you have seen your fair share of people who manually enter nonparametric dimensional text into a note, and then write themselves a note to remember to update that text if the design changes. This can be as effective as trying to cut the grass after every rain storm; sometimes you will forget. Forgetting to update notes on a drawing can be a costly mistake; developing and using parametric notes can reduce or eliminate the second guessing that you may encounter when updating drawings. And above all it ensures that the documentation truly captures the design intent of the product you are developing.

Using Seed Data

For companies who have been using other CAD/CAM systems, having the ability to link the design's material, finish, and other user attributes to the drawing has, in most cases, been either difficult or impossible. The key limitation of these systems is their inability to preserve data in case of database corruption. In addition to that, some CAD/CAM systems, like Pro/ENGINEER, don't keep the drawing within the part or assembly file. Hence there is no direct link to the drawing from a three-dimensional database for material handling or finishing instructions, which are generally left with the drawing file.

I can remember working on a rush detail drawing for 12 long hours, when we had a system crash that corrupted several drawings that had already been completed, including the one that I was working on. After I rebooted, cleaned the system up, and wiped the remaining tears from my cheek, I sat down to start over on my drawing. This particular design was a sand cast component that required a lot of general information, that is, wall thickness, corner/edge radii, draft angles, finish stock, etc., to be included on the drawing's title block.

Before You Detail 185

All of this information was lost with the print and took at least 15 to 20 minutes to enter, size, reposition, and finalize.

We have seen, in previous chapters, how information can be passed from one module or design to another using parametric relationships. This ability to pass information between components and modules opens up a new and powerful door within Pro/ENGINEER—the ability to parametrically link specific parameters to the drawing. You may have seen general examples that use Pro/REPORT for the querying of component information within an assembly. But this goes further and involves the sharing of key information about the design such as the material, finish, and other drawing-specific information—information that you may decide is better kept *with* the design instead of in a separate file. This information is the seed data with the variables filled in.

The following illustration is an example of the seed data as it would appear in the seed file.

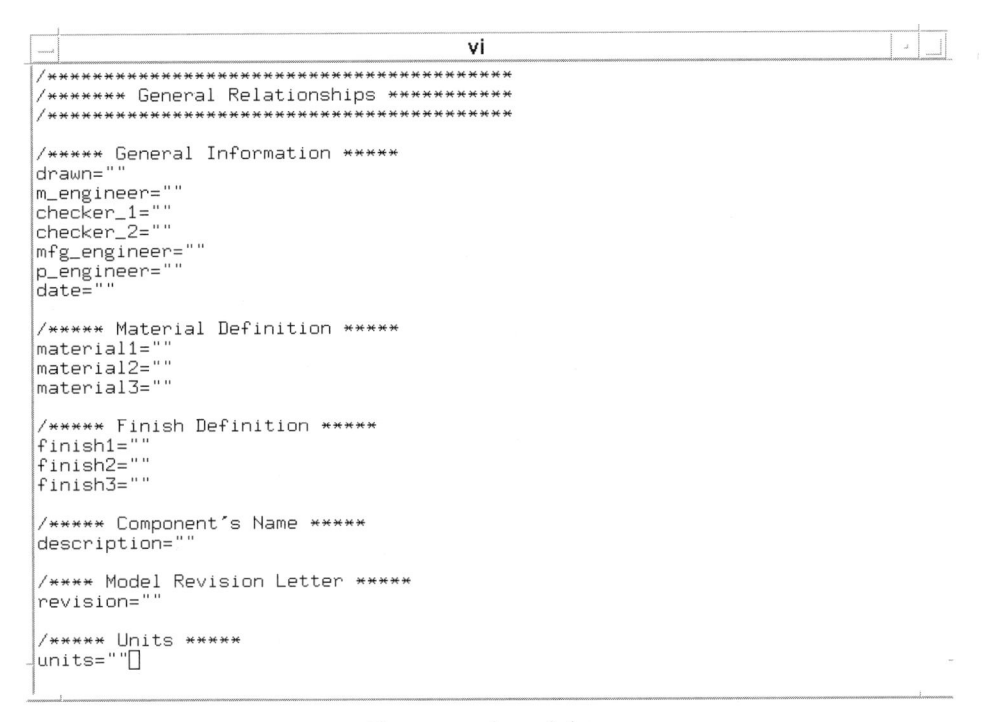

```
                                 vi
/***************************************
/******* General Relationships ************
/***************************************

/***** General Information *****
drawn=""
m_engineer=""
checker_1=""
checker_2=""
mfg_engineer=""
p_engineer=""
date=""

/***** Material Definition *****
material1=""
material2=""
material3=""

/***** Finish Definition *****
finish1=""
finish2=""
finish3=""

/***** Component's Name *****
description=""

/**** Model Revision Letter *****
revision=""

/***** Units *****
units=""
```

The original seed data.

Chapter 8: Detailing

The seed data for a part that has been completed and is ready to be detailed may look like that shown in the following illustration.

```
/*******************************************
/******* General Relationships ***********
/*******************************************

/***** General Information *****
drawn="DHB"
m_engineer="JKC"
checker_1="MDS"
checker_2="LRS"
mfg_engineer="SHF"
p_engineer="DTB"
date="02-24-95"

/***** Material Definition *****
material1="1020 LC CR STEEL"
material2="0.91mm^A#^B0.1 THICK"
material3=""

/***** Finish Definition *****
finish1="BLACK ZINC CHROMATE"
finish2="0.0127-0.0254 THK"
finish3="MUST PASS 24 hr. SALT SPRAY"

/***** Component's Name *****
description="SUPPORT BRACKET"

/**** Model Revision Letter *****
revision="A"

/***** Units *****
units="METRIC"
```

Seed data with actual data.

Remember, this information is included in and kept with the part or assembly with which you are working. Once this data has been completed and the drawing has been prepared to receive and display the information, Pro/ENGINEER automatically passes the variables to any preformatted or manually placed locations on the drawing.

For example, for the purposes of demonstration, a drawing will be generated using the system's defaults, and a general view will be placed on the drawing. Once the drawing references the part, it is not only referencing the model geometry, but the entire model and any relationships that have been established.

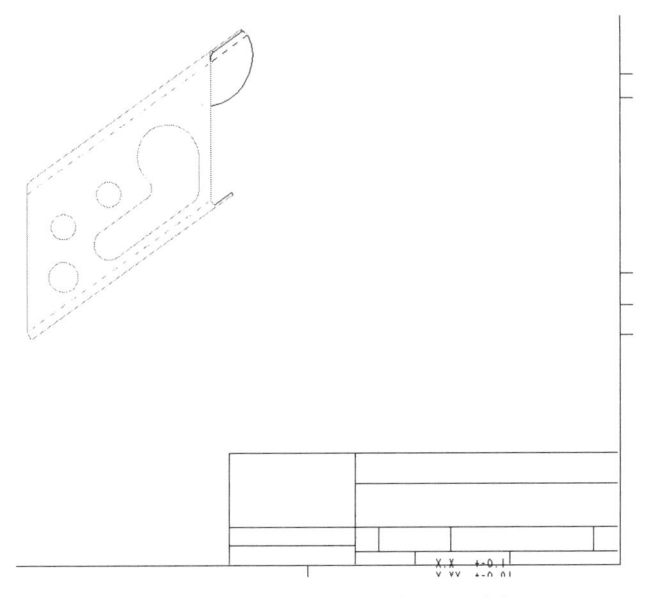

Generic drawing with a general view of the part.

By simply entering a set of notes on the drawing using the &#### format, where #### is the variable you wish to link to the note, you can access the parametric relationships that have been developed from the seed data. The drawing after the notes have been added to the drawing is shown in the following illustration.

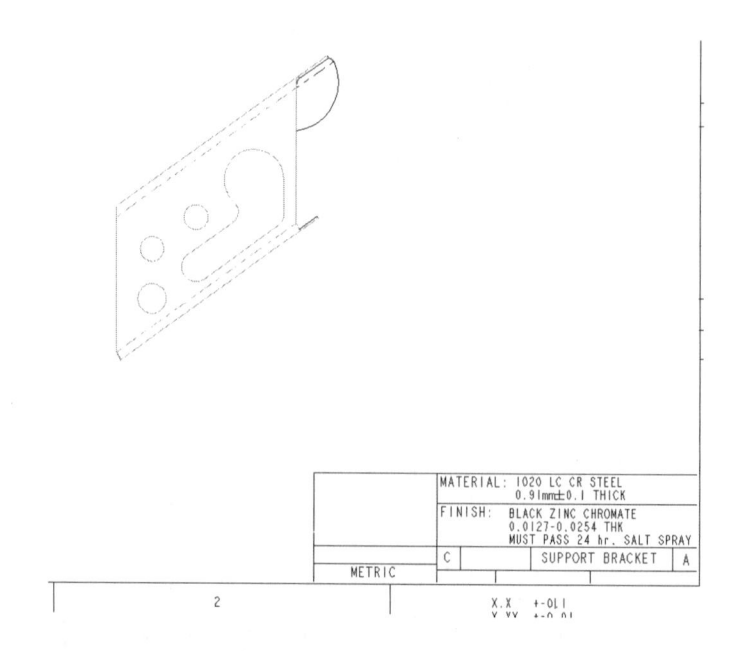

Generic view with notes that access the part's parametric relationships.

As you can see from the previous illustration, the information that was developed and remains with the part is linked to the drawing. The only thing that you would have to do, is enter the &#### formatted text to access the parametric relationship, format, and locate the text. If the relationships within the part were to change, the note on the drawing would automatically update upon regeneration. Hence, you would not burdened with the redundant tasks of updating the information on the drawing. This way you are ensuring that the drawing always has the latest information.

Parametric Formats and Seed Data

Another advantage to using the seed data lies in your ability to make major changes in the presentation of your information, the drawing format size, almost effortless. Have you ever worked on a drawing in Pro/ENGINEER or another CAD/CAM system and been required to change the drawings size from B to D? In general, it is not difficult to change the size of the drawing format to a larger size. The catch lies in the amount of rework or adjustments

Before You Detail

to all of the notes and views that you have developed. Once you have changed the size of the drawing, you usually must go in and relocate or reenter the entire title block of information, and in some cases, a bill of materials that may be included on the drawing.

By using the parametric relationships that have been established and are maintained in the part, you will be able to quickly recover from this change by simply regenerating the model or assembly that contains the information.

For example, the following illustration shows a drawing in which all of the information for the title block has been manually entered into the title block and is not parametrically linked to the part. After the drawing size has been changed from B to D, all of the text must be relocated and positioned in the title block.

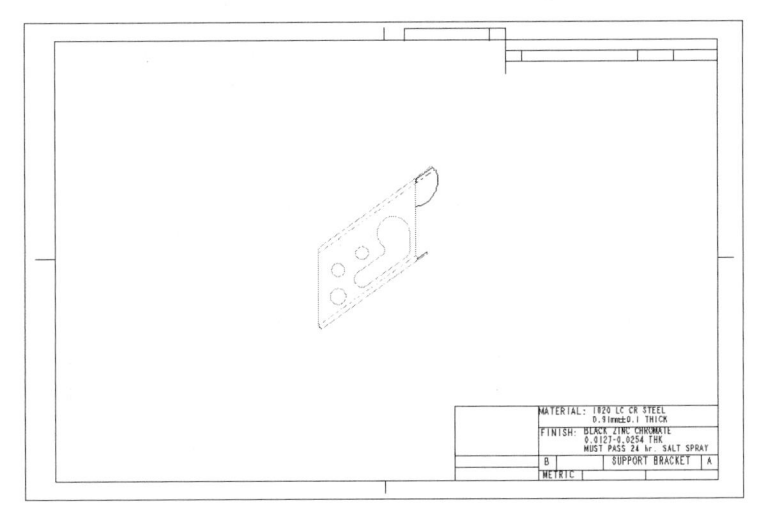

Drawing prior to change in size.

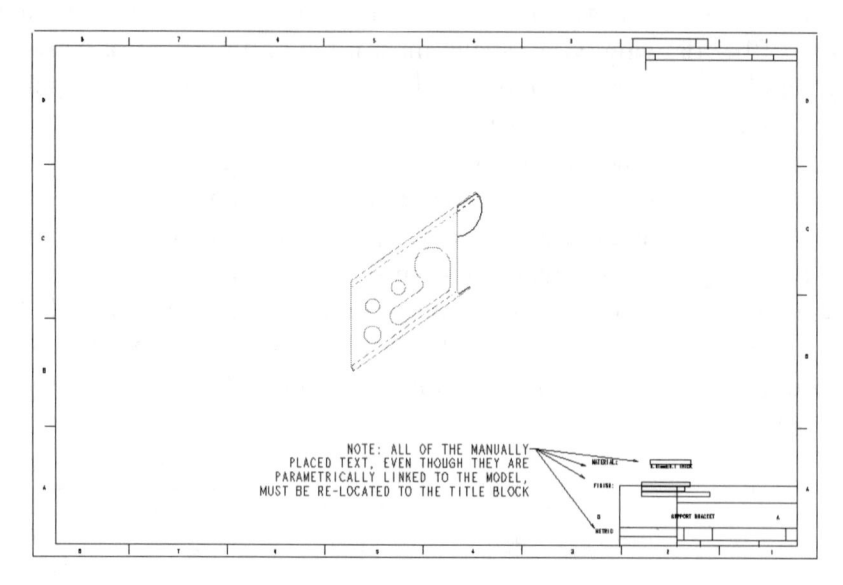

Chapter 8: Detailing

Drawing after change in size.

Notice in the previous illustration how each manually placed note must be independently relocated to its proper location on the drawing. But just manually placing parametric variable calls on the drawing does nothing to help reduce the amount of work that you have to do.

If the previous example was developed using a format that had all of the locations, sizes, and fonts predefined, all of the information would fall into place at the right size, location, and font. The following example shows how the use of parametric formats can reduce or eliminate the amount of work that must be done during a drawing size change.

Before You Detail 191

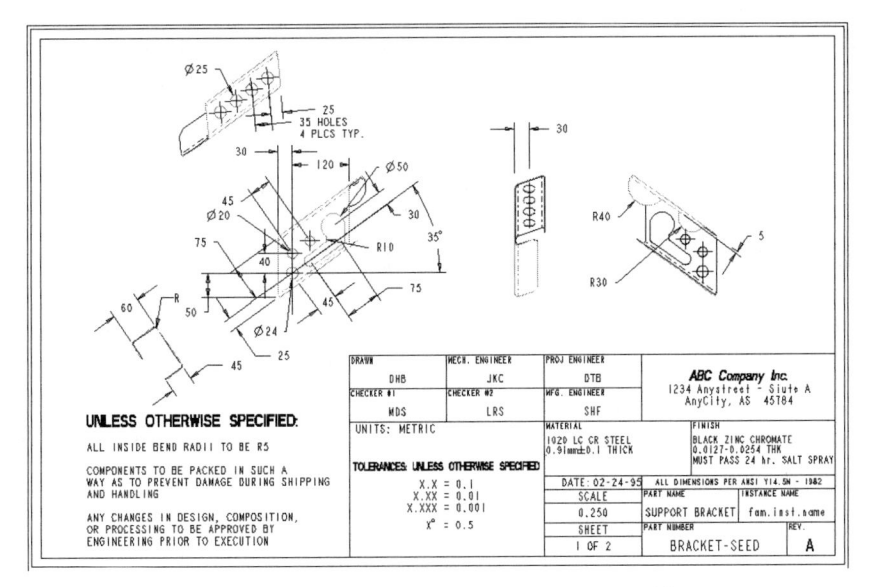

Original drawing size using parametric variables.

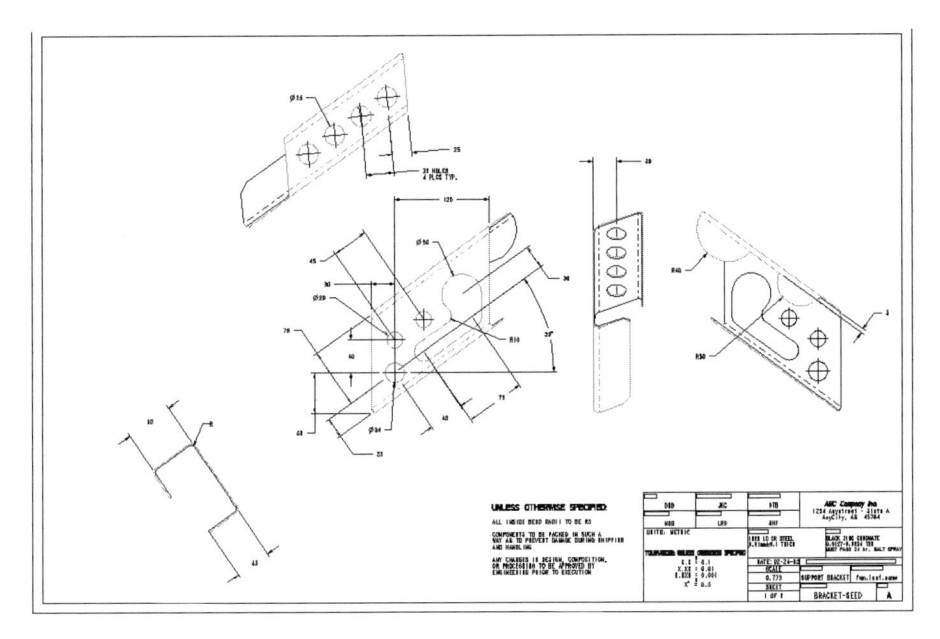

Final drawing size using parametric variables.

The change was made by simply selecting a new format size. Because each format was predefined with the seed variables for their location, size, and font, all of the seed data was regenerated automatically. Therefore, you did not have to rework the drawing.

Developing Parametric Formats

As we have seen from the previous section, parametric formats can remove a lot of the redundant and boring drawing management and maintenance tasks that you are required to do. But to have this level of flexibility and efficiency, you must take the time to set up and test the formats that you will be using to automate some of your detailing functions.

As in modeling, there are many ways to accomplish the same visual results on a drawing. The question is, which method is most efficient for your purposes? The key words in this question are *for your purposes*. The methods and techniques may or may not capture everything that you are looking for; they are to provoke thought and interest in alternatives to the usual approaches.

Manually Placed Text

The use of manually placed text within the format is not a new approach to controlling the location, size, and font of the seed data that the format will be accessing during detailing.

Developing Parametric Formats 193

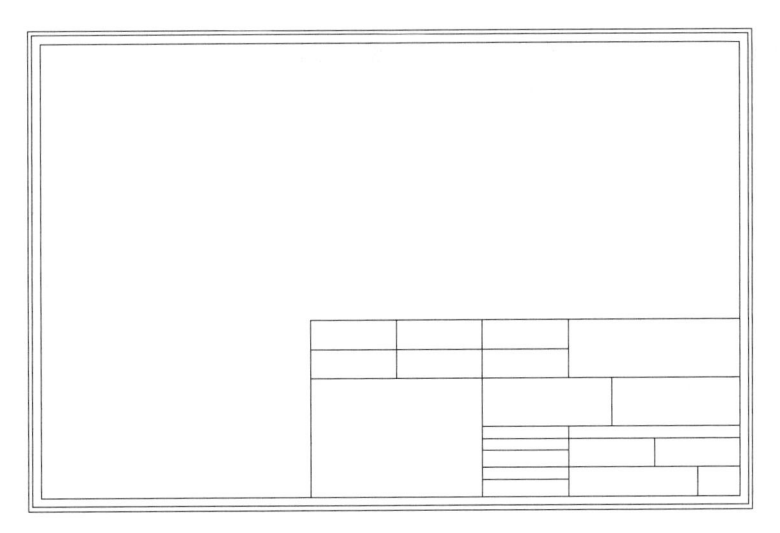

Generic format prior to text location.

For the format shown above, you would simply add, format, and locate the parametric notes on the drawing, one for each variable that the format will be accessing from the model. This may look like the following illustration.

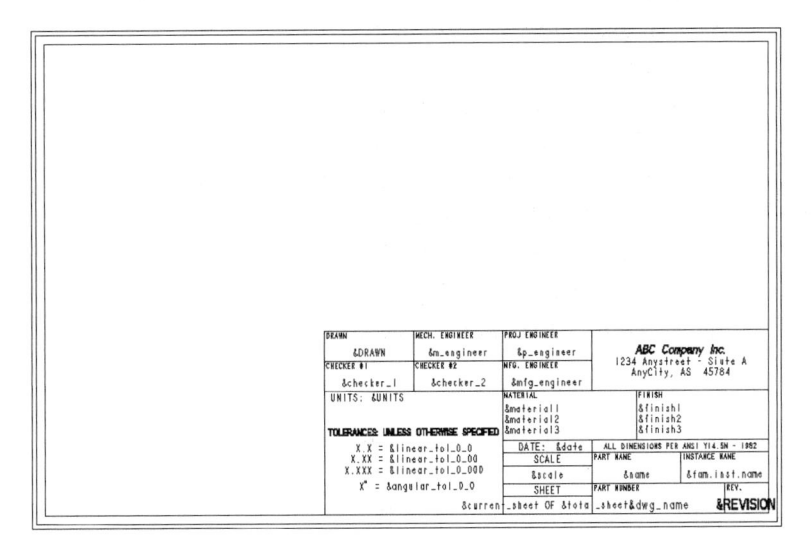

Generic format after text placement.

This looks pretty good, and it will be functional for the reporting of the seed data when a model is being detailed. It took approximately 15 to 20 minutes to set up this format and place, size, and format all of the parametric text within the title block. Now that this format is completed, you have all of the other sizes to complete.

This is a viable method of development for the format, and the results will produce the expected results. The problem with this development is that it will require you to reproduce the same information across all of the formats that your company uses, which introduces the possibility that the text from one format may not be in the same location as the previous format. In addition, it takes a long time to set up accurately.

Symbols

Using symbols has some distinct advantages over the manual placement and formatting of text. Most people think of a symbol as a group of geometry that is used to represent a special process requirement or procedure. But in this case, a symbol can be used to locate and manage a block of text or geometry. For our application, a symbol can be used to locate text within a title block. The symbol could be developed during the creation of a format, saved onto your hard drive, and then quickly called into the next format that you develop. The advantage is that all of the text would be located in the same place from one format to the next. The disadvantage is that the symbol must be accurately placed on the new format such that all of the text does not appear to be out of location relative to the title block. The following is an illustration of a symbol that was created with its origin at the lower right corner of the format.

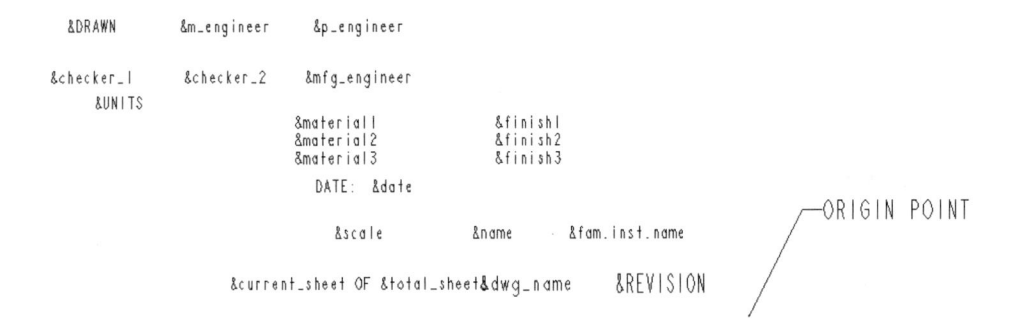

Developing Parametric Formats

```
&DRAWN          &m_engineer     &p_engineer

&checker_1      &checker_2      &mfg_engineer
     &UNITS
                                &material1      &finish1
                                &material2      &finish2
                                &material3      &finish3
                                DATE: &date

                                &scale          &name       &fam.inst.name

                  &current_sheet OF &total_sheet&dwg_name   &REVISION
```
                                                                        ─ORIGIN POINT

Symbol with parametric variables.

The following is a format that has the symbol's origin located at the lower right corner of the format.

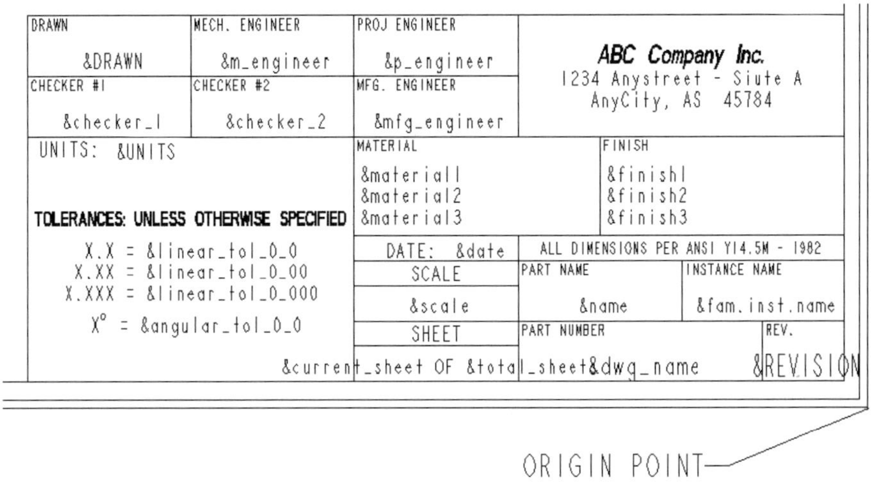

```
| DRAWN           | MECH. ENGINEER  | PROJ ENGINEER   |                               |
|     &DRAWN      |    &m_engineer  |   &p_engineer   |   ABC Company Inc.            |
| CHECKER #1      | CHECKER #2      | MFG. ENGINEER   |   1234 Anystreet - Siute A    |
|     &checker_1  |    &checker_2   |   &mfg_engineer |     AnyCity, AS  45784        |
| UNITS: &UNITS                     | MATERIAL          | FINISH                      |
|                                   |   &material1      |   &finish1                  |
|                                   |   &material2      |   &finish2                  |
| TOLERANCES: UNLESS OTHERWISE SPEC |   &material3      |   &finish3                  |
|   X.X   = &linear_tol_0_0         | DATE:    &date    | ALL DIMENSIONS PER ANSI Y14.5M - 1982 |
|   X.XX  = &linear_tol_0_00        | SCALE             | PART NAME    | INSTANCE NAME |
|   X.XXX = &linear_tol_0_000       |   &scale          |   &name      | &fam.inst.name |
|   X°    = &angular_tol_0_0        | SHEET             | PART NUMBER             | REV. |
|                     &current_sheet OF &total_sheet&dwg_name           | &REVISION |
```
                                                    ORIGIN POINT─

Format that uses a symbol to locate parametric variables.

Again the advantage here is that all of the text can be located within the title block quickly and easily. The disadvantage is that you must be consistent with your placement from one format to the next. Another disadvantage is that the text within the symbol cannot adapt to changes in location within a specific block of information. Variations in location may be a desired attribute of text within a title block. Because the symbol's text uses a fixed reference, this would not be possible. In the end, you may have a situation where you are forced to change all of your formats to accommodate a piece of information that was not predicted during development.

Tables, Tables, and More Tables

Tables can make your life easy when it comes to the development of parametric formats. For many, this is the preferred method for a number of reasons. A table enables you to have all of the key pieces of information controlled and managed on one entity. This gives you a great level of consistency from one format to the next. In addition, you will have greater control over individual text formats and their location, that is, justification within each cell in the table. The following is a title block that was developed using a single table.

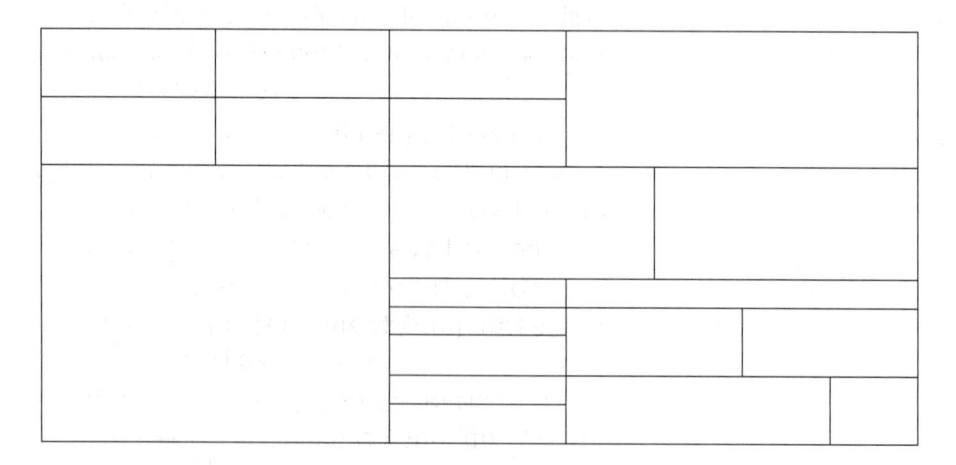

Title block that was developed using a single table.

By entering all of the text that you will require for the title block and the parametric variables, you will ensure that each piece of information is properly placed and sized and is aesthetically pleasing. The final title block with formatted text and parametric variables is shown in the following illustration.

Developing Parametric Formats 197

DRAWN	MECH. ENGINEER	PROJ ENGINEER		
&DRAWN	&m_engineer	&p_engineer	**ABC Company Inc.** 1234 Anystreet - Siute A AnyCity, AS 45784	
CHECKER #1	CHECKER #2	MFG. ENGINEER		
&checker_1	&checker_2	&mfg_engineer		
UNITS: &UNITS		MATERIAL	FINISH	
		&material1	&finish1	
		&material2	&finish2	
TOLERANCES: UNLESS OTHERWISE SPECIFIED		&material3	&finish3	
X.X = &linear_tol_0_0		DATE: &date	ALL DIMENSIONS PER ANSI Y14.5M - 1982	
X.XX = &linear_tol_0_00		SCALE	PART NAME	INSTANCE NAME
X.XXX = &linear_tol_0_000		&scale	&name	&fam.inst.name
X° = &angular_tol_0_0		SHEET	PART NUMBER	REV.
		&current_sheet OF &total_sheet	&dwg_name	**&REVISION**

Title block with standard text and parametric variables.

Now that this title block has been completed, you can save the table to your hard drive and reuse it on other formats. Another advantage to using tables as your primary method of management is their ability to accept Pro/REPORT variables. This introduces a level of flexibility that is just not possible with other methods of format development.

Assume that the title block shown previously needed to be reformatted so that it could be used to generate a parts/assembly list for top level or assembly drawings. Integrating repeat regions into the table will allow you to automate the querying and counting of components within an assembly. A possible revised title block is shown in the following illustration.

&rpt.index	&asm.mbr.name	&asm.mbr.description		&rpt.qty	
ITEM	**PART NUMBER**	**DESCRIPTION**		**QUANTITY**	**COMMENTS**
DRAWN	MECH. ENGINEER	PROJ ENGINEER			
&DRAWN	&m_engineer	&p_engineer		*ABC Company Inc.*	
CHECKER #1	CHECKER #2	MFG. ENGINEER		1234 Anystreet - Siute A	
&checker_1	&checker_2	&mfg_engineer		AnyCity, AS 45784	
UNITS: &UNITS		MATERIAL		FINISH	
		&material1		&finish1	
		&material2		&finish2	
TOLERANCES: UNLESS OTHERWISE SPECIFIED		&material3		&finish3	
X.X = &linear_tol_0_0		DATE: &date	ALL DIMENSIONS PER ANSI Y14.5M - 1982		
X.XX = &linear_tol_0_00		SCALE	PART NAME	INSTANCE NAME	
X.XXX = &linear_tol_0_000		&scale	&name	&fam.inst.name	
X° = &angular_tol_0_0		SHEET	PART NUMBER		REV.
		&current_sheet OF &total	_sheet&dwg_name		**&REVISION**

Revised title block with repeat regions for assembly drawings.

As you can see from the previous examples and methods, there are a number of advantages and disadvantages to each technique; it all depends on what your requirements are for documenting the design.

Proper View Development

This is one area of Pro/ENGINEER that does not receive a lot of attention, but is just as important as how you develop your models and set up your drawing formats. If you are like most people, when you started to detail a design, you selected a drawing size, placed a general view, oriented it, and set up the rest of the views from that base view. An example of this sequence is shown in the following illustration.

Proper View Development 199

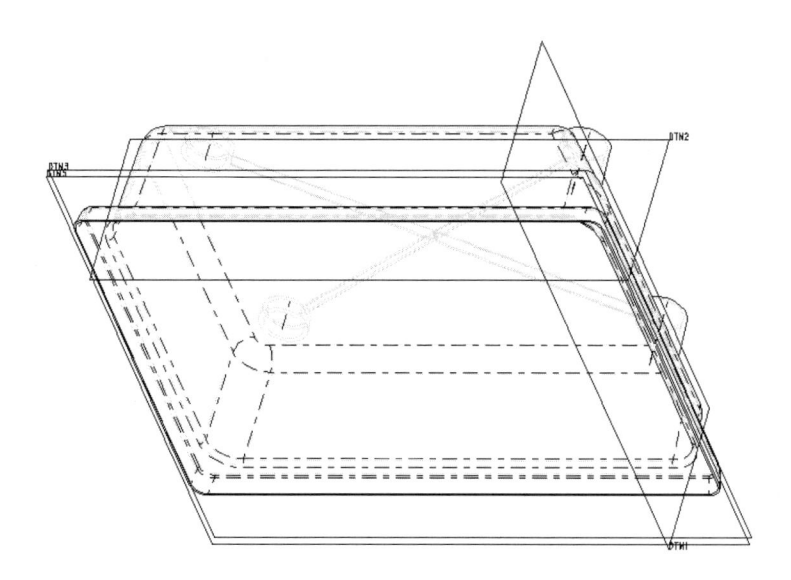

Placed general view on drawing.

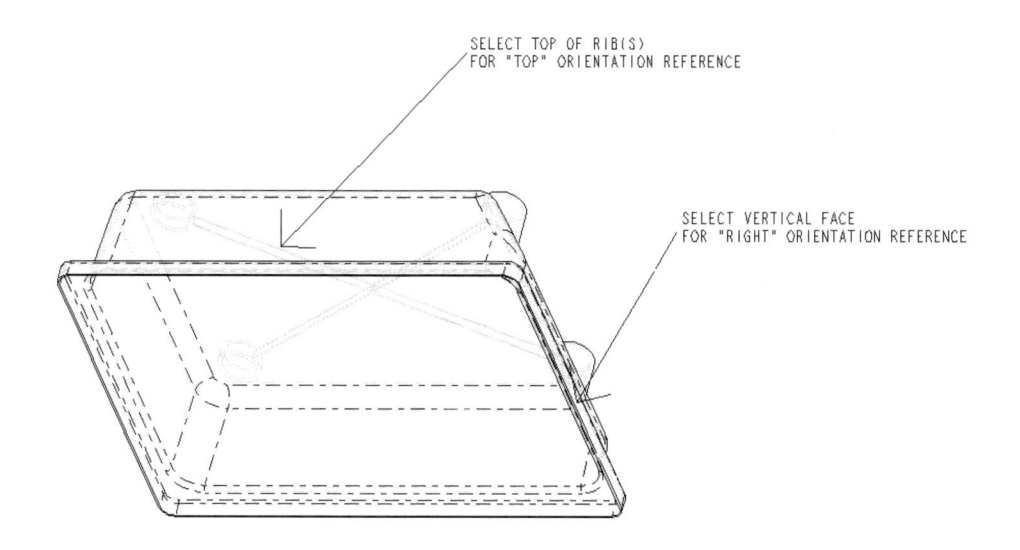

Selected surfaces for orientation.

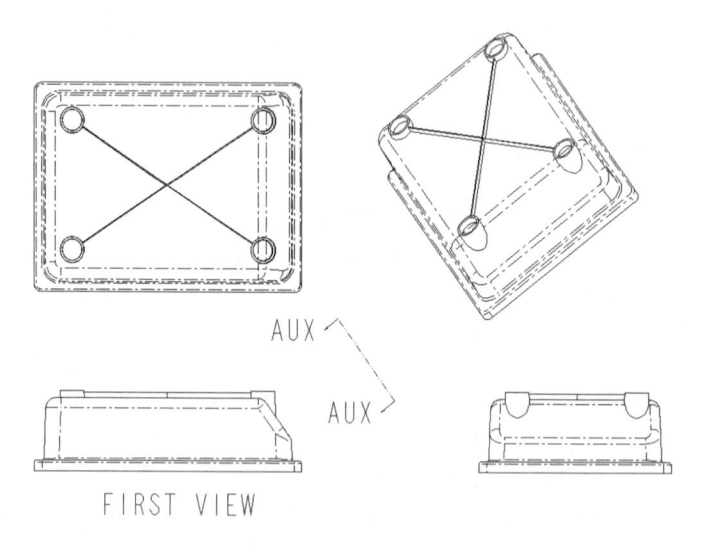

Added projection views from first view placed on drawing.

This sequence may seem familiar to you. If this is the case, then you have accidentally placed yourself, and your company, at a high level of risk for a lot of drawing rework.

What is wrong with this situation? Even though it looks good on the drawing, there are a number of setup issues that could cause serious problems at a later date. Just as features can have parents and children when you are modeling a component or assembly, the views on a drawing can have parents and children. In this case, the parents for the first view on the drawing are the surfaces that were used for orientation. In addition, the views that were developed as projections from the first view are children of that view. What does this mean? The answer can be found in the following illustration.

Proper View Development 201

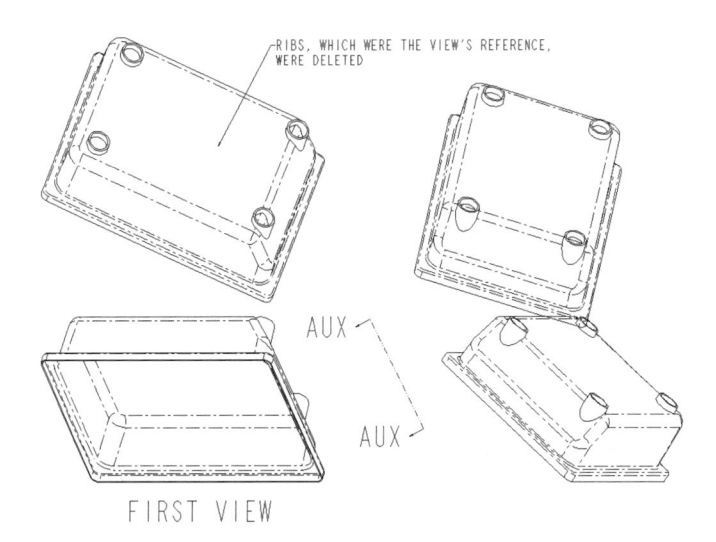

Views after parent geometry was deleted through engineering change.

In the previous illustration, a feature was deleted due to a required engineering change. The results of this are obvious; all of the views are out of alignment. Why? Because the feature that was deleted was the geometric reference for the primary and all of the subsequent views that were developed.

How do you get around this problem? If you had developed a set of default datum planes as your base feature, something that I highly recommend, then you would have a stable view reference from which you can develop all of your primary views. If the previous example were to be redefined using the default datum planes, all of your geometry would be children of the datum planes, which most likely will not be deleted. Therefore, your model can be modified without having an impact on view orientation. The results of this are shown in the following illustration.

202   Chapter 8: Detailing

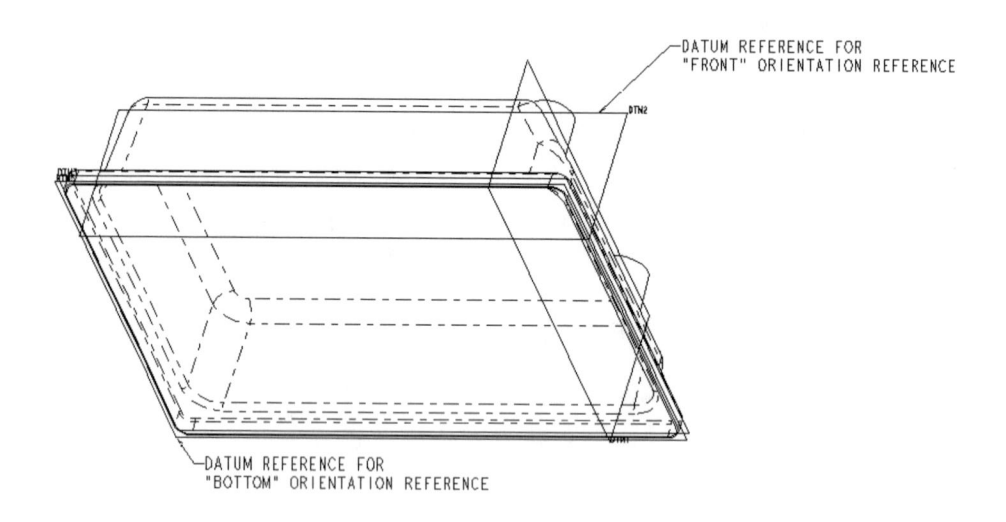

Selected surfaces for orientation.

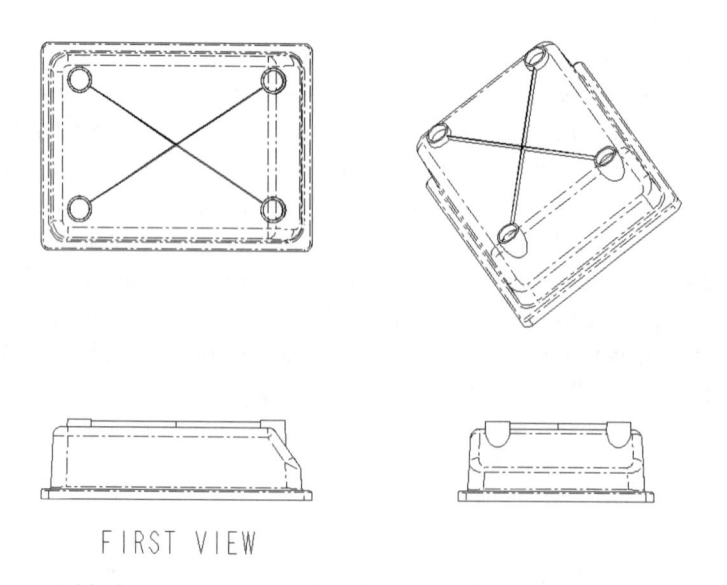

FIRST VIEW

Added projection views from first view placed on drawing.

Once these views have been developed, suppose that the same geometry was to be deleted because of an engineering change. The following illustration shows the results of that design modification.

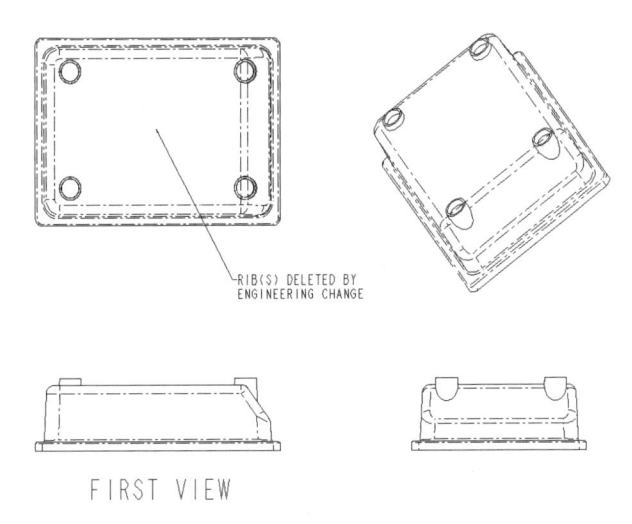

Views after geometry was deleted through engineering change.

As you can see from the previous illustrations, view placement follows the same rules that all of the other geometry must follow. Parent/child relationships must be considered when setting up and working with views. Mistakes made in the early phases of your view development can mean lots of rework later. Be sure to take the time to plan and properly execute your view development. Nothing hurts more than spending several days detailing a design, only to have to rework and redefine it later.

Showing Off

If you were to select one area of Pro/ENGINEER that impressed you the most when you were sitting in your PTC demo of the software, I am willing to bet that it was the reverse associativity between the designs and the drawings. This functionality is truly impressive and has introduced a more efficient and functional method of detailing designs to the engineering community. But

204   Chapter 8: Detailing

what are the requirements for using this technology to its fullest extent? If you have followed everything up to this point, you should have already figured it out.

If you have successfully completed your design and it satisfies all of the process and design issues, all of your dimensions and tolerances should have already been determined and incorporated into the design. Having all of this information integrated into the actual model ensures that the design intent is captured and that the dimensioning and tolerancing scheme is functional to the design. Because you have taken great care during your design's development to select the proper tools for modeling, you should make every effort to use all of that information when you develop your drawings. The following illustration highlights a fully parametric drawing that uses all of the dimensions and tolerances that were developed in the part.

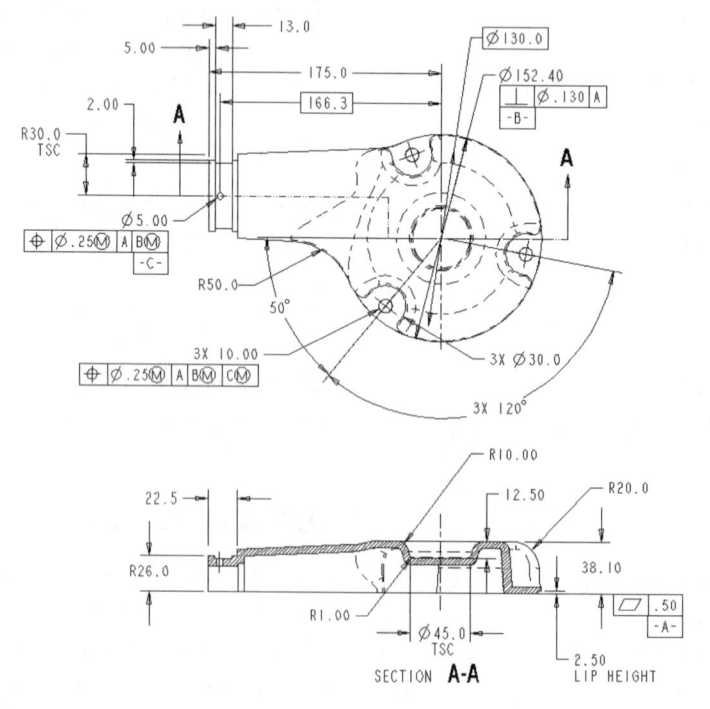

Fully parametric drawing that uses driving dimensions and tolerances.

Showing Off 205

I have seen a number of examples where the user spends a lot of time working on developing a model and then applies manually placed or driven dimensions on the drawing. The end results of this are obvious; the next user to modify the design will have to hunt for the feature's dimensions in the model, even for small modifications. Another risk is that the user will not replicate the dimensioning scheme that was used to develop the model in the first place. The following illustrations highlight the dimensional differences between the model and the drawing.

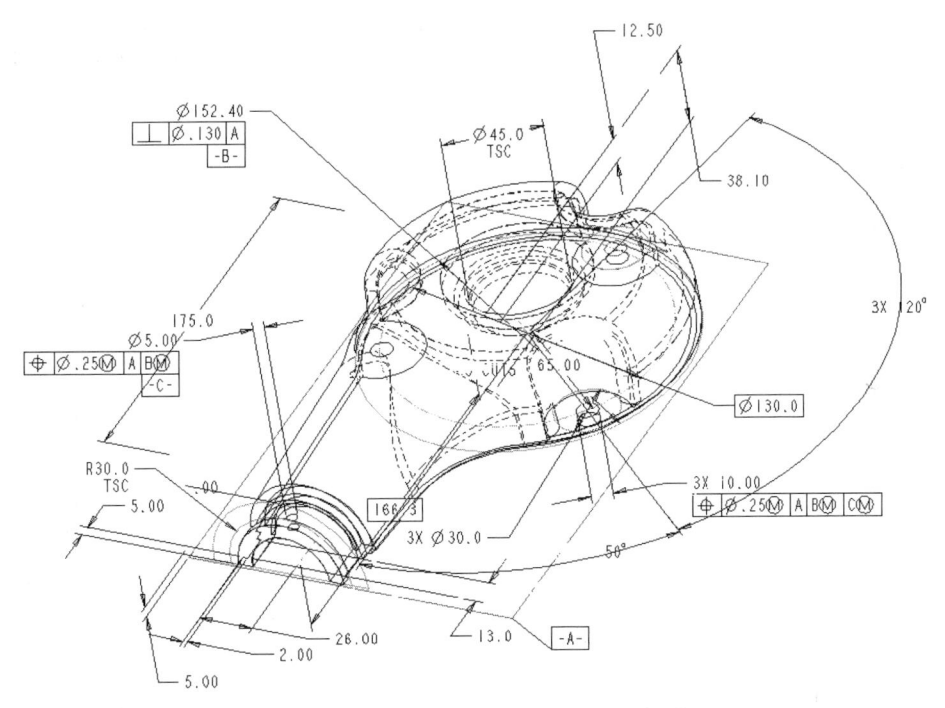

Fully parametric model that captures the design intent.

Chapter 8: Detailing

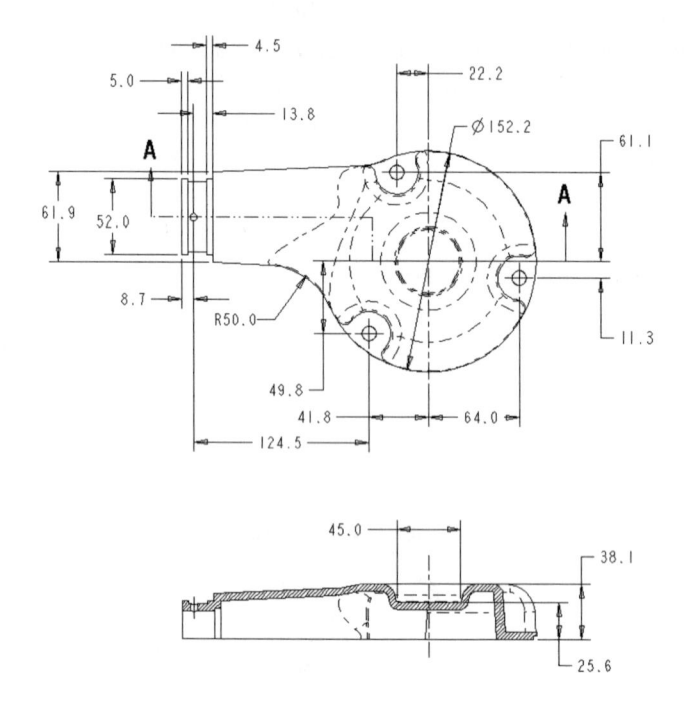

Nonparametric drawing that uses different dimensioning and tolerancing schemes.

    As you can see, having a difference in the dimensioning and tolerancing scheme can cause big problems when it comes to modifying the part. If and when a change is required to the part, the user will have to review the model closely to ensure that the parametric dimensions that they will be modifying produce the desired size and location modifications that may be required on the nonparametric drawing. Then after a change has been made, there is always that question in the back of your mind as to what parent/child relationships may have been established that may have a dimensional effect on an area of the part that did not need to be changed.

    In the end, the quality of the drawing is directly proportional to the quality of the models that you have developed. As you develop more accurate databases, use dimensioning schemes and tolerances that are functional to the final design and inspection requirements, your documentation and modeling link will remain parametric. However, if you are working with a design that has not been properly developed or uses dimensioning and tolerancing schemes that are not functional, your success rate for maintaining a parametric link with the drawing will be much lower due to the required driven dimensions.

What is involved in using the design's dimensions and tolerances on the drawing? Quite simply, all you have to do is (1) make sure the view is properly developed, (2) access the SHOW DIM menu, and (3) select the features in the drawing view for which you want to reveal the dimensions. For more information on the menus, selections, and options, please refer to the *Pro/ENGINEER Drawing User's Guide*. This same technique can be used to show any geometric tolerances or reference dimensions that you may have added to the design.

For example, the following illustration is a parametric design that captures the design intent. The dimensioning and tolerancing scheme has been established and is functional to the inspection requirements. The goal is to use the SHOW menu options when the drawing is being created to use the dimensions and tolerances on the drawing, therefore maintaining a parametric link with the part.

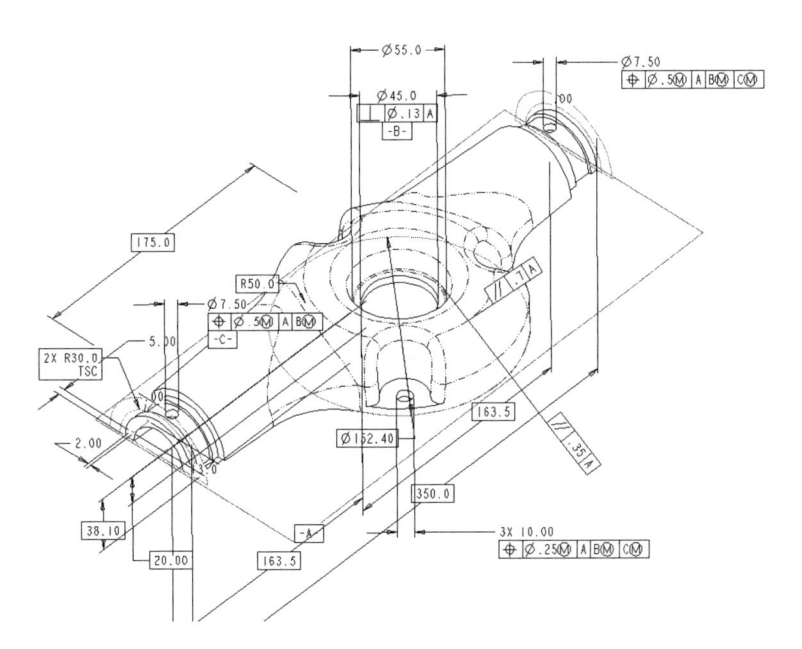

Original parametric design with tolerances.

Chapter 8: Detailing

By creating a drawing and placing the views that may be required to detail the component, we are now ready to *Show* the part's design and inspection information.

After a drawing has been created and the views placed on the drawing, you can selectively, by view, feature, or other methods, reveal the dimensional and tolerance information that was used to develop the design. The previous illustration might look like the following illustration after it has been placed on the drawing.

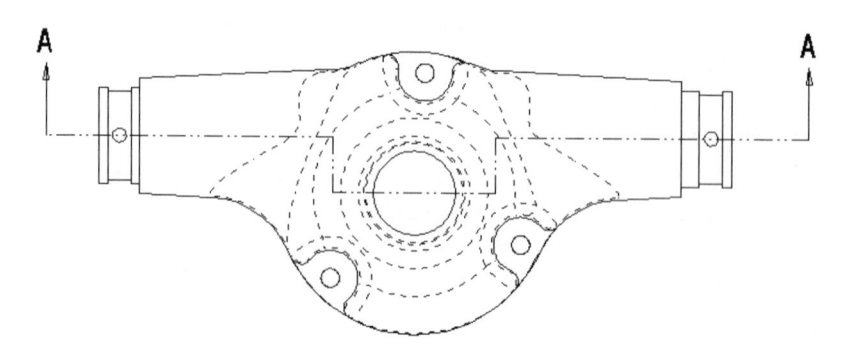

Drawing with views of the part.

By selecting the features of interest to show their dimensional information, the drawing may look like the following.

Showing Off 209

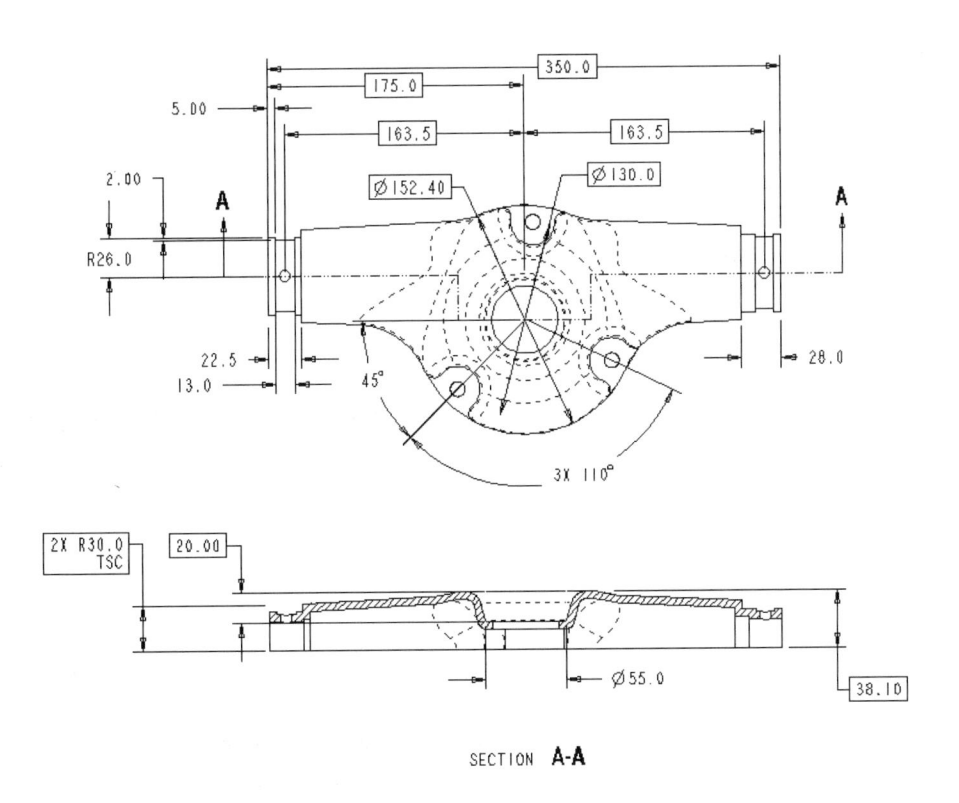

Drawing with some features' dimensions shown.

Using this same technique, the feature's GD&T can also be shown. The following illustration highlights the results of showing the GD&T.

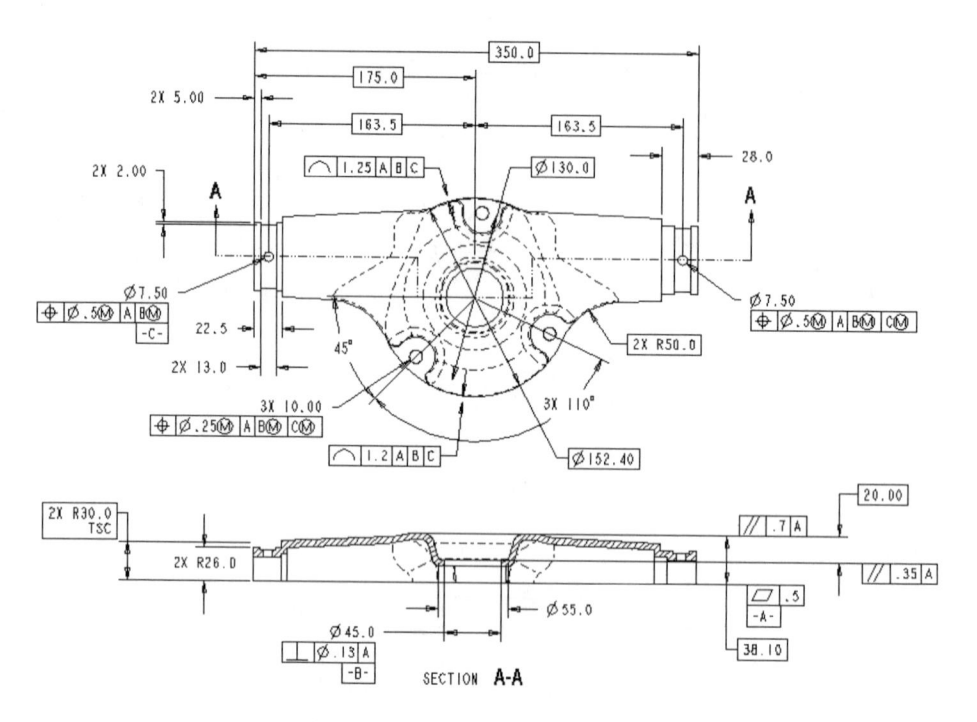

Drawing with some features' geometric tolerances shown.

Once all of this information has been *shown* on the drawing, your next step may be to relocate the dimensions and tolerances to an aesthetically pleasing location or view on the drawing. The final result of using this technique over manually detailing the design is a reduction in time and an increase in accuracy and flexibility. The advantages to using this technique for detailing your components far outweigh the alternative, provided that your designs are set up properly.

Summary

Pro/ENGINEER's detailing capabilities have been plagued with the verbal reputation among new users of being difficult to use. However, Pro/DETAIL has been unfairly labeled. The strengths of this module outweigh the limitations, and when used properly can result in a fast and accurate detailing cycle of the design, using the dimensions and tolerances that you have taken the time to integrate into the design.

Pro/DETAIL is a logical extension of the Pro/ENGINEER product line and can, if used properly, reduce your development time by maintaining parametric links with the design and drive the design from the drawing. This ability to directly link the design to the drawing and make changes from either mode of operation is a significant leap in the CAD/CAM industry and ensures that your drawings will always have the latest information that was included in the model. This ability ensures that any manufacturing, material, or processing requirements that you include with the design, stay with the design.

From consolidating notes and applying tolerances in the model to simplifying the communication of a number of operations or features to the development of fully parametric formats, Pro/DETAIL has a lot of standard and user-definable functionality. But there are more fundamental requirements for efficient detailing in Pro/ENGINEER. Just as you must plan for and deal with parent/child relationships during the modeling of a design, these same parent/child relationships can create some headaches when you are developing your drawings. By not taking the time to properly set up your views for detailing and placing views that are dependent on model geometry, you may end up redetailing your design at a later date when your original view orientation references may be removed.

Just as the quality of the inputs to your design is important for capturing the design intent, the quality of the inputs for detailing are just as important. People who spend most of their time working on completing a model by sculpting it in Pro/ENGINEER or arbitrarily placing the features and illogically placing the dimensions in the design are creating difficulties in communicating the design on the drawing. A popular workaround for detailing a sculpted design is to manually add dimensions to the drawing to describe the design. Aside from the significant amount of time that is required to add all these dimensions, the user's ability to modify the design is crippled because it is more difficult to locate and modify the appropriate dimension.

Overall, when models and assemblies have been properly developed, capture the design intent, and can adapt to change, Pro/DETAIL is an excellent tool for the communication of that design intent.

Improving Design Execution

Introduction

Suppose that your project leader or department head has given you a ground zero design task to complete within a week. Because your final product should be flexible and functional for future use, you go through the process of generating *quality input* from all the departments and manufacturing support personnel who will be involved with the design. Once you have the design worked out on paper, you begin to model the component in Pro/ENGINEER. Because it was decided by all of the groups involved that the design would be a plastic injected component, you take care to ensure that the part is not only functional to the design intent but also to the manufacturing processes.

After you develop the foundation for the component (the "Christmas tree"), you begin to add the manufacturability features (the "ornaments"), such as draft, ribs, gussets, etc. Because you have never used macros, or any other method, for speeding up your use of Pro/ENGINEER, successfully placing all of this information within the model takes quite a bit of time. As you work, you find yourself reexecuting the same command sequences over and over to properly add all the features to the part. Once you complete the model, you send it for review at the molder. A day later, you receive a memo from the molder requesting that the parting line for the component be moved from its current reference to a new reference.

The change that the molder requests does not appear to affect the design intent of the component, but it requires that all of the drafted surfaces on the part be redefined. With only a few days left to complete the design, you sit down at the computer and begin to redesign all of the ornaments that you have hung on the part. Once again you execute the same command sequences over and over again. During this rework of the part, you discover that the new references will create some very thin wall thicknesses for some features. This complicates the rework and forces you to use some split drafts to ensure that the part will still satisfy the design's requirements. By now your development time has shrunk to almost nothing, and you are receiving notice from the management that the drawing must be completed within the next day. With this new deadline, you quickly finish the design, review the changes with all of the parties involved, obtain acceptance of the changes, and proceed to the detailing of the design.

You begin the drawing by accessing a standard drawing format from your library of corporate formats and placing the views on the drawing. Because you have taken the time to obtain input from all the parties involved and have a rational dimensioning and tolerancing scheme, you are able to simply *Show* each feature's information on the drawing views. Since you do not want all of the features' dimension and tolerance information to show up at once, you *query* each feature within each view that you feel best describes that geometry, and then move those dimensions to their final position on the drawing. To do this, you are required to execute a repetitive list of commands to tell Pro/ENGINEER that you are going to *Show* the dimensions of a feature by querying that feature by the view and then moving the dimensions. Because your part has almost 100 features, the manual selection of each feature proves to be a time-consuming task.

After working an extra 6 hours to complete the drawing, you meet the deadline that was established earlier in the week. But could all of this been done more efficiently? And could you have opened up some additional design options if you had additional time to experiment with or tweak the design? The answer to both of these questions is undoubtedly, yes.

Options For Initiating Repetitive Execution

The previous example may not be too far from reality for you. There are still experienced users who hunt and peck through the Pro/ENGINEER menu structure looking for each and every command. If you have a basic understanding of the features that you are intending to use, you should be able to execute them rapidly, without scanning through four or five menus to get to the command. One of the major keys to success in designing is iteration: the more successful iterations that you can accomplish before a design is finalized, the better the design is likely to be. If time is the limiting factor in your designs, then you need to improve your use of the tools at your disposal. One way that you can improve your use of Pro/ENGINEER is in the execution of repetitive command sequences or tasks. This can be done any number of ways, with many levels of sophistication. One of the fastest and most common methods of execution for these repetitive tasks is by using a macro.

Macros

In Pro/ENGINEER, a macro is basically a one-line, user-defined list of commands that can be manually executed by the user. You may have been exposed to macros in word processor or spreadsheet software. With those types of software, macros are commonly used to execute command sequences to reformat text or query and calculate data. The same principles apply to the definition and use of macros within Pro/ENGINEER.

Using macros in Pro/ENGINEER can eliminate redundant tasks, improve your use of the software, and buy you more time to try other design options. Looking back at the introductory example, the user was manually applying a lot of the same feature type—draft—to the model. Assume that the user knows how the draft feature works, what its requirements are, and when to use one type of draft over another. If the user was continuously executing the following menu command sequence,

    `Feature, Create, Tweak, Draft, Done, Done`

and then querying the neutral plane and the features (solid surfaces) to be altered, this would take quite a bit of the user's time, especially on larger or

Chapter 9: Improving Design Execution

more complex components. By writing a macro that is executed by a key sequence, all of those commands would be executed automatically, leaving you to define the neutral plane and the features (solid surfaces) that will receive the draft feature and eliminating the hunting and pecking through all the menus to execute the command. The advantage would be a significant reduction in the amount of time to execute a command sequence, which would increase the efficiency of using Pro/ENGINEER.

Where Are They Kept and How Are They Defined?

Although you can develop independent files for macros, they are generally developed and maintained in your *config.pro* file. This is the same file that contains all your environment and directory search settings for Pro/ENGINEER. Refer to the *Pro/ENGINEER Fundamentals* guide for additional information on the *config.pro* file. Each user can have his or her own *config.pro* file, and therefore his or her own configurations and macros for Pro/ENGINEER. The *mapkey* is the *config.pro* configuration option that tells Pro/ENGINEER that the associated, or following, characters and command string are a user-defined macro. A typical mapkey configuration line within the *config.pro* file is shown in the following figure.

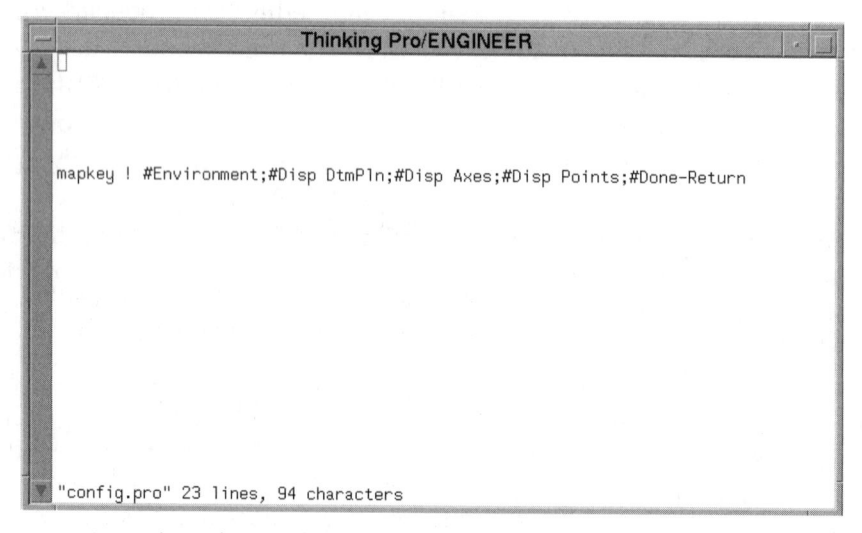

```
mapkey ! #Environment;#Disp DtmPln;#Disp Axes;#Disp Points;#Done-Return
```

"config.pro" 23 lines, 94 characters

Typical mapkey configuration option that defines a user's macro.

Options For Initiating Repetitive Execution

As you can see from the illustration, the macro has been defined to select the Datum Plane Display (*Disp DtmPln*), Axes (*Disp Axes*), and Datum Points (*Disp Points*) within the ENVIRONMENT menu when the exclamation point (!) is entered by the user. A dissection of the macro reveals the following:

- **mapkey** (configuration option): This lets Pro/ENGINEER know that the following key sequence is a user-defined and executable command string.

- **!:** This is the alphanumeric key that Pro/ENGINEER recognizes as the command to execute the macro. Multiple characters and function keys can also be used.

- **#Environment;#Disp DtmPln;#Disp Axes;#Disp Points;#Done-Return:** This is the list of command sequences (menu selections) that you would normally have to execute or select to obtain the results. The command sequence would access the ENVIRONMENT menu, select the menu options, and finally perform a *Done-Return* to exit the menu.

✍ **NOTE:** *The above macro could be executed from any submenu within Pro/ENGINEER because it is a MAIN menu option.*

This sample macro can be helpful when you are working on large parts that have a lot of holes, datum planes, or scanned datum points. What the macro does is, once the user enters the !, Pro/ENGINEER automatically enters the ENVIRONMENT menu and selects the *Disp DtmPln*, *Disp Axes*, and *Disp Points* menu selections, which switches them from their current settings. By using this method of command execution, you would be turning a 3- to 10-second operation into less than a second. You are probably thinking, "This is great. But how can this be applied when modeling parts or detailing components?"

Improving Design By Using Macros

There are several ways to improve, optimize, and perfect a design. This is a subject that cannot be covered within a single chapter, and I am not trying to claim that the methods discussed in this book are the only options. Realistically, improving and optimizing designs would require an entire book (or two). But for the purposes of our discussion, an optimal design can be developed if you only have enough time to design, analyze, and tweak a developing design. In your search for design perfection, you must have time to *iterate* a design. Because time is not a luxury for most companies, you must do all that you can to produce a design that satisfies the requirements of your company and customer within the available time.

But what are some of the factors that limit you? We have seen in previous chapters that a design's development can be improved tremendously by simply involving all parties early in the development and maintaining their involvement. But on the modeling level, you must find ways to reduce the amount of development time by looking at the things that you spend most of your time doing. Whether you are spending most of your time sketching geometry or adding relatively sketchless features such as draft, rounds, and shells, there is room for improvement.

The Sketcher is one area that is a "time vacuum" for users of Pro/ENGINEER. It is not sketching the geometry that takes the most time, it is all the time you spend executing commands to manipulate geometry. By programming macros to automate the selection and execution of Sketcher functions, you can spend more time sketching and actively working with the geometry, rather than searching the menus for commands.

Of course, this is just one area where you can reduce a significant amount of your development time; there are others that could use just as much attention. For this example, the final part is shown in the following illustration.

Final part of several protrusions and cuts.

Options For Initiating Repetitive Execution 219

If this part were to be started by developing the base, or flange, as the first feature, your sketch might look like the following figure.

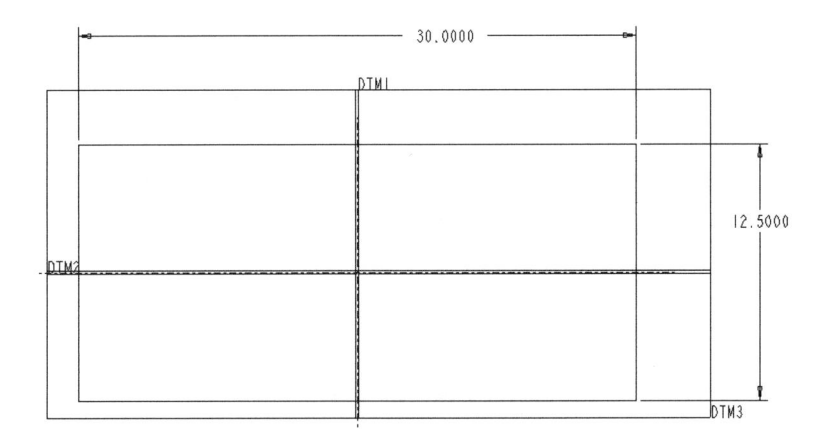

Part's flange sketched protrusion.

The previously shown sketch might have taken anywhere from 1 to 5 minutes (depending on the user) to generate, using the mouse for menu selection and sketching. If you had taken the time to program macros for executing alignment, dimensions, and the sketching of vertical or horizontal lines, you would not only have reduced the amount of time necessary to develop the geometry, but you would have spent more time working on what's important—the geometry.

The next feature that was sketched for this part is shown in the following illustration.

220   **Chapter 9: Improving Design Execution**

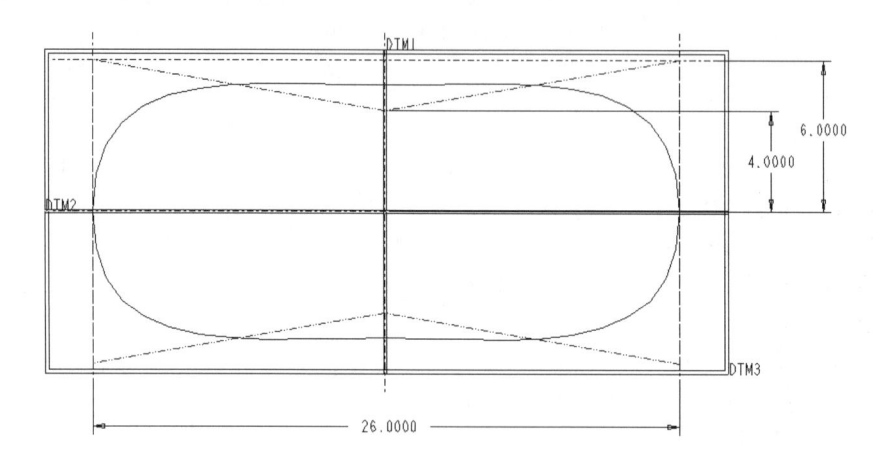

Second feature sketched datum curve.

Notice that this sketch is a little more complicated than the first sketch and requires more development. As before, the use of macros for the geometry's development can significantly reduce the amount of time you spend working on the sketch.

If you were to start and complete the design using the mouse exclusively for all of the menu selections and the sketching of the geometry, you would have spent most of your time picking menus instead of actively working on the geometry. On the other hand, if you used macros to perform most of the menu executions, you would most likely be putting an idle hand to work (punching in the macros on the keyboard), and spending more time working with the geometry. The end results would be a significant reduction in the amount of time you spent developing the part. If there was a problem with design, the time you saved by using the macros could be used to try a different approach to the design's development or improving model flexibility.

The same principles of macro development and execution can be applied to all other areas of Pro/ENGINEER. When detailing in Pro/ENGINEER, common functions such as showing dimensions by view, moving text, and alignment of dimensions are all examples of redundant command use. Whether you are modeling a component, assembly, or detailing a design, macros can significantly reduce the time required for initial development or rework of existing geometry. The number of macros that you program is entirely up to you. My only suggestion is that you have an understanding of the features or commands that you are programming in a macro. Misuse of a feature when you are blindly executing the macro can be a real headache if you do not understand what the features will be doing to the model. Also, it is not a good idea to program every possible command sequence or option into macros. You can do it if you wish, but I am sure that you will find that you will use only a few of the most common functions over and over. In addition, the more macros that you have programmed, the harder it is to remember all the key combinations. Simplicity in optimal feature selection and execution will be key to reducing development time and increasing efficiency.

Multiple Macro Execution By Nesting

One area where macros can be especially useful is in the multiple execution of commands within Pro/ENGINEER. This typically involves the execution of other macros, from a macro, to perform multiple operations. A common application might be to execute the *Purge* command after every *Save* command that you execute. The reason for this may be to preserve space on your hard drive.

To do this you may have a macro programmed to a function key that is set up to *Save* whatever you are currently working on. In addition, you may have an additional macro programmed to a function key that *purges* the current file. Those macros may look like those shown in the following illustration.

Chapter 9: Improving Design Execution

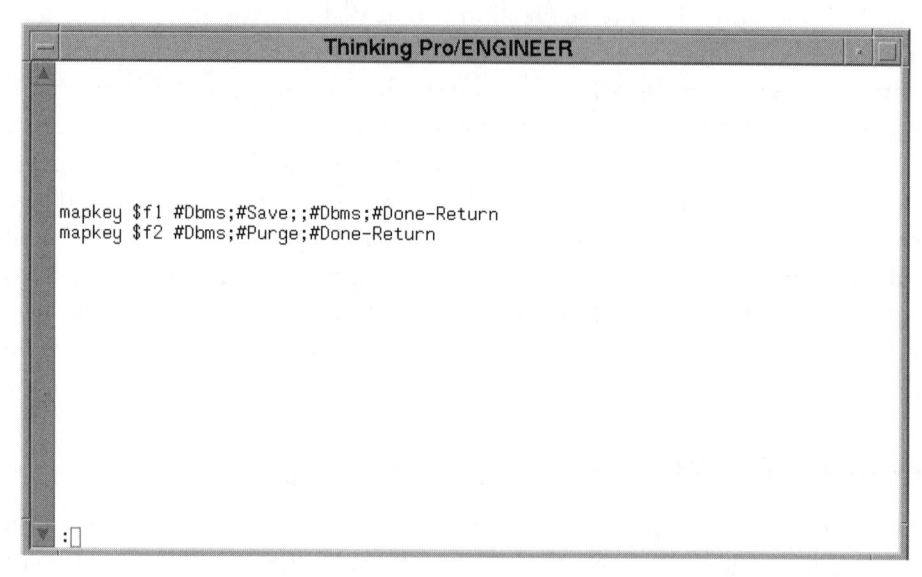

```
┌─────────────────── Thinking Pro/ENGINEER ───────────────────┐
│                                                              │
│                                                              │
│   mapkey $f1 #Dbms;#Save;;#Dbms;#Done-Return                 │
│   mapkey $f2 #Dbms;#Purge;#Done-Return                       │
│                                                              │
│                                                              │
│                                                              │
│                                                              │
│   :                                                          │
└──────────────────────────────────────────────────────────────┘
```

Save and purge macros programmed into a function key.

Because the intent is to have a macro execute another macro, you have a couple of options to accomplish this. The first would be to program a new macro that executes the *save* macro and then follow it with the *purge* macro. That new nested macro may look like the following, when added to the previously shown macro list.

Options For Initiating Repetitive Execution

```
mapkey $f1 #Dbms;#Save;;#Dbms;#Done-Return
mapkey $f2 #Dbms;#Purge;#Done-Return
mapkey $f3 %$f1;%$f2
```

Nested macro added to macro listing.

When you are programming macros in Pro/ENGINEER, you have the option to execute other macros by simply adding a % followed by the other macros' keyin code, to execute the other macro. If the user were to execute F3, Pro/ENGINEER would execute F1 (the *save* macro), followed by the execution of F2 (the *purge* macro). But some of you may not want to add an additional macro to your list of macros. You may want to *nest* the F2 macro call within the F1 macro so that it automatically calls the *purge* macro immediately after execution. This twist to the F1 (*save* macro) scheme may look like the following.

Chapter 9: Improving Design Execution

```
mapkey $f1 #Dbms;#Save;;#Dbms;#Done-Return;%$f2
mapkey $f2 #Dbms;#Purge;#Done-Return
```

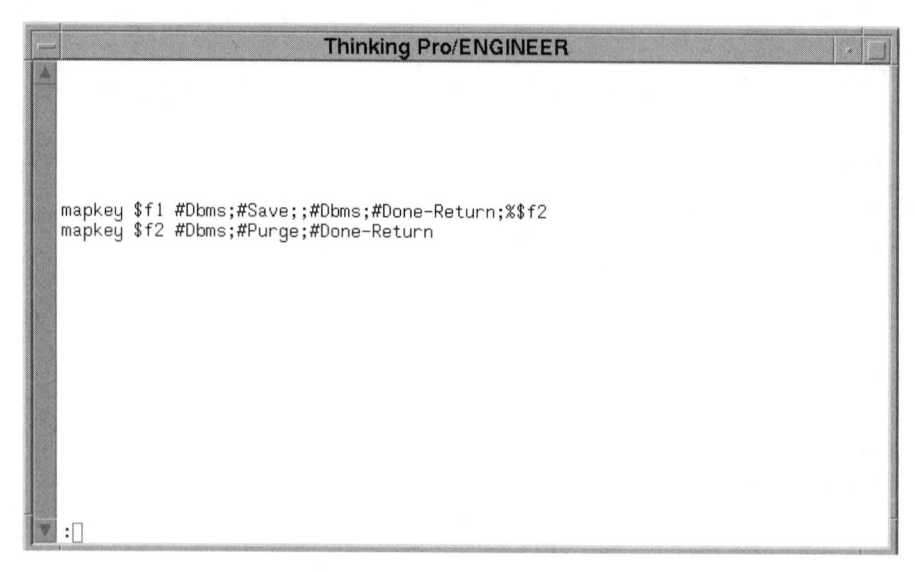

Save macro calls purge macro.

Of course if you wanted to really save keystrokes, you could just add the *purge* functionality into the *save* macro and eliminate the nesting all together. Ultimately, macro setup and functionality is completely up to you. The previous example is only intended to open the door to some additional possibilities for using macros. This technique can come in handy when you are dealing with long macro command sequences.

Another popular example of nesting macros can be found in shading and spinning a model. *Shading* and *spinning* geometry is a fairly common set of executions that the user makes to visualize the design. Shading and spinning are also used commonly as independent functions. This is a good case for the integration of a nested macro to execute the commands sequentially. The following illustration shows a sample macro listing.

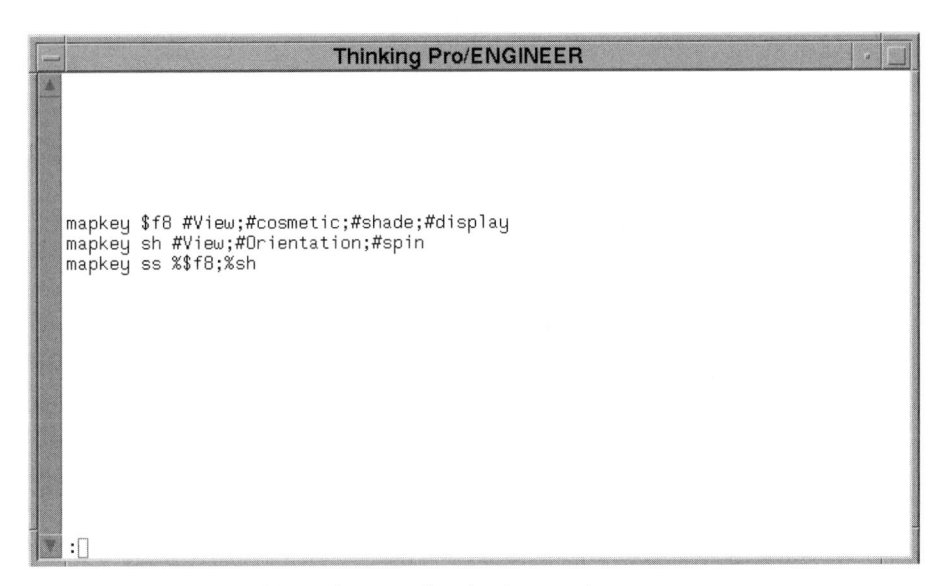

```
mapkey $f8 #View;#cosmetic;#shade;#display
mapkey sh #View;#Orientation;#spin
mapkey ss %$f8;%sh
```

Nested macro for shading and spinning.

As in the previous illustration, the programming of an additional (nested) macro to execute other macros can be useful. Nesting macros can be a powerful tool and ally within Pro/ENGINEER. You must be careful about any nesting that you try to do. The risk is that you may be executing extra commands or performing extra operations and adding time to your designs. In addition, you will be adding additional macros to your list; this means that you will have more to remember. The level of sophistication that you program into your macros is dependent on how much you want the computer to do for you. To save time and space, I recommend that you use nested macros only when you cannot get everything done in one macro, or when it is advantageous, such as the *shade* and *spin* combinations. In the long run, it is better to resolve bulk instructions into one macro and have less to worry about from a setup and execution standpoint.

Things To Keep in Mind

When working with macros, you must keep in mind that a macro will only execute if you are at the right menu location within Pro/ENGINEER to execute

226   **Chapter 9: Improving Design Execution**

the macro. For example, suppose the macro was defined per the following illustration.

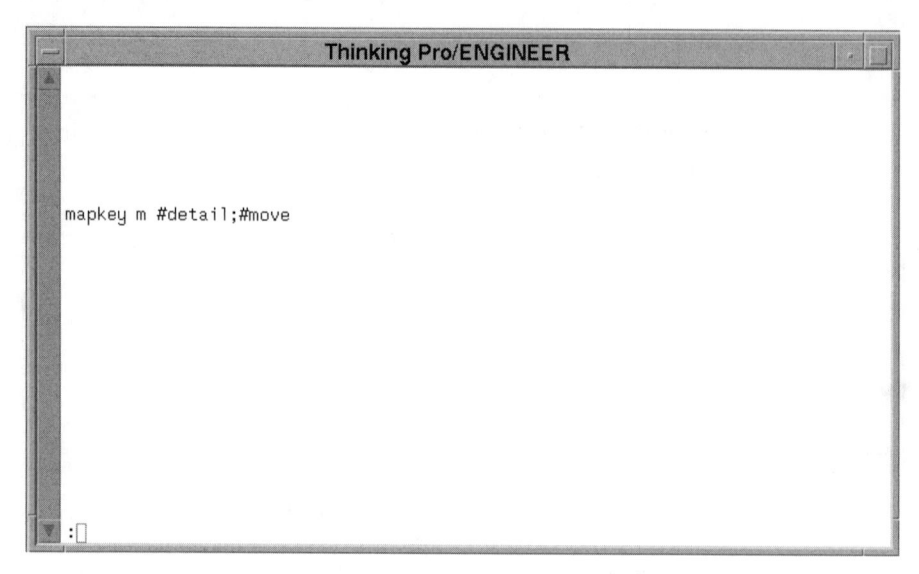

```
Thinking Pro/ENGINEER

mapkey m #detail;#move


:
```

Macro to execute the Move command.

If you were looking at the MODIFY menu, under the DETAIL menu, you might see the following submenu.

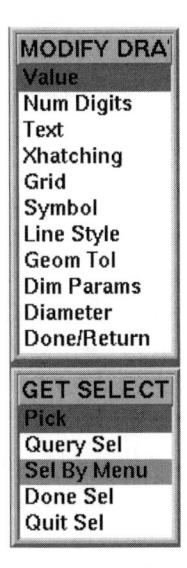

MODIFY menu, submenu of the DETAIL menu.

Because you are not within the top level of the DETAIL menu, you will not be able to execute the move macro that you have programmed. Therefore, you must be at the top level menu or within the menu that your command is located to execute the macro properly.

The creation of macros within Pro/ENGINEER can be time consuming, especially if you are just using the Table Editor for programming the macros. Experienced users have found that it can be easier and faster to manually edit the *config.pro* file using *vi* or some other text editor. This is a nice option because you can edit the file in a separate window, while you are using Pro/ENGINEER. The advantage is that you will be able to accurately transpose the menu command sequences to the *config.pro* file as you select them from the Pro/ENGINEER menus. This gets around being locked into the Table Editor and trying to remember what command was next and whether or not there was a *Done* or a *Done-Return* at the end of the command sequence.

Menu Items

Adding menu items is another technique for improving your use of Pro/EN-GINEER. As briefly discussed in Chapter 3, you have seen that by adding a menu item you don't have to remember a long list of commands to execute a centrally located script or program within Pro/ENGINEER. The addition of a menu item can also be used to navigate a large network or even load multiple configuration files.

Suppose that you are working on several design projects, each of which are deeply located on completely different machines within completely different departments in your company, and that you are not using a product data management system. You could either spend quite a bit of time using the Pro/ENGINEER menus to swim through directories to get to the location of your designs, or you could type in the locations manually (don't lose those Post-It notes on your computer that have all of those directories written down). Either way, you may be taking a lot of time to search through your company's network, or even your own workstation, to locate designs. If you could change from one location, within your network, to another by the click of a mouse, you could virtually eliminate all of the searching through countless directories.

By programming a menu item into your Pro/ENGINEER menu structure you could change to a desired location by simply selecting that menu item. For example, your home directory may look like the following.

```
/usr/people/eng1/
```

If you had to work on three projects that existed on the network, in one day, the directory structures may look like the following.

```
Project = Stampings: Local Drive;
/usr/people/eng1/development/stampings
Project = Japan: Remote Host;
/usr2/manft40/guest/eng_dpt9/japan/osaka/plastics/
    molds
Project = Analysis: Remote Host;
/usr4/anlys3/guest/eng_dpt9/experimental/thermal_
    fluids
```

If you had to float from one area to another several times a day, you could spend a good chunk of your day just changing directories. For some of you, the directories shown previously may seem small.

The addition of a menu item would simplify your transition from one project to another and reduce the amount of time required to perform the operation. To ensure that you don't accidentally select one of the menu items that you will be adding, I recommend that you place them within a submenu. For the

Options For Initiating Repetitive Execution 229

purpose of demonstration, all these new menu items will be placed within the MISCELLANEOUS menu. The new menu looks like that shown in the following illustration.

MISCELLANEOUS menu with new menu items.

As you can see, the project names have been added to the MISCELLANEOUS menu. But as an added bonus, you can program a description of the new menu items so that you will not have to remember each and every aspect of that new menu item. This will also help if another user needs to access a file or directory from your workstation; they will be able to quickly navigate through the network to your projects with ease. When I am traveling and one of my designs is needed by someone back in the office, I can instruct a designer over the phone to click the menu item "XXXXX," which is a lot easier than having to type in a thousand characters for a directory on the network.

Where Are They Kept and How Are They Defined?

Menu items can be added to the Pro/ENGINEER menu structure by simply adding a line of information to the *menu_def.pro* file. This file is generally located within the */proe/text* directory and is only read at the startup of

Chapter 9: Improving Design Execution

Pro/ENGINEER. Therefore, any additions or subtractions to this file can only be accessed if you restart Pro/ENGINEER. The previous menu items *menu_def.pro* definition strings are shown in the following illustration.

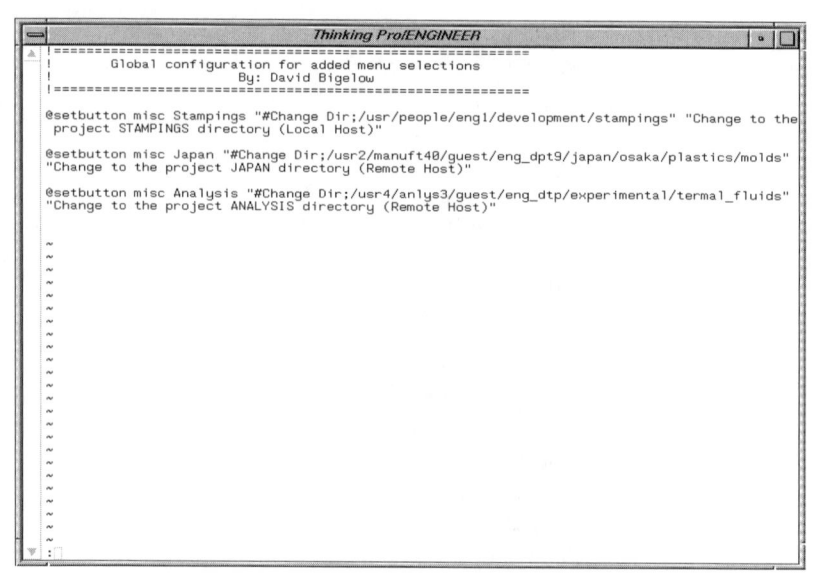

```
!===========================================================
!         Global configuration for added menu selections
!                          By: David Bigelow
!===========================================================
@setbutton misc Stampings "#Change Dir;/usr/people/eng1/development/stampings" "Change to the
project STAMPINGS directory (Local Host)"
@setbutton misc Japan "#Change Dir;/usr2/manuft40/guest/eng_dpt9/japan/osaka/plastics/molds"
"Change to the project JAPAN directory (Remote Host)"
@setbutton misc Analysis "#Change Dir;/usr4/anlys3/guest/eng_dtp/experimental/termal_fluids"
"Change to the project ANALYSIS directory (Remote Host)"
```

The menu_def.pro file contents.

Referencing the above *menu_def.pro* file, you will notice a pattern of definition for the menu items. A dissection of the first menu item within the *menu_def.pro* file would reveal the following:

- ❑ **@setbutton:** Pro/ENGINEER recognizes this as a flag to add the following strings of information into the Pro/ENGINEER menu structure.

- ❑ **misc:** This is the menu that the menu item will be added to.

- ❑ **Stampings:** This is actual menu item name that will be added to the menu (what the user will see on the screen).

- ❑ **"#change Dir;/usr/people/eng1/development/stampings":** This is the command sequence that is executed when the menu item is selected by the user.

- ❑ **"Change to the project STAMPINGS directory (Local Host)":** This is the description that would be presented in your message window as you placed your mouse over this menu selection.

All of this may seem like a lot of definition for a simple menu item. But if you use this technique for quickly accessing different directories, or even executing other commands within the Pro/ENGINEER environment, I am sure that you will find that they can save significant amounts of time.

Things To Keep in Mind

Menu items can be a method of improving your speed and use of Pro/ENGINEER. However, they should be used sparingly and properly placed so that they are functional to your needs. Most people who use menu items have added items such as *shading* and *spinning* functionality to the MAIN menu to improve access to these functions. The MAIN menu would look similar to the following illustration with these additions:

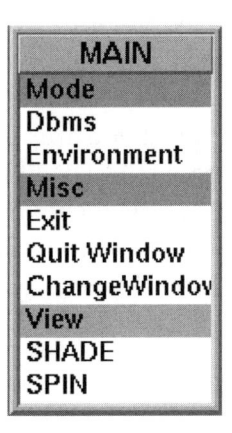

MAIN menu with added view functions.

If you are dedicated to using the mouse instead of programming a macro for this simple addition of a menu item, then this very well may help to reduce a few menu picks. But the additional menu items that you have placed on the menu tend to clutter the screen, especially if the commands you are executing are only one menu away.

Use menu items for more complex or in-depth command execution, such as showing dimensions by a view, changing to directories with long character listings, or whatever you think could be simplified by the addition of a menu item. For other guidelines and suggestions for definition and execution, please refer to the *Pro/ENGINEER Fundamentals* guide.

Running Multiple Configurations

Have you ever been working on a design in Part mode when a rush detailing job gets pushed to the front of your stack? There are many people who are actively using macros to improve execution, and quite a few who have also discovered the power of using menu items. What is surprising is the number of people who will either have a very large *config.pro* file that contains all of the users macros for modeling, detailing, manufacturing operations, etc., or they will have several configuration files that they rename to *"config.pro"* and then restart Pro/ENGINEER.

One of the problems with having all of your macros located within a single file, aside from the difficulty in remembering a lot of key sequences, is that you may not have the ability to use the same macro keys for different functions. For example, you may prefer to have the *m* key programmed to execute the *Modify* command when in Part mode, the *Move* command when you are detailing, or *Mod part* when working in an assembly. This could present some problems, especially if you are spending a lot of time renaming configuration files and restarting Pro/ENGINEER every time you change from one mode of operation to the next. Is there an easier way? You bet there is.

Suppose that the following macros were programmed into your *config.pro* file, which was automatically loaded when you started Pro/ENGINEER.

```
                  Thinking Pro/ENGINEER
mapkey k #sketch
mapkey tb #Geom Tools;#Trim;Bound
mapkey tc #Geom Tools;#Trim;#Corner
mapkey go #Sec Tools;#Grid;#Grid On/Off
mapkey m #Modify
mapkey zz %k;#Line;#Centerline
mapkey z+ %k;#Line;#Centerline;Vertical
mapkey z- %k;#Line;Centerline;Horizontal
mapkey ++ %k;#Line;#Vertical
mapkey -- %k;#Line;#Horizontal
mapkey 2t %k;#Line;#2 Tangent
!/ *************************************

!/ ************ Modeling Macros ***************
mapkey crd #Feature;#Create;#Tweak;#Draft;%d
mapkey csc #feature;#create;#surface;#new;#copy;#done
mapkey csd #feature;#create;#tweak;#draft;#split;#done
mapkey csm #feature;#create;#surface;#merge
mapkey cso #feature;#create;#surface;#new;#offset;#done
mapkey e #Enter
mapkey gt #set up;#geom tol
mapkey gck #info;#geom check
mapkey l #loop
mapkey pp #misc;#design;#quit window;#part;#search/retr;#in session
mapkey pd #misc;#detail;#quit window;#drawing;#search/retr;#in session
mapkey q #wuery sel
mapkey u #delete;#undelete last
mapkey m #modify
mapkey h #chain
mapkey o #Okay
mapkey f #Flip
mapkey rdf #Feature;#Redefine
mapkey rc #Feature;#Create;#Round;%d
mapkey rss #Feature;#Create;#Round;#Surf-Surf;%d
mapkey rv #feature;#create;#round;#variable;#done
mapkey x #quit
mapkey 1 #center
mapkey 2 #tangent
!/ *************************************
```

Original config.pro file.

The macros shown may be designed for modeling components in Part mode. If you need to switch from Part mode to Drawing mode and want to load a configuration file that used some of the same keys to execute the macros, what do you think would happen? Do you think that Pro/ENGINEER would simply overwrite the existing mapkey definition with the new one in the new file? Or would Pro/ENGINEER simply default to the mapkeys that have already been programmed? Before you answer, look at the following configuration file; to avoid confusion with the original *config.pro* file we will call this file *config.dtl*.

Chapter 9: Improving Design Execution

```
Thinking Pro/ENGINEER
mapkey $f7 #View;#Pan/Zoom;#Reset;;
mapkey $f8 #View;#cosmetic;#shade;#display;;
mapkey $f9 #View;#Names;#iso;;
mapkey $f10 #detail;#show;#Dimension;#feat & view
mapkey $f11 #Dbms;#Save;;#Dbms;#Purge;;
mapkey $f12 #View;#Repaint;#done-return;;
mapkey s #View;#Orientation;#spin
mapkey d #Done
!/ ***************************************

!/ **********  Drawing Macros  **********
mapkey a #detail;#move Attach
mapkey b #Pick many;#pick box
mapkey e #detail;#erase;#dimension
mapkey f #detail;#flip arrows
mapkey gt #detail;#create;#geom tol
mapkey i #detail;#create;#draft;#tools;#intersect
mapkey k #detail;#create;#draft;#sketch
mapkey l #detail;#clip
mapkey m #detail;#move
mapkey nd #modify;#num digits
mapkey o #okay
mapkey q #query sel
mapkey pp #misc;#design;#quit window;#part;#search/retr;#in session
mapkey pd #misc;#detail;#quit window;#drawing;#search/retr;#in session
mapkey w #detail;#switch view
mapkey v #modify;#text;full note
mapkey x #quit
mapkey 1 #center
mapkey 2 #tangent
mapkey 3 #detail;#create;#draft;#sketch;#arc;#3 points
mapkey 4 #detail;#create;#dimension
mapkey ` #return
mapkey tb #detail;#tools;#trim;#boundry
mapkey tc #detail;#tools;#trim;#corner
mapkey ++ %k;#line;#vert line
mapkey -- %k;#line;#horiz line
!/ ***************************************
```

User-defined detailing configuration file config.dtl.

Comparing these two short configuration files, it is obvious that there are a number of macros that have been programmed to the same mapkey. If you were to load this new *config.dtl* file over the original *config.pro* file, you would find that the *m* mapkey would be executing the *Move* command. But on the other hand, some of the other macros that do not overwrite the original *config.pro* file are active and do execute properly. Why is this so?

Suppose that you had mapkeys loaded when you started Pro/ENGINEER. When you load a new configuration file with mapkeys programmed to a specific key sequence that may already be active in Pro/ENGINEER, Pro/ENGINEER will execute whatever mapkeys are currently in memory, even if you load five different configuration files that do not overwrite mapkeys from when you first started Pro/ENGINEER. This can present some serious problems if some of your configuration files use nested mapkeys. Picture loading several configuration files to work in different modules of Pro/ENGINEER. During this process, you have loaded a nested macro that executes other key sequences that have been overwritten by later configuration files. For example, a key sequence that once instructed Pro/ENGINEER to select a tool and save the part, now quits the part and tries to shade an image. These multiple configuration problems can interfere with efficient design execution and force you to spend time fighting the system.

If you are bound and determined to use the same character sets for other configurations, you can introduce what I call a *config.clear* file. This is basically a way to eliminate the possibility of executing false instructions because of dysfunctional mapkey relationships. This will permit you to use the same *m* key for both *Modify* (in Part mode) and *Move* (in Drawing mode), as well as use nested macros specifically designed for a particular mode, *without* exiting, renaming files, and restarting Pro/ENGINEER. The key is to develop a completely new file that comments out the mapkeys that have been loaded into memory. The following illustration shows the new file.

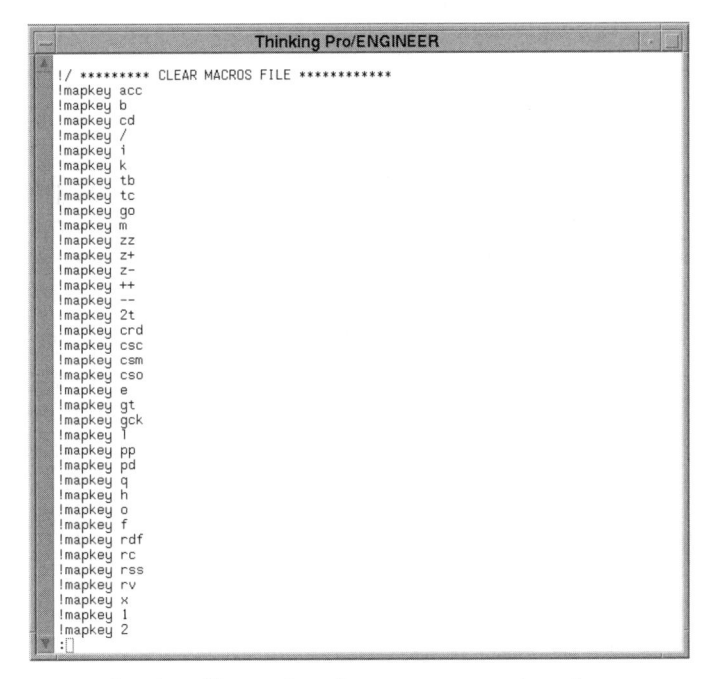

```
!/ ********* CLEAR MACROS FILE *************
!mapkey acc
!mapkey b
!mapkey cd
!mapkey /
!mapkey i
!mapkey k
!mapkey tb
!mapkey tc
!mapkey go
!mapkey m
!mapkey zz
!mapkey z+
!mapkey z-
!mapkey ++
!mapkey --
!mapkey 2t
!mapkey crd
!mapkey csc
!mapkey csm
!mapkey cso
!mapkey e
!mapkey gt
!mapkey gck
!mapkey l
!mapkey pp
!mapkey pd
!mapkey q
!mapkey h
!mapkey o
!mapkey f
!mapkey rdf
!mapkey rc
!mapkey rss
!mapkey rv
!mapkey x
!mapkey 1
!mapkey 2
:
```

Same config.clear file used to clear existing mapkeys from memory.

Suppose that you loaded Pro/ENGINEER, which references the *config.pro* file that contains all of the macros for modeling in Part mode, and you were required to detail some components. By simply loading the *config.clear* configuration file, which will "comment out" the existing mapkeys, and then loading the *config.dtl* configuration, which contains all of your macros for detailing, you would have successfully loaded all the detailing macros. In essence, you are now able to use the same key sequences cross-functionally, without having to worry about dysfunctional nested macros, rename a bunch of files, or exit the system.

Once you finish with your detailing functions or just need to do some more modeling, you simply reload the *config.clear* file and then the original *config.pro* file. The only difference here is that you would be clearing out the mapkeys for the *config.dtl* file so that you could use the mapkeys in the *config.pro* file for modeling in Part mode. But what are the risks of using this method of clearing and reloading configurations?

Probably the biggest thing that you must remember for loading and using multiple configuration files is that you must be sure that each and every mapkey that you have programmed in all of your configuration files must be included within the *config.clear* file. The reason for this is simple: if you forget to include a mapkey within the *config.clear* file, you may accidentally execute a macro that uses nested mapkeys. This is not a high risk; your new macro will not work, but it can be a frustration to debug as you are pounding the keyboard in a futile attempt to execute that macro. The implementation of a *config.clear* file can be used to maintain order from one configuration to the next.

This technique may not be optimum for each and every user of Pro/ENGI-NEER. You ultimately must decide what methods of configuration and execution you are comfortable with, and I strongly urge you to take the time to experiment with each method until you find the ones that work for you.

Making the Transitions Slick

So you have learned a little about improving your execution of commands within Pro/ENGINEER. And you have also learned about adding menu items and running multiple configurations. Which brings us to the next obvious step—bringing it all together to make your transitions from one mode to another as slick and seamless as possible.

By adding menu items and executing commands through macros, you can integrate some of the configurations within the Pro/ENGINEER menu structure. But why would you want to do this? If you recall, the addition of a menu item can relieve you from remembering a whole list of commands and can place needed or commonly used functionality at a location that is easy for the user to access.

Let's say that you would like to be able to change from one configuration to the next, without having to manually execute all of the commands to successfully change from one mode of operation to the next. You could add a menu item for each configuration file that managed the execution of all of the commands, and the loading of all of the files necessary to change to a new configuration. That menu item, within the *menu_def.pro* file, may look like that shown in the following illustration.

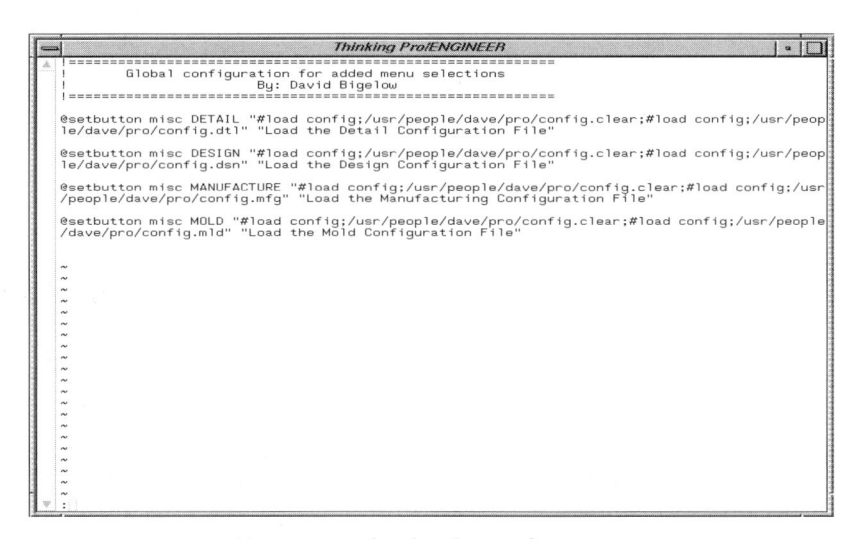

```
!==============================================================
!          Global configuration for added menu selections
!                        By: David Bigelow
!==============================================================
@setbutton misc DETAIL "#load config;/usr/people/dave/pro/config.clear;#load config;/usr/peop
le/dave/pro/config.dtl" "Load the Detail Configuration File"
@setbutton misc DESIGN "#load config;/usr/people/dave/pro/config.clear;#load config;/usr/peop
le/dave/pro/config.dsn" "Load the Design Configuration File"
@setbutton misc MANUFACTURE "#load config;/usr/people/dave/pro/config.clear;#load config;/usr
/people/dave/pro/config.mfg" "Load the Manufacturing Configuration File"
@setbutton misc MOLD "#load config;/usr/people/dave/pro/config.clear;#load config;/usr/people
/dave/pro/config.mld" "Load the Mold Configuration File"
```

Menu items that load a configuration.

As you can see from the *menu_def.pro* file, a *config.clear* file is being loaded prior to the configuration file that you are intending to use. What you are doing by configuring the menu item definition string like this is ensuring that the *config.clear* file overwrites any mapkeys that are currently loaded in memory. When the configuration file is loaded, immediately and automatically after the *config.clear* file, all of the macros will be usable. All you would see when you were running Pro/ENGINEER would be the following.

Chapter 9: Improving Design Execution

```
         Misc
List Dir
Show Dir
Change Dir
System
Load Config
Edit Config
Trail
Train
SystemColors
List Options
Product Info
Picture
Time
Done-Return
DETAIL
DESIGN
MANUFACTUR
MOLD
```

MISCELLANEOUS menu with added configuration items.

Therefore, the selection of any of the new menu items would automatically load that configuration file and ensure that you could use the contents of that file. But how can this be improved further?

Simply developing a macro, or set of macros, in the *config.pro* file that will automatically take you from one mode to another can automate the transitions and give you more time to work on fulfilling the requirements of the design. For example, the addition of the following mapkey to the *config.pro* file will *quit* you from your existing window, load a new configuration file for detailing, access the Drawing mode, and search for any drawings that are currently in session.

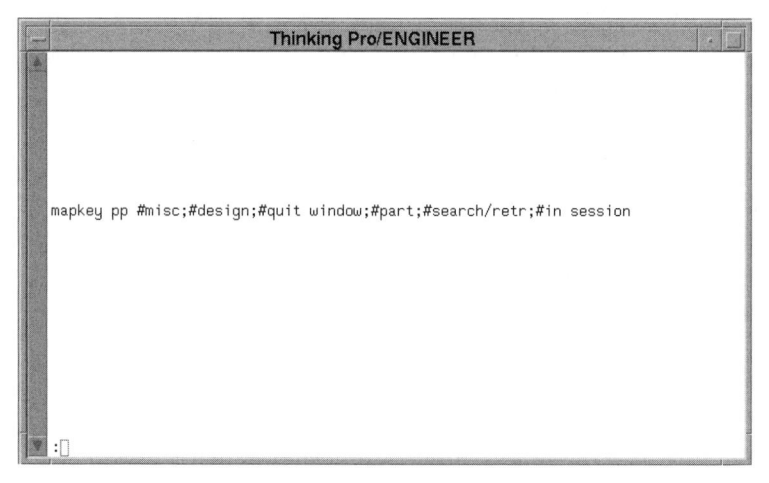

```
mapkey pp #misc;#design;#quit window;#part;#search/retr;#in session
```

New macro to execute switching from one mode to another.

The amount of time that these two key macros will save may not seem like a lot, but by just executing these two key macros, you are performing a whole list of redundant tasks that you would have to do anyway, and as an added bonus you will be loading the proper configuration file to operate in the new mode that you will be accessing.

Summary

There are several ways to improve, optimize, and perfect a design. An optimal design can be developed if you only have enough time to design, analyze, and tweak a developing design. In your search for design perfection, you must have time to iterate a design. Because time is not a luxury for most companies, you must do all you can to produce a design that satisfies the requirements of your company and customer within the available time. You must find ways to reduce the amount of development time by looking at the things that you spend most of your time doing. Whether you are spending most of your time sketching geometry or adding relatively sketchless features such as draft, rounds, and shells, there is room for improvement!

This chapter focused on a number of user-definable methods for improving your use of Pro/ENGINEER by reducing the amount of time you spend performing operations. Use the examples and topics that were discussed as some options for the future or for solving current problems by improving execution of command sequences.

Use macros, menu items, or combinations of the two with caution. It can be frustrating to program hundreds of macros in an attempt to cover each and every option within Pro/ENGINEER. In the end, you may have programmed too much to remember, which could lead to misexecution of commands. Avoid the headaches of overprogramming by keeping things functional and simple and only for features that you understand and use frequently.

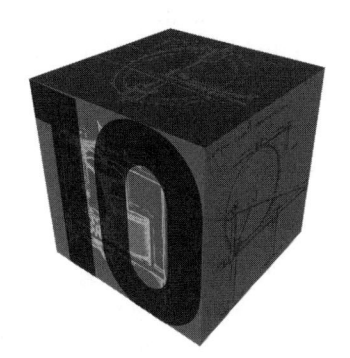

Analysis

Introduction

After several days working on completing a design, you send off the database for analysis. The person in charge of setting up, running, and interpreting the results spends another several days tearing apart the design to reduce the amount of data to only the critical elements necessary for performing the analysis. After the database has been reduced to its minimum amount of geometry, the analyst transfers the database out of Pro/ENGINEER and into the analysis package. Once in the analysis package, the analyst then develops all the constraints and any additional element definition that may be required. Once the conversion, setup, and definition have been completed, the analysis is run, and the results are logged for future comparison. From the first round of analysis, it becomes apparent to the analyst that the design could be improved by adding some ribs and adding or increasing some radii on some sharp corners.

Because the initial results were not promising, a series of design iterations are performed within the analysis package to try and improve the design. Because your company has invested in software that can iterate to a solution based on geometric design constraints within the analysis package, your design can be improved and refined to reduce the amount of mass and minimize the stress in the part. After the design has been optimized in the finite element analysis (FEA) package, your analyst returns with a list of dimensional and geometric modifications that should be made to the design.

During your review of the recommendations, you discover that a significant amount of rework will be required to satisfy any optimization that may have been completed in the analysis package. Now you have some difficult decisions to make. Should you take the time to incorporate the design suggestions and computer optimizations, knowing that it may take anywhere from a few hours to a few days, or can you live with the additional weight and a little bit more stress in the component? These are some big questions, and there are many opinions as to whether or not to incorporate the results given to you by the analyst. Based on the levels of stress and weight of the current design, you decide that the amount of rework required would not be warranted due to the amount of time that is needed to incorporate the changes. Sometimes there is more emphasis on meeting your timing for the design rather than getting into the cycle of design optimization.

Could anything have been done to improve the design cycle that was just outlined? Are there areas that could be improved to reduce time and communicate the design intent? The answer to both of these questions is, of course, yes.

Improving Communication

What would have happened if the analysis cycle was performed with the wrong grade of material or an improper set of constraints? Most likely, you would have had to go back and reestablish the design intent and rerun and optimize the models. One of the biggest communication gaps of the design intent is in the transfer of the design problems and goals from the engineer to the analyst. A number of you wear many hats in your company. But in general, the design's requirements, limitations, operating conditions, and goals can be difficult to communicate. This lack of communication can bring a design to its knees, especially when the results are misinterpreted or the constraints improperly applied to the FEA model.

Improving Communication 243

You can do several simple things to improve the preparation and transfer of the design from a production model to a model that is functional for the purpose of analysis. Whether you are preparing data for transfer via the IGES format or another method into a separate analysis package or preparing the information for a package that is closely integrated in Pro/ENGINEER, these techniques can be used for both methods. Suppose that you are designing a sand casting, and the final design looks like that shown in the following illustration.

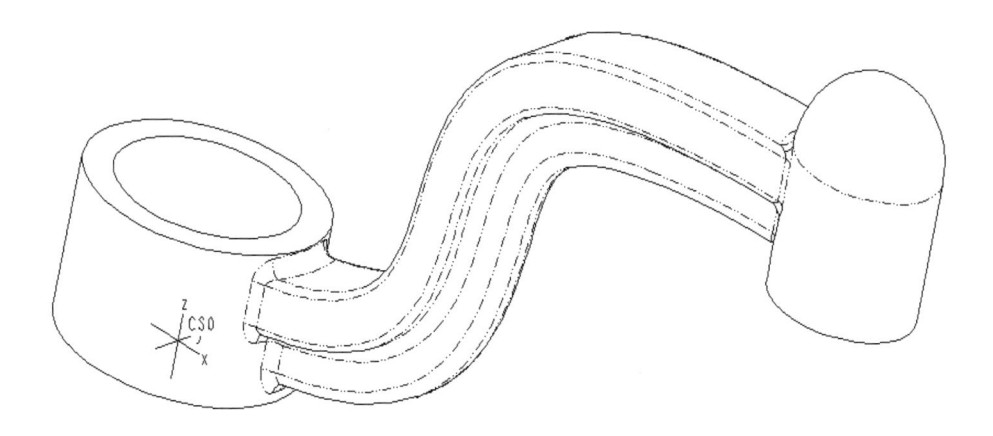

Final design of sand casting.

As you can see from the illustration, there are a number of small rounds that were added to the model to improve the manufacturability of the component. For all you "purists" who want to get down to the nitty gritty, these rounds could contribute to reducing the stresses at the corner interfaces. But for the purpose of analysis, a straight-walled geometry could be used to establish an approximation of the stresses and displacements in the component for a given set of loads. Because this detail may not be necessary to perform FEA on this component, you may have to eliminate, or temporarily remove, some of the geometry that is nonessential to FEA.

Remember, this is done to improve the analysis phase by eliminating the need for the analyst to remodel or alter your valuable data. When working with the Pro/ENGINEER database, I have found that a number of analysts request that geometry that is not essential to FEA be layered so that those

Chapter 10: Analysis

features can be selectively suppressed, thereby simplifying the database for mesh generation. The thinking behind this is that there are some features that may be required for the production of the component, but may not have a significant impact on the overall design for analysis. The suppression of nonessential geometry will help to reduce the size (i.e., number of elements) of the finite element mesh, which is directly related to the amount of time it takes to perform the calculations.

For example, the previously shown design may be marked to have the following rounds layered and suppressed from the model so that a finite element mesh can be easily generated.

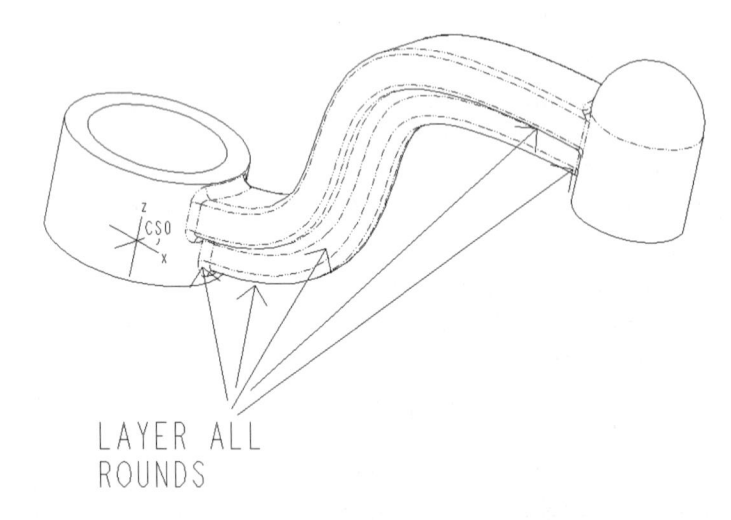

Markup of casting, round suppression.

By simply creating a layer called *ROUNDS* for the part, you will be reducing the amount of effort required to prepare the model. The previously shown markup indicates the analyst's requirements for submission of the database. Some companies who regularly engage in analyzing designs from the Pro/ENGINEER database have adopted an internal standard for how designs are to be submitted for analysis. These requirements extend beyond the basic requirements for design flexibility and functional dimensioning schemes and are geared toward preserving the data that will serve as the master. This ensures that the design and detailing on the drawings that you will be sending

Improving Communication 245

to production will perform as mathematically anticipated by using FEA. The final finite element model of the design might look like the following illustration in Pro/ENGINEER.

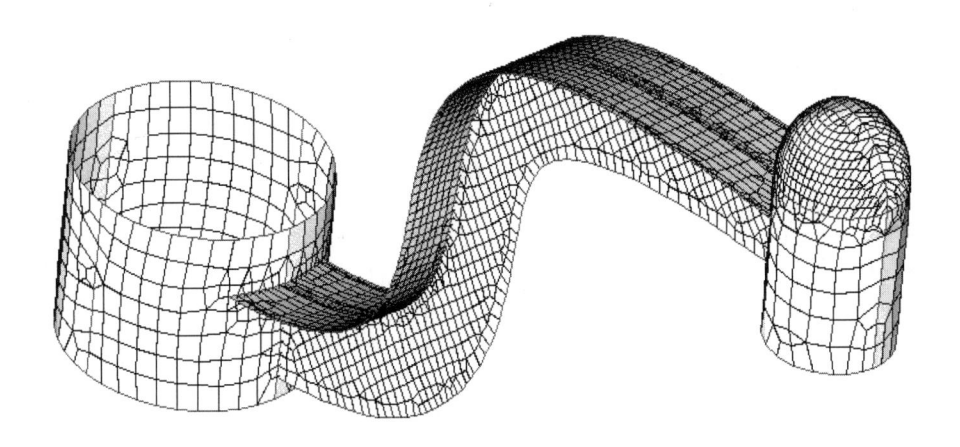

Finite element mesh of the simplified casting (with no loads, mesh only).

What if the analysis results of the mesh contained too much stress in the corner of the part? Remember, this design's finite element mesh is currently being described with a sharp corner (a high stress concentration). If the master database was not being used as the reference for the analysis, any attempts to reduce the levels of stress by the addition of a round may require the analyst to manually add radii into the model. If the part was required to have a shell follow the application of the round to ensure constant wall thickness, the analyst may spend more time trying to find a location in the database to which the geometry could be added versus just analyzing the design. If you have included the radii on the *Layer* that is being used to suppress all geometry not essential to FEA, the analyst could maintain the design intent of the component by unlayering the features of interest, remeshing the design, and interpreting the results.

This does several positive things at once:

1. It ensures that the model that is being used satisfies your design requirements.

2. Your master data is preserved.

3. Evaluation of any modifications to the design will be much easier to interpret.
4. Once the analysis has been completed, any modifications to the original design can be created to improve the communication of any design change proposals.

Whether or not you are using Pro/MESH to apply all your load cases to the Pro/ENGINEER database, you should send along a list of design goals and requirements for the design in general. Sending the file with the ability to be simplified for finite element mesh generation and the application of the load cases is not enough. It is important that you spend time with the person who will be setting up, running, and interpreting the results. You must educate the analyst as to the purpose of the analysis and what you hope to gain from the process, that is, simple static load analysis, forced response, weight reduction, topology optimization, etc. If you do not take the time to educate the people who will be performing the analysis, you should not expect miracles when the results come back. Taking the time to discuss and explain the objectives can save days of work and rework due to possible misinterpretation in analysis requirements.

Meshing

The mesh shown previously, as you might suspect, was developed in Pro/ENGINEER using Pro/MESH. There are a number of advantages to using this module, just are there are some disadvantages. But for this application, Pro/MESH proved to be easy to use for the generation, application of loads, and mesh constraints. But Pro/MESH may not be for everyone. There are some types of analysis software available that do not even use the types of elements that Pro/MESH generates (H-Elements). But aside from the obvious, there may be a number of other limitations that you encounter. Some types of analysis require things such as node coupling (which mathematically constrains an element node to move with a relationship) or specific element types that may not be currently available such as eight-node quadrilateral or "brick" solid elements (which may be preferred because of model accuracy).

If you were to look at your analysis software manuals, you may find anywhere from three to well over a hundred types of elements, each with a specific set of properties and requirements. Pro/MESH is not the answer to all of your analysis setup and computational requirements. However, if your intent is to use the database as much as possible to ensure that the finite element mesh truly captures the design intent, you can perform all of your meshing and a good portion of your constraints development prior to exporting the mesh into your analysis package. There are of course several analysis packages that either can be executed from within Pro/ENGINEER or use an automated conversion and meshing program to seamlessly transfer your design from Pro/ENGINEER into the analysis package. This saves time, and you will not have to work on recreating the geometry either from scratch or by fitting mesh geometry to an IGES database. The real payoffs come when a change to the design is required.

Looking at the following initial design, it is estimated that the hole in the top of the part needs to be opened up to approximately 1.5 times its current size. This may seem like a simple change to the finite element model, and for most systems it would not take long to integrate the change. But using Pro/MESH this change can be accomplished just by simply modifying the dimension for the opening and remeshing.

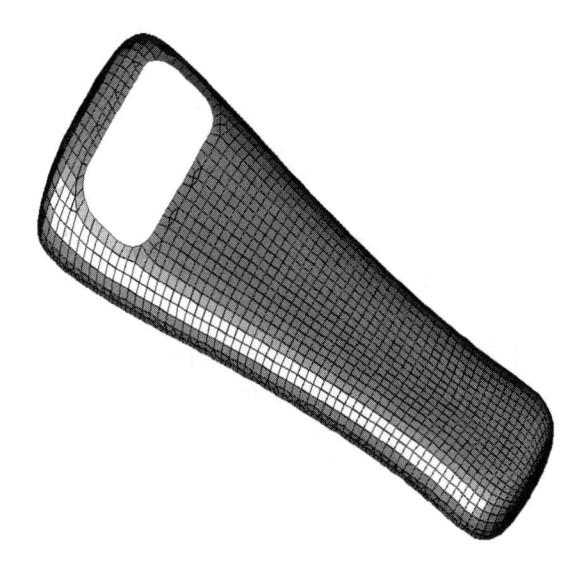

Finite element mesh.

Finite element mesh after model change.

Efficient changes in the design can be easily accomplished provided that the model and mesh have been properly constrained to accept the change in design. This is another advantage to using this module for mesh generation in Pro/ENGINEER. The ability to have the mesh adapt to changes in the design leads to another exciting area of the design process—optimization.

Design Optimization

The concept and application of design optimization have been discussed and performed for a number of years. But the tools and techniques for design optimization have generally only recently (within the last 5 to 7 years) captured the eye of a much larger engineering community. Currently, there are a number of analysis packages available that include tools to perform routine analysis and also to iterate to a solution based on the user's constraints for the size of the components' features. This new technology and approach to design has and will continue to improve the way we all do business and design components.

Design Optimization 249

For those of you who have spent any amount of time setting up, performing, and interpreting finite element models, you know that in the past, your hands were tied to the current design under consideration. Once your analysis and evaluation of the results were complete, you probably made your best guess as to the modifications to the model that would be required for the change. For this primitive attempt at design optimization, you took the time to correct the model and rerun the analysis. This best-guessing method of design optimization is like shooting a gun at a target blindfolded. You are not exactly sure what your results will be but you at least know there is a target out there. The risk was, and still is, that the changes that you are making to the design may or may not be feasible, cost effective, and necessary.

Using the old method of design optimization, your initial model of a typical corner interface might look like the one in the following illustration.

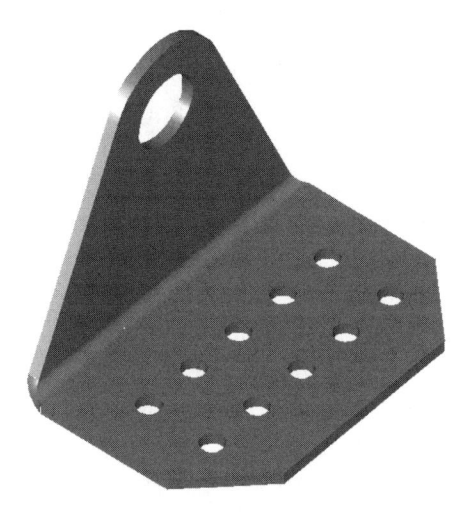

Original design, corner with radii.

Suppose that the stress levels at the base of this intersection were too high for the design's requirements; you select a different radii size in Pro/ENGINEER, remesh the model, export the design, and reanalyze the component. Your new model looks like that shown in the following illustration.

250   Chapter 10: Analysis

First manual iteration of original design, larger radii.

If this new radii value were not large enough to reduce the stress levels to an acceptable level, you would have to go and generate a new finite element mesh and rerun the analysis with yet another radii value. You could have set up several instances of the part, each instance with a different value to be evaluated. This is of course a form of design iteration. But I'm sorry to inform you that in all of that time you spent modifying the part and remeshing and analyzing all the design options, you could have optimized the design by just establishing the feature's size limits and letting the computer do all the work for you.

Your limits of size might look like those shown in the following illustration.

Design Optimization 251

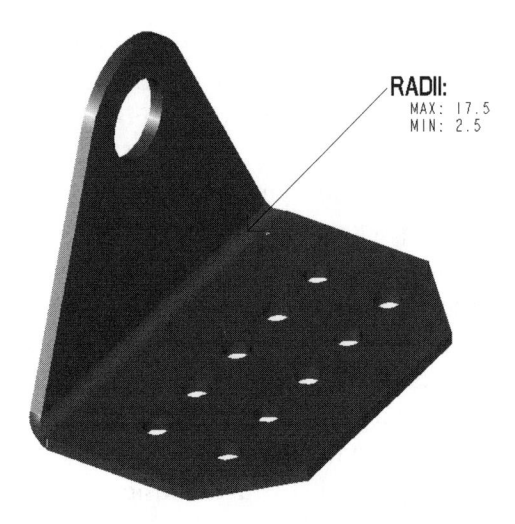

Original radii with limits of size (maximum and minimum values).

The illustration shows the user-defined maximum and minimum values for the feature. These limits may have been established to satisfy packaging, manufacturing, or any other number of design- and process-related requirements. And the limits of size that you have established may not satisfy the optimization requirements that you are looking for. But, if the range of possible values has been realistically established and the model that you have developed can adapt to the iterative changes that may be required, you can quickly optimize this design problem and obtain results with a higher level of confidence than with the traditional method of using the next best guess. For this simple example, with one design variable, optimization may be achieved rather quickly.

✍ **NOTE:** *However, the more variables that you designate for design optimization, the longer your computer will take to achieve convergence to your design constraints.*

Using the Design for Optimization

Optimization of a design can generally be accomplished in either one of two ways: (1) using the Pro/ENGINEER database and Pro/MESH or (2) using the analysis software's mesh to define and iterate model features (independent of the Pro/ENGINEER database). Each method of geometry manipulation is valid and can help to reduce the amount of design time required for a design. But if you are going to be successful in your design, you must be sure that the design is capable of adapting to change, that is, the design must be flexible. If the design is not flexible, any optimization attempts that you try can give you a headache quickly, at least for FEA packages that use the Pro/ENGINEER model for design iterations. This is a key example for the need to ensure that your designs are flexible and accurate. If your designs are not flexible, you will not only create problems when it comes to making simple changes, but also when it comes to using more advanced design and manufacturing tools within Pro/ENGINEER where the design's flexibility can make all the difference.

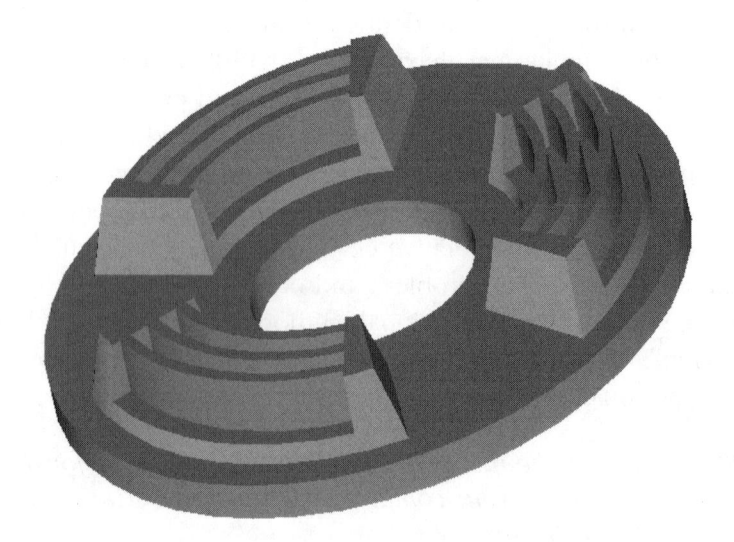

"Sculpted" nonfunctional design.

Suppose that the design shown previously was developed by a master Pro/ENGINEER "sculptor." This design has a number of imperfections, such as thin edges that were the result of all of the individual cuts performed to the model. Pro/MESH may not allow shell element geometry due to the system's inability to pair surfaces. And during an attempt to generate the mesh you are required to use tetrahedral mesh elements with a very fine resolution, just to get a mesh. The mesh is shown in the following illustration.

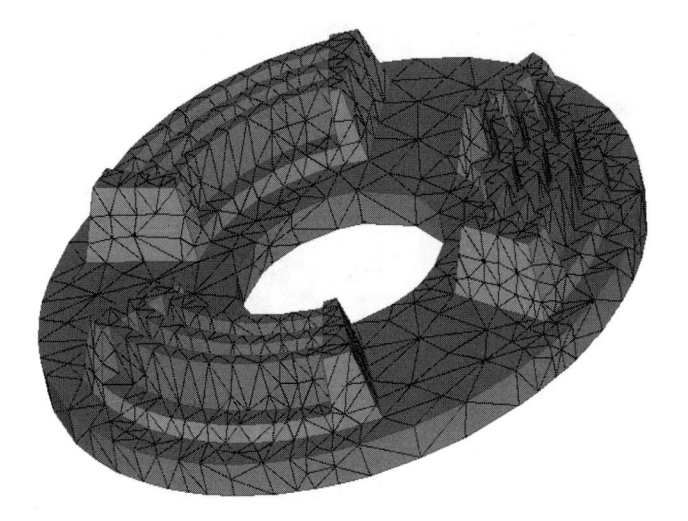

FEA mesh of sculpted design.

Suppose that the design was exported to the FEA package, and the results took several hours to compute due in part to the number of elements in the model. The results of the analysis may indicate that a change in the thickness of the mating flange will vastly reduce the stress levels in the component and yield a better design. With this information, you try to change the flange thickness to improve the design. Because the model was not developed to ensure flexibility, you have to sit through and evaluate several parent/child conflicts and geometry errors that prompt you to review the problems using *Geom Check*. After you finally manage to regenerate the model after searching for all the features and children of those features to modify to ensure the correct results, you access the FEA module and try to remesh the model. This time you have to work around several aspect ratio and distortion issues that have arisen because of the changes. No matter how you look at it, in order to perform design optimization, you must be set up to quickly make transitions in design from one stage to the next with ease and efficiency.

254   Chapter 10: Analysis

The same design developed with a logical approach to the model development, properly established and maintained parent/child relationships, and easy to modify is shown in the following illustration.

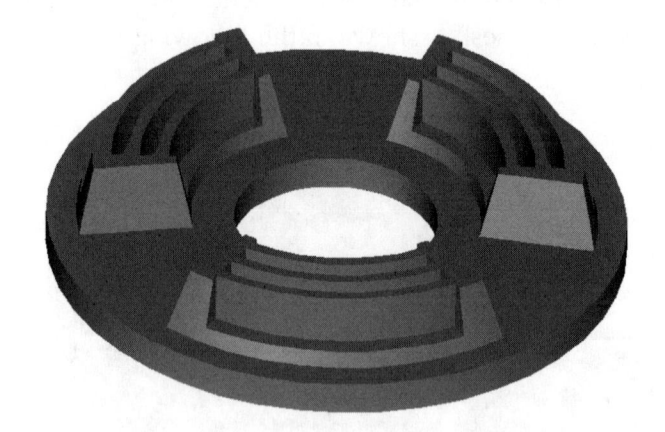

Same design, fully parametric and flexible.

In this case, because the design was properly developed in Pro/ENGINEER to ensure flexibility and proper feature relationships, you do not have any geometry errors in the model. This correlates to the user's ability to investigate the use of larger elements, and even the possibility of using shell elements extensively throughout the design, which ultimately reduces the size of the FEA model and therefore the amount of time required to perform the computations.

The FEA model for this parametric/flexible model might look like the following illustration.

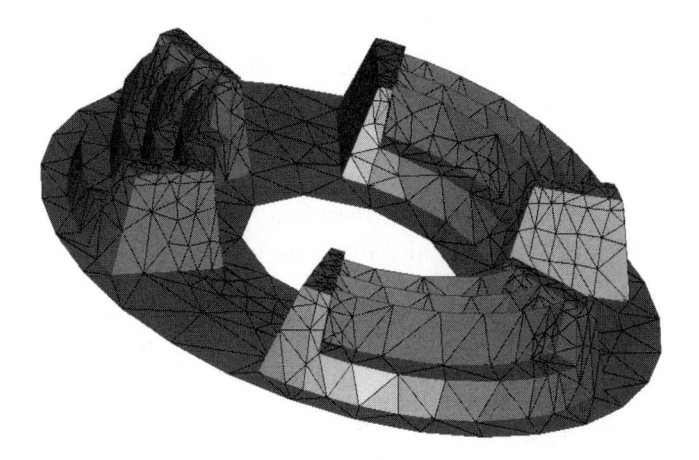

Design Optimization 255

Mixed mesh FEA model of parametric design.

Now, because the model was developed properly, a modification to the design and the resulting finite element mesh would look like the following illustration.

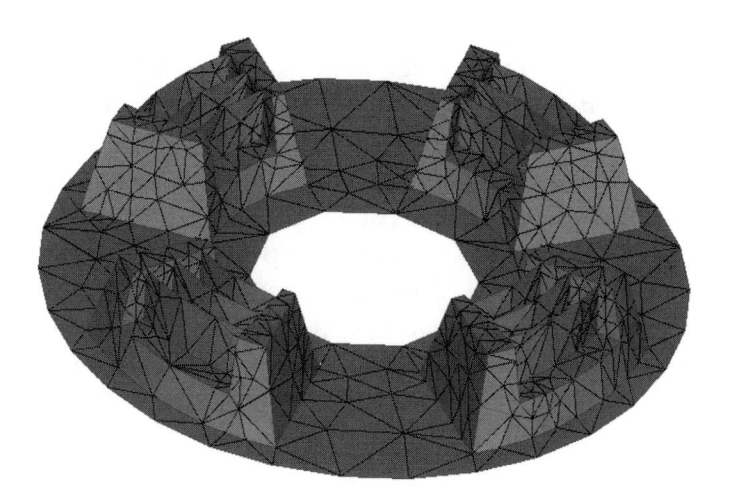

Mixed mesh FEA model of modified parametric design.

Notice that I did not say that you had to sit at the computer and fight the regeneration problems that we had in the previous model. This was because the part was well thought out and capable of responding to the dimensional changes that were being given. Note that this design, and other examples in this chapter, could have been simplified by developing half, third, or quarter symmetry models. Basically, by dividing the model into equal and symmetrical portions, you can establish the boundary conditions such that the revised model mathematically represents the whole part. The advantage is a much smaller model that can be processed quicker than a full FEA model, thus giving you more time to design and evaluate new design options.

> **NOTE:** *Care must be taken when implementing symmetry models. Improperly developed boundary conditions can result in improper results.*

Adapting to changes in the models that you create is a fundamental requirement to performing successful design optimization; the number of dimensional variables can be just as important.

Dimensions and Iteration

Design optimization is a useful tool for any engineer who wants to improve certain aspects of design, that is, localized stress levels. The thing that you must keep in mind is this: each dimension that you declare as a variable that can be iterated within a set of design limits is directly related to the number of equations that your computer will use for iteration of a solution. The more dimensions that you declare as variables, the more equations that your computer will have to manipulate, which could produce some very long iteration times for your design. The risk in selecting too many dimensions as variables is that you could be introducing the possibility of having more than one result due to the number of variables that the computer is solving for. For example, the following design was developed so that the model was flexible and capable of reacting to changes during design iterations.

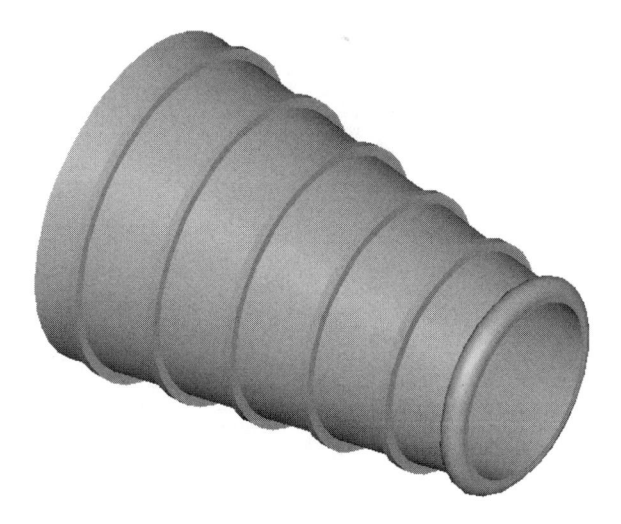

Original design.

The objective for this design is to limit the stress levels and minimize the mass in the design (for the sake of demonstration, assume that the model has been designated overstressed after an initial analysis cycle).

258   Chapter 10: Analysis

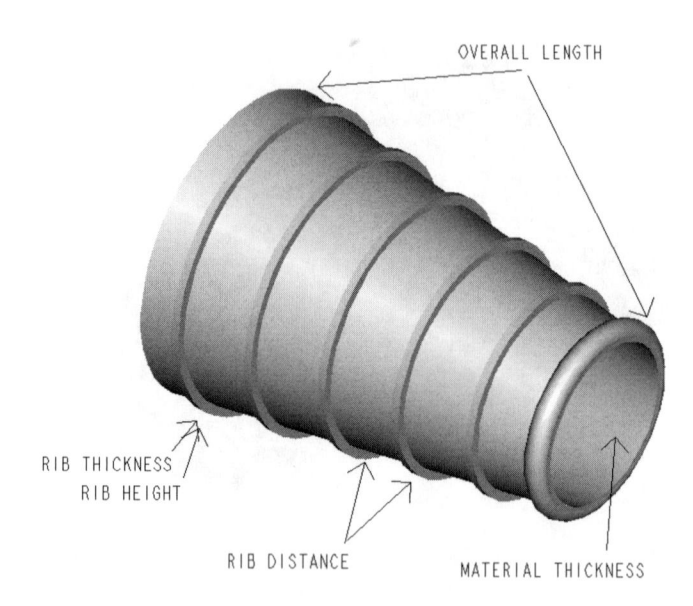

POSSIBLE DESIGN VARIABLES

Original design with features that will be used as design variables.

If the previously shown features' dimensions were to be selected as design variables, it would be possible to have some of the following results from the iterative process, given the number of variables that were declared.

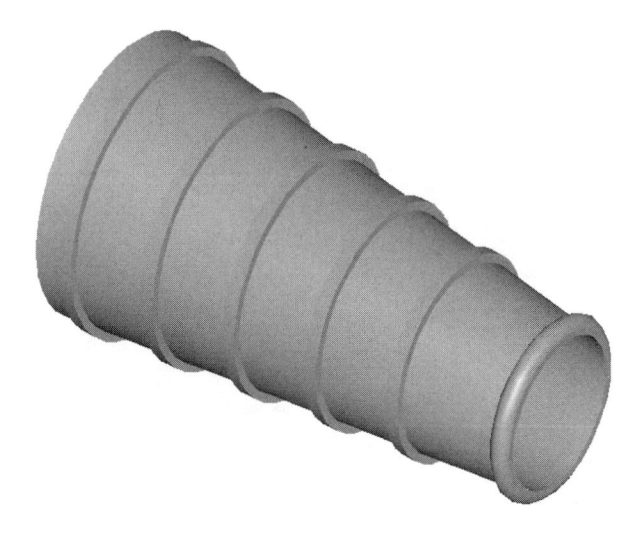

Design Optimization 259

Possible result of a design iteration.

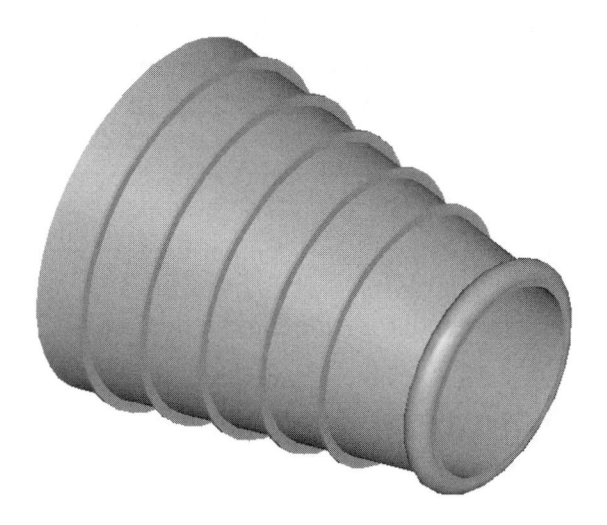

Possible result of a design iteration.

Chapter 10: Analysis

Possible result of a design iteration.

Most of the FEA packages available use mathematical tests for convergence that basically act as mathematical gates within the computer as it is calculating the design. These gates determine and predict whether or not the iteration that the computer is performing will be significant or whether the computer should abort the cycle and try a new value or set of values. Ultimately these gates help you to avoid executing a 10-hour analysis when the job could be done in 2 hours. Keep in mind that each analysis package has a set of guidelines for the maximum number of dimensional or feature iterations to perform at once. Please reference your analysis package's recommendations and guidelines for additional information and guidance.

Topology Optimization

Just having the ability to define the limits of size or location for a dimension or feature in Pro/ENGINEER, or within the analysis package you are using, and then having the geometry iterate to optimize the design based on those constraints is impressive in and of itself. But there is another new ability of some analysis packages that goes beyond the somewhat routine methods of optimization. This new area deals with fundamental questions such as, "Have I chosen the proper number of holes to satisfy the design?" or "Are there

Design Optimization 261

enough ribs in the design to adequately support the loads that components will be under?" I am sure that you can add your own fundamental questions to this short list.

Topology optimization is most likely the next big leap in design optimization for engineers. The advantage to this type of optimization is that you will now, or in the near future when it becomes more widely available, have the ability to optimize the number of features that would be required to satisfy a design's requirements. For example, the following illustration shows a typical flange bolted cap for the end of a pipe.

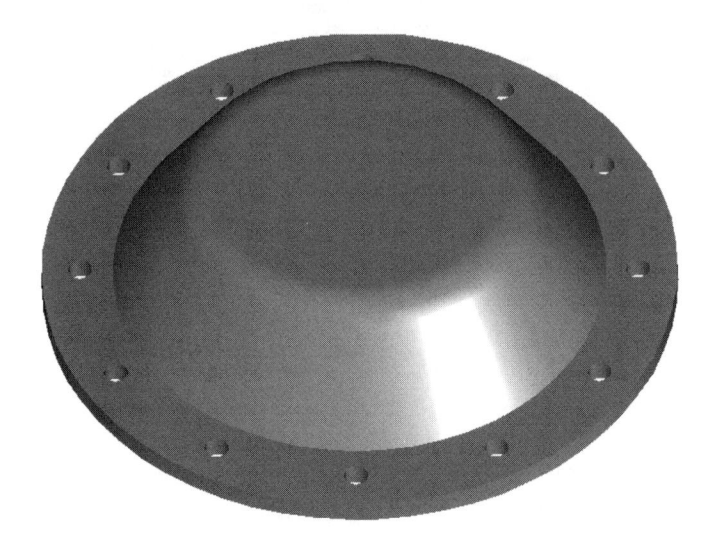

Original design of pipe cap.

As you can see, there are quite a number of holes, which are used as bolt clearance holes, in the flange of the cap. The selected number of holes could have been selected based on the manufacturer's recommendations for the anticipated pressure levels within the pipes, or the number may have been extracted from an industry standard table for flange designs. Either way, you may be adding cost to the program or design unnecessarily with the addition of bolts, nuts, and manufacturing operations to produce this component.

If you knew enough about the loads that the component would be exposed to, the available materials for the design, and the types of bolts (or whatever method you will be using) available, you could add these parameters into the model along with the minimum and maximum number of openings. After the analysis was run, you might find that a reduction in the number of bolts could be achieved by simply using a slightly larger bolt size. The results might look like those shown in the following illustration.

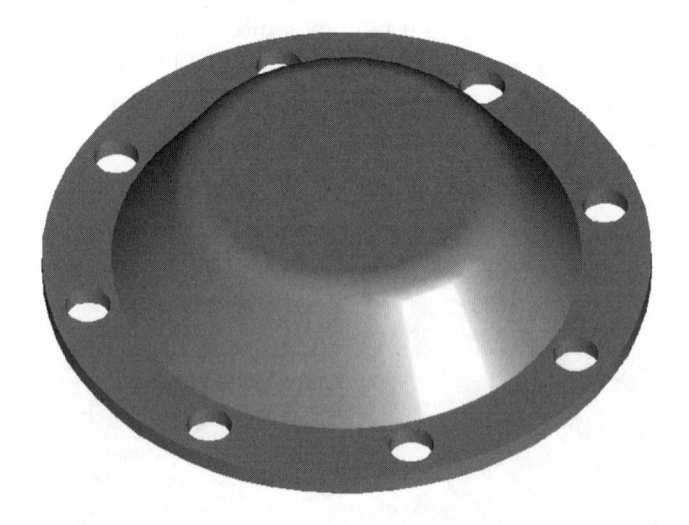

Optimized topology for pipe cap.

As you can see from the topology optimization, this method of design accounts for more than just what size and location would be required to optimize the design. This method focuses more on the fundamentals of design optimization, and then adds to it by introducing the ability to iterate the number of features. This technology can have a significant impact on the cost of the components by ensuring that the amount of material and the geometry is capable of satisfying the design's requirements. But having all of this power at your fingertips can either be a help or hindrance unless you are capable of setting up, running, and interpreting the results.

Who Should Conduct the Analysis?

With all of the high-end, easy to use FEA packages that have come out recently, the power of FEA has moved much closer to the design phase. Part of this

Who Should Conduct the Analysis? 263

move is to reduce the amount of time required for proving a design mathematically, and then making the necessary adjustments to improve the design. But there is quite a bit of background that the users of this technology must be familiar with, not to mention the experience needed to properly apply the loads and constraints, and ultimately interpret the results of the analysis. For example, the following illustration shows a design markup with the types of loads that the component must sustain.

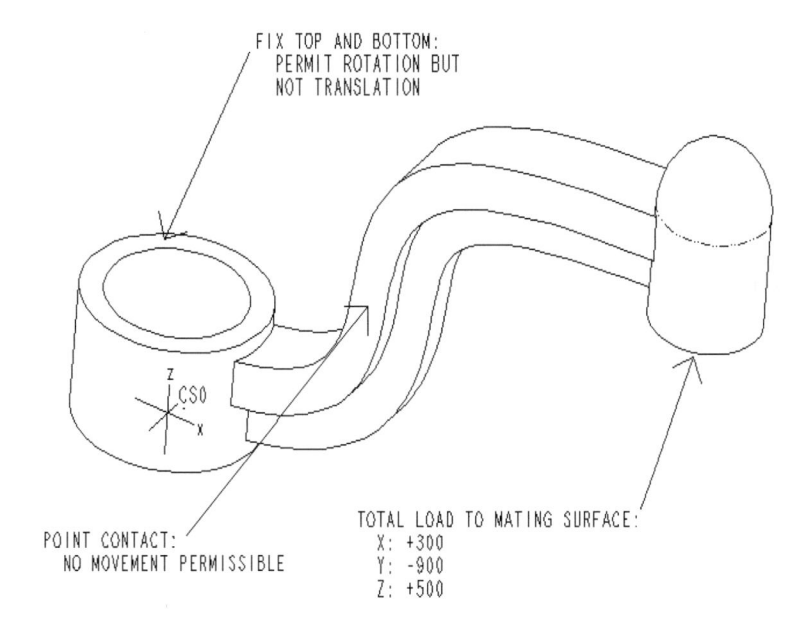

Markup of FEA model's requirements.

One aspect of the analysis that needs to be properly set up in the design is the constraints for the part. If the constraints were not properly set up for the part, the results that you receive could indicate that the design is not under the stress levels that the design would actually experience in the real world. Your FEA model without any constraints might look like the following illustration.

264 Chapter 10: Analysis

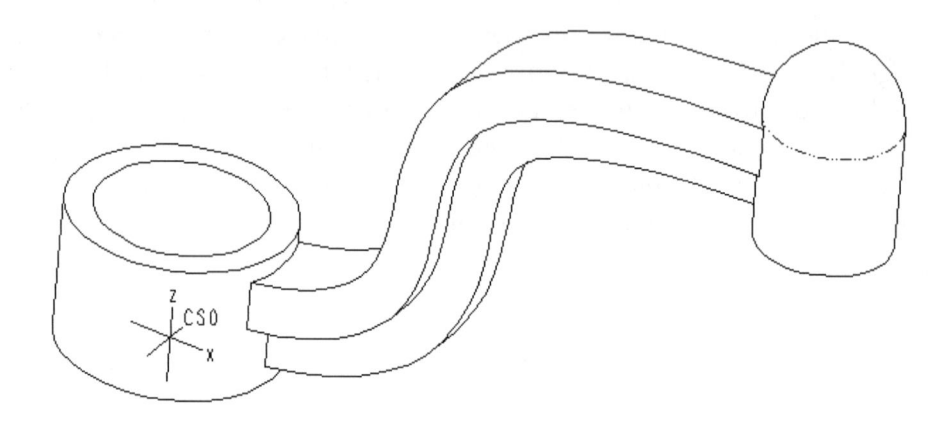

FEA model with no constraints applied.

The loads for the FEA model shown above are presented in the following illustration.

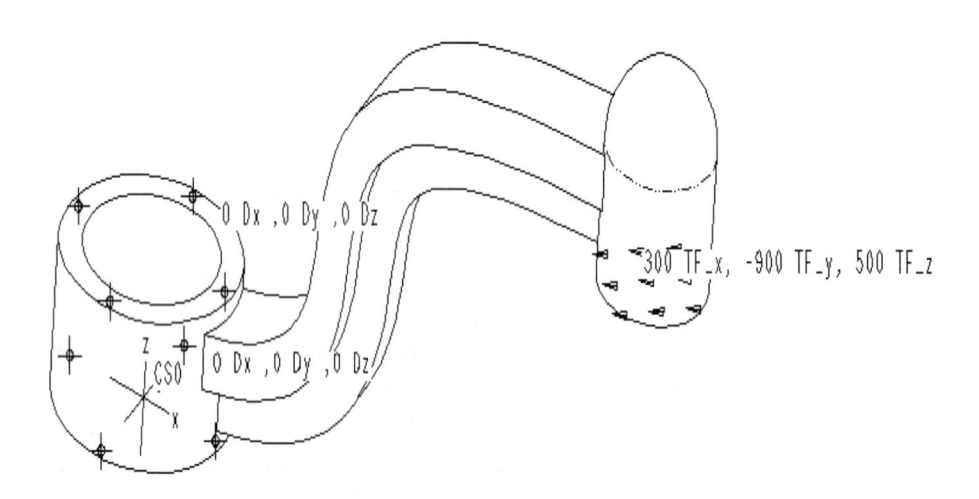

FEA model with loads and constraints.

Looking at the markup for the component, and the previous illustrations, you may notice that the constraints for the side of the component do not

Who Should Conduct the Analysis? 265

capture the intent. The addition of an immovable point constraint will better represent the FEA model and associated constraints to satisfy the analysis requirements. That revised FEA model with the new constraints is shown in the following illustration.

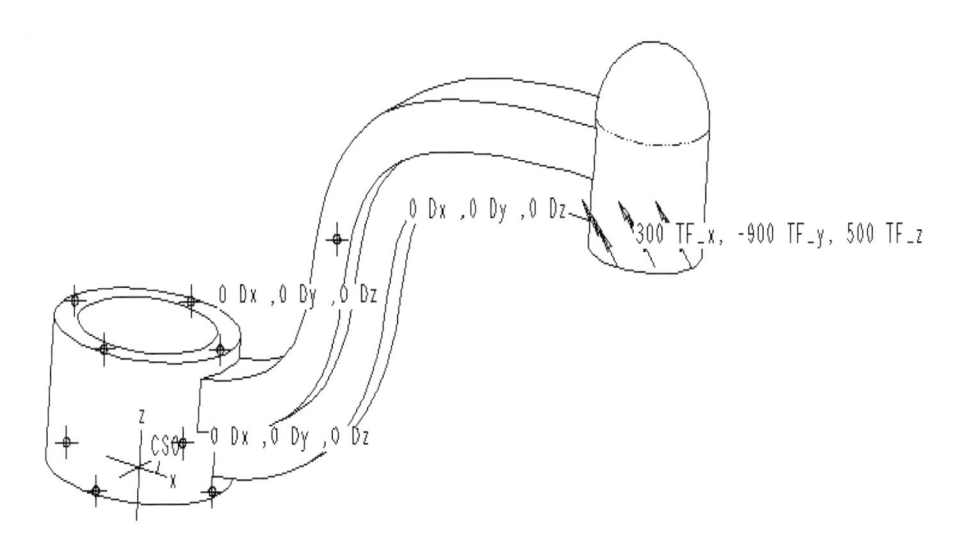

Revised FEA model and constraints.

This is a somewhat fundamental example of finite element meshing and application of the design constraints. But if you were not experienced in the setup of finite element mesh and the loads and constraints for the components, you may be performing analysis that does not produce any useful information. This situation can be compounded when you have overlooked a required constraint and are in the process of optimizing a design based on your initial results. This can cause some real problems, especially if the design is permitted to continue into the prototype or production phase of development. Some FEA packages provide a postprocessor to integrate the results of the analysis, most of which require a fairly in-depth understanding of the software to use. Pro/FEM-POST is a postprocessing module within the Pro/ENGINEER product line that provides you with a graphical interface to the FEA results. The key advantage of this module is that you can analyze the results within the Pro/ENGINEER environment and actively interact with the results using a number of tools. Review the Pro/MESH and Pro/FEM-POST users' guides for a full description of features and functionality.

FEA is a relatively large area of the engineering community, and with the tools and methods of setting up and analyzing designs becoming easier to work with, the technologies of design and analysis are rapidly coming together. Experience has been a hard lesson in the need to understand the fundamentals of FEA. There is a lot that you can learn and put to use for improving your designs by properly setting up and performing analysis. However, for the novice, FEA can be an overwhelming experience, due to the amount of detail that you must keep track of.

Engineers qualified to develop, analyze, and interpret the results of the analysis can be worth their weight in gold. If you are interested in getting into FEA, I strongly suggest that you start out with small models and master the fundamentals of meshing; this can be a challenge for both the new and experienced users of FEA. Once you have learned about the development of FEA meshes, the application of loads and constraints for the designs can be just as much of a challenge, and then there is the analysis itself, followed by the interpretation of the results. Of course, for each phase of the analysis process, there are a number of things to consider and keep track of to ensure that the results of the analysis are representative of how the actual design will perform.

Summary

The cycle of design, analyze, modify, analyze, modify, etc., is still a viable method for improving a design. But this method relies heavily on your next best guess for improving the design. This process of anticipating which modifications to the design will produce the desired results, while trying to minimize the amount of materials and stress levels and satisfy the manufacturing requirements, can be a time-consuming and frustrating process. This entire process can be compounded when your design must be exported to the analysis package and then remodeled for the finite element mesh. At times it may seem as if you are spending most of your time remodeling and remeshing the design.

With the power of parametric modeling, and an analysis community that is eager to develop applications that are more flexible and integrated with the design process, you now have the ability to not only analyze the design, but establish the limits of size and location of design features, truly optimize for the design's requirements, and evaluate the results. But having this optimization capability does not mean that you are exempt from committing yourself to generating quality and flexible databases. Whether you are using a FEA package that is integrated into Pro/ENGINEER or a package that manipulates its own geometry, you must be sure that your inputs to the FEA packages are accurate and capable of change.

The rules for modeling in Pro/ENGINEER also apply for the modeling of components for analysis. If the modeling quality of your design is not high, then there is the possibility that you will have to use a finer resolution mesh to adequately describe the geometry, the results of which will increase processing time. Therefore, it is important that your modeling not only be accurate but have the ability to be easily modified. But the quality of the design goes beyond the number of geometry errors that you may have in the model. In order to be able to use some optimization software, your designs must respond to change; flexibility is crucial for efficient setup and execution of advanced design optimization techniques.

But having all of these analysis optimization tools integrated with Pro/ENGINEER or within the execution of a program that will seamlessly transfer the geometry into the analysis package is useless if you do not know whether or not your loads and constraints are properly set up. With the advanced tools becoming easier to use and more integrated into the design process, there is the risk that users may be performing analysis that they are not properly trained to make or making adjustments in the design without fully understanding what the results of the analysis are. If users are going to use these analysis tools, education and training is a must.

Rapid Prototyping

Introduction

After spending several weeks completing a design, your group comes to the next critical phase of development—building prototypes. With your time frames for development at a premium, your group comes to a difficult crossroads in the development of the design. Do you take the time to fully develop a set of toleranced drawings, or do you try to use the CAD data as the master reference for prototyping as many components as possible? The answers to these questions are dependent on what types of materials each component in the design must be, the types of prototyping processes available for those materials, and the quality level that your designs require.

Assume that the prototype phase of development is required to produce structurally sound components that can be used for minor assembly and design verification requirements. Knowing that your first-phase prototypes have to be finished within the next week and a half, you obtain some quotes, decide on a service bureau, and prepare the databases for export. Because your group has decided on obtaining stereolithography apparatus (SLA) components, and this particular service bureau does not have Pro/ENGINEER, you are required to generate some surfaced IGES files of the designs. The service bureau that you have chosen will use this surfaced geometry to generate the STL file, which the SLA machine uses to lase the cross-sections of the design.

After the IGES files have been generated, you send them to the service bureau. Two days later, you receive a call from the service bureau. It seems that the IGES files that you generated could not be completely read into their CAD system. Frustrated, you decide to send the designs to another service bureau that has Pro/ENGINEER. Once the files arrive at the new company, you receive another call; this time the database that you sent has a number of complex geometry errors that are complicating the STL file development, which is required for the SLA machine. The service bureau indicates that the errors can be quickly corrected by simply removing a couple of rounds, suppressing a number of cuts in the part, and reducing the resolution of the STL file parameters. The cost of doing this is obvious: the final prototype component will not completely represent the design intent.

Reluctantly, you agree to the removal of some of the geometry that is causing problems, and a week later you receive the prototype parts. While reviewing the components, you notice that a significant amount of your component's ribbing detail was lost during the removal of the support structure for the component, which was required to support the part during its growth in the photoreactive fluid. In the end you are able to use the components for "show and tell" and construct a package model of the design using the various SLA components of the design.

Ultimately, once your component designs were completed, your design group could have chosen any number of possible methods for producing the prototype components, ranging from SLA all the way up to computer numeric control (CNC) machining of each component out of a solid material. This area of rapid prototyping has blossomed into its own industry, which continues to change as the various technologies become less expensive and more efficient.

Which Technique Is Right for You?

The rapid prototyping industry is currently changing about as rapidly as Pro/ENGINEER. It seems that every few months there is either an improvement or new approach to the processing, manufacture, quality, accuracy, and material options for prototyping designs. Writing about all of the methods, materials, and options available could take an entire book. On top of that, a number of the methods that were discussed may be replaced or made obsolete by newer, faster, and more cost-effective methods or techniques. Ultimately, the methods that you use must satisfy the needs of the prototype-level design. You must answer questions such as, will the prototype components be used for just show and tell purposes or as a functional prototype that can retain screws, be painted, or withstand operating loads for the intended application?

Historically, when working with a design that will be developed using rapid prototyping techniques, there are a number of things that you must keep in mind. Your department's expectations for the components may differ from the expectations of other departments in your company, or even worse, your customer's expectations. It can be to your advantage to not only understand the capabilities and expectations of each rapid prototyping process, but to have samples of each process in your department. This will give you the opportunity to have a physical sample of the materials that your final product will be made of. These samples of each process are not hard to come by; most companies who possess the rapid prototyping equipment can supply you with calibration or rejected components from other customers.

You also should have an understanding of some of the limitations for each process. Limitations may be in the form of the level of detail that may be obtained from each of the processes, and how much finishing work is required for the component once the design has been processed. Processes that require a lot of finishing work, especially on small complex components, can create a number of problems when it comes to delivering the final product. Generally, try to avoid processes that could potentially distort or remove geometry that may be important for the design. Research the various processes at your disposal and determine which will satisfy your needs.

For example, a component of the design that you will be developing may look like that shown in the following illustration.

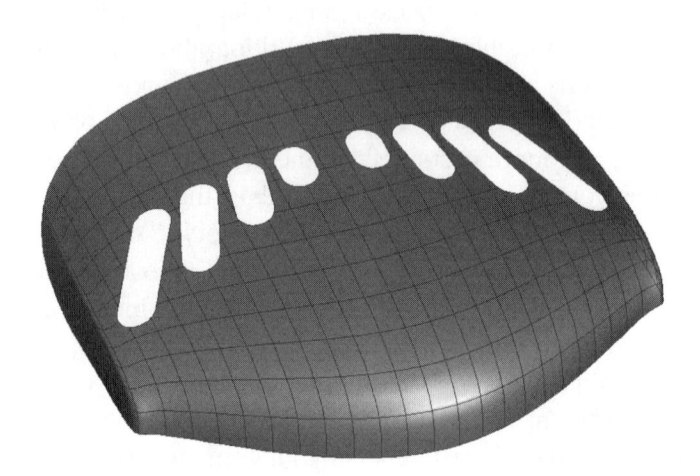

Final design that needs to be made into a prototype (meshed for visualization purposes).

Suppose that the manufacturing group would like to use this component as a prototype to prove some fixturing that is being designed. The fixture will basically hold the component in place while another component is assembled to the design. If your design intent is to make the above design out of plastic, then you should only have to decide on the rapid prototyping process that will produce a component that is robust enough to take the stresses of torquing a screw into the design.

With this additional requirement for the design, the prototyping process and material should be obvious, right? Maybe not. A few years ago, the selection of a prototyping process may have been simple, but with the number of systems and processes available today, you must consider not only the robustness of the final prototype component, but the price and turnaround time of the designs. In this case, if you were to simply select SLA, without specifying a particular type of resin or the applications that the component will be used for, you may receive a component that is brittle once it has dried out and hardened.

The effects of this can be dramatic: have you ever seen a boss explode while trying to torque in a screw? It can be disappointing, frustrating, and expensive, especially if the boss's failure causes a large crack or even the destruction of other important geometry near that boss. I can't count the number of times that I have seen a prototype component damaged or destroyed because of an accidental fall from a table or overloading the design by trying to make the prototype do more than was physically possible.

I remember one instance where a prototype component was being carried to a presentation with the client. The person got out of his car, set the prototype component on the roof of his car, and bent down to retrieve some other materials from the back seat. The part slid from the roof, bounced off the trunk, and finally smashed onto the parking lot. Luckily, this individual had some duct tape in his trunk. As you might expect, however, the customer was not impressed with the part or the duct tape and was not willing to pay the $5000+ bill for the component.

If you were to specify a resin, or outline the strength requirements for the final prototype component, or even change the process from SLA to selective laser sintering (SLS), then you may be able to obtain components that can be used for more than just show and tell purposes. But, as with any process or design, there is a balance between the amount of money you are willing to invest and the quality levels that you are expecting for the components.

Price, Quantity, and Process

But what if the design mentioned previously, because of other department's, and your customer's, intentions, required that a total of ten prototype components be developed? Would the rapid prototyping processes be capable of producing the required quantities within the required time frames? Depending on how aggressive the quoting is for the design, and the turnaround time, you may be able to obtain the prototype quantities in the required time frames. But suppose that you are looking to build 30 functional prototype components of the following design.

Plastic design for which you wish to build 30 prototypes (meshed for visualization purposes).

If your prototype sources for laser or optically developed components quoted $2300 for the first component and then $1900 for each additional component, the cost of obtaining the required number of components would most likely be prohibitive. But there are other options for development that can be used to produce a sizable number of prototype components, with an acceptable level of quality at reasonable prices.

Using CNC

If your company has access to CNC machines, you could use your Pro/ENGINEER database of the design as the master reference for the generation of CNC tool paths. This can be an effective method of producing a number of prototype components rather quickly. The advantage is that, once your tool paths, feeds, and speeds have been proven, you will have a set of CNC programs that can be used over and over. All of this is dependent on the availability of your company's CNC equipment and the amount of time required to program the tool paths, obtain the materials, and run the programs. Having the ability to program a set of CNC tool paths and run multiple components is definitely an advantage and can be cost effective. But what if

Which Technique Is Right for You? 275

your department wanted to try two additional design options of the above design that looked like the following?

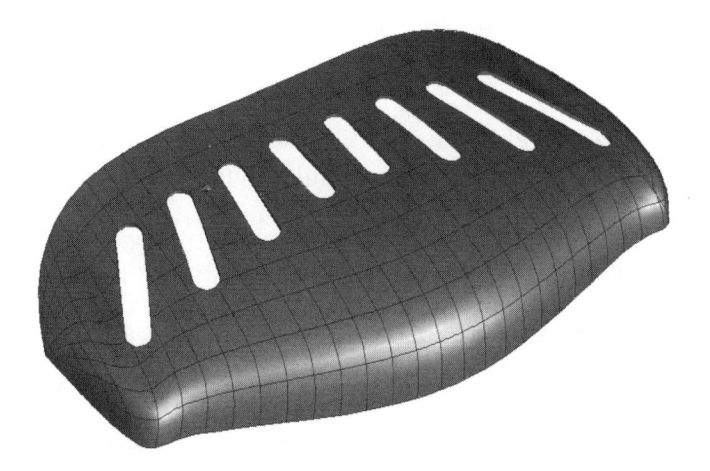

Design option 2 (meshed for visualization purposes).

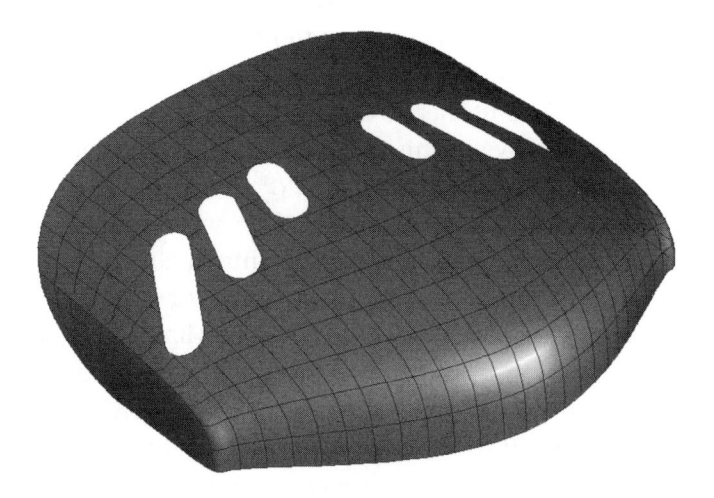

Design option 3 (meshed for visualization purposes).

Suppose also that the total number of prototypes were to stay at 30 pieces, 10 pieces of each design option. The use of the original prototype option would definitely be fast and produce several design options quickly. But the cost of producing all of the components may still be an issue. Using your CNC equipment to machine the various designs out of plastic is still an option but you may experience a delay in generating all those CNC tool paths. But, if your company is fortunate enough to have a seat of Pro/MANUFACTURING, you can take your prototyping to an entirely new level by quickly developing several design options and having the CNC tool paths automatically update to the design's change. Please review Chapter 12, "Pro/MANUFACTURING," for additional information on this powerful functionality.

Other Options

To produce multiple prototypes of the initial design, the use of urethane molds can be a relatively low tech, cost-effective alternative to running 30 individual components. This process has been used for a number of years and can be an attractive method for short runs. The design shown previously could probably have been produced using a urethane mold for approximately $5,000 to $10,000. The development of the mold is dependent on the development of a master pattern that will be used to generate the negative impressions in the urethane. The current trend is to use a finished prototype model that was developed from a process similar to the SLA process as the master for the mold. The results of this technique for the development of a urethane mold can be very attractive from a timing standpoint. The advantage is that your master model can be generated directly from the database, which eliminates the need to machine a single master part.

Other rapid prototyping processes for short-run, higher quality components such as spray metal and aluminum tooling, castings, or other popular methods, have benefited as the various technologies have improved. But no matter which method you choose, there will always be a give and take for each option, in essence a balance between cost and quality. Ultimately, you and your company must analyze which methods and techniques satisfy you and your customer's needs. You must be aggressive in your search for emerging technologies and develop a concise understanding of the advantages and disadvantages of each method, process, and option. But in the end, this subject could easily encompass volumes of books due to the number of options and variations currently available.

The Common Link: The Database

No matter which methods or technologies you are using for your rapid prototype components, there is one common link between all of these processes—the database. The quality, and often the cost, of the prototype components that you receive are directly related to the quality of the information that you will be giving to the people who develop the prototype components. This has been a common theme in this book, and the quality of the design can make all the difference when it comes to not only obtaining rapid prototype components but having success in all other areas of manufacturing. The quality of the design is probably the most important variable in the rapid prototyping equation. Occasionally, there are variables that are added to the equation that can make rapid prototyping a difficult and time-consuming process; those variables are also known as geometry errors.

Geometry Errors

Errors in the database such as overlapping geometry (which usually can be found in older designs), alignment issues, and the occasional mathematical "hiccup" can not only cause problems with the modifications of a design, but also with your efforts to obtain prototype components. Common development problems such as not using the right tool for the job, which may be part of the reason that some of your models are very complex, can definitely contribute to modeling and geometry problems. These problems can be perpetuated throughout the design process and into the development cycle, potentially affecting the analysis, prototyping, drafting, and manufacturing phases.

The following illustration highlights an area in the model that can cause problems with the evolution of a design from the Pro/ENGINEER model into physical components.

Chapter 11: Rapid Prototyping

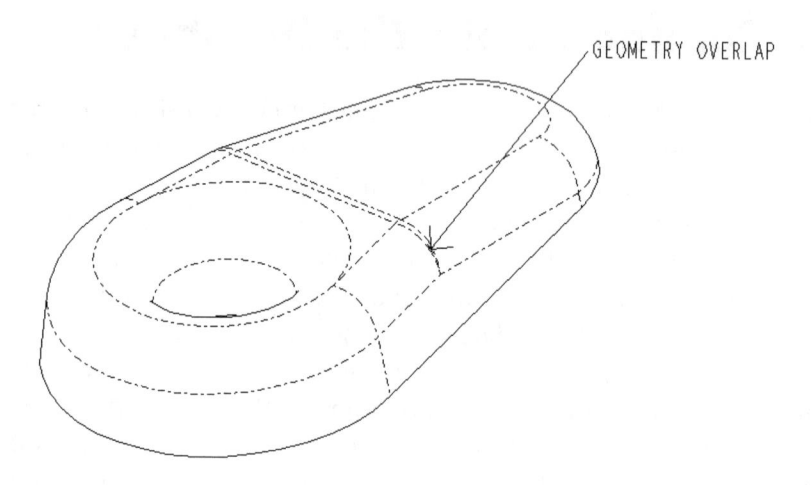

Design with a geometry problem.

If the above design was developed using "sculpting" techniques, where the user simply starts off with a block of material and then skillfully cuts geometry away from the block, there would be a greater chance of having difficulty during regeneration than if the model was properly developed. With this in mind, you might expect that the model would be more prone to regeneration problems that go above and beyond basic parametric relationship errors. As you continue to develop a sculpted design, you are placing yourself at greater risk for geometry errors that can affect the efficient transformation from a database to a physical part.

For example, assume that the design shown previously is to be used for development of an STL file that is used as the input for SLA. If you are going to send a Pro/ENGINEER database, or IGES file, to a service bureau for the generation of a prototype component, you can save a lot of time by debugging the design prior to the generation of the STL file. The STL file basically is constructed of triangles. These triangles look like a poor finite element mesh of your component. Just as you can control the size of elements in a finite element mesh, you can control the size of the triangles (elements) that are being generated for the STL file. The following illustration represents the typical parameters that govern the size of the triangles used for the STL file.

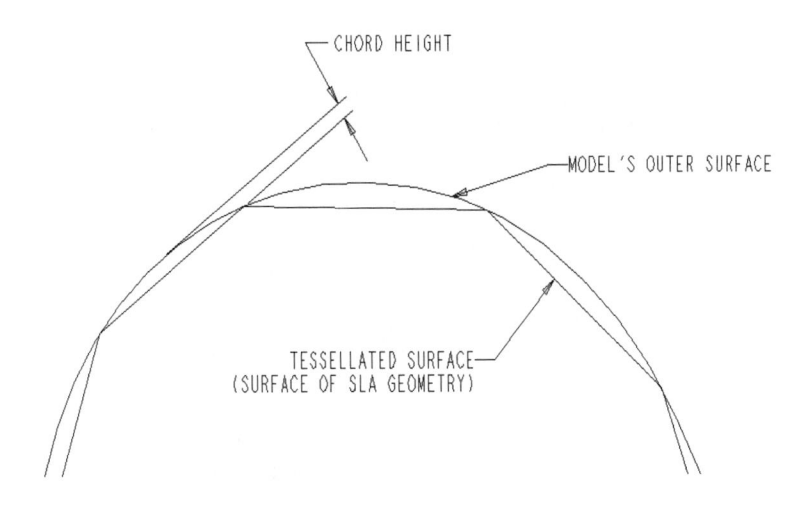

General parameters for an STL file.

Please notice that there is a definite relationship between the size of the triangles and the geometry that you will be processing.

One way to ensure that your geometry is usable for the chosen prototyping process is to generate an STL file on your own, before releasing the design for prototyping. But before you do this, obtain the cord height and angle control values from the service bureau that you will be using. The advantage to this is that you will be able to debug the model of areas that may cause problems during the STL file generation. It is important that you obtain a set of recommended values for the type of process with which your components will be produced.

For this example, an STL file of the previous design will be generated using a set of chord height and angle control values that were provided by the service bureau.

Chapter 11: Rapid Prototyping

STL file generated from original design, Chord Height = 0.008; Angle Control = 0.7.

The previous illustration is what the file would look like, given the current values for the STL file. If the file could not be generated, because of the number of geometry errors in the model, you have a number of options. You can either try to fix the geometry problems or reduce the resolution of the STL file. Each option has its downside. Fixing the geometry is by far the most important of the two options, but it requires you to debug the problems, which takes time. On the other hand, if your design is permitted to contain geometry errors, your service bureau may decide to reduce the resolution of the file that is being generated. The effects of reducing the resolution are a smaller STL file that does not represent the database as accurately, and you will ultimately produce a rougher part. Testing your databases can be a quick way to make sure that your rapid prototyping service bureau will not have any problems working with your data. But what if you are not using a SLA type of process for your rapid prototyping needs?

Geometry Errors and CNC

Whether you are using Pro/ENGINEER or another CNC programming package, geometry errors can translate into big CNC programming problems. If you are sending the database to a service bureau for the development of prototypes that will be developed using a machining process, assume for the moment that the service bureau does not have Pro/MANUFACTURING and the database must be exported via the IGES format into the CAM software that will be used to program the tool paths. A Pro/ENGINEER database with geometry errors is shown in the following illustration.

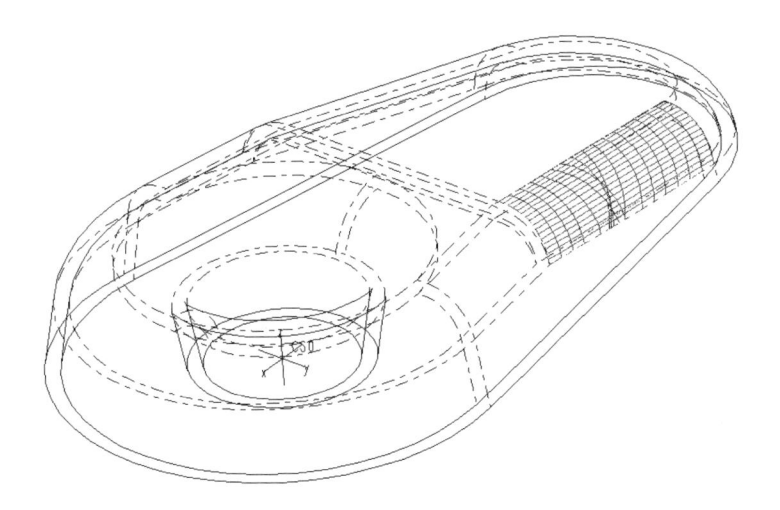

Design option with geometry errors.

The IGES process, basically copies the solid surfaces of the design and translates them into a neutral format that can be accessed by other CAD/CAM systems. But this process of translation is not always 100% accurate. Aside from some geometry that might not translate, there is the possibility that the incorrect geometry may be translated into the target CAM system. An enlarged view of some incorrect geometry in the above design is shown in the following illustration.

282   Chapter 11: Rapid Prototyping

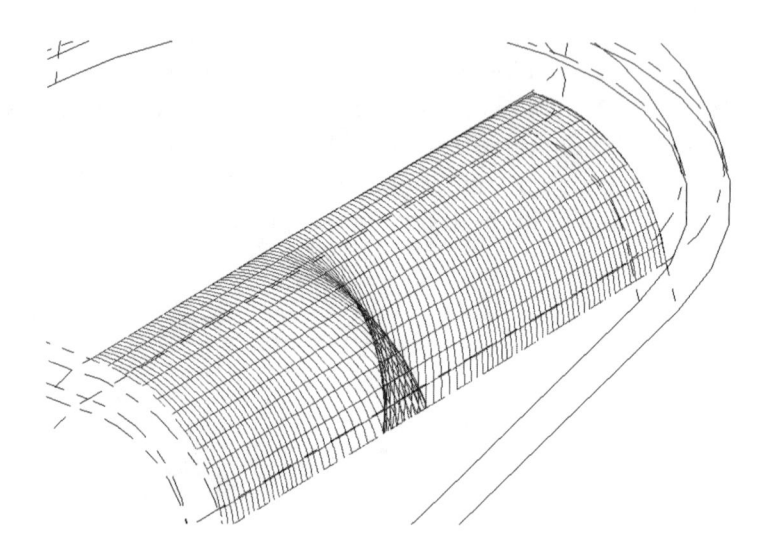

Enlarged view of incorrect geometry (meshed for visualization purposes).

    This geometry can cause some big problems for the CAM system that will be used for programming the tool paths, especially when tool paths are generated over multiple surfaces. The results may be irregular tool paths that gouge the piece that will be machined, or the loss of a number of tool paths that may be dependent on portions of this geometry. Either way, this method of rapid prototyping can be fast, cost effective, and produce some relatively high-quality prototype components.

    Looking back at the beginning of this book, we discussed the importance of generating quality input for your designs. Having this input is important and necessary to ensure success no matter what your designs will be used for. What you must remember is that your designs are the inputs into other people's areas of expertise. Because you cannot accomplish your job without putting quality information into your system of design, you must take the time to ensure that your inputs to others will be useful. It does not matter if you are going to use the design for a lasing or CAM process for rapid prototyping; the quality of the materials that will be returned to you will be only as good as the information that you provide to the people and companies who will be working toward satisfying your prototyping goals and needs.

Summary

As your designs evolve, there comes a time in the development process when you need to prove a design or concept before releasing a production-level tool. Only a few years ago rapid prototyping was thought of as a fairly expensive and delicate process. But as the various technologies have evolved, this area has blossomed into an industry that uses several processes and approaches to producing prototypes.

You must ask questions such as "Will the prototypes be used for show and tell or as functional components that must act as part of an assembly?" The use of CNC machines, urethane moldings, as well as other short-run prototype processes are still popular and cost-effective methods relative to the latest laser and optical techniques for development. But each method has its own list of advantages and disadvantages that you must carefully consider. Some methods require quite a bit of finishing work, which can put aspects of your design at risk for being damaged or removed. For this reason, it is important that you have an understanding of the available processes and their limitations. By obtaining samples of each rapid prototyping process available, you can help decide which methods will be used for which types of components.

No matter which methods you decide to use, there is a common link to the development of prototypes when using Pro/ENGINEER or any other CAD/CAM system: the quality of the information that you input into the prototyping process. Quality input is heavily dependent on the involvement of other departments and people who will be involved in the development of a design. All of that input was designed to act as the foundation for the development of the models and assemblies in Pro/ENGINEER. The successful development of a functional, accurate, and flexible model in Pro/ENGINEER can make all the difference in some types of prototyping processes. It is important that your designs are clean and without geometry errors, not only for the prototyping phase but for the production phase as well.

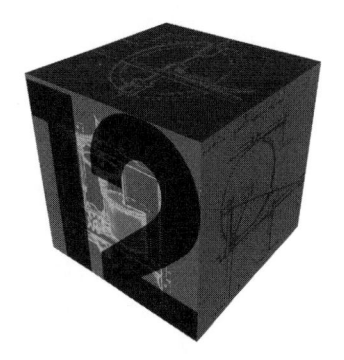

Pro/MANUFACTURING

Introduction

Having gone from the conceptual phase to layout, design, analysis, detailing, and prototyping, it is fitting that manufacturing be discussed in the last chapter. As the level and quality of designs have improved over the years, the manufacture of prototype or production components and equipment has also improved. These new and higher levels of design often require sophisticated programming tools and techniques. This use of advanced tools and techniques is especially necessary when a design uses free-form three-dimensional surfaces or complex intersecting geometries that are dependent on the existence of other types of geometry. The subject and use of machine tools is a large and rapidly changing field in manufacturing. Indeed, this subject is so large that several books could be written on it alone. But for the purposes of our discussion, we will look at some functionality of Pro/MANUFACTURING that can save you and your company a lot of time and money in the short

286 Chapter 12: Pro/MANUFACTURING

and long runs. Because the subject of Pro/MANUFACTURING and Pro/NC-CHECK are large enough to cover a whole book, the examples in this chapter have been developed around the most common of computer numeric control (CNC) operations: three-axis milling and drilling.

Suppose that the following design is to be manufactured using conventional three-axis methods of CNC programming.

Design that is to be manufactured using three-axis CNC machining.

Suppose also that the design shown previously was developed in Pro/ENGINEER and is intended to be a prototype of a plastic injected component. Because your company had a machining package prior to purchasing Pro/ENGINEER, you are forced to export your Pro/ENGINEER database via the IGES format into the CAM package so that the CNC tool paths can be generated. Once the design was translated in the CAM package, the programmer spent two days setting up the model and programming the tool paths to machine the design. A day later, halfway through the cutting of the part, a change from another design group requires that your prototype be redesigned to accommodate several design options for the part. The design options might look like those shown in the following illustrations.

Introduction 287

Design option 2.

Design option 3.

Design option 4.

Because your current Pro/ENGINEER design will have to be redefined due to some hole locations that can't be used, you quickly complete the new designs. After the new design options are completed and output as IGES files, you sit down with the CNC programmer to discuss the design changes. As you review the design options with the CNC programmer, it is decided that because the changes are significant, it would be quicker for the programmers to simply program new tool paths for each design version. This would ultimately produce a complete set of four CNC machining sequences that would take upward of a week to complete. The design changes were not anticipated, nor was the additional time that will now be added to the development of your prototypes. In the end, the initial design and additional options were completed, even though your development schedule was compromised.

Does the above situation seem familiar? I am sure a number of you have bumped into this at least once in your design career. Ultimately, there are a number of CAM packages that are very good at quickly programming CNC sequences, usually due to the tools within the software. And there are even some packages available that can adapt to subtle changes in the design. But it is difficult to find CAM packages that are cost effective and capable of adapting to changes in design on the fly. This is probably the strongest aspect of Pro/MANUFACTURING—having the ability to adapt to changes in design.

Adapting To Change

Just as Pro/ENGINEER is famous for its ability to capture the design intent in a flexible and robust model, Pro/MANUFACTURING has paralleled these abilities and evolved into a powerful module. One specific area in which Pro/MANUFACTURING seems to excel is the system's ability to be parametrically linked to the designs that will be used as the references for manufacturing operations. Referencing the previous example and design options, the original design within Pro/MANUFACTURING is shown in the following illustration.

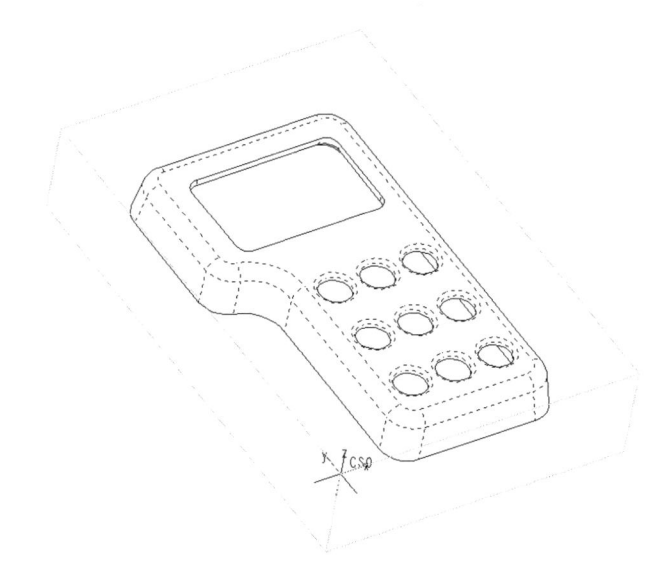

Original design within the workpiece.

    Please note that the original design is assembled to a location within the workpiece. You can think of the workpiece as the stock that is to be machined down to the original design part. Basically, you are working in an assembly of the workpiece and the original design. Tool paths are developed by referencing the original design part. Based on the tool paths and the workpiece geometry, the manufacturing process can be simulated on the screen. The tool paths for the top of the above design are shown in the following illustration.

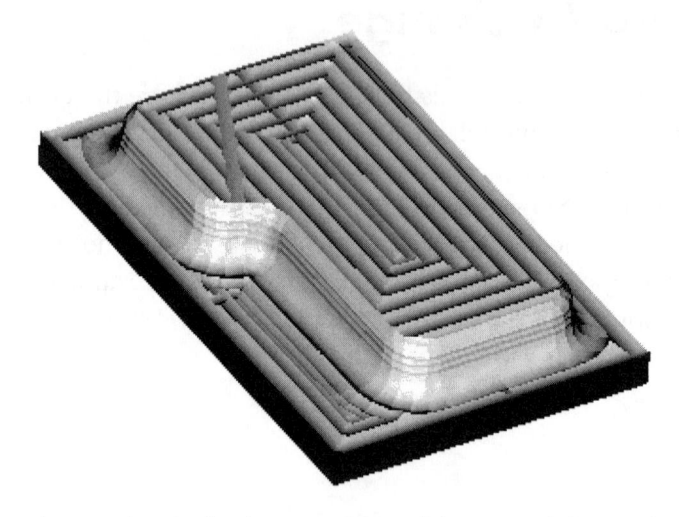

Roughing tool paths for the top volume of the original design. (NC-check shown for visualization purposes.)

These roughing tool paths were generated using traditional three-axis machining operations that reference the part's geometries within Pro/MANUFACTURING. You could have chosen from a number of other methods for the development of these tool paths. But for the purpose of this demonstration, assume that the tool paths shown previously were satisfactory for your purposes. To finish this set of tool paths, you select a smaller tool size, reduce the step over of the tool, and increase the spindle speed to perform a set of finish cuts.

Those finish cuts are shown in the following illustration.

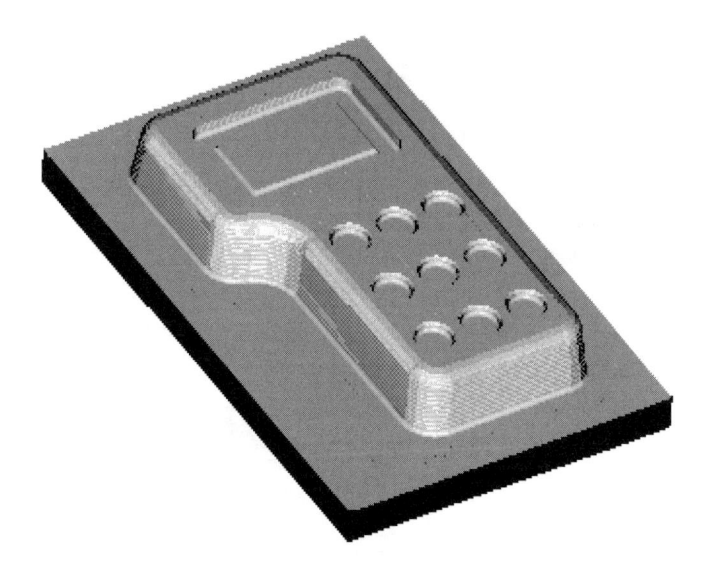

Finish tool paths for the top volume of the original design. (NC-check shown for visualization purposes.)

Now that the rough and finish tool paths have been programmed and accepted, assume that a design change was made to design option 2. If you were using any ordinary CAM system, you would have most likely had to import the new geometry or try to change the existing geometry and reprogram the tool paths. But because the types of changes that will be occurring in the design involve changes in the size and location of some geometry, you have some interesting options at your disposal. You could either delete the existing tool paths and reprogram the tool paths to the new design option, or you could simply regenerate the existing tool paths.

The roughing and finishing tool paths would look like the following illustrations.

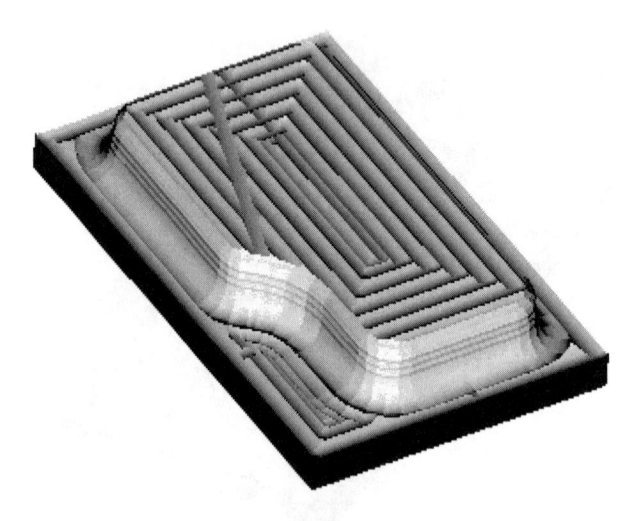

Roughing tool paths for design option 2. (NC-check shown for visualization purposes.)

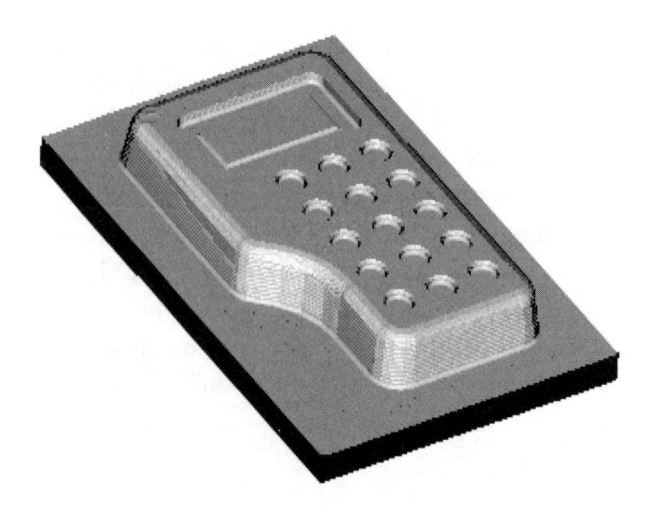

Finishing tool paths for design option 2. (NC-check shown for visualization purposes.)

As you can see, the mill volumes and tool paths are parametrically linked to the design. Therefore, the amount of reprogramming time was almost nonexistent. This of course may seem too easy to do, especially when the types of changes that are required do not involve major reworks in design. It is this ability to adapt to changes rapidly that can make the difference between a week's worth of reprogramming and simply regenerating the model based on a number of design options and changes. By using this ability within Pro/ENGINEER, all three design options could have been quickly developed by simply regenerating the tool paths after each design change and saving the tool paths for each design option. In the end, you would have only had to use one model to develop all of the tool paths for each of the design options.

Patterns

Another area where Pro/MANUFACTURING can really shine is in its ability to regenerate after changes are made in the size and locations of features in the design. Having the ability to not only regenerate the model but have the tool paths automatically update can be carried to a new level when dealing with patterned geometries. For example, the following design has a pattern of holes drilled in the top.

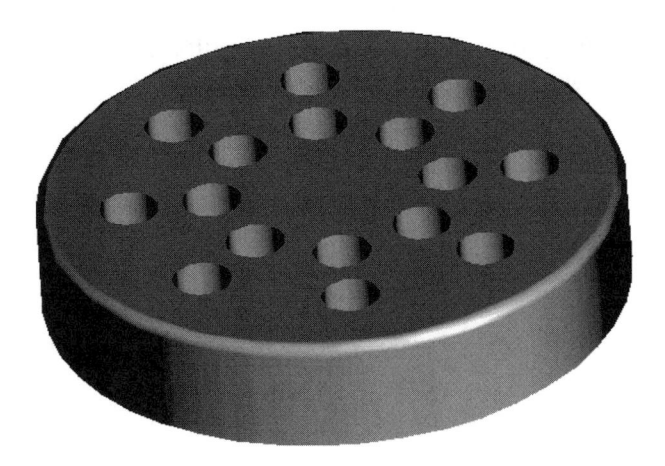

Design that has a pattern of holes.

294   Chapter 12: Pro/MANUFACTURING

After the design was delivered to be machined, a change in the design was requested that would change the location of the holes and the number of holes that will be used in the design. The tool paths for the above design are shown in the following illustration.

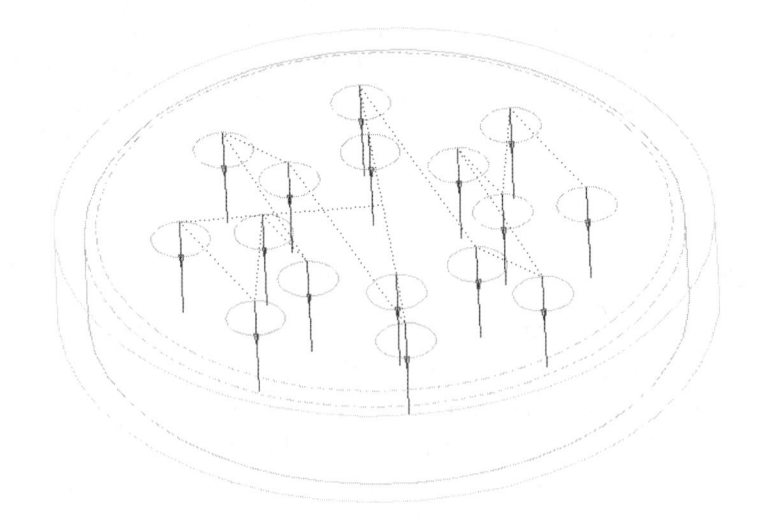

Tool paths for original design.

After the change was made to the design and the tool paths regenerated, the tool paths are shown in the following illustration.

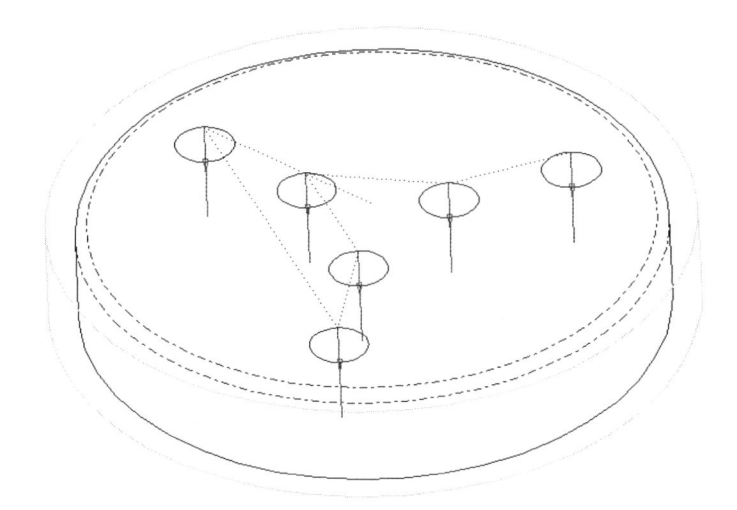

Tool paths for the hole pattern that changed in location and number of holes.

Once again, this ability to adapt to changes in the design can be a real time saver. This may not seem like a major change in the design, but for some CAM systems, a change like this may require quite a bit of time to reevaluate and edit the tool paths for this geometry. With Pro/MANUFACTURING, you can quickly update the tool paths, with little or no rework, often by just regenerating the manufacturing model.

Adapting to changes in design is definitely one of the strongest aspects of Pro/MANUFACTURING. But there are a number of other advanced features that can make the software not only easy to use but help the programmer to understand where they are in the machining process.

Ease of Use + Powerful Tools = Productivity

The removal of material can vary from system to system and user to user, but the basic principles are the same. The big difference from surfaced wireframe systems and some solids-based machining systems lies in the user's ability to understand where they are in the programming sequence. For example, if the following design were to be machined in another CAM system, the programmer may develop a wireframe or surfaced set of machining volumes to work the tool up to the design, layer by layer. To keep the sequences in order, a popular method of keeping track of machining volumes may be to layer the construction geometry and maintain a log of which machining sequence is related to which layer in the CAD database. Nevertheless, this can be a time-consuming and delicate process.

Sketching Mill Volumes

Interactively programming tool paths can increase your understanding of where you are in the programming process. To do this, a general approach would be to define a milling volume, the volume of geometry that will act as the "boundary" for the tool path. The following is to be made into a prototype using a three-axis machining process.

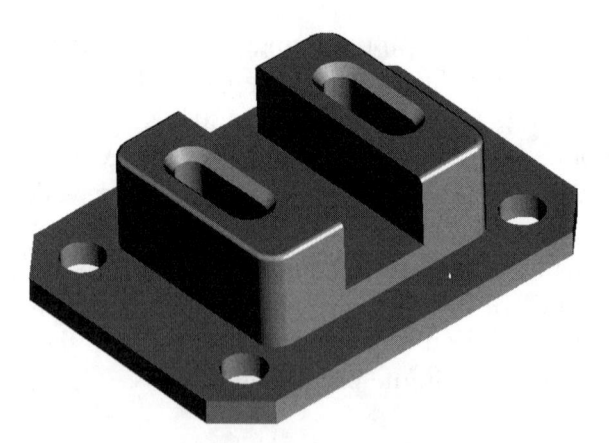

Design to be machined.

The design and workpiece assembly would look like that shown in the following illustration.

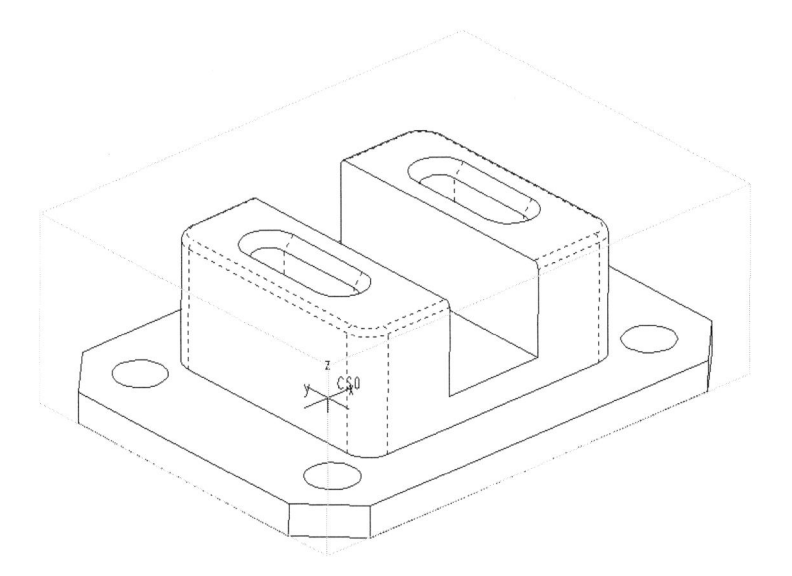

Ease of Use + Powerful Tools = Productivity

Workpiece with design; the manufacturing model.

Of course, there will be a number of different opinions as to how this model should be set up for the generation of the tool paths for a rough cut. There are a number of methods and techniques within Pro/MANUFACTURING that could be used for the development of the tool paths. But for the previous example, let's investigate a method that involves definition of a mill volume by sketching a cross-section at some distance from the top of the design within the workpiece that goes up to the top of the workpiece.

The sketch of this cross-section is shown in the following illustration.

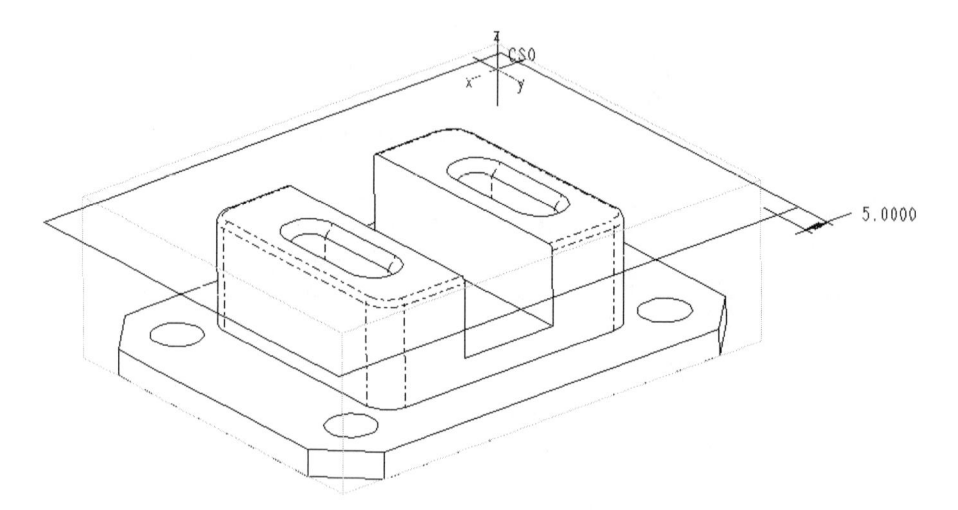

298   **Chapter 12: Pro/MANUFACTURING**

Sketched cross-section for mill volume.

The final mill volume is shown in the following figure.

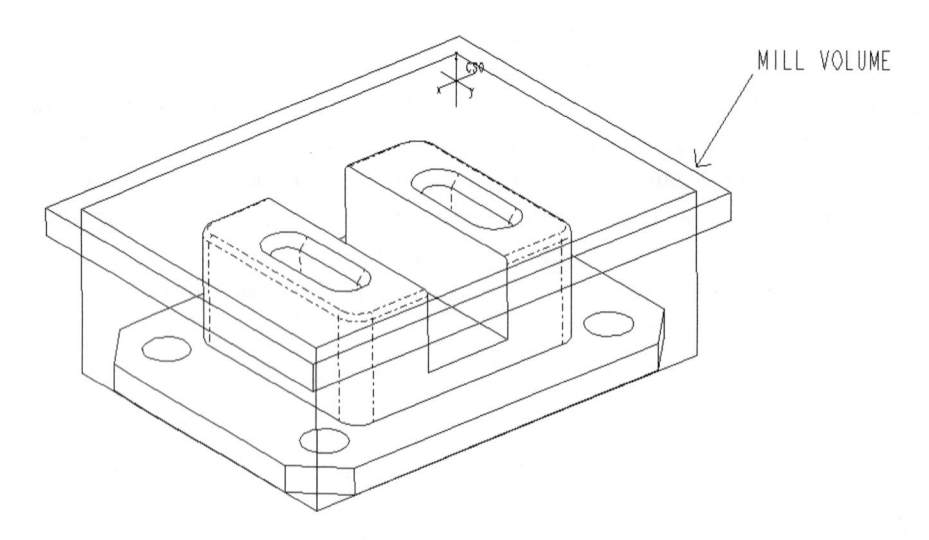

The defined mill volume.

Once this mill volume has been developed, you have basically defined the volume of geometry in the workpiece from which the tool paths can be generated. After defining some of the tool's movement parameters, that is, step over and step depth, and turning over the generation of the tool paths to the computer, you can really save yourself a lot of time. The above mill volume's tool paths might look like the following illustration.

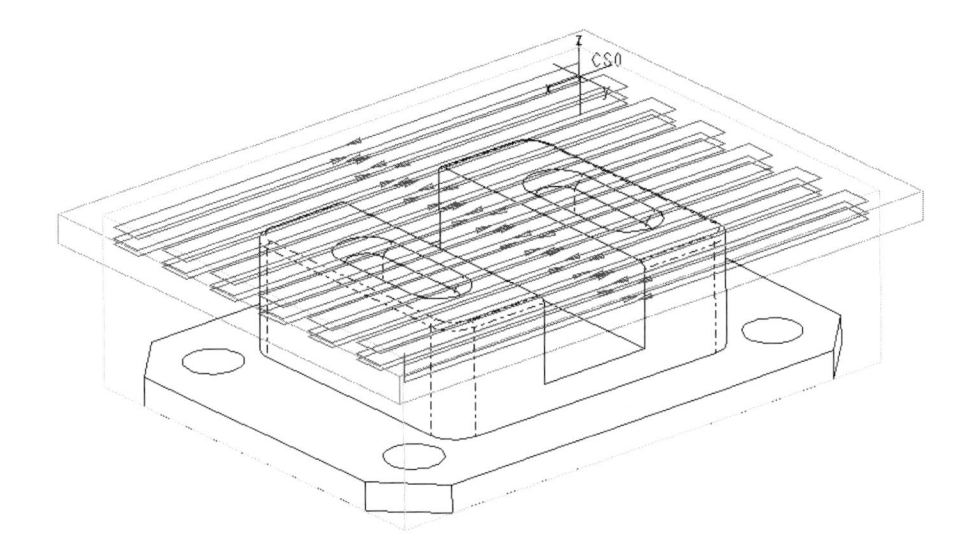

Tool paths for mill volume.

Please note that the previously shown tool paths could be manually, interactively programmed. But, if you were satisfied with the mill volume and tool paths that were generated within the volume, you could simply save the tool paths to a file and have Pro/MANUFACTURING perform a material removal of the mill volume that was just programmed. Like carving out a piece of pie, the use of an *Automatic* option within the *Matrl Remove* command sequence will basically tell the system to subtract the mill volume from the workpiece. This gives you a visual representation of the geometry that has already been machined.

At this point, your model might look like that shown in the following illustration.

Chapter 12: Pro/MANUFACTURING

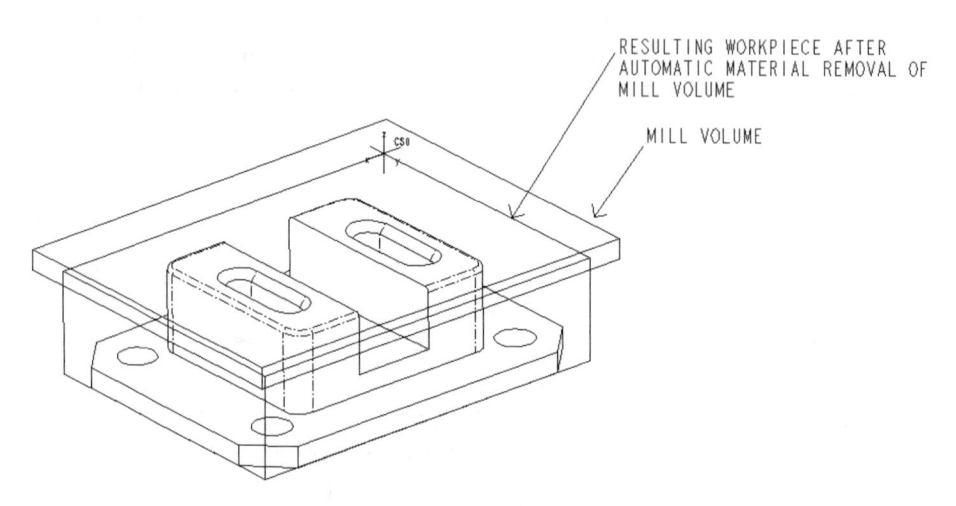

Approved mill volume removed from workpiece.

I cannot count the number of times that a CNC programmer, using other CAM packages, has stopped in the middle of a complex CNC programming sequence for lunch, a meeting, or the weekend, and come back having to retrace his or her steps to find where they left off in the CNC programming sequence. With Pro/MANUFACTURING, all of the mill volumes that you have programmed, tested, approved, and removed from the workpiece give you a graphical understanding of what has been completed and what has not.

Surfaces for Mill Volumes

But, as you may be aware, in addition to sketching, other utilities may be needed to define complex geometries. The following design has some geometries that you cannot capture by simply sketching a mill volume to mill up to.

Ease of Use + Powerful Tools = Productivity 301

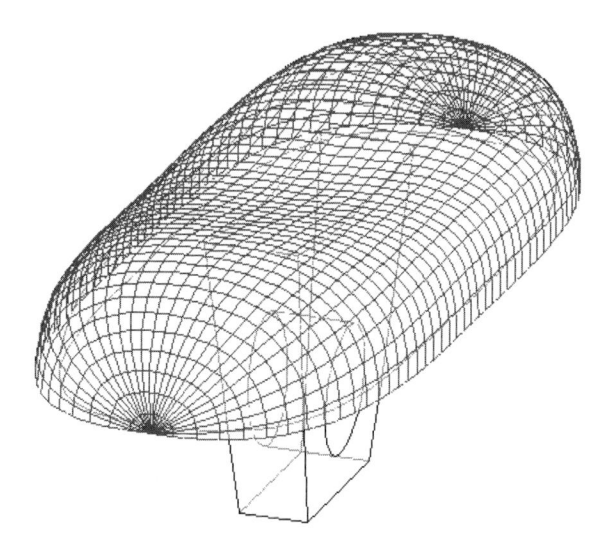

Design that will be used for tool path generation. (Top surface meshed for visualization.)

There are many approaches to defining mill volumes, some of which are combinations of a user's sketched mill surfaces and the actual design's surfaces.

In this case, the actual part geometry will be used as the reference for the mill volume definition. This can be done for both roughing and finishing tool paths. The mill volume might look like that shown in the following illustration.

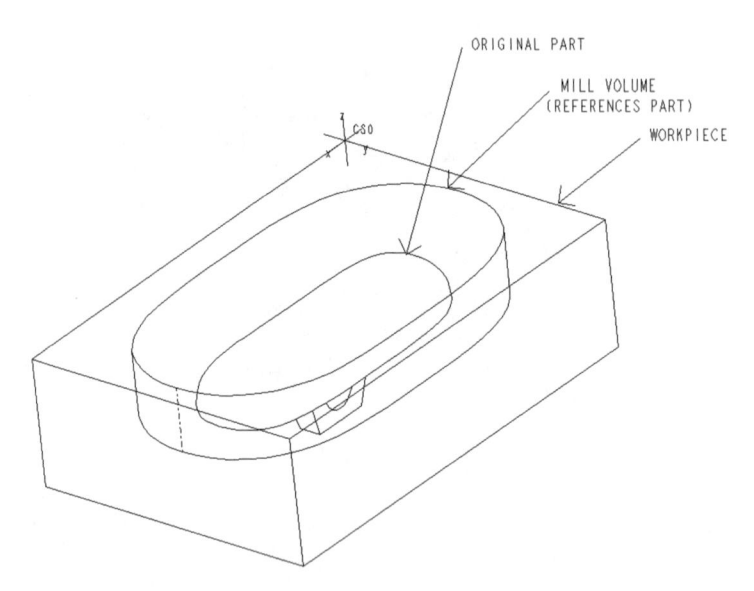

Mill volume for roughing tool paths.

After the tool paths were generated for the above mill volume, the tool paths may be accepted as usable code and the mill volume material removed from the workpiece. The new manufacturing model is shown in the following illustration.

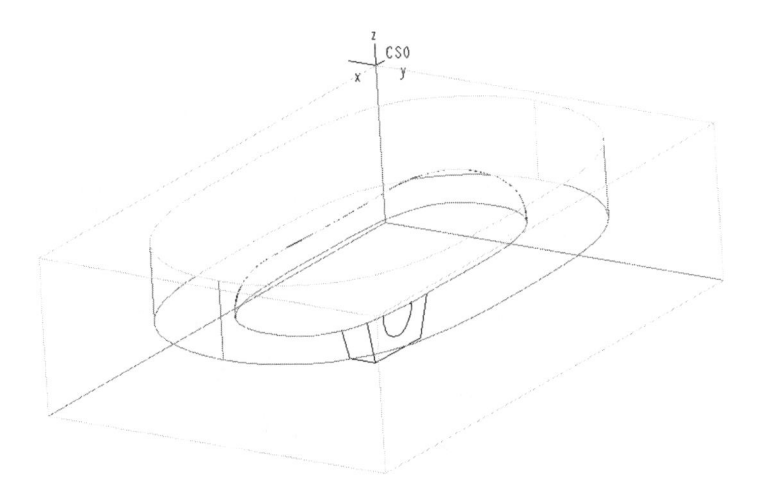

Manufacturing model with the mill volume removed.

Assume that the next step would be to generate a finishing tool path of the design's surfaces. Because the mill volume had been programmed and successfully removed from the workpiece, you can simply use the same mill volume without any rough offset. Your final verification might look like that shown in the following illustration.

Chapter 12: Pro/MANUFACTURING

NC-check of rough and finish tool paths for part.

Once again, after the final tool paths have been generated and accepted by the programmer, the mill volume for the finishing tool paths can be removed from the workpiece. This leaves you with a visual cue as to what has been completed and what still needs to be programmed. Imagine how much time it would have taken to generate and keep track of all of the tool paths using a wireframe and surface-based CAM system. For some systems, this may not have taken long at all, but what if the design were to change? The likelihood of the tool paths being reprogrammed in other CAM system would be very high. But, with Pro/MANUFACTURING these dimensional changes would only require the regeneration of the manufacturing model and the tool paths you automatically update.

As you can see from the previous examples, Pro/MANUFACTURING is a powerful and easy-to-use tool that can definitely increase productivity. There is no question that the technology that Pro/MANUFACTURING uses to maintain a parametric link to the model is impressive and useful. But in the end, there are some ground rules that you must be aware of in order to ensure maximum flexibility and efficiency. Any ideas as to what that might be? You guessed it, a flexible and accurate database.

Design Quality and Manufacturing

A flexible and accurate design can make all the difference when it comes to generating tool paths in Pro/MANUFACTURING or any other CAM package for that matter. We have discussed the benefits of having flexible designs, but even though it is possible to input and use designs from other CAD systems or designs sculpted in Pro/ENGINEER, geometry misalignments and errors in construction can plague the development of tool paths. Remember, misalignments and geometry checks are information provided by Pro/ENGINEER to indicate that a part may not be manufacturable. Common problems importing geometry from other CAD/CAM systems, such as tangency inconsistencies or other transition or mismatch problems from one surface to the next, can definitely affect the development of tool paths.

Inaccurate Data

Inaccurate or incomplete geometries in Pro/ENGINEER can create some interesting problems. For example, the following design was developed in Pro/ENGINEER.

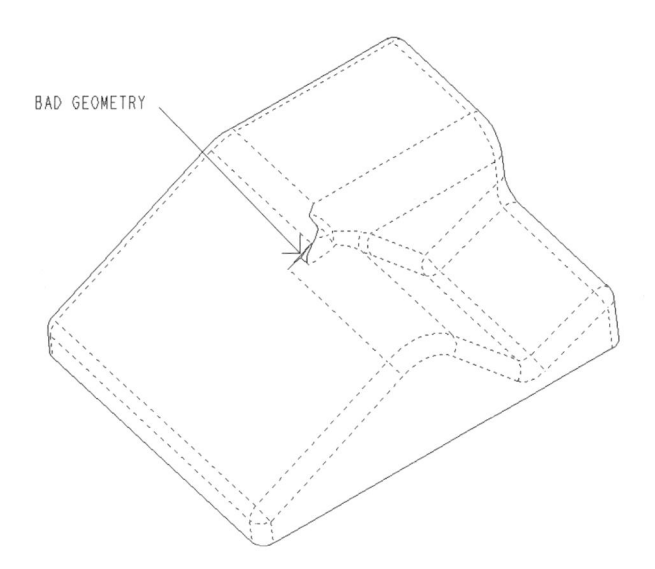

Design developed in Pro/ENGINEER with incomplete geometry.

Chapter 12: Pro/MANUFACTURING

As you can see, the previous design has some problems with the rounds that were developed to describe the geometry. This model can still be used for the generation of some tool paths, but you are at a greater risk of gouging the part or adding unnecessary complexity to the tool path's development. A three-axis milling operation for this part may look like the following illustration.

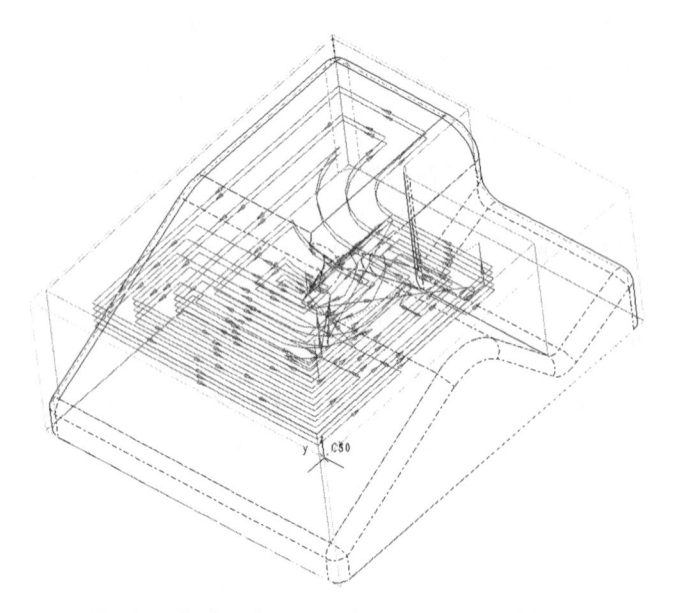

Tool paths for design with geometry problems.

As you can see from the previous illustration, there is an increased number of tool paths in the localized area where the geometry is not completely described. If you were to perform an NC-check on this tool path, you would see the following results.

Design Quality and Manufacturing 307

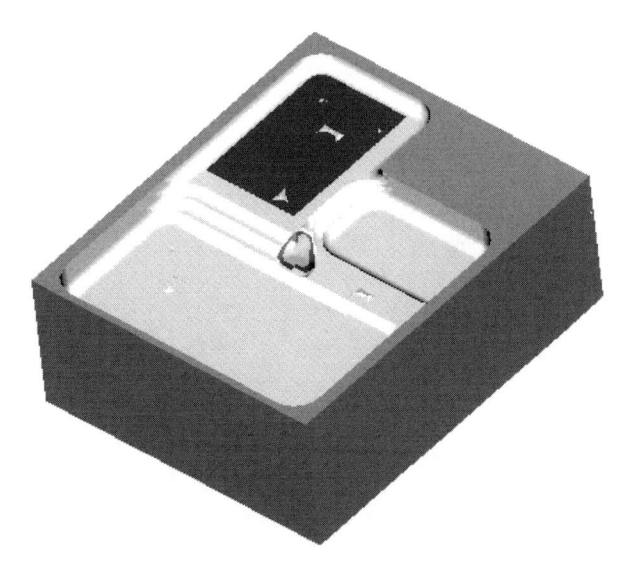

NC-check of tool path.

Notice that there are some gouges in the part with this tool path. It is possible to try to eliminate the problem by interactively programming the tool paths for this area of the geometry, but the time that it would take to fix the problem with Pro/MANUFACTURING would not be a good use of your time. In the end, the design should have probably been sent back to be reworked so that the geometry was developed properly.

Suppose that the previous design was sent back to get reworked, and the final design looked like that shown in the following illustration.

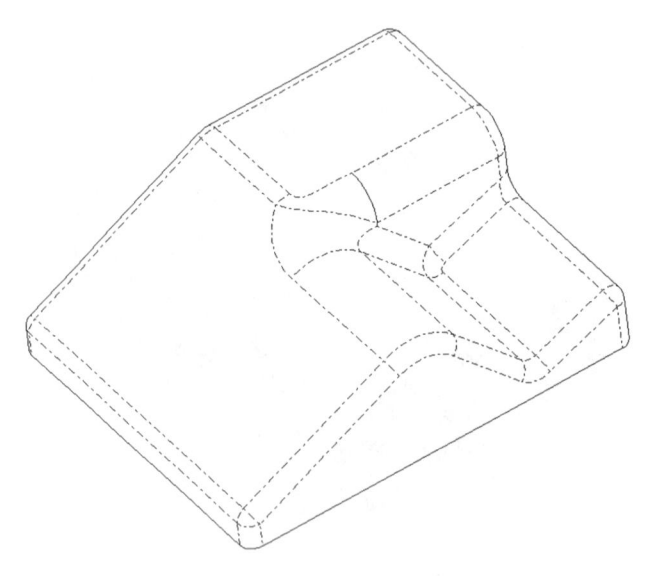

Corrected database.

After reprogramming the mill volume and generating the tool paths, the NC-check would look like the following illustration.

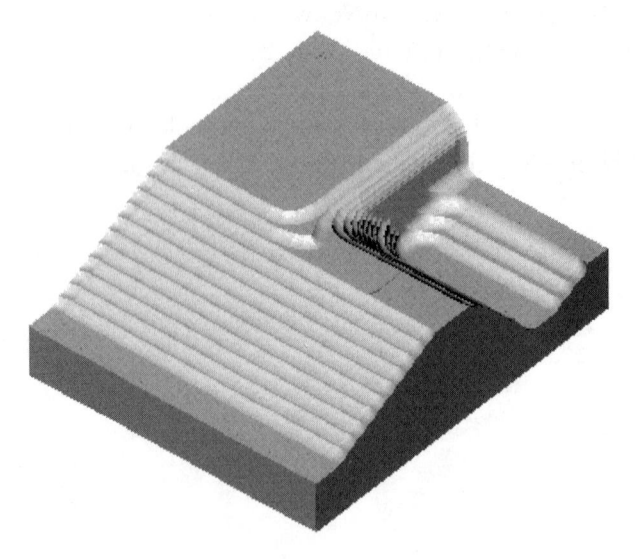

NC-check of corrected design with no gouges.

Design Quality and Manufacturing 309

Another area where you can run into some big problems is when a design is developed where you are making a hole and then filling it. Probably the best example of this can be found with a pattern of holes. The following design was developed in Pro/ENGINEER and uses a radial pattern of holes on the top of the part. Suppose that this design looked like the following example.

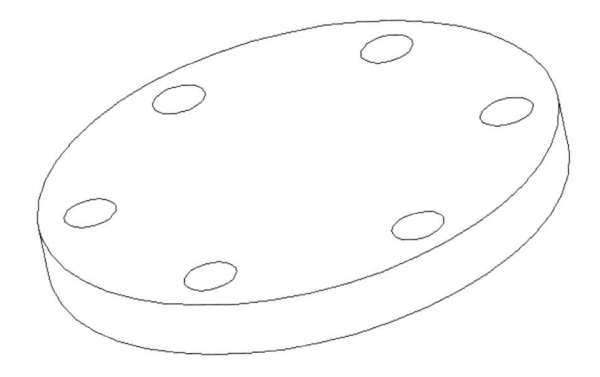

Design with pattern of holes.

Because all of the holes in the design are the same size, you have selected a drilling operation for these features in Pro/MANUFACTURING.

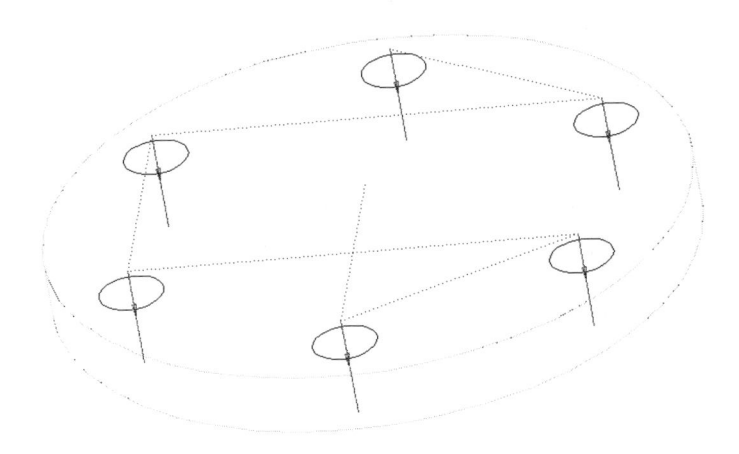

Tool paths for hole pattern.

Chapter 12: Pro/MANUFACTURING

After the tool paths were developed, a change in the design was encountered that added a tab to the top of the part. This new design would look like that shown in the following illustration.

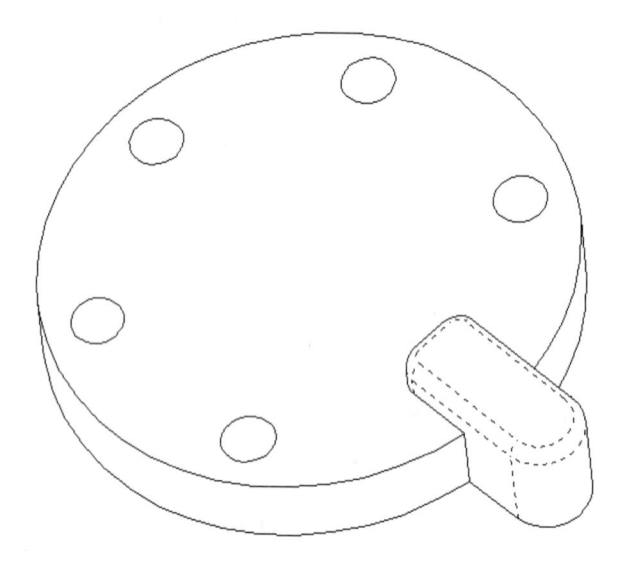

New design with tab added to top.

But during the generation of this new design, the pattern was not updated to allow for this additional geometry. Basically the designer filled one of the holes with geometry from the new tab. The hole is still there; it is just not visible. So what do you think will happen to the tool paths that were generated for the drilling operation? Let's see.

Design Quality and Manufacturing 311

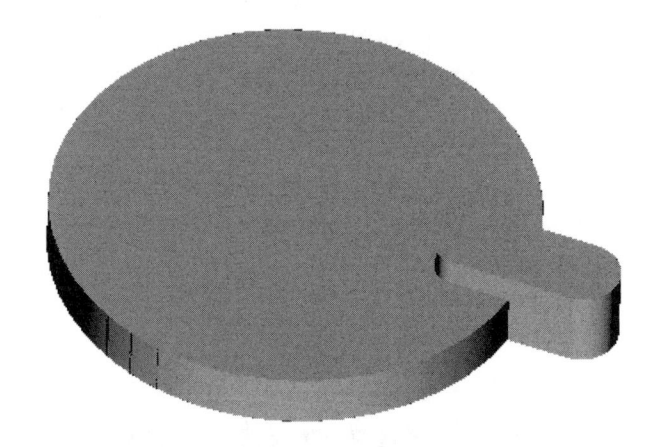

NC-check for design with new tab minus the drilling operation.

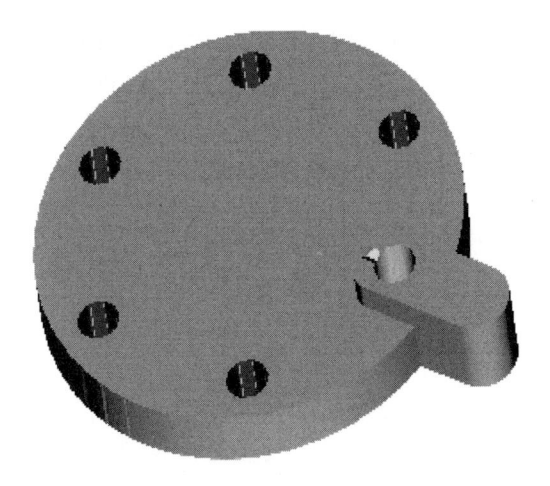

NC-check for design with new tab and drilling operation added.

As you can see, the drilling operation is still referencing geometry that has been covered up by the design change. This can be a big problem when it comes to quickly updating the design from one stage to the next. If you did not notice that the design still had an active hole in the part, and simply developed the tool paths to remove the geometry around the new tab without checking the rest of the code, you may have ruined the tool or part that you were machining. The obvious solution would be to redesign the pattern of holes so that the design change could be accepted and is functional.

As you can see from the previous examples, the quality of the design can have an impact on the generation of tool paths in Pro/MANUFACTURING. The quality of the design can depend on a number of things, such as using the right tools for the design's development and making sure that the design is flexible and can adapt to changes. These safeguards may seem fundamental, but are necessary to ensure the long-term success of all phases of the design and manufacturing process.

Configuration State and Simplified Representation Machining

Talk about a cool tool; Pro/MANUFACTURING comes with the ability to develop your mill volumes and tool paths at a particular stage of the part's development. This is easier to show than to explain, so let's look at the following design.

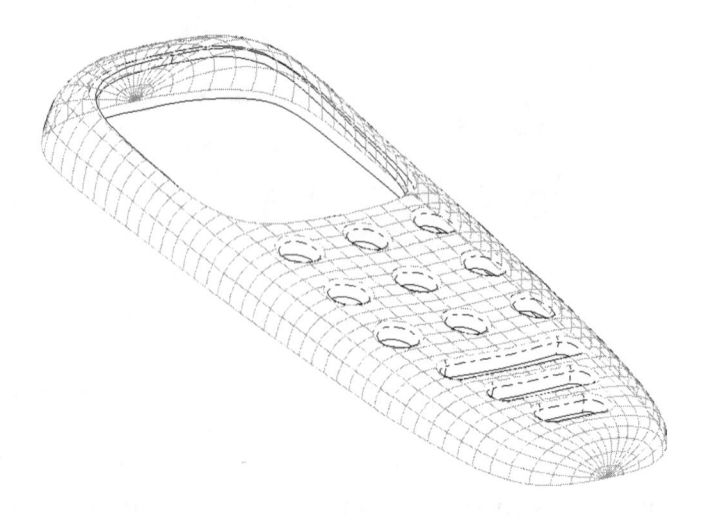

Complex design that is to be machined. (Free-form surface meshed for visualization purposes.)

Configuration State and Simplified Representation Machining

This particular design uses some free-form three-dimensional surfaces and complex transitions from the free-form surface to geometry that acts as geometry within the design. The complexity of this design can complicate the development of the mill volumes and the tool paths. For this example, the objective will be to develop a rough cut that will follow the contour of the free-form surface minus the openings in the part. But how will you obtain all the free-form surface geometry that is missing?

If you were using another CAD/CAM system, you would have to track down the master surface geometry that was used for the development of the part. Once this geometry was located, you would most likely offset the surface and then develop the tool paths up to this geometry. This can be time-consuming, and the geometry would not be dependent on the design if a design change was made.

You have the ability to develop a number of versions or instances of your design using family tables or simplified representations within Pro/ENGINEER. This ability to develop instances of your model can be helpful when developing milling volumes and tool paths in Pro/MANUFACTURING. Basically, you reduce the amount of information presented by adding the features that you do not want to review to a family table, and then turning off those features by developing an instance of the part that does not use those features, or you can selectively suppress features by developing simplified representations of your design. For example, the previously shown design will be machined using conventional three-axis machining techniques.

The following is an instance of the original design that does not have all of the holes in the design.

314   Chapter 12: Pro/MANUFACTURING

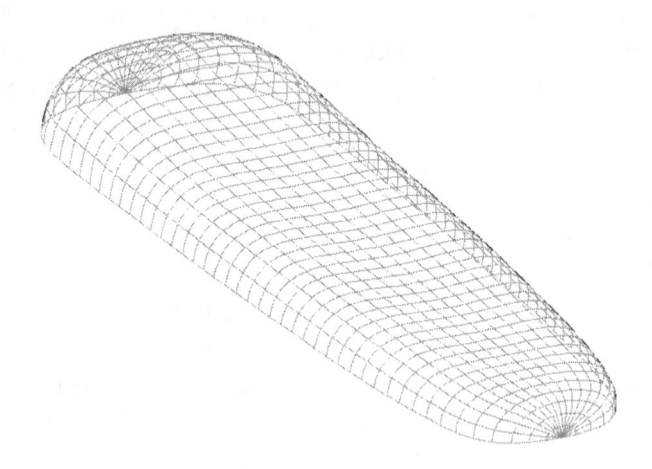

Instance or simplified representation of original design without holes. (Surfaces meshed for visualization purposes.)

The top surface of this instance will be used as the reference for the mill volume of the roughing tool path. Looking at the manufacturing model that contains the top-level design and the workpiece, you would see the following model.

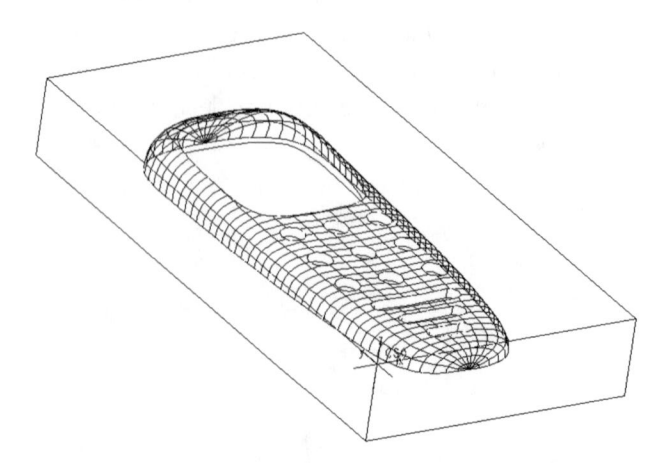

Manufacturing model of design and workpiece. (Part meshed for visualization purposes.)

Configuration State and Simplified Representation Machining 315

By simply accessing the MFG MODEL menu and setting up an instance by either replacing the existing model with a family table instance or substituting a simplified representation of the design, you can quickly swap out the top-level model for an instance of the design. The manufacturing model would look like that shown in the following illustration.

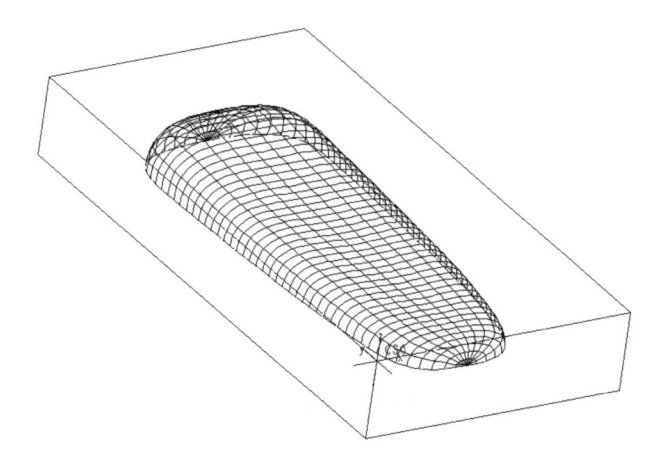

Manufacturing model design instance and workpiece. (Instance or simplified representation meshed for visualization purposes.)

Now you have the opportunity to quickly and easily develop the mill volume for the roughing cuts. The following is an illustration of the tool paths that were generated using a mill volume that was based on the instance of the part.

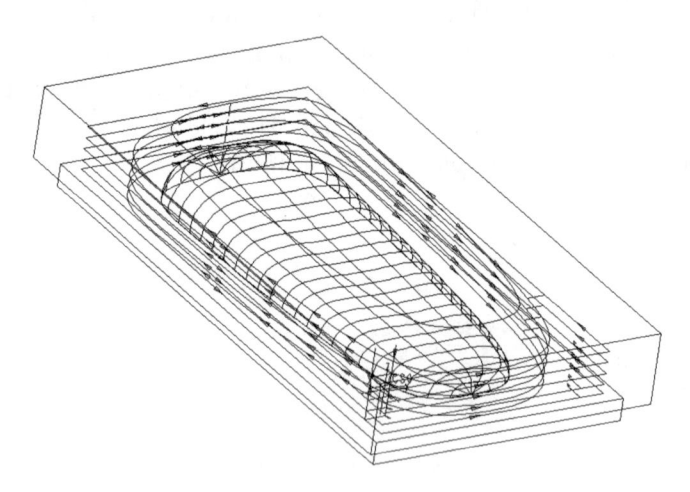

Mill volume with tool paths developed using instance of design. (Instance meshed for visualization purposes.)

Now that this roughing operation is completed, you can either generate the finishing tool paths, change the current design instance for another design instance, or change the design instance for the top-level design (the generic instance). For this example, let's assume that the previous instance was set up for another instance of the design so that some rough cuts for the holes can be machined.

Configuration State and Simplified Representation Machining 317

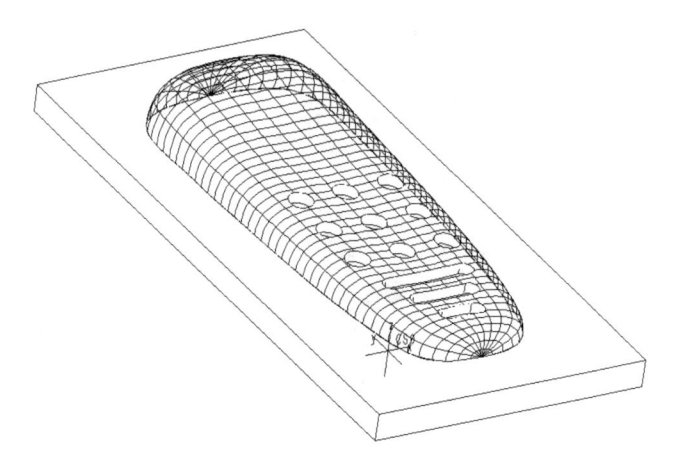

Manufacturing model design instance (with holes) and workpiece. (Top meshed for visualization purposes.)

The tool paths for the holes in the design might look like the following illustration.

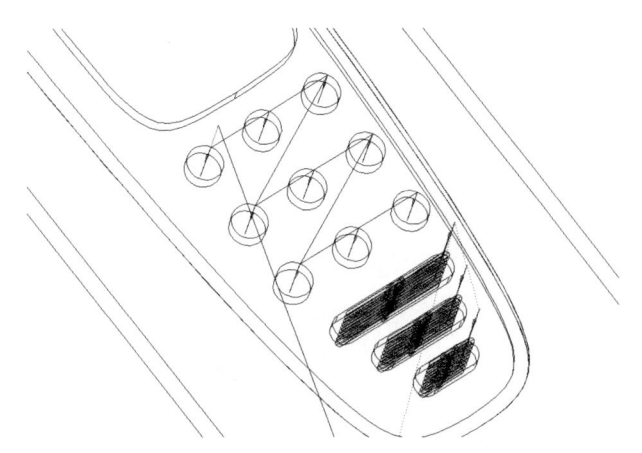

Tool paths for roughing of holes in design.

To show what the workpiece would look like at this stage in the programming, the following is an NC-check of the two previously shown roughing tool paths.

318   Chapter 12: Pro/MANUFACTURING

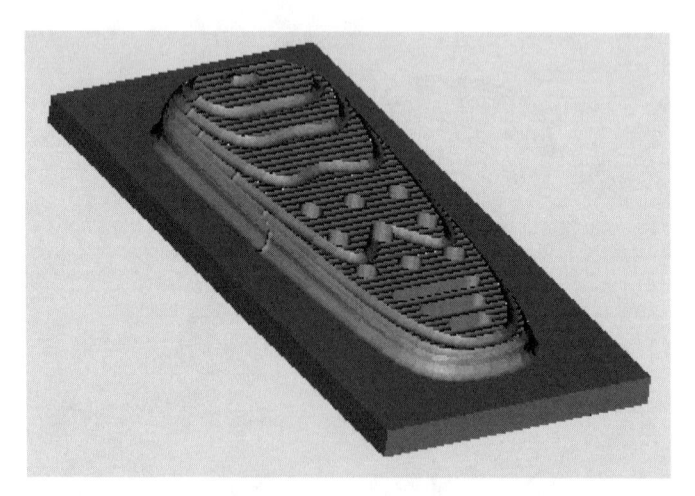

NC-check of the two roughing tool paths.

Now that you have programmed, tested, and accepted the roughing tool paths, a finishing pass over all of the surfaces could be generated based on the design's surfaces. To do this, you would change the design instance to the top level (generic instance) and generate the mill volume based on the design's actual surfaces. The resulting tool paths would look like those shown in the following illustration.

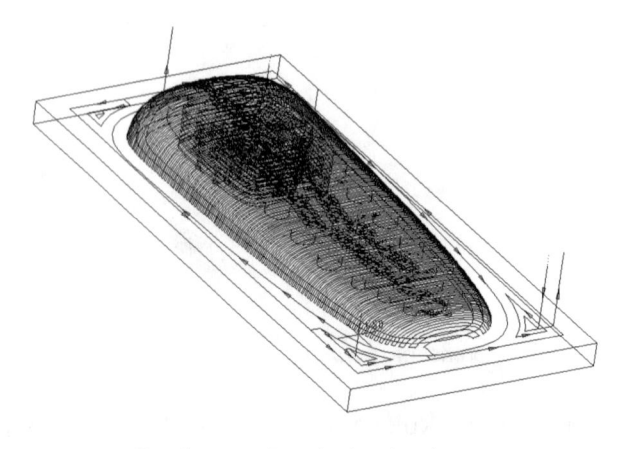

Finishing tool paths for the design.

After all of these tool paths were generated from the design at various stages in the design's development, the NC-check file would look like the following illustration.

NC-check of all tool paths.

As you can see, the user is not limited to the features and surfaces that are currently visible in the master model. This is a distinct advantage over other CAM systems and can be a real time saver, especially when working on complex and ever changing surface geometries. Having the ability to set up instances of the design to simplify the manufacture of the components opens a number of doors for the development of tool paths within Pro/MANUFAC-TURING. However, as you may have suspected, the powerful functionality can only be put to use if the database is clean and capable of developing functional instances of the design. The reason for this is the number of problems that can crop up from undesirable parent/child relationships. Once again the quality of the design and the database can make all the difference.

Pro/NC-CHECK

Pro/NC-CHECK has been shown periodically in this chapter to show how the tool paths that you have programmed interact with the workpiece. There are

Chapter 12: Pro/MANUFACTURING

a number of positive reasons for using this module, but the biggest one is its ability to prove your tool paths prior to running the tool paths on actual parts. This module dynamically simulates the removal of material from the workpiece as the tool paths are replayed. For example, the following manufacturing model is composed of a core developed in Pro/MOLDDESIGN and a workpiece.

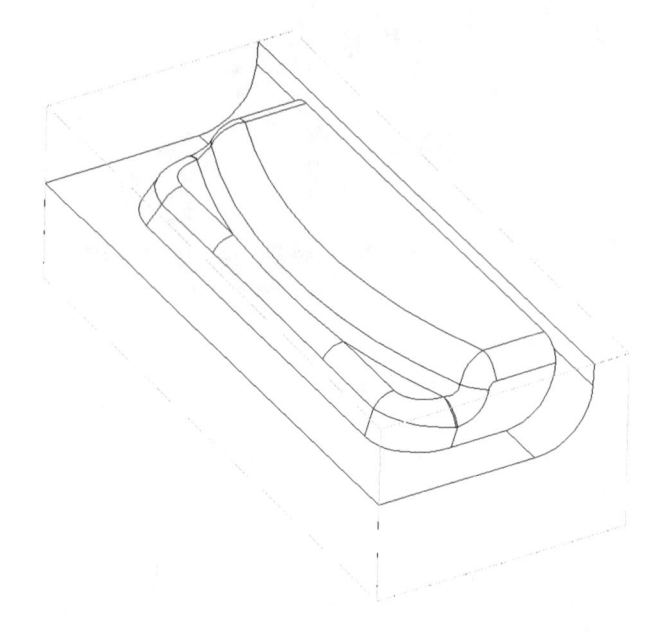

Core of a design developed in Pro/MOLDDESIGN with workpiece; the manufacturing model.

A mill volume along with the tool paths for the roughing of the core geometry is shown in the following illustration.

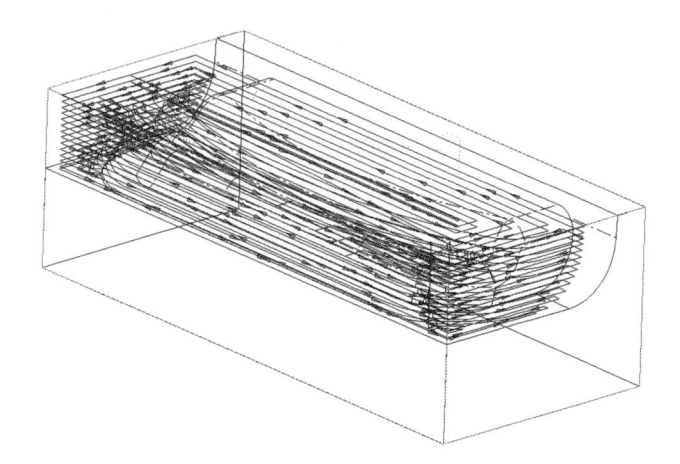

Roughing tool paths for the core side of the mold.

To ensure that the tool paths have been generated properly and are not accidentally gouging the part, you can perform an NC-check prior to accepting the tool paths. This can be a handy tool for proving your machining parameters and how they interact with the model.

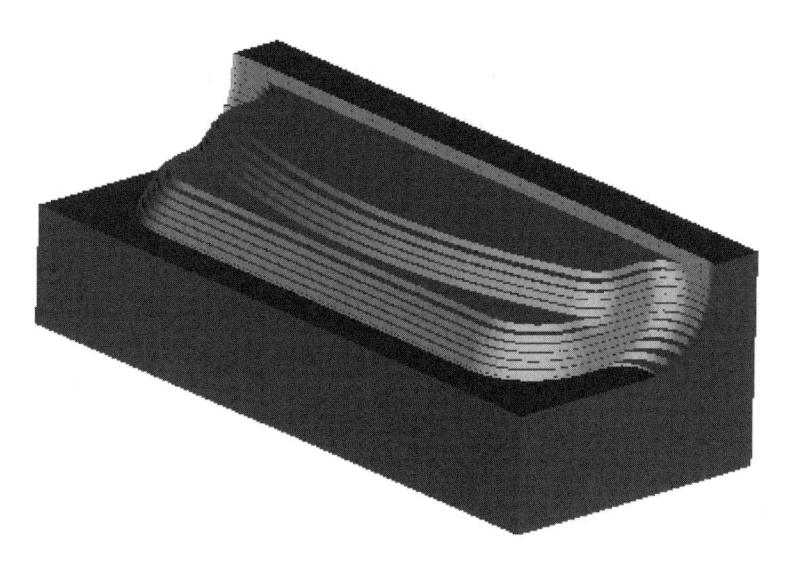

NC-check of the roughing tool paths for the core side of the mold.

Most other CAM systems do not have the ability to verify the tool paths using a material removal simulation technique. The advantage in applying this technology is that instead of just accepting the tool paths and removing the material from the workpiece, the NC-check simulates the actual tool geometry that will be used for the operation. Typically, when you are programming a set of tool paths in other CAM systems, you would develop several sets of tool paths and then export the tool paths to a verification package. In some cases, in order to verify the tool paths that you generated, you would have to translate or reformat the NC file so that the verification package could process the information. In addition, you would most likely be required to program into the verification package all the parameters for the types of operations that will be used, including the size of the workpiece.

Pro/MANUFACTURING and Pro/NC-CHECK are a powerful combination because you can perform all of your programming, tool path modifications, and verification within the same environment on the fly. The ability to verify your tool paths, before continuing with your next programming sequence, ensures that you will be getting more use out of your tools and throwing away less material in the form of scrap because of gouges or poor judgment.

Clipping Planes

Another impressive and useful tool within Pro/NC-CHECK can be found in the user's ability to set up clipping planes. Clipping planes are similar to the *"Clip"* functionality when spinning shaded objects in Pro/ENGINEER, provided you have the ability to use this option. Basically, clipping planes can help you to visualize areas of a design that are difficult to view. For example, the following design is a small fixture that will be machined out of plastic.

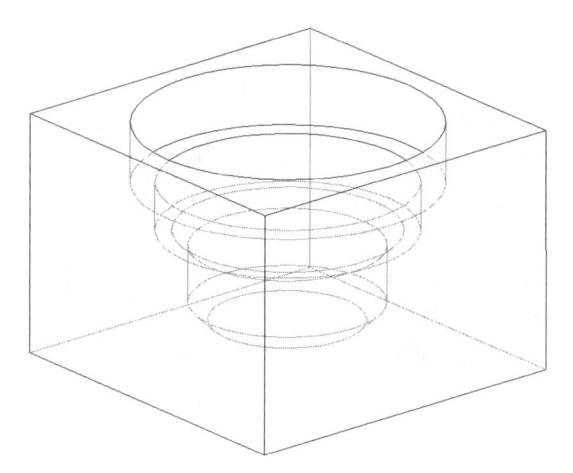

Design that will be machined.

The manufacturing model of the piece shown above is shown in the following illustration.

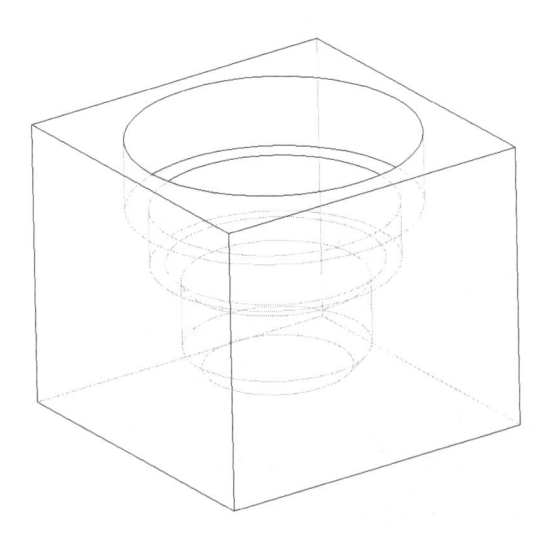

Manufacturing model design with workpiece.

Note that the mill volume will not be visible because the workpiece and design are the same size.

NC-check of roughing mill volume.

Notice that the previously shown NC-check does not communicate the full story for how the geometry was machined. At this point, you could either reorient the view to an angle whereby you could see the verification, or you could set up a clipping plane to temporarily remove some geometry that may be in front of the areas you are interested in.

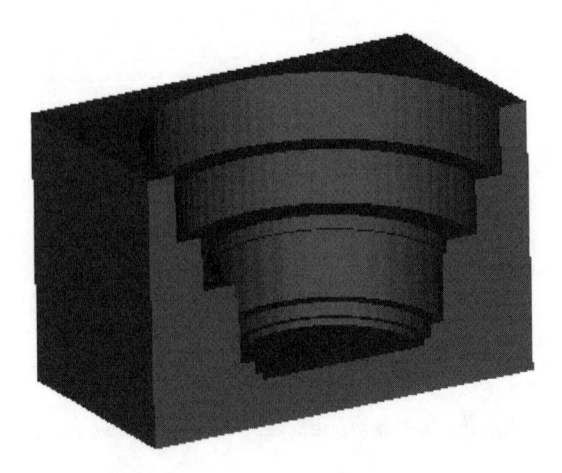

NC-check with clipping plane through the workpiece.

Pro/NC-CHECK could be classified as a must-have module when you are using Pro/MANUFACTURING. The amount of time that this can save you and your company, not to mention all the tools and materials, can pay for the module within a short period of time. Just think what it would be like to develop several sets of tool paths only to find that your workpiece gouged in several places because of an error in the setup, or have to go through the time-consuming task of reformatting your NC files for a third-party NC-verification package, only to find an error, and then reprogram the tool paths, reformat, and run the new tool paths to verify the code. With Pro/NC-CHECK comes the ability to prove your tool paths on the fly, without saving a whole bunch of files, reformatting, programming workpiece parameters, or even exiting Pro/ENGINEER.

Postprocessing

No matter what type of manufacturing operations you have programmed with Pro/MANUFACTURING, you would most likely not be able to do anything with the CL files until they are reformatted, or postprocessed, for the type of machine tool that you will be using. Basically, all the tool paths that you have generated are a generic listing of the tool's location relative to the reference coordinate system. As you continue to build tool paths upon tool paths and play back the NC sequences, you are simply developing and replaying the locations of the tool. All of this information is written to a file in ASCII format, with an APT syntax.

Because there are so many manufacturing tools available in the industry, and therefore so many proprietary codes and controllers, postprocessing packages serve a much needed function as a link between CAM packages and the tools of manufacturing. For a listing of available postprocessing packages that are compatible with Pro/MANUFACTURING, please reference the user's manual or contact your local authorized Parametric Technology Corporation Sales Office or authorized VAR.

Summary

Pro/MANUFACTURING is a powerful, flexible, and easy-to-use module within the Pro/ENGINEER family. Having the ability to quickly develop tool paths by working from the surfaces of the design is a common operation that many CAM packages have, but the thing that really separates Pro/MANUFACTURING from the rest of the pack is its ability to adapt to changes in the design rapidly and efficiently. However, adapting to changes in the design can only be done efficiently if the designs are capable of adapting to changes. This of course means that the quality of the design will enter and dominate the equation of parametric manufacturing.

Above and beyond the development of tool paths in Pro/MANUFACTURING lies the area of NC verification. For a number of years, NC verification has been in the user's ability to predict how well the programming sequence is progressing by third-party software that required that the NC files generally be reformatted for processing and all of the tooling and workpiece parameters be programmed just to verify the tool paths. By using Pro/NC-CHECK for the verification of the tool paths, prior to accepting and saving the tool paths, you can prove your code without having to wait until the end of a programming sequence to verify a set of NC files. Pro/NC-CHECK uses a verification technique that actually simulates the tool's geometry removing material from the workpiece, therefore, reducing the risk of accidentally gouging the part or any other geometry that you may wish to avoid, such as fixtures for machining.

We have seen some examples of advanced techniques for the manufacture of complex geometry. Techniques such as the use of configuration state or simplified representation machining can improve your ability to quickly develop complex geometries. Having the ability to program tool paths over geometry that normally would not be available to the user can make all the difference when it comes time to make changes in the design. But having all of this power at your fingertips will not do you any good unless you are able to postprocess the CL file into a format that can be used to drive your machine tools.

Postprocessing is the final stage that is required to convert your CL files into usable code that can drive your machine tools. Because Pro/MANUFACTURING develops CL files in a standard format, the files are not useful for driving machine tools by themselves because there are so many machine tools available in the manufacturing community, and each manufacturer has its own requirements for NC files. Because of this, you will not be able to use the information contained in the CL files unless the information is postprocessed, essentially converting the generic code into a machine-specific code that can be used to manufacture the design.

Overall Pro/MANUFACTURING coupled with Pro/NC-CHECK gets a strong "two thumbs up" from this user. The number of changes that have been incorporated into the modules is a strong indication of the manufacturing community's support and interest in an evolving technology and tool. As a user of Pro/ENGINEER you may find areas of the software that need improvement, and by filling out the enhancement request forms, being active in your local Pro/USER groups, and taking the time to attend national meetings, you may be surprised at how fast your changes get implemented.

Appendix

Hardware Configurations

Memory, Graphics, and Processing

Imagine what it would be like to have a computer that responded to your every command with lighting speed, looked and felt robust in all areas of processing, and allowed you to iterate through a number of design options quickly and efficiently. For a select few of you reading this book, you have a workstation that satisfies all of your memory, graphics, and processing needs: congratulations, you are very fortunate. For the rest of us using Pro/ENGINEER, we are forced to look at a small intermittent reminder that we are sitting idle; it is shown in the following illustration.

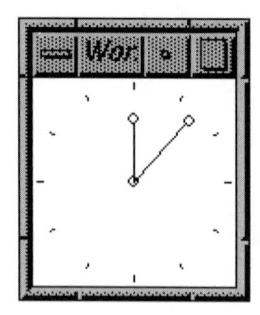

The Pro/ENGINEER clock.

Working with the *minimum* configuration requirements for Pro/ENGINEER can be a real time vacuum for those of us who work on complex parts and assemblies. Even if you have optimized your use of Pro/ENGINEER through the use of macros, menu items, or a number of other productivity tools that you can develop, there will always be a bottleneck. And the last time I looked up the definition of *minimum,* the word *optimum* was not included in the description.

Bottlenecks

If you were to break down a workstation into its fundamental components that would have an impact on your ability to work efficiently, you would basically be looking at (1) memory, RAM and hard drive, (2) graphics, and (3) processing. As you might expect, each of these areas go hand in hand and are equally important when it comes to manipulating your designs in Pro/ENGINEER, or any other CAD/CAM/CAE system. Try to perform modeling and analysis tasks on underequipped systems, and the results are usually the same—hours and hours of lost time. Within the eternal battle to satisfy your design and analysis requirements, while still meeting the development schedule, lies a balance between the three fundamental areas of your workstation and the bottlenecks that each of these areas can create.

Memory

Some of these bottlenecks are more noticeable than others, and most can be found in your system's ability to manipulate data in memory and represent that information on the screen with graphics. The amount of memory that you have in your computer can make all of the difference when it comes to manipulating large databases in Pro/ENGINEER. I can't count the number of times that I have been working on a computer that only had 32 MB of RAM and listened to the hard drive *scream* to me that it was working. This *scratching* of the hard drive is an indication that the memory requirements have not been met, the results of which are an increase in system activity and regeneration time. Because you are working with Pro/ENGINEER databases, which are intrinsically large, the amount of memory can make a difference when it comes to making a large number of changes.

Graphics

The type of graphics that you have can be just as large a bottleneck as the amount of memory. Graphics and memory are probably the most noticeable bottlenecks in your system, mostly because it may seem that you see the Pro/ENGINEER Clock more than your design. The type of graphics that you have can make a significant difference in the quality of the designs that you produce and the amount of time that you spend working on the overall design. A low-end graphics accelerator, like an 8-bit or 24-bit system that will drop its resolution back to an 8-bit image during any manipulation of the geometry, can seem like you are playing a game of steps and ladders. A low-end graphics accelerator can be a boat anchor to your system on large or complex components. These delays are usually due to lengthy regeneration, resulting from the calculation of a hidden line removal or some other display option. On the other hand, a high-end graphics accelerator, like a buffered 24-bit system, can improve your visualization of the design and significantly reduce your regeneration time, not to mention that complex parts and assemblies are much easier to decipher when you can actually see where one part ends and another begins.

There is a difference in the speed and performance of hardware- and software-based graphics accelerators. Hardware-based accelerators generally use a separate graphics-dedicated engine to process graphics computations.

Whereas software-based accelerators do have an advantage over running in X-Windows only, there is a penalty due to the additional computations that your CPU will be performing. Once again, run a benchmark test on available options to find an accelerator that satisfies your needs.

Processing

The final major bottleneck can be found in the speed and processing capabilities of your processor, or CPU. During my career, I have worked with a number of machines, each with their own unique configuration. The area of processing has not come up as often as the other two primary bottlenecks, but it has been an issue, especially on large parts and assemblies. This type of bottleneck can present some frustrating problems when it comes to performing computationally intensive processing functions such as FEA or NC programming work. You may have lots of memory and the fastest graphics in the department, but if your processor is not robust enough to tackle the numeric operations that you require in an timely manner, then don't be surprised to see the Pro/ENGINEER Clock at the base of your screen.

In the end, it all comes down to your ability to fulfill your design requirements within the time frames available. If you are going to be able to produce quality designs in an acceptable time frame, you must have a balance of the tools necessary to perform all of your design and documentation functions. But above and beyond that, you must have the ability to iterate your designs so that they can evolve. Iteration is one of the most important keys to a successful design and development phase. And with time at a premium, it is important to minimize the amount of idle time in the development process. One way to do that is to invest in the fastest processor available, a realistic amount of memory for the types of applications that you will require, and a graphics accelerator that will satisfy your needs and be there when you need more functionality.

The Price of an Optimal Configuration

All of this of course is relative to the amount of money that you, or your company, are willing to spend on each of these items. But in making your

The Price of an Optimal Configuration

decision, you must weigh carefully the amount of down time you may experience with a system at its *minimum* configuration relative to an *optimally* configured system, which will enable you to make quick work of tough modeling and analysis problems and be there for future changes. Always remember, *minimum* does not mean *optimum*.

By now you are probably asking, "What is an optimally configured system for Pro/ENGINEER?" If I were to say that one specific type of system was better than another, you might think that I had sold out. Besides there are a lot of workstation manufacturers out there who want your business, and by the time you read this section of the book, my personal recommendation may be leap frogged by a competing manufacturer or an entirely new technology. But if I were to configure my *optimum* system, based on the number of systems that I have worked on, relative to Pro/ENGINEER, my shopping list would look like the following:

```
Memory: 128-144 MB
Disk: 2.0+ GB
Processor: PA-RISC 125 MHz+ or MIPS 200 MHz+
Graphics: 24-bit GL (HP's 48Z or SGI's XZ or
    Extreme Graphics)
```

Of course, each of these above options are my selections; you probably have your favorites and this list is not intended to sell computers for one company over another. I do, however, recommend that you and your company use the above configurations as a reference for what works well with Pro/ENGINEER. The amount of money involved for an optimally configured system can and does vary from manufacturer to manufacturer. In general, you should be able to obtain an optimally configured system from anywhere between $37,000 and $65,000 (keep in mind that the price of workstations has and will continue to decrease). There is a tendency to let these figures scare the people writing the checks away from these high-end systems. But remember, you have a choice, spend the money now and enjoy the speed and flexibility or pay for it later in lost time. Either way, I strongly suggest that you look for a system that will satisfy your current and future engineering as well as your financial needs.

Index

A

Add sequence, developing, 51–54
Alignment of dimensions, macros used for design improvement, 218–221
Alignment, rapid prototyping, errors in database, 277–279
Alternative module selection, corporate standards, 75–76
Aluminum tooling, rapid prototyping, 276
Analysis
    Design intent communication, 241–242
    Dimensions and iteration, 256–260
    Finite element analysis, 241–245, 260, 262–266
    Geometry layering to suppress features, 242–245
    Optimization of design, 248–249
    Pro/MESH, 246–248, 252–253
    Shell elements, use, 254
    Topology optimization, 260–266
Approval of design, layouts, 22–23
Assemblies
    Concurrent assembly development, copies of layouts for, 22–23
    Declaring models and assemblies, 22–23
    Drawings, modifying designs from, 153
    Functionality, 10–11
    Interchangeability, 10–11
    Layout illustration, 16
    Layouts, relationship management, 14, 16
    Multiple layouts and assemblies, 24–25
    Planning design, 10–11
    Stack up analysis, 121–122
    Subcomponents, effect of changes, 112–113
Assembly mode
    Assembly modifications, 138–140
    Selection, 99, 101–102
    Stack up analysis, 121–122
Automatic assembly of components, 14, 16, 23–24
Automatic feature relationship management, 85

B

Blanking components, 151
Brainstorming
    Documenting, 5–6
    Early consensus, 6–7
    Group think, 5–6
    Mediating, 5–6
    Planning design, 5–6, 10–11
    Quality input, generating, 4
    Timing, 5–6

C

CAM systems
    Pro/MANUFACTURING, 286–287
    Rapid prototyping, errors in database, 280–282
Case Study, layouts, 19, 21
Changes
    See Design modifications
CL files, Pro/MANUFACTURING, postprocessing, 325–327
Classroom instruction, 98
Clipping planes, Pro/NC-CHECK, 322, 324–325
CNC
    See Pro/MANUFACTURING
Communication of corporate standards, 62–63
Components
    Automatic assembly, 14, 16
    Corporate standards, 65–73, 75–76, 78
    Cost control, topology optimization, 260–266
    Cross-sectional view, 85
    Declared, 14, 16
    Dimensional relationships, outlining, 6–7
    Evaluation in design planning, 7
    Floating, 102–105
    Generating, 14, 16
    Inspection relationships, outlining, 6–7
    Interchanging, 27–29
    Layout, 7

Index

Mode selection, 99, 101–102
Modeling priority, 98–99
SLA, 269–270
Computer numeric control, rapid prototyping, 274–275
Config.clear file
 Design execution improvement, 236–240
 Multiple configurations, 235
Config.pro file
 Macros, 216–217, 227–228, 236–240
 Multiple configurations, running, 232
Configuration files, menu item addition, 228–229
Configuration state
 Machining with Pro/MANUFACTURING, 312–313
 Simplifying design view, 143–146, 148–150
Consensus, planning design, 6–7, 10–11
Consolidation of dimensions, parametric notes, 179–181, 183–184
Constraints
 Finite element analysis, 262–266
 Layouts, relationship management, 14, 16
Contract elements, 246–248
Contracted resources
 Benchmark test, 66–67
 Contractor's role, 65–73, 75–76, 78
 Corporate standards' effect on, 77–78
 Resource's role, 65–73, 75–76, 78
Corporate standards
 Alternative module selection, 75–76
 Analysis submittal standards, 242–245
 Approved modeling method definition, 65–73, 75–76, 78
 Benchmark test for contracted firms, 66–67
 Communication among departments, 62–63
 Component standardization, 65–73, 75–76, 78
 Contracted resources, effect on, 77–78
 Contracting with other firms for component modeling, 65
 Defined, 57–58
 Design modification, 133–134
 Design verification and manufacturability, 109–112
 Developing, 65–73, 75–76, 78
 Educating firm members of need, 65–73, 75–76, 78
 Enforcement, 75–76
 Flexibility, 75–76
 Future use, preserving information for, 77–78
 In-house Pro/ENGINEER experts, 72–73, 75
 Involvement of other departments in development, 65–73, 75–76, 78
 Layouts, 23–24
 Novice users, 75–76
 Planning design, 10–11
 Remodeling, 62–63
 Roles in relationship with contracted firms, 65–73, 75–76, 78
 Selective enforcement, 77–78
 Supplier input, 72–73, 75
 Tool selection, 72–73, 75
 Uniformity of product, 75–76
 Uses, 57–58
 Worksheet, 60
Cross-functionality, module selection, 8–9
Cross-sectional view, design intent, 85

D

Database
 Flexibility, Pro/MANUFACTURING, 304
 Rapid prototyping, 277–279
Datum planes
 Layouts, relationship management, 14, 16
 Seed files, 32
Datum points, layouts for relationship management, 14, 16
Declaring layouts to other design units, 27–29
Declaring models and assemblies, 22–23
Default datum planes
 Seed files, 32
 View development, 201–203
Definition pattern, menu item additions, 229–230
Deletions
 Design intent, 89–92
 Design modifications, 137–138
Design constraints, finalizing design plans, 7
Design execution improvement
 Additional options, 215
 Config.clear file, 235–240
 Config.pro file, 216–217, 227–228, 232, 236–240
 Efficiency improvement, 213–215
 Macro keys, 232–234
 Macros, 215–216
 Menu item addition, 228–229
 Menu items, menu_def.pro file, 229–230

Index

Menu location, macro execution, 225–227
Menu_def.pro file, 236–240
Multiple configurations, running, 232
Multiple configurations, transitions among, 236–240
Multiple projects, transition among, 228–229
Nesting, multiple macro execution, 221–224
Repetitive executions, 215
Save and purge commands, 221–224
Shading and spinning geometry, 224–225
Table Editor, menu creation within, 227–228
Design for assembly analysis, 120
Design instances, Pro/MANUFACTURING, versions developed with family tables, 313
Design intent
   Automatic feature relationship management, 85
   Communication to improve analysis, 241–242
   Component modeling priority, 98–99
   Consequence anticipation, 89–92
   Cross-sectional view of component, 85
   Deletions, 89–92
   Detailing, 179
   Feature applications, 89, 91–92
   Feature development, 89–92
   Feature selection, 95, 97–98
   Flexibility, 95, 97–98
   Flexibility of generated designs, 81–82
   Intersecting walls, 83
   Layouts, 22–23, 98–99
   Lead time, 98–99
   Manufacturing requirements, 98–99
   Mode selection, 99, 101–102
   Modeling techniques, 79–81
   Module selection, 92, 94
   Order of execution, 89, 91–92
   Parametric relationship generation, 102–105
   Parent/child relationships, 86–89
   Pro/MESH, 246–248
   Problem-solving, 79–81
   Protrusions, 82
   Risk assessment, 98–99
   Rounds, adding, 84–85
   Shell the model, 84–85
   Speed and efficiency, 102–105
   Tool selection, 89, 91–92
Design modification
   Assembled components, modification, 140–143

Assembly modifications in Assembly mode, 138–140
Assembly modifications using layout, 134–137
Assembly regeneration for development process, verification, 138–140
Blanking components, 151
Configuration state use to simplify view, 143–146, 148–150
Corporate standards, 133–134
DECLARE menu for reference verification, 138
Design intent, assembly regeneration for development, 140–143
Design verification and manufacturability, 109–112, 118–120
Dimensioning scheme, redefining, 169–170
Drawing format size changes, 188–189, 191–192
Drawings, modifying designs from, 153
Geometry reordering, 158
Geometry rerouting, 166–169
Insert mode, 159, 161–164
Layers use to simplify view, 151
Layouts, assembly modifications, 134–137
Modify-Modify Dim command sequence, 143–146, 148–150
Modify-Modify Part command sequence, 143–146, 148–150
Module selection, 95, 97–98
Parametric notes, 179–181, 183–184
Parent/child relationships, 158
Part geometry modifications, 154–155
Part mode, 143–146, 148–150
Pro/MANUFACTURING, mill volumes, 302–304
Pro/MANUFACTURING, strengths, 289–290
Querying features, 158
Regen Info command, 154–155
Resuming features, 164–165
Simplification of reference components, 151–152
Subassembly components, dimension value changes, 134–137
Subcomponents, 112–113
Suppressing components, 151
Suppressing features, 164–165
Tool path modifications, 289–290
Tracking feature development sequence, Regen Info command, 154–155
Trail files, 157

View development, 203
Design requirements, topology optimization, 260–266
Design verification and manufacturability
   Alterations of design, 118–120
   Assembly mode, stack up analysis, 121–122
   Changes in design, 109–112
   Corporate standards, 109–112
   Design For Assembly analysis, 120
   Design intent, 109–112
   Detailing, 109–112, 121–122
   Dimension changes, 124–127, 129–131
   Dimensional relationships, 109–112
   Dimensional requirements, 107–109
   Draft Check, 112–114
   Finite Element Analysis, 120
   Flexibility, 107–109, 112–113
   Gaussian curvature analysis, 116
   Geometric dimensioning and tolerancing, 124–127, 129–131
   Geometric relationships, 109–112
   Inspection requirements, 107–109
   Necessary development phase, 107–109
   Part mode, stack up analysis, 121–122
   Pattern relationships, 109–112
   Porcupine command, 116
   Pro/SCAN-TOOLS module, 116–117
   Process requirements, 118–120
   Reference dimension use, 124–127, 129–131
   Sectioning, 112–113
   Shaded images, 114–115
   Slope Surface Analysis, 112
   Stack up analysis of assembly part, 121–122
   Subcomponents, 112–113
   Supplier input, 118–120
   Surface geometry analysis, 114–115
   Tolerance format change, 122–124
   Tolerances, application, 120
   Tolerancing requirements, 109–112
Detail prints, layouts, 14, 16
Detailing
   Default datum planes, 201–203
   Design verification and manufacturability, 121–122
   Dimensional call outs, 173
   Drawing format size changes, 188–189, 191–192
   Driven dimensions, 171–172
   Feature control frame, 177

Flexibility of design, 173–175
Free form, 171–172
Parametric formats, 188–189, 191–192
Parametric notes, 179–181, 183–184
Parent/child relationships, 178
Regen Info command, 173–175
Reverse associativity, 203–206
Seed data, 184–185
Symbols, 197–198
Tables, 197–198
Tolerances developed in model, 175–177
View development, 198–201, 205–206, 208, 210
Detailing requirements, 109–112
Dimensional call outs, detailing, 173
Dimensional references, design modification, DECLARE menu use, 138
Dimensional relationships
   Assembly layout illustration, 16
   Corporate standards, 57–58
   Design verification and manufacturability, 109–112
   Planning design, 6–7
Dimensional requirements, 107–109
Dimensioning scheme
   Design modification by redefining, 169–170
   Process requirement verification, 118–120
Dimensions
   Design optimization, dimensions and iteration, 256–260
   Design verification and manufacturability, 124–127, 129–131
   Detailing, driven dimensions, 171–172
   Macros used for design improvement, 218–221
   Parametric notes, 179–181, 183–184
   Reverse associativity, 203–206
   Value changes, design modifications, 134–137
Draft Check, 112–114
Drawing format size changes, detailing, seed data, 188–189, 191–192
Drawings, design modification from, 153
Driven dimensions, detailing, 171–172

E

Efficiency
   See also Design execution improvement
   Mode selection, 99, 101–102
Enforcement of corporate standards, 75–76

Index   339

Errors, rapid prototyping, geometric errors in database, 280–282
Exclamation point (!), config.pro file, macros, 216–217
Experimentation, 98–99
Extruded cut, parent/child relationships, 89

F

Family tables, design instance developed with family tables in Pro/MANUFACTURING, 313
Feature control frame, detailing, 177
Feature relationships, corporate standards, 57–58
Features
    Design intent, 89–92
    Design modification by querying features, 158
    Design requirements, topology optimization, 260–266
    Macros used for design improvement, 218–221
    Parametric notes, 179–181, 183–184
    Relationship management, 85
    Selection for design intent, 95, 97–98
    Suppression, 242–245
Finite element analysis, 120, 241–245, 260, 262–266
Flexibility
    Design intent, 81–82
    Design verification and manufacturability, 107–109, 112–113
    Detailing, 173–175
    Feature selection, 95, 97–98
    Module selection, 95, 97–98
    Parametric formats, tables, 197
    Pro/MANUFACTURING, database flexibility, 304
    Pro/MESH, optimization of design, 247, 252–253
Free form detailing, 171–172
Free form modeling, planning design, 4–5
Function keys, nesting multiple macro execution, 221–224
Functional prototype, rapid prototyping, 270–273
Functionality, assemblies, 10–11

G

Gaussian curvature analysis, 116
Geometric dimensions and tolerances
    Design verification and manufacturability, 124–127, 129–131
    Detailing, 205–206, 208, 210
Geometric references, design modification, DECLARE menu use, 138
Geometric relationships, 109–112
Geometry
    Case Study, verifying calculations by, 19, 21
    Layering, 242–245
    Rapid prototyping, errors in database, 277–279
    Reordering, design modification, 158, 166–169
    Rerouting, design modification, 166–169
    Shading and spinning geometry, 224–225
Graphics requirements, 330–333
Group think, 5–6

H

Hardware configurations
    Graphics, 331
    Memory, 329
    Optimal configuration requirements, 330–333
    Processing capabilities, 332
Holes, Pro/MANUFACTURING, 309

I

IGES file, 269–270
    Pro/MANUFACTURING, 286
    Pro/MESH, 246–248
    Production model to analysis model, 242–245
    Rapid prototyping, errors in database, 280–282
In-house experts, corporate standards, 72–73, 75
Indirect relationships, assemblies managed with, 13
Insert mode, design modification, 159, 161–164
Inspection relationships, outlining, 6–7
Inspection requirements, 107–109
Interchangeability, assemblies, 10–11
Interchanging components, 27–29
Intersecting walls, design intent, 83
Iterations, design optimization, 256–260

K

Key sequences, macros, 215–216

L

Layering geometry, 242–245
Layers use, simplifying design view, 151
Layout mode, planning design, 10–11
Layouts
    Accessing other layouts and linking data, 24–26
    Approval of design, 22–23
    Assembly layout illustration, 16
    Assembly modifications, 134–137
    Automatic assembly of components, 23–24
    Case Study, 19, 21
    Changing layouts, 27–29
    Copies of layouts for concurrent assembly development, 22–23
    Corporate standards, 23–24
    Declaring layouts to other design units, 26–29
    Declaring models and assemblies, 22–23
    Design intent, 22–23, 98–99
    Detail prints, 14, 16
    Dimensional relationships, 19, 21
    Minimum sublayout requirements, 24–25
    Multiple layouts and assemblies, 24–25
    Parameter definition by minimum sublayout requirements, 24–25
    Parametric relationships, managing, 102–105
    Parent component modification, 23–24
    Quality input, generating, 14, 16
    Rough layout development, 22–23
    Standardizing the assembly process, 24–25
    Sublayout requirements, 24–25
    Tables, managing relationships, 21–22
Layouts, design management
    Assembly constraints, 13
    Automatic assembly of components, 14, 16
    Component declared, 14, 16
    Component generation, 14, 16
    Free-form and Pro/ENGINEER layouts, illustration, 15
    Layouts described, 15
    Parametric relationships, assemblies managed with, 13
    Quality input, generating, 15
Lead time, component modeling priority, 98–99
Localized stress levels, design optimization, dimensions and iteration, 256–260

M

Machining operations, Pro/MANUFACTURING, 289–290, 312–313
Macros
    Design execution improvement, 215–216
    Execution method, seed files, 42–43
    Mapkeys, config.clear file, 236–240
    Mapkeys, running multiple configurations, 232–234
    Menu location, 225–227
    Multiple macro execution, nesting, 221–224
    Shading and spinning geometry, 224–225
    Table Editor, creation within, 227–228
Manually placed text, parametric formats, 192, 194
Manufacturing requirements
    Component modeling priority, 98–99
    See also Design verification and manufacturability
Mapkeys
    Config.clear file, 236–240
    Config.pro file, macros, 216–217
    Multiple configurations, 232–234
Material removal, Pro/NC-CHECK, 319–322
Mathematical errors, rapid prototyping, errors in database, 277–279
Memory requirements, 329–333
Menu execution method, seed files, 43–45
Menu items, design execution improvement, 228–229
Menu location, macro execution, 225–227
Menu selection, macros used for design improvement, 218–221
Menu_def.pro file
    Design execution improvement, 236–240
    Menu item additions, 229–230
Milestones, project development outline, 6–7
Mill volumes, Pro/MANUFACTURING, 293, 296, 298–300, 302–304, 314
Misc, menu item additions, 230
Modeling techniques
    Corporate standards, 72–73, 75
    Design intent, 79–81
Models
    Adding new information to old models, 45–48
    Declaring models and assemblies, 22–23

Index 341

Detailing, tolerances developed in model, 175–177
Pro/MANUFACTURING, swapping top-level model for design, 315
Production model to analysis model, 242–245
Modes
   Selection, design intent, 99, 101–102
   Transitions among, 236–240
Modification of design
   See Design modifications
Modify-Modify Dim command sequence, design modification, 143–146, 148–150
Modify-Modify Part command sequence, design modification, 143–146, 148–150
Module selection
   Corporate standards, 75–76
   Design intent, 92, 94
   Planning design, 8–11
Multiple configurations
   Menu item addition, 228–229
   Menu_def.pro file, transitions, 236–240
   Running, 232–234
Multiple layouts and assemblies, standardizing assembly process, 24–25
Multiple macro execution, nesting, 221–224
Multiple projects, menu item addition for transition among, 228–229

N

NC sequences, playing back, 325
NC-check
   See also Pro/NC-CHECK
   Tool paths, 306–308, 311, 317, 319
Nesting, multiple macro execution, 221–224
Networks, menu item addition, 228–229
Node coupling, 246–248

O

Offset datum planes, seed files, 32
Optimization of design, analysis, 248–249
Order of execution, design intent, 89, 91–92
Overlapping geometry, rapid prototyping, errors in database, 277–279
Overprogramming, 240

P

Parameters, adding new parameters, seed files, 45–48
Parametric formats
   Detailing, 188–189, 191–192
   Developing, 192
   Manually placed text, 192, 194
   Pro/REPORT variables in tables, 196–197
   Symbols, 194–196
   Tables, 196–197
Parametric link, seed files, 32
Parametric notes, detailing, 179–181, 183–184
Parametric relationships
   Add sequence, developing, 51–54
   Adding to seed script, 49, 51–53
   Assemblies managed with, 13
   Copying and replacing existing relationship, 49, 51–53
   Design intent, 102–105
   Design modifications, 137–138
   Layout, managing with, 102–105
   Seed data, accessing, 186–188
   Seed files, 32
Parent component modification, layouts, 23–24
Parent/child relationships
   Design intent, 86–89
   Design modification, 158
   Detailing, 178
   Extruded cut, 89
   Pro/MESH, optimization of design, 247, 252–253
   Sketched cut, 86–89
   View development, 198–201
Part mode
   Selection, 99, 101–102
   Stack up analysis, 121–122
Parts
   Drawings, modifying designs from, 153
   Geometry modifications, 154–155
   Parametric relationships maintained in part, 188–189, 191–192
   Planning design, 10–11
Pattern relationships, design verification and manufacturability, 109–112
Patterned geometries, pro/MANUFACTURING, 293–294

Physical models, planning design, 4–5
Planning design
    Assembly function, 10–11
    Brainstorming, 5–6, 10–11
    Component evaluation, 7
    Component layout, 7
    Consensus, 10–11
    Corporate standards, 10–11
    Dimensional relationships, outlining, 6–7
    Final markup copies, 6–7
    Free form modeling, 5
    Free-form modeling, 4
    Inspection relationships, outlining, 6–7
    Layout mode, 10–11
    Meeting minutes, 6–7
    Module selection, 8–11
    Objectives of project, satisfying, 4–5
    Paper sketches, 4–5
    Parts, 10–11
    Physical models, 4–5
    Planning the plan, 6–7
    Pro/Sheet Metal example, 8–9
    Problems, brainstorming, 4
    Quality input, generating, 4, 10–11
    Sequence of development steps, 6–7
    Thinking through design, 4
    Thinking through design intent, 10–11
Porcupine command, 116
Postprocessing, Pro/MANUFACTURING, 325
Price, rapid prototyping process selection, 273–274
Pro/CABLING, 94–95
Pro/ENGINEER, menu item additions, 230
Pro/HARNESS-MFG, 94–95
Pro/MANUFACTURING
    Clipping planes, Pro/NC-CHECK, 322, 324–325
    Configuration state machining, 312
    Database flexibility, 304
    Functionality, 285
    Holes, making and filling, 309
    Inaccurate data, problems created, 305
    Incomplete geometries, problems created, 305
    Machining operations, parametric link to references, 289–290
    Mill volume surfaces, 296, 298–300, 302–304
    Mill volume, dimensional design changes, 302–304
    Mill volume, sketching, 296, 298–300, 302–304
    Mill volume, tool paths for, 296, 298–300, 302–304
    Patterned geometries, 293–294
    Postprocessing, 325
    Pro/NC-CHECK, 319–322, 326–327
    Rapid prototyping, 276
    Tool paths, 289–290
    Tool paths, removal of material, 295
    Versions of design developed with family tables, 313
Pro/MESH, 246–248, 252–253
Pro/NC-CHECK, 326–327
    Clipping planes, 322, 324–325
    Tool paths, 319–322
Pro/REPORT, 185, 197
Pro/SCAN-TOOLS module, 116–117
Pro/USER groups, 326–327
Problem-solving, design intent, 79–81
Problems, brainstorming, 4
Process requirements, 118–120
Processing requirements, 330–333
Prototypes
    See Rapid prototyping
Protrusions, design intent, 82

Q

Quality input generation, 3, 77–78
    Layouts, 14–16
    Rapid prototyping, errors in database, 280–282
Quantity, rapid prototyping process selection, 273–274
Querying features, design modification, 158

R

Rapid prototyping
    Aluminum tooling, 276
    Castings, 276
    CNC process, 280–282
    CNC use, 274–275
    Database quality, 277–279
    Functions, 270–273
    Geometry errors in database, 277–279
    Limitations of processes, 270–273
    Method selection, 269–270
    Price, 273–274
    Pro/MANUFACTURING, 276

Index 343

Quantity, 273–274
SLA, 269–270
SLA process, 280–282
Spray metal, 276
Time limits, 273–274
Urethane molds, 276
Redefining dimensioning scheme, 169–170
Redundant data
   Macros, 215–216
   Seed files, 33
Reference components, simplication, 151–152
Reference dimensions, 124–127, 129–131
Regen Info command
   Detailing, 173–175
   Tracking feature development sequence for design, 154–155
Regeneration
   Assembly regeneration for development process, 138–140
   Changes in design, 118–120
Relations, editing in seed files, 45–48
Relationship management, features, 85
Relationships
   See Parent/child relationships
Remodeling, corporate standards, 62–63
Renaming trail files, 39–41, 45–48
Repetitive executions, improvement, 215
Replaying features with trail files, 35
Return, semicolon, 230
Reverse associativity, 153, 203–206
Risk assessment, component modeling priority, 98–99
Rounds, design intent, 84–85

S

Save and purge commands, nesting, 221–224
Sculpting, rapid prototyping, errors in database, 277–279
Sections, 112–114
Seed data, detailing, 184–185
Seed files
   Add sequence, developing, 51–54
   Copying and replacing existing parametric relationship, 49, 51–53
   Creation, 33–34
   Defined, 32

Detailing, 184–185
Macro execution method, 42–43
Menu execution method, 43–45
Naming part, 39–41
New information to old models, adding, 45–48
New parameters, adding, 45–48
Parametric link, illustration, 32
Parametric relationships, adding to seed script, 49, 51–53
Regenerating entire file, 51–54
Removing exit command from trail file, 35
Replaying features with trail files, 35
Seed data selection, 37–39
Seed data turned into seed file, 39–41
Seed script creation, 33–34
Seed script, updating, 49, 51
Trail files used to develop seed files, 35
Update execution, improving, 51–54
Value portion of equation, saving, 37–39
Seed script
   Creation, 33–34
   Updating, 49, 51
Selective enforcement of corporate standards, 77–78
Selective laser sintering
   See SLS
Semicolon, return, 230
Shaded images, 114–115
Shading geometry, 224–225
Sharing information, corporate standards, 61–62
Shell elements, use, 254
Shell, design intent, 84–85
Simplified representation, 149
   Machining operations, 312
   Resuming features, 164
   Suppressing features, 164
Simplifying design view, 143–146, 148–150
Size limit establishment, 248–249
Sketched cut, parent/child relationships, 86–89
Sketcher session, Case Study, verifying calculations by, 19, 21
Sketching, macros used for design improvement, 218
SLA
   Components, 269–270
   Rapid prototyping process selection, 270–273
   Rapid prototyping, errors in database, 278–280

Slope Surface Analysis, 112
SLS, rapid prototyping process selection, 270–273
Solid surface geometrics, trail files use, 49, 51–53
Speed, mode selection, 99, 101–102
Spinning geometry, 224–225
Spray metal, rapid prototyping, 276
Stack up analysis, 121–122
START OPTS menu, 139
Stereolithography apparatus
   See SLA
STL files, 269–270, 278–280
Subassembly components, dimension value changes, 134–137
Subcomponents, 112–113
Subcontractors, corporate standards, 65–73, 75–76, 78
Submenus
   Macro execution from, 217
   Menu item addition, transition between projects, 228–229
Suppliers
   Input in developing corporate standards, 72–73, 75
   Process requirement verification, 118–120
Suppressing components, 151
Suppressing features, design modification, 164–165
Surface geometry analysis
   Design verification and manufacturability, 114–115
   Porcupine command, 116
Surfaces for mill volume, Pro/MANUFACTURING, 296–304
Symbols, parametric formats, 194–196

T

Table Editor, macro creation, 227–228
Tables
   Managing relationships, 21–22
   Minimum sublayout requirements, 26
   Parametric formats, 196–197
   Pro/MANUFACTURING, 313

Tangents, brainstorming sessions, 5–6
Text
   Macros used for design improvement, 218–221
   Symbols, parametric formats, 194–196
Thinking through design, generating quality input, 4
Time limits, rapid prototyping process selection, 273–274
Time savings, module selection, 8–9
Timeliness project development outline, 6–7
Tolerances
   Design verification and manufacturability, 109–112, 120
   Detailing, tolerances developed in model, 175–177
   Format change, 122–124
   Process requirement verification, 118–120
   Reverse associativity, 203–206
   Stack up analysis, 121–122
   Tables, managing relationships, 21–22
Tool paths
   Pro/MANUFACTURING, 289–290, 293
   Pro/MANUFACTURING, configuration state machining, 315–317, 319
   Removal of material, 295
Tool selection
   Design intent, 89, 91–92
   Rapid prototyping, errors in database, 277–279
Tools, corporate standards, 57–58, 72–73, 75
Topology optimization, 260–266
Trail files
   Design modification, 157
   Relations editing in seed files, 45–48
   Removing exit command from trail file, 36
   Replaying features, 35
   Used to develop seed files, 35
Transitions among multiple configurations, menu_def.pro file, 236–240

U

Uniformity of product, corporate standards, 75–76
Update script, developing, 51–54
Urethane molds, rapid prototyping, 276

V

Value portion of equation in quotes, 37–39
Variables, design optimization, dimensions and iteration, 256–260
Verification of design
  See Design verification and manufacturability

View development
  Default datum planes, 201–203
  Detailing, 198–201
  Dimensions and tolerances shown on drawing, 205–206, 208, 210
Views
  Macros used for design improvement, 218–221
  Pro/NC-CHECK, clipping planes to help visualize design, 322, 324–325

More OnWord Press Titles

Pro/ENGINEER and Pro/JR. Books

INSIDE Pro/ENGINEER
Book $49.95 Includes Disk

Thinking Pro/ENGINEER
Book $49.95

Pro/ENGINEER Quick Reference, 2d ed.
Book $24.95

INSIDE Pro/JR.
Book $49.95

Pro/ENGINEER Exercise Book
Book $39.95 Includes Disk

Interleaf Books

INSIDE Interleaf
Book $49.95 Includes Disk

The Interleaf Quick Reference
Book $24.95

Adventurer's Guide to Interleaf Lisp
Book $49.95 Includes Disk

Interleaf Tips and Tricks
Book $49.95 Includes Disk

The Interleaf Exercise Book
Book $39.95 Includes Disk

MicroStation Books

INSIDE MicroStation 5X, 3d ed.
Book $34.95 Includes Disk

MicroStation for AutoCAD Users, 2d ed.
Book $34.95

MicroStation Reference Guide 5.X
Book $18.95

Adventures in MicroStation 3D
Book 49.95 Includes Disk

MicroStation Exercise Book 5.X
Book $34.95
Optional Instructor's Guide $14.95

MicroStation Productivity Book
Book $39.95
Optional Disk $49.95

MicroStation 5.X Delta Book
Book $19.95

MicroStation Bible
Book $49.95
Optional Disks $49.95

Build Cell
Software $69.95

101 MDL Commands
Book $49.95
Optional Executable Disk $101.00
Optional Source Disks (6) $259.95

101 User Commands
Book $49.95
Optional Disk $101.00

Bill Steinbock's Pocket MDL Programmer's Guide
Book $24.95

MicroStation for AutoCAD Users Tablet Menu
Tablet Menu $99.95

Managing and Networking MicroStation
Book $29.95
Optional Disk $29.95

The MicroStation Database Book
Book $29.95
Optional Disk $29.95

The MicroStation Rendering Book
Book $34.95 Includes Disk

INSIDE I/RAS B
Book $24.95 Includes Disk

The CLIX Workstation User's Guide
Book $34.95 Includes Disk

SunSoft Solaris Series

The SunSoft Solaris 2.* User's Guide
Book $29.95 Includes Disk

SunSoft Solaris 2.* for Managers and Administrators
Book $34.95
Optional Disk $29.95

The SunSoft Solaris 2.* Quick Reference
Book $18.95

Five Steps to SunSoft Solaris 2.*
Book $24.95 Includes Disk

One Minute SunSoft Solaris Manager
Book $14.95

SunSoft Solaris 2.* for Windows Users
Book $24.95

Windows NT

Windows NT for the Technical Professional
Book $39.95

The Hewlett Packard HP-UX Series

The HP-UX User's Guide
Book $29.95 Includes Disk

Five Steps to HP-UX
Book $24.95 Includes Disk

The HP-UX Quick Reference
Book $18.95

One Minute HP-UX Manager
Book $14.95

CAD Management

One Minute CAD Manager
Book $14.95

Manager's Guide to Computer-Aided Engineering
Book $49.95

Other CAD

CAD and the Practice of Architecture: ASG Solutions
Book $39.95 Includes Disk

INSIDE CADVANCE
Book $34.95 Includes Disk

Using Drafix Windows CAD
Book $34.95 Includes Disk

Fallingwater in 3D Studio: A Case Study and Tutorial
Book $39.95 Includes Disk

Geographic Information Systems/ESRI

The GIS Book, 3d ed.
Book $34.95

ArcView Developer's Guide
Book $49.95

INSIDE ARC/INFO
Book $74.95 Includes CD

INSIDE ArcView
Book $39.95 Includes CD

ARC/INFO Quick Reference
Book $24.95

DTP/CAD Clip Art

1001 DTP/CAD Symbols Clip Art Library: Architectural
Book $29.95

DISK FORMATS:
MicroStation
DGN Disk $175.00
Book/Disk $195.00

AutoCAD
DWG Disk $175.00
Book/Disk $195.00

CAD/DTP
DXF Disk $195.00
Book/Disk $225.00

Networking/LANtastic

Fantastic LANtastic
Book $29.95 Includes Disk

The LANtastic Quick Reference
Book $14.95

One Minute Network Manager
Book $14.95

OnWord Press Distribution

End Users/User Groups/Corporate Sales

OnWord Press books are available worldwide to end users, user groups, and corporate accounts from your local bookseller or computer/software dealer, or from HMP Direct: call 1-800-223-6397 or 505-473-5454; fax 505-471-4424; write to High Mountain Press Direct, 2530 Camino Entrada, Santa Fe, NM 87505-8435, or e-mail to ORDERS@ BOOKSTORE. HMP.COM.

Wholesale, Including Overseas Distribution

High Mountain Press distributes OnWord Press books internationally. For terms call 1-800-4-ONWORD or 505-473-5454; fax to 505-471-4424; e-mail to ORDERS@ IPG.HMP.COM; or write to High Mountain Press/IPG, 2530 Camino Entrada, Santa Fe, NM 87505-8435, USA. Outside North America, call 505-471-4243.

Comments and Corrections

Your comments can help us make better products. If you find an error in our products, or have any other comments, positive or negative, we'd like to know! Please write to us at the address below or contact our e-mail address: READERS@HMP.COM.

OnWord Press
2530 Camino Entrada, Santa Fe, NM 87505-8435 USA